EMPOWERING SURVIVORS OF ABUSE

Sage Series on Violence Against Women

Series Editors

Claire M. Renzetti
St. Joseph's University

Jeffrey L. Edleson
University of Minnesota

In this series . . .

EMPOWERING SURVIVORS OF ABUSE

Health Care for
Battered Women
and Their Children

Jacquelyn C. Campbell
Editor

Sage Series on Violence Against Women

Association of Women's Health,
Obstetric and Neonatal Nurses

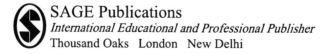

SAGE Publications
International Educational and Professional Publisher
Thousand Oaks   London   New Delhi

For information:

SAGE Publications, Inc.
2455 Teller Road
Thousand Oaks, California 91320
E-mail: order@sagepub.com

SAGE Publications Ltd.
6 Bonhill Street
London EC2A 4PU
United Kingdom

SAGE Publications India Pvt. Ltd.
M-32 Market
Greater Kailash I
New Delhi 110 048 India

Printed in the United States of America

Library of Congress Cataloging-in-Publication Data

Main entry under title:

Empowering survivors of abuse: Health care for battered women and
  their children / [edited by] Jacquelyn C. Campbell.
      p. cm.—(Sage series on violence against women ; vol. 10)
    Includes bibliographical references and index.
    ISBN 0-7619-1121-9 (cloth : acid-free paper)
    ISBN 0-7619-1122-7 (pbk. : acid-free paper)
    1. Women—Abuse of—Prevention. 2. Abused women—Health aspects.
  3. Children—Abuse of—Prevention. 4. Victims of family violence—Care.
  5. Pregnant women—Abuse of—Prevention. 6. Abused women—Cross-cultural studies.
  7. Abused women—Services for. I. Campbell, Jacquelyn. II. Series: Sage series on
  violence against women ; v. 10.
    RA1122.E46 1998
    616.85′822—ddc21   98-25308

98 99 00 01 02 03 04 10 9 8 7 6 5 4 3 2 1

Acquiring Editor: C. Terry Hendrix
Production Editor: Wendy Westgate
Production Assistant: Lynn Miyata
Typesetter/Designer: Marion Warren
Indexer: Juniee Oneida

Contents

PART II. DYNAMICS OF DOMESTIC VIOLENCE

PART III. ABUSE AND PREGNANCY

PART IV. CHILDREN AND ADOLESCENTS

PART V. CLINICAL APPLICATIONS AND INTERVENTIONS

PART VI. CULTURALLY SPECIFIC CLINICAL INTERVENTIONS

Preface

Leading nurse researchers and clinicians in violence and abuse address major issues in providing care for abused women and their children in this volume. The text includes a compilation of original research and clinical, policy, and education applications. The women's perspective is fundamental and embedded throughout the chapters. From this perspective, practitioners, educators, and researchers will gain a clearer understanding of women's experiences with abuse. *Empowering Survivors of Abuse* is based on and explains the latest health care research that addresses woman abuse. The book is relevant to practitioners from a variety of fields, including nurses, social workers, shelter and system advocates, policy-makers, health planners, physicians, criminal justice practitioners, and any others in the health and social services arena.

The book is one of the first that addresses issues and interventions specific to women of special populations, including chapters on adolescent, African American, Native American, Hispanic, migrant, and rural abused women and their children. In addition, recommendations for health care practice for abused women and their children in varied health settings are made. Strategies for prevention of violence, early identification, clinical interventions, and policy reformation also are included, an important addition to the scholarly based practical literature on violence against women.

Acknowledgments
and Dedication

Thanks go to my coauthors, who are all friends and colleagues. I respect so much all that you do: the direct care that most of you provide to battered women and the indirect advocacy all of you provide through our research, teaching, and/or policy activities. I know that you are somewhat overwhelmed at times by all that needs doing, and I appreciate your contributions to this volume. Thanks also go to AWHONN for its idea to put the first version of this book together as a special issue of *AWHONN's Clinical Issues* and its subsequent support for its publication with Sage. And thanks to Jeff Edleson and Claire Renzetti, for their support and inclusion in their very important series, and to C. Terry Hendrix and Dale Grenfell at Sage, who are incredibly supportive editors and responsible for compiling and marketing the most amazing collection of books on violence, providing all of us in the violence scholarship business a forum and readership for our work.

I would like to dedicate this book to several groups of people.

First, to Evan Stark and Anne Flitcraft for their early vision, for their unswerving commitment to principle, and for showing all of us in the health care system how it might be changed to be an empowerment zone. In that same category of trailblazers, to Rebecca and Russell Dobash, Diana Russell, and Mildred Daly Pagelow for changing all of our ideas about battered women so that we could see the responsibility of our history, our societal arrangements, and our systems for their victimization and for being especially influential to my work. Also to Susan Schechter and Ellen Pence and the rest of the advocacy movement for battered women for their incredible struggle long before it was fashionable, and uncompromising commitment to the safety and empowerment of battered women—we try to follow your example. And finally to Christine King, Judith McFarlane, Barbara Parker, Anne Helton, and Linda Bullock for their pioneering leadership and organization against woman abuse in nursing practice and nursing research. There are many of us in nursing and in the rest of the health care system, with diverse strengths and areas of expertise, who have gone after, and I also salute us all.

Second, to all the battered and formerly battered women I have known personally and well and those I have known indirectly. I always especially think of Anne, who was the first and has now been gone almost 20 years; of Vickie, who has become a friend and a colleague in the struggle; and of Carla, who will soon be free. I am always awed by all battered women's strength and courage. I cannot adequately express how you have paid me back a million times for anything I have ever done on your behalf and how much more I know the health care system can do.

Third, to my new group of colleagues and research staff at Johns Hopkins, who make me look good. In that group Jackie Dienemann, Andrea Gielen, Nancy Glass, Joan Kub, Linda Lewandowski, Phyllis Naumann, Linda Rose, and Daniel Webster especially come to mind, with Cathy Barenski, Carolyn Erwin-Johnson, Julie MacPhee, Janet Schollenberger, Rose Smith, Jo Ellen Stinchcomb, and Louise Lancaster directly contributing (or indirectly by taking care of other things!) to the production of this volume. And I will never forget the wonderful group of colleagues and students at Wayne State University that I will always miss and whose scholarship has and will contribute substantially to nursing science and to the body of literature on violence against women.

And last, I want to dedicate this book to my family. To my brother and sister and their spouses and families, who are more of a joy every year. To my wonderful now grown children, Christy and Brad, who make me proud every day both of their accomplishments and because they aren't afraid to show it when they love somebody.

To two wonderful mothers, my love's who left us too soon, and my own, thankfully healthy and still taking care of us all. These two loving women came from totally different backgrounds, but both epitomize the best of what it means to be a lady and a mother and a woman of courage all at once.

And to my father, who has shown me all my life how a man can combine strength and gentleness, the combination that I treasure so much in the man I now love.

PART I

SYSTEM CHANGE: POLICY AND PROFESSIONAL EDUCATION

1

Making the Health Care System an Empowerment Zone for Battered Women

Health Consequences, Policy Recommendations, Introduction, and Overview

Jacquelyn C. Campbell

The most recently published, national random survey estimates that 4.4 million adult women are abused by a spouse or partner in this country every year (Plichta, 1997). The Commonwealth Fund survey of women's health demonstrated an 8% prevalence rate of American women being physically abused in the prior year and a 3.2% rate of severe abuse. In another national survey of violence, the National Crime Victimization Survey (NCVS) (more sensitive to other forms of violent crime, less sensitive to domestic violence), adult women were significantly more likely to be victimized by a current or former intimate partner than by anyone else, including strangers (Bachman & Saltzman, 1995). The NCVS also demonstrated that separated women were significantly more likely to be abused than were married, divorced, or unmarried women. Such evidence, coupled with international data and smaller, non-population-based studies, suggests that battered women are at increased risk for violence when they leave their abusive partner (Campbell, Sullivan, & Davidson, 1995; Wilson, Johnson, & Daly, 1995).

3

The mental and physical health effects of this violence are significant. Research from many disciplines over the past decade has resulted in a much clearer picture of the extent of these health effects, and the combination of research and clinical experience has begun to establish appropriate interventions in the health care system. It has been an exciting 10 years. The decade has resulted in a glimpse of a health care system that can go beyond sanctuary for abused women, beyond advocacy, and actually provide prevention of further violence plus increase the power and efficacy of battered women to make their lives violence free—a health care system as an empowerment zone.

This chapter presents an overview of the latest research on the physical and mental health effects of domestic violence, a brief history of the nursing and health care evolution on the subject of domestic violence, a delineation of suggested policy initiatives in the area, and a description of the kind of empowerment zone I envision. Readers will be referred to the chapters in this volume that further develop various topics as they are introduced. The book is a combination of revisions and updates of most of the contributions to a special issue of *AWHONN's Clinical Issues in Perinatal and Women's Health Nursing* on domestic violence published in 1993 (Lewis, 1993) and four entirely new chapters. Most of the leading nursing researchers in the field, along with other discipline collaborators, have contributed to this volume.

The book is organized into six major sections: System Change, Dynamics of Domestic Violence, Abuse and Pregnancy, Children and Adolescents, Clinical Applications and Interventions, and Culturally Specific Clinical Interventions. The first and last sections synthesize prior research, trace clinical developments, and present clinical applications; the middle four are primarily original research. A general literature review for each section can be found in its first chapter and will not be repeated in subsequent chapters.

Physical and Mental Health
Effects of Battering

Battering is defined here as repeated physical and/or sexual assault by an intimate partner within a context of coercive control (Campbell & Humphreys, 1993). The emotional abuse that is almost always part of the coercive control also has serious psychological consequences according to women themselves, but the actual effects on women's health have seldom been measured separately.

Health Effects of Forced Sex

The forced sex aspect of battering has also often been neglected in prior research. Approximately 40% to 45% of all battered women are forced into sex by their male partners (Campbell, 1989a). Forced sex can range from unwanted roughness and painful or particular sexual acts through threatened violence if sexual demands are not met to actual beatings prior, during, or after sex and/or sex with objects (Campbell & Alford, 1989). Relationship sexual abuse probably results in the increased risk of pelvic inflammatory disease, sexually transmitted diseases (STDs) including HIV/AIDS, vaginal and anal tearing, bladder infections, sexual dysfunction, pelvic pain, urinary tract infections, and other genital- and urinary-related health problems documented for battered women in several population-based shelter and health care setting studies (Bergman & Brismar, 1991; Campbell & Alford, 1989; Chapman, 1989; Plichta, 1997). Eby, Campbell, Sullivan, and Davidson (1995) documented that the increased risk for STDs including HIV/AIDS in one sample was related to the lack of using protection during intercourse (67%), primarily at the male partner's insistence or when sex was forced, rather than other risky behavior on the woman's part (e.g., multiple casual sexual partners or IV drug usage).

Sexually abused battered women in shelters surveyed by Campbell and Alford (1989) reported other gynecological problems such as dysmenorrhea, and the battered women in the Saunders, Hamberger, and Hovey (1993) HMO study were noted as having unexplained vaginal bleeding. Battered women in focus groups also linked forced sex in battering relationships as well as male partner control of contraceptive use with unintended pregnancy, a link also shown in a large population-based study in one state (Campbell, Pugh, Campbell, & Visscher, 1995; Institute of Medicine, 1995). When asked directly by health care professionals about sexual abuse, women respond without objection, and the health care system is the only place where women are likely to receive appropriate care for this aspect of their battering experience.

Abuse During Pregnancy

Pregnancy can be a direct result of forced relationship sex, and abuse during pregnancy a continuation of the general battering. Chapter 7 in this volume further addresses the dynamics of abuse during pregnancy with an overview of the most recent research related to that subject. Much of the leading research on the subject has been nursing research, using the Abuse Assessment Screen (AAS; Parker & McFarlane, 1991) to identify pregnant women who are abused. The AAS is also being used widely to screen for abused women in a variety of both inpatient and outpatient health care settings. Chapter 16 gives the latest psychometric information on this increasingly important screening instrument.

Physical Health Effects of Violence

Increased health problems and health care seeking of battered women are well documented. In two population-based national surveys, physically abused women were significantly more likely than other women to define their health as fair or poor (Gelles & Straus, 1990; Plichta, 1997). They were also more likely to say they had needed medical care but did not get it (Plichta, 1997), and severely battered women had almost twice the number of days in bed due to illness than other women (Gelles & Straus, 1990). In a survey of battered women who had ended the violence, the majority of women had sought help from medical professionals, a higher proportion than from other sources of help (Bendtro & Bowker, 1989).

Injury is the most obvious health effect of battering, and since Stark, Flitcraft, and Frazier's (1979) groundbreaking study of battered women in the emergency department (ED), large proportions of female ED patients have been documented as abused. Although prevalence varies considerably depending on the identification criteria (self-report, disclosure to professionals, record review) and the denominator of the equation (all women seen, all young adult women seen, all trauma patients), clearly domestic violence is a major cause of both injury and noninjury visits to the ED by women (Abbot, John, Loziol-McLain, & Lowenstein, 1995; Dearwater et al., in press; Goldberg & Tomlanovich, 1984; McLeer & Anwar, 1989b). Chronic pain was found to be the most frequent reason for visiting the ED in one sample (Goldberg & Tomlanovich, 1984) and is a common symptom of battered women in other settings (McCauley et al., 1995). Although frequently described as somatization, this pain may well be the result of old, misdiagnosed or never treated injuries.

The aftermath of injuries from abuse such as pain, broken bones, facial trauma (e.g., fractured mandibles), and tendon or ligament injuries is usually followed in outpatient settings (Goldberg & Tomlanovich, 1984; Grisso et al., 1991; Varvaro & Lasko, 1993; Zachariades, Koumoura, & Konsolaki-Agouridaki, 1990). Because battered women frequently report untreated loss of consciousness as a result of abuse, the chronic headaches they often describe (Gelles & Straus, 1990; McCauley et al., 1995) may be an inadequately diagnosed sequelae of neurological damage from beatings. Undiagnosed hearing, vision, and concentration problems reported by battered women also suggest possible neurological problems from injury (Eby et al., 1995). In recent studies of primary care settings, the percentage of women currently abused from self-report (rather than record review) has ranged between 5.5% and 25% (Gin, Rucker, Frayne, Cygan, & Hubbell, 1991; McCauley et al., 1995; Rath, Jarratt, & Leonardson, 1989; Saunders et al., 1993). Rath et al. (1989) found that not only the battered women in the HMO studies but also their children used health services 6-8 times more often than controls.

Other symptoms and conditions shown in controlled investigations to be associated with physical violence from intimate partners may be more related to the results of stress, including chronic irritable bowel syndrome, digestive problems, eating disorders, and other stress-related physical symptoms (Bergman & Brismar, 1991; Breslau, Davis, Andreski, & Peterson, 1991; Campbell, 1989a, 1989b; Drossman et al., 1990; Kerouac, Taggart, Lescop, & Fortin, 1986; McCauley et al., 1995; Stark & Flitcraft, 1985). Other studies suggest that physical conditions with both biologic and environmental components such as hypertension are related to abuse (Kerouac et al., 1986; McCauley et al., 1995; Rodriguez, 1989). Although the suppression of the immune system from chronic stress has been investigated in other populations, the role of stress in the etiology of the frequent communicable diseases of battered women and their children (Kerouac et al., 1986) has not been investigated.

Mortality Related to Abuse

Obviously, the most severe health consequence of intimate partner violence is homicide, causing more than half the homicides to women in the United States each year (Browne, 1988). The majority of adult women who are killed are killed by a husband, partner, or ex-husband or ex-partner, and in the majority of those homicide cases, the woman was battered before she was killed (Campbell, 1995). The trajectory of the most severe kinds of abuse is often an increase in severity and frequency over time that may culminate in a homicide if the woman does not leave or the man does not receive either treatment or incarceration for violence. The majority of battered women do eventually leave the abuser, but they are probably most at risk for homicide after they have left the abuser or when they make it clear to the abuser that they are leaving for good (Campbell, 1995; Wilson & Daly, 1993). There is also some indication that battered women who have been abused during pregnancy are particularly at risk for eventual femicide and/or for killing their abuser, as discussed in Chapter 8.

Women's Mental Health Consequences

Mental health sequelae to abuse are significant and prompt women to seek health care services as frequently as for physical health problems. The primary mental health response of women to being battered in an ongoing intimate relationship and the main reason for battered women going to a primary health care setting is depression (Saunders et al., 1993). In controlled studies from a variety of settings, battered women are consistently found to have more depressive symptoms than other women on various instruments (e.g., Jaffe, Wolfe, Wilson, & Zak, 1986a; McCauley et al., 1995; Ratner, 1993). Prevalence of depression in abused women has ranged from 10.2% (Weissman & Klerman, 1992) to 21.3% (Kessler et al., 1994) to 31.9% when also including anxiety diagnoses (Plichta, 1997) in general population studies. In two different community samples of battered women, Campbell (1989a; Campbell, Kub, Belknap, & Templin, 1997) found 39% to 43% of women to be in the moderately severe to severe categories of depressive symptoms on the Beck Depression Inventory.

Using psychiatric diagnostic procedures, Gleason (1993) found a significantly higher prevalence of major depression in 62 shelter battered women than a comparison group and a higher prevalence of major depression (63%) than of diagnosed posttraumatic stress disorder (PTSD) (40%). In comparison, depression in women in general is estimated at 9.3% and 20% to 25% lifetime risk. Other shelter samples (e.g., Cascardi, Langhinrichsen, & Vivian, 1992; Tolman & Bhosley, 1991) have been reported at similar levels of depression. There are increasing recommendations for the treatment of depression in primary care settings (U.S. Department of Health and Human Services, 1993). Yet the need to assess for and intervene if necessary for domestic violence as well as depression has seldom been recognized (Campbell, Kub, & Rose, 1996).

In studies exploring the dynamics of depression in battered women, significant predictors include the frequency and severity of current physical abuse and stress, more strongly than prior history of mental illness or demographic, cultural, or childhood characteristics (Campbell et al., 1997; Campbell et al., 1995; Cascardi & O'Leary, 1992). Self-care agency, or women's ability to care for themselves, was found to be a protective factor for depression in one study (Campbell et al., 1997). Similar concepts (agency, survival strategies) have been found in other studies, indicating the need to investigate the strengths of battered women as well as their problems (Gondolf, Fisher, & McFerron, 1988; Lempert, 1996).

Trauma Framework. Many current mental health researchers and practitioners are conceptualizing the psychological effects of domestic violence within a traumatic response framework (e.g., Dutton, 1992, 1993). Higher rates (31% to 84%) of PTSD have been documented in battered women in shelters than in other women (Astin, Lawrence, & Foy, 1993; Gleason, 1993; Kemp, Green, Hovanitz, & Rawlings, 1995; Saunders, 1992; Woods & Campbell, 1993). The prevalence of PTSD in battered women in the general population has been less than would be expected but still substantial (1.7% to 12.3%) (Kessler et al., 1994; Resnick, Kilpatrick, Dansky, Saunders, & Best, 1993; Saunders et al., 1993). So far, the strongest predictor of PTSD in battered women has been the severity of current abuse (Astin et al., 1993), but other experiences of trauma (e.g., childhood sexual abuse, rape) were not well measured in that study. The association of PTSD and battering has only fairly recently been documented and primarily in the violence or trauma literature rather than in mainstream health or mental health publications. Battered women would generally not complain of PTSD to a health care provider, but rather of sleep disorders or stress (McCauley et al., 1995). Thus, there is substantial probability of misdiagnosis or lack of diagnosis of PTSD by non-mental health providers.

Herman's (1992) work suggests that a complex (or chronic) traumatic stress response, where the person is subjected to ongoing control and terror, may be more adequate to explain the responses seen in battered women than a single traumatic event. These somewhat different responses include alterations in (a) affect (the predominance of depressive affect), (b) perception of the perpetrator (the tendency of severely battered women to see their abuser as omnipotent), and (c) sense of self (the self-blame and disappearance of a sense of self described by severely abused women) (Campbell et al., 1997; Dutton, 1993). Attachment to the abuser should not be underestimated as part of the psychological responses of battered women and their children, making the response to trauma more complex (Dutton, 1993).

Substance Abuse. Substance abuse is frequently seen as part of a trauma response—part of the avoidance dynamic. Abuse of both alcohol and illicit drugs has been found to be a substantiated correlate of abuse during pregnancy in all of the studies where it was measured as well as in several studies of clinical and shelter samples of battered women (Amaro, Fried, Cabral, & Zuckerman, 1990; Bergman, Brismar, & Nordin, 1992; Campbell, Poland, Waller, & Ager, 1992; McCauley et al., 1995; McFarlane & Parker, 1994a). Although Ratner (1993) found a substantial association of alcohol abuse and battering in a recent Canadian random sample survey, Plichta (1997) did not find an association between intimate partner violence and alcohol use (abuse not measured) in the United States, although an association with illicit drug (but not tranquilizer) use was found. Clearly, substance abuse treatment programs for women need to address domestic violence, and shelter programs need to become more inclusive of substance-abusing battered women in their interventions.

History of Health Care Response to Battering

The pioneering work of Evan Stark and Anne Flitcraft (Stark et al., 1979) first drew attention to the potential of the health care system encounter to be another victimization experience for battered women. They were also the first to outline how the health care system could be used to empower battered women (Stark et al., 1981). Their leadership in scholarship, training of health care professionals, and health policy change over the past two decades has been crucial to the growing awareness of domestic violence in the health care system. Karil Klingbeil (1986), in the family violence program of hospital-based interventions at Harborview in Seattle, was also a pioneer in demonstrating the potential effectiveness of health care system interventions for battered women. Former Surgeon General C. Everett Koop (U.S. Surgeon General, 1985) convened a groundbreaking conference in 1985 to advance using the public health perspective to address violence. Mark Rosenberg, Jim Mercy, Linda Saltzman, and Denise Johnson have since then provided leadership at the Centers for Disease Control in providing research funding directed at primary and secondary prevention of violence, including all forms of violence against women.

In medicine, Ronald Chez and Robert Jones were instrumental in starting the American Association of Obstetrics and Gynecology initiative for educating physicians to screen for and appropriately refer abused women. As president of

the American Medical Association (AMA), Robert McAfee made family violence his first priority and started the highly visible and effective AMA initiative
against family violence in 1992 (American Medical Association, Council on
Ethical and Judicial Affairs, 1992). The Family Violence Prevention Fund, under
the direction of Esta Soler and her staff, especially Debbie Lee and Janet
Nudleman, received funding in 1992 to become the National Health Resource
Center under the Department of Health and Human Services. They have been
leaders in providing training for health care professionals on domestic violence
and in producing health-related training materials. On the international front,
Lori Heise has led efforts to document the health care effects of abuse for women
around the world and has been successful in gaining recognition for the health
care costs of domestic violence from the World Bank (1993) and the need for a
violence against women initiative from the World Health Organization (WHO;
1997).

Nursing has been part of and provided leadership in all these efforts. The
first nursing research study on domestic violence was Barbara Parker's (Parker
& Schumacher, 1977) controlled study of risk factors published in 1977. At least
20 nurses attended the Surgeon General's Task Force in 1985 and in the same
year held the first nursing conference on violence against women organized by
Christine King (Chapter 4) and Peggy Perry. At that conference, the Nursing
Network on Violence Against Women was started, in 1995 adding *International*
and becoming NNVAWI. This organization is dedicated to ending violence
against women and transforming the health care system to become more responsive to the health care needs of victimized women and their children. The
organization has nursing membership from every state, holds a meeting every
other year, publishes an occasional newsletter, and maintains a directory of
nurses knowledgeable and committed to the issue of violence against women and
their particular specialty. The American Nurses Association (ANA) passed major
resolutions on domestic violence in 1987 and 1991 calling for nursing screening
of women for domestic violence in all health care settings. Daniel Sheridan
initiated the first nursing-social work hospital-based family violence intervention program at Rush-Presbyterian-St. Luke's Medical Center in Chicago. In
Chapter 2, he describes the current generation of such programs, and in Chapter
17, Deborah Page-Adams and Susan Dersch present findings from one of the
programs currently under way.

Nursing research has contributed significantly to the body of knowledge
about the health effects of domestic violence. The first nursing research study on
abuse during pregnancy was published in 1986 (Helton, 1986), and Judy
McFarlane and Barbara Parker have conducted a sustained program of nursing
research on this aspect of domestic violence for more than a decade (Chapters 8
and 16 in this volume; see also Parker, McFarlane, & Soeken, 1994). They have
currently completed an evaluation of a nursing intervention for abused pregnant
women with exciting results (McFarlane, Parker, Soeken, Silva, & Reel, 1998).
My own program of research began with domestic homicide (Campbell, 1981)

and is currently returning to that issue as described in this volume and elsewhere (Campbell, 1995). I have also examined the health effects of forced sex in battering relationships (Campbell, 1989b), and women's physical, emotional, and behavioral responses to battering over time (Campbell et al., 1996; J. C. Campbell, Miller, Cardwell, & Belknap, 1994). There are other leading nursing researchers who have contributed substantively to what is known about battered women and their children and what can be done to address their health and safety needs. Notable programs of research and scholarship include Kären Landenbur-ger's (Chapter 5) development and testing of her theory of entrapment and recovery, Christine King and Jo Ryan's (Chapters 4 and 14) development of primary care and preventive interventions, Janice Humphreys (Chapter 11) and Janet Ericksen and Angela Henderson's (Chapter 12) in-depth investigations with the children of battered women, and the emphasis on culturally competent interventions for women of color and other special populations, represented in this volume by Doris Campbell and Faye Gary (African American women), Sara Torres (Latinas), Rachel Rodriguez (migrant women), Diane Bohn (Native American women), and Nancy Fishwick (rural women). A comprehensive and critical review of nursing research in this area will be published this year (Campbell & Parker, in press).

Nursing research has been characterized by its activist and/or feminist (woman centered) assumptions and stance. This conclusion is supported by the close collaboration of nursing researchers with shelters for abused women, particular concern for the safety of women and their children (Parker & Ulrich, 1990), clear concern for the empowerment of women as part of the research process as well as in the use of research results (Hoff, 1990), documentation of battered women and their children's strengths as well as problems, and an assumption that the locus of responsibility is with individual perpetrators and our societal structures and attitudes that facilitate or fail to sufficiently sanction or prevent battering. There has also been a beginning (but ahead of the field in general) inquiry into and sensitivity to cultural effects on women's responses to battering (e.g., J. C. Campbell, Miller, et al., 1994; Torres, 1987, 1991). Nursing has often been a bridge between the activist battered women's movement and the rest of the health care system. There have also been serious shortcomings in nursing research, with too many studies with small and/or nonrepresentative samples, a lack of intervention testing studies (true of the field in general), and generally a lack of visibility of this research to the rest of the field.

Policy Recommendations
for the Health Care System

For the health care system to become an empowerment zone for battered women, policy-level initiatives are needed. These recommendations have also been made by several health-related organizations such as the ANA, AMA,

AWHONN, the American College of Obstetricians and Gynecologists (ACOG), the Association of Nurse Midwives (ANMW), and the NNVAWI. The first group of recommendations relate to screening for domestic violence in health care settings.

Recommendation for Health Care Settings

Universal screening of women for abuse at all health care visits should be routine. All women coming to a health care setting for any reason should be routinely screened for abuse (see Chapters 16 and 17 for methods and tools for screening). Universal screening of all women (including adolescents) for intimate partner abuse at each health care system is warranted as routine practice for the following reasons: (a) the general prevalence of abuse is greater in young women than are other conditions routinely screened (e.g., hypertension), (b) the change in abuse status over time (during pregnancy, before and after pregnancy, and throughout the woman's life) (J. Campbell, Pliska, Taylor, & Sheridan, 1994; Gielen, O'Campo, Faden, Kass, & Xue, 1994; McFarlane, Parker, Soeken, & Bullock, 1992), (c) the variety of physical and mental health problems (most often *without* injury) battered women experience (Goldberg & Tomlanovich, 1984; Ratner, 1993), (d) the lack of consistently identified personal or demographic characteristics (risk factors) that can identify women more likely to be abused in any setting (Chapter 17 in this volume; see also Hotaling & Sugarman, 1990) or more likely to continue in battering relationships than other abused women (J. C. Campbell, Miller, et al., 1994), and (e) abuse can aggravate an existing condition or compromise the treatment of an existing condition as well as directly or indirectly cause a health problem.

In EDs, the screening should not be limited to women presenting with trauma, because of evidence that women are more likely to present with other conditions (Goldberg & Tomlanovich, 1984). Urgent care settings also need to be conducting routine screening. As more and more of health care is delivered as managed care, there is even more need for universal screening (at least for those under age 60) and interventions for abuse of women in those settings. Because of the frequency of abuse during and after pregnancy, routine screening of women at all prenatal care visits, at delivery, and at the postpartum checkup is mandatory. Intimate partner abuse should also be particularly assessed at well-child visits, and all programs directed to childbearing women such as Special Supplemental Nutrition Program for Women, Infants, and Children (WIC), Healthy Mother-Healthy Baby programs, and adolescent pregnancy and parenting programs.

All screening protocols need to include a procedure for regularly separating the woman from all male partners and family members during the abuse screen-

ing process. Women who do not speak English should not be asked about abuse using a family member as an interpreter. Separation of partners needs to be a built-in, routine part of the health assessment so that abuse screening administered in private does not seem unnatural. Health care providers need to realize that a male partner is not the only problem when screening for abuse. Female family members may also make women feel uncomfortable about disclosing.

Nontraditional health and public health settings should be used as opportune settings to prevent future and address existing intimate partner violence. School-based clinics and STD clinics are excellent examples of settings where health care providers can be used in prevention of domestic violence and to assess for and intervene with both victims and perpetrators of intimate partner violence.

Mandatory reporting of domestic violence by health care providers to criminal justice agencies should not become policy or law until subsequent safety is investigated by research. Mandatory reporting of domestic violence (less serious than a felony assault or domestic violence involving a weapon) by health care providers may well make women less likely to tell a health care provider about their abuse (Hyman & Chez, 1995). She may be afraid that he will hurt her more as a result of the health care provider's report. There has been no research to indicate whether women are safer or less safe as a result of mandatory reporting (Chalk & King, 1998). The potential inhibiting effect may be even more true in the military where a report might not only engender more violence but also can adversely affect the male partner's career. If a woman is still invested in the relationship, his career also is part of her future.

Civilian criminal justice authorities already have difficulty in responding to all the domestic violence 9-1-1 calls and are not equipped to handle more reports of domestic violence. If the criminal justice response to such calls is uncertain, it is problematic to make the reports. Finally, mandatory reporting takes away the battered woman's agency to make her own decisions about what should be done next. It may be that it would be helpful for a health care professional to make the report to the criminal justice system, because it would take the onus of responsibility off the woman. In fact, that can and should be one of the options offered to her. But she is in the best position to make that decision—it is her life and well-being that are on the line, and she is empowered only if she is facilitated in making her own decisions.

Sexual Abuse-Related Recommendations

Because of the frequency of sexual assault in battering relationships, the following recommendations take into account the interface of health care providers and women's sexuality in a variety of settings.

All women coming to family planning centers (e.g., Planned Parenthood) should be routinely screened for intimate partner violence with interventions for those abused provided. The significant physical and mental health effects (lower self-esteem) specific to forced relationship sex and possibility of unintended pregnancy clearly support such a mandate (Campbell, 1989a; Campbell & Alford, 1989; Campbell, Pugh, et al., 1995; Eby et al., 1995). It also has been demonstrated that women can be successfully screened for abuse in planned parenthood settings with indication that face-to-face interviews using the AAS were more successful than using a written history form, although both methods yielded significant disclosure of abuse (Bullock & McFarlane, 1989). In family planning settings, a brief nursing intervention of thorough gynecological assessment and treatment for identified problems, counseling about increased STD and HIV/AIDS risk, referral to domestic violence specific services (criminal justice, shelter) as desired, safety planning, and follow-up appointments would be appropriate on site because the majority of these women may not be ready or able (in terms of transportation or other obstacles) to seek services elsewhere. Weingourt (1985, 1990) has also described nursing interventions in mental health settings for women sexually abused by an intimate partner.

All HIV/AIDS prevention programs and STD interventions/special programs for women should include careful assessment and interventions for intimate partner abuse. It is clear that battered women, especially those also sexually abused, are at increased risk for HIV/AIDS and other STDs (Eby et al., 1995; Gielen et al., 1994; Ratner, 1993). Complex interactions are related to this issue that need to be investigated further. Some data indicate that abusive men may be particularly reluctant to use condoms and/or that their sexual partners would be afraid to insist on condom use (Campbell, Harris, & Lee, 1995; Eby et al., 1995). Other abusers, already prone to jealousy, may interpret a request for safe sex practices as meaning that the woman has been sexually unfaithful. In actuality, the reverse is more likely to be accurate. To place the onus of responsibility on women to insist that their partners use a condom may put women at risk for violence.

Because of the intimate partner violence issues related to HIV/AIDS transmission and safe sex practices, advocacy is needed to urge increased resources directed toward the swift development of vaginal HIV antiviral agents. The basic development of these agents is already completed, but their progress to clinical trials has been relatively slow. The National Institutes of Health (NIH) should be urged to complete clinical trials on these agents because pharmaceutical companies are not progressing as swiftly as possible. Because of violence and sexual autonomy issues, this could be the most significant advance in the prevention of the spread of HIV/AIDS to women short of a vaccine.

All research involving HIV/AIDS and other STDs needs to take into account the potential for domestic violence in partner disclosure protocols. Research related to domestic violence needs to have particular regard for women's safety. A recent investigation of HIV/AIDS in Africa resulted in a third of the women who had tested positive being beaten by their husbands as a result of informing them of the test results according to the researchers' directions. The possibility of domestic violence to women in situations involving research needs to be taken into account in institutional review board deliberations. Nursing researchers (Parker & Ulrich, 1990) have collaborated to publish a protocol of safety for domestic violence research to be used as a starting point in designing such studies, and leading ethical scholars Tilden and Limandri have collaborated in Chapter 3 to fully explicate ethical issues related to domestic violence.

Collaborative Systems Approaches

Treatment for depression and substance abuse (in primary care and other settings) needs to include assessment and interventions for domestic violence. Based on the research documenting depression as the primary mental health response to battering, interventions in the health care system for depression need to include abuse assessment and interventions. Even if health care providers conceptualize major depression as a primarily neurophysiological genetically based disorder with abuse as an episode-triggering stressor, treating only the depression will not end the violence. Specific and separate interventions are needed. The same is true for substance abuse treatment for both perpetrators and survivors. Similarly, community domestic violence interventions such as shelters need to include routine screening and referral for depression and substance abuse. These systems can benefit from close collaboration with cross-training and jointly designed interventions to make them appropriate for both problems.

Programs addressing child abuse as well as inpatient nursing care for abused children need to include domestic violence assessment and intervention. Research indicates a strong overlap between woman abuse and child abuse, with as many as 77% of couples with severe wife abuse also abusing a child (Straus & Gelles, 1990). Indications are that children are at even higher risk when the abusive partner is not the biological father (Daly & Wilson, 1990). Programs designed to address child abuse (e.g., family preservation programs; Healthy Mothers, Healthy Babies; child protective services; hospital multidisciplinary child abuse teams) all need to assess mothers of children abused or at risk for abuse for domestic violence and intervene accordingly. Programs such as Advocacy for Women and Kids in Emergencies (AWAKE) at Children's Hospital of Boston have been designed to specifically address the needs of abused mothers of abused children (see Chapter 2). Although not yet rigorously evaluated, preliminary indications are that this program is helpful not only in protecting the abused mothers but also the children (Chalk & King, 1998). Pediatric nurses can provide assessment and interventions for domestic violence for the mothers of hospitalized abused children in hospitals where programs like AWAKE do not exist.

Collaborative, interdisciplinary research efforts among health care system professionals and among the health care, legal, and advocacy systems are needed, especially partnerships to implement longitudinal and intervention evaluation studies. This kind of partnership research is characterized by true "interdisciplinarity," respect for complementary areas of expertise rather than the sometimes patronizing attitudes of researchers in the past, understanding for the past and present realities that cause distrust between disciplines and between researchers and advocates, a commitment to long-term working relationships and working through inevitable conflicts and misunderstandings, and mutual commitment to inclusion of the communities served by interventions (Short, Hennessy, & Campbell, 1996). Several recent documents have made excellent, specific recommendations as to the type of research that is needed (Chalk & King, 1998; Crowell & Burgess, 1996).

Special Populations

International health as well as human rights organization initiatives need to address domestic violence. There has been limited international research related to domestic violence, but population-based surveys are beginning to emerge from several different countries (Heise, Pitanguy, & Germain, 1994). There have also been a few ethnographic investigations. For instance, Counts, Brown, and Campbell (1992) used primary ethnographic evidence collected from 14 different societies representing a range of geographic locations, industrialization, household arrangements, and degree of spousal violence to examine evidence supporting the primary Western social science theoretical stances about battering. Although the feminist theoretical premises received considerable support, several aspects were brought into question. The review suggested that all forms of violence against women could not be considered as facets of the same phenomenon and that status of women is an extremely complex, multifaceted phenomenon that may have a curvilinear rather than direct relationship with wife battering. The review also demonstrated the importance of societal influences on individual couples. In that study, wife beating (occasional, nonescalating, without serious or permanent injury, seen as ordinary by most members of the culture, and occurring in almost all societies in the world) was differentiated from wife battering (the continuing, usually escalating, potentially injurious pattern of physical violence within a context of coercive control, not seen as normative) most often described in Western social sciences and health research. The factors that discouraged the escalation of wife beating to battering across societies included community-level sanctions against battering and sanctuary for beaten wives enacted in culturally specific and appropriate forms. It is possible that some of these community-level strategies could be adapted as prevention measures in the United States.

More international research is needed and could be conducted collaboratively through such entities as the WHO and the World Bank. In Vienna in 1993, violence against women was first officially recognized as a human rights violation by the international community. Such international organizations as the WHO and the Pan American Health Organization are just beginning to conceptualize intimate partner violence as a health problem and strategize how to include domestic violence initiatives in international maternal child and mental health initiatives. Although the health ministries of many developing countries are beginning to address domestic violence, much more attention is needed.

Interventions and research with battered women need to be culturally specific and sensitive. Recently, Doris Campbell and colleagues (D. W. Campbell, Campbell, King, Parker, & Ryan, 1994) reported a study on the use of the Index of Spouse Abuse (ISA) with African American women. They found somewhat different psychometric categories of the instrument in this group with evidence of Oliver Williams's (1989) formulation suggesting that "when black males engage in violence against black females, it is because they have defined the situation as one in which the female's actions constitute a threat to their manhood" (p. 265). The study suggested the importance of developing culturally sensitive assessment for battered women and considering ethnic specific interpretations of abuse when providing interventions. Translation issues also are complex. Back-translation procedures and standards and differences in dialects within the Spanish language often are not fully taken into account in research instruments or in health care system assessment forms and resource materials (Porter & Villarruel, 1993). Both the AAS and the Danger Assessment (Campbell, 1995) have been translated into Spanish and used successfully with Spanish-speaking women from many countries.

Nursing research has begun to address issues of ethnic influences on battering (e.g., Torres, 1987), a field in which the state of the science is underdeveloped. Several clinical nursing articles have delineated nursing care of battered women, taking culture into account (e.g., Campbell & Campbell, 1996), and this text has a section of chapters (19-23) detailing suggested nursing and health care interventions specific to various cultural and geographic groups. In nursing research with important clinical implications, McFarlane and colleagues (1992) examined the prevalence and severity of abuse in African American, Hispanic, and Anglo pregnant women. They found prevalence significantly lower among Hispanic women and severity lowest among African American women. In investigations of the influence of ethnicity on depression and subsequent violence in battered women, little difference was found between African American and Anglo women (Campbell et al., 1994; Campbell et al., 1997).

Culturally sensitive research also involves careful strategies for recruiting ethnic minority samples and interpreting results within a cultural context (Henderson, Sampselle, Mayes, & Oakley, 1992). Unfortunately, many members of health care professions are convinced that battering is primarily a problem with poor women of color. Many of the recent medical research studies on abuse have used samples of primarily poor women and therefore disproportionately more women of color, because it is difficult to gain access to private patients for research on sensitive issues. Unfortunately, this supports the impression that only these women are affected. Issues of race and ethnicity are sensitive in violence research, and it is extremely important to include economically heterogeneous samples and use class and/or income as well as ethnicity in multivariate analysis (Hawkins, 1993; Porter & Villarruel, 1993).

Advocacy Issues

Continuing efforts for legal and industry mandates and constant vigilance are needed to ensure that battered women are not denied health care insurance because of being abused. Although much headway has been made in addressing this issue thanks to the leadership of the Pennsylvania Coalition Against Domestic Violence, this era of capitation and managed care presents a constant threat of health care business using documentation of abuse as a preexisting condition for insurance denial.

Nurses and other health care professionals need to be part of the collaborative efforts to address the needs of battered women in the process of welfare reform. Beginning research efforts have demonstrated that battered women are disproportionately affected by welfare reform, and may be less able to take advantage of work training programs because of the interference and threats of a violent partner. In addition, battered women often need to use welfare temporarily to escape from a violent relationship. Sara Buel (1994) and Vickie Coffey (1998) are two heroines who eloquently describe their history of going from welfare and battering to advanced degrees and are inspirations to us all. At the same time, actions to protect battered women on welfare should not be taken at the expense of other poor women and their children. Nurses and other health care professionals need to be part of the search for solutions of these dilemmas, in terms of specific input related to Medicaid health care for these families as well as addressing the issues in general. Clearly, back-to-work programs for women on welfare need to assess for domestic violence in women's homes and to collaborate with shelters, advocates, and the health care system to address the issue of violence and the issues of work and welfare.

All health care professionals, including nurses, need to continue efforts to decrease the availability of handguns in general and to join with the domestic violence advocacy community to decrease the availability of handguns to batterers. The overwhelming majority of homicides in general and homicides of women specifically are perpetrated with a handgun. Handguns kept in the home are far more likely to kill family members than intruders (Bailey et al., 1997). All experts in the field agree that a gun in the home is a risk factor for homicide in battering relationships (Campbell, 1995). In addition, the threats of abusive men often are backed up with and made more frightening with a gun. The experience of being threatened with a handgun is more traumatic and emotionally devastating than that of being threatened with a fist.

Public funds pay for approximately 70% of hospital costs of gun-related injury (Martin, Hunt, & Hulley, 1988), draining our resources from other badly needed health care initiatives (Kassierer, 1991). Where handguns are illegal (e.g., Canada, Western Europe), all forms of violent crime and injury related to violence are substantially less than that of the United States, arguing against the notion that criminals will continue to obtain handguns and use them against innocent citizens. Public opinion polls indicate that most Americans favor stricter gun-control laws, and it is hoped that new federal restrictions on convicted domestic violence offenders owning handguns will increase the safety of battered women. It is important, however, that these restrictions be addressed in state law also so that a gun can be impounded when there is an order of protection. In a recent case in Maryland, an abuser was removed from a woman's home by the police under an order of protection, but his gun was not taken from him. The next day, he used that gun to kill the woman.

Nurses as Intervenors

Nursing, in collaboration with other disciplines and depending on the setting and its staffing roles, should be providing interventions for abused women, not just screening and referral. There is some debate as to who should be providing interventions in the health care system as well as what kinds of interventions should be provided. However, nurses are the most numerous health care professionals, of all the health care professionals interact the most amount of time with women, and are present in inpatient health care settings 24 hours a day. In addition, one of the first completed evaluations of interventions for abuse provided in the health care setting has demonstrated that a brief intervention conducted by prenatal care nurses was effective in increasing safety behaviors (McFarlane et al., 1998). Although screening and referral may be the primary roles for staff nurses in settings where social service staff are readily available, and/or there is a domestic violence program in house, nurses in most settings should be trained to provide at least active listening, an assessment of lethality, safety planning, and an explanation of a woman's legal, medical, and shelter/counseling options (Campbell & Humphreys, 1993). Nurses may be the principal health care intervenors in settings where they are providing primary care or community health care.

Obviously, to be competent providers of interventions for battered women, nurses need more training about domestic violence (see Chapter 4). Although all the major nursing texts contain at least a chapter about family violence, there is not systematic inclusion of domestic violence in all nursing curricula. The ANA has called for such inclusion, and addition of questions on all licensure and certification exams would do much to ensure curricular attention to the issue. Continuing education offerings have been and continue to be held as part of most of the specialty nursing conferences as well as training in EDs and hospitals. However, it is questionable if individual provider education and training will result in widespread and sustained system change. Training that involves interdisciplinary teams of providers, community domestic violence advocates, and institutional managers (e.g., Family Violence Prevention Fund; Warshaw & Ganley, 1996) has the greatest chance of creating an empowering health care setting, where interventions with battered women are supported and expected.

Empowerment Zone Interventions

No matter what the setting, the ideal health care setting intervention is provided as an interdisciplinary process with the woman herself determining who and when is the most appropriate person for her to disclose her abuse to and to intervene. The empowerment zone concept means that the woman herself should be in charge of the process, with her autonomy and her strengths acknowledged and respected, and the health care professionals partners with her in providing the interventions she needs.

The desired outcome of interventions is not necessarily leaving the relationship, at least immediately. New and innovative interventions are needed that are preventive in nature and seek to transform controlling and abusive relationships to nonviolent and supportive ones. The assumption of many advocates and much of the literature on domestic violence is that the best outcome for abused women is that they leave the battering relationship. In fact, research suggests that the majority of battered women do eventually leave the violent relationship (Campbell et al., 1994). However, it is a process of leaving that often involves returning several times—a process that needs to be interpreted as normal rather than pathological (see Chapters 5 and 6).

Interventions also need to recognize that women experience considerable abuse after they leave, ranging from mild forms of harassment to serious property destruction, stalking, and physical violence (Campbell, McKenna, Torres, Sheridan, & Landenburger, 1993; Campbell & Parker, in press). In a recent analysis of longitudinal data from a community (not clinical or shelter) sample of 57 women, Campbell, Sebbio, and associates (Sebbio, 1996) found that after 3 years, a greater proportion of those who had left the abusive relationship (14 of 18 or 77.7%) were still being battered by the original partner than those who had stayed (16 of 25 or 64%). This is not to argue that battered women should stay in the relationship, but that health care professionals should be aware of the continued abuse that most often occurs if they do leave and their need for continued protection as well as the possibility that an abusive relationship can become nonviolent, although this is not the usual pattern. Several studies suggest that abusive relationships *can* become not only nonviolent but also noncontrolling and non-emotionally abusive (D. W. Campbell et al., 1994; Fagan & Browne, 1994; Feld & Straus, 1989). Public health principles would predict that identifying and intervening with battering relationships early would increase our chances of successful relationship transformation.

Abused women in health care settings are often not seeking intervention for the abuse per se and, if in the early stages of a violent relationship, usually do not even define themselves as abused or battered (Campbell, Anderson, et al., 1993; see also Chapter 5 in this volume). They most often wish to maintain the relationship, usually out of concerns for children, although also because of financial issues, love for the spouse, pessimism that she will find another relationship that is better, or a sense that the partner has other problems that are causing the abuse (e.g., substance abuse, unemployment, discrimination) that can perhaps be solved (Campbell, Rose, & Kub, in press; Ulrich, 1994). Minority cultural groups also express the concern that criminal justice or relationship dissolution solutions for domestic violence are destructive for their communities and families. Thus, nursing and the health care system need to continue to be proactive in designing interventions in conjunction with the battered women's community and women themselves who promote the transformation of relationships to nonviolent and noncontrolling. Evaluations of such programs as WomanKind (Hadley, Short, Lesin, & Zook, 1995; see also Chapter 2 in this volume) that provide domestic violence interventions in the health care system should be encouraged and new and innovative interventions developed and tested.

Research indicates that women are most at risk for homicide from an intimate partner and that her abuse is the major identifiable precursor of the homicide (e.g., Campbell, 1992). There is also indication that women are most at risk for homicide when they leave the battering relationship (Wilson & Daly, 1993). Although there are no domestic homicide risk factor lists with actual evidence of predictive validity, several have been developed and published with widespread support for some sort of lethality assessment conducted. The Danger

Assessment was specifically designed for health care system administration to increase battered women's awareness of the potential for homicide and thereby enhance their self-care agency (Campbell, 1986). It has some construct validity support and has been used widely in many different kinds of health settings (Campbell, 1995). It can be obtained either from the author or on page 93 in this volume.

The health care provider best suited to provide interventions related to domestic violence is the provider that the woman trusts the most. Providing a thorough assessment of all aspects of the abuse (physical, emotional, and sexual) and the physical and mental health effects, lethality assessment, immediate problem and solution identification, safety planning, follow-up provisions, and appropriate referral are all within the professional scope and abilities of nurses, social workers, and physicians. So too are diagnosis and treatment of their mental and physical health care problems; assessment of their psychosocial conditions and the full context of their situation, including their children; and help in developing their ability to care for themselves and their children. The health care system can become a place for battered women and their children to find safety, to find respite, to find support, and to find affirmation for their strengths.

2

Health Care-Based Programs for Domestic Violence Survivors

Daniel J. Sheridan

Hospital-based domestic violence (DV) programs were first created in the mid-1970s; however, by the early 1990s there were probably no more than 10 hospital-based DV programs in the country (Sheridan & Taylor, 1993). Today, interest in creating specialized health care services for battered women and their children is at an unprecedented high, and hospital or health care system-based DV intervention and prevention programs are almost too numerous to count. The physical, emotional, and sexual abuse of women by intimate partners is now seen as a major public health problem deserving of specialized services and education.

Four Early Model Programs

After recognizing four of the earliest hospital-based DV programs, this chapter will briefly highlight a variety of current health care system-based DV programs. These DV programs can serve as models for the growing number of institutions wanting to provide much needed services to domestic violence survivors. Because of space considerations, many excellent and nationally known health care system DV programs are not mentioned. The criteria for choosing the highlighted programs were based on trying to present differing models coupled with the availability of written program descriptions at time of press.

The first hospital-based DV program reported in the literature (Hadley, 1992) was the Battered Women's Program at Hennepin County Medical Center in Minneapolis, which was created in 1975. This program, initiated by Betty Cavanaugh, an emergency department (ED) nurse, had one paid staff member and a core of trained volunteers who provided in-depth advocacy to domestic violence survivors and provided training to interested ED nurses and physicians. By the early 1990s, the program had served over 2,500 battered women survivors and included a support group for older battered women.

In 1986, in a suburb of Minneapolis, Susan Hadley, a community-based battered women's advocate, created WomanKind at Fairview Southdale Hospital (Hadley, Short, Lesin, & Zook, 1995). WomanKind, which was initially a separate agency, was started as a one-person, around-the-clock, domestic violence crisis intervention and advocacy program that provided services primarily to battered women in the ED. In addition to advocacy, WomanKind provided education of ED and hospital staff. As a core of trained volunteers became available, the program developed domestic violence support groups and more in-depth education programs for any interested health provider, and it continued to expand its communication and networking services.

The Advocacy for Women and Kids in Emergencies (AWAKE) program at Children's Hospital in Boston was created by Susan Schechter in 1986. It was the first program in a pediatric setting to provide dual advocacy for battered women and their abused children. The philosophy of the AWAKE program was and is that by providing advocacy, support, and counseling to battered women in conjunction with services to their abused children, both patient populations are better served. This philosophy is empowering of women and increased the safety of children and women, but is a philosophy still not readily embraced by child protective agencies and child advocates, who too often chose a punitive approach toward battered women for failing to protect their children.

Later in 1986, the Family Violence Program (FVP) at Chicago's Rush-Presbyterian-St. Luke's Medical Center was created by this author to provide 24-hour crisis clinical services to family violence survivors throughout the life cycle who presented for ED treatment (Sheridan & Taylor, 1993). Although crisis intervention and systems advocacy were the primary objectives of the FVP, thorough, accurate documentation, including photographic documentation, in the health care record was also prioritized. Training of interested ED, hospital, and university personnel on domestic violence recognition and documentation was also conducted. The FVP also trained and coordinated a core of volunteers who provided on-call advocacy services to sexual assault survivors. With increased funding from community and governmental sources, the staff of the FVP grew to where it provided battered women support groups and community outreach and networking. The FVP primarily served ED patients but was beginning to expand its services throughout the medical center and its clinics just prior to being restructured out of existence in 1993.

WomanKind, on the other hand, prospered, expanded, and became a formal department within the Fairview health care system (Hadley et al., 1995). Today, WomanKind has program services in three Minnesota hospitals, Fairview Ridges Hospital, Fairview Southdale Hospital, and Fairview Riverside Hospital. Services within these hospitals from WomanKind staff, either paid or from a core of trained volunteers, include 24-hour case management, advocacy, crisis intervention, and ongoing assistance. Clinical services and education and training has expanded well beyond the ED to serve the entire Fairview health care system.

Current Programs

Domestic Violence Project

As information on the above programs began to be disseminated through conferences, battered women's networks, and by word-of-mouth, additional programs slowly began to develop around the country. In 1991, the Domestic Violence Project began as an independent, nonprofit organization to provide hospital-based domestic violence advocacy to patients in hospitals in Kenosha, Wisconsin. Combined systems advocacy from a local cardiologist and former director of a local battered women's shelter convinced two local hospitals and the local order of Catholic Dominican Sisters to provide seed money to develop an innovative advocacy and training program. Through a small paid staff and trained volunteers, the Domestic Violence Project provides services throughout the hospital system including working to create an abuse-free workplace for employees of Kenosha Hospital and Medical Center. In an effort to prevent further violence, for the past several years Domestic Violence Project staff are also making telephone outreach to victims identified through local law enforcement records.

Hospital Crisis Intervention Project

In 1992 in Chicago, a partnership between Cook County Hospital and the Chicago Abused Women's Coalition resulted in the creation of the Hospital Crisis Intervention Project (HCIP), which began providing clinical services in February 1993. HCIP is a program of the Chicago Abused Women's Coalition that is provided space and a variety of in-kind support from Cook County Hospital, which provides health care to a primarily poor, medically indigent, and culturally diverse population from Chicago's inner city. Most of HCIP's staff are bicultural and bilingual, and crisis intervention and advocacy services are provided in at least five different languages, reflecting the diversity of the patient population. Most services are focused on Cook County Hospital's enormous ambulatory care clinics and ED services and consist of individual counseling and referral into needed services ranging from emergency shelter to parenting skill training and drug and alcohol treatment. Ongoing education of hospital staff is conducted in conjunction with a few highly trained direct care providers from within the hospital staff. HCIP staff routinely network with multidisciplinary professionals interested in child abuse and neglect, women with HIV issues, high-risk pregnancies, and community-based organizations.

AWAKE Program

In 1994, the AWAKE program expanded its services, primarily through the use of paid staff, to the community health care site in a low-income housing development and routinely makes outreach to pregnant adolescents. Services include crisis response; risk assessment; safety planning; individual and support group counseling for battered women and abused children; and assistance and referral into emergency housing, legal services, court advocacy, and immigration services. The goal of the AWAKE program is to make the hospital and/or clinic a safe place to disclose abuse, to empower and validate battered women so that they can better protect themselves from further violence and coercion, and to keep women and their children together whenever possible.

AWARE Program

In 1994, the Assisting Women with Advocacy, Resources, and Education (AWARE) program was created by nurse advocate Susan Dersch at Barnes and Jewish Hospital in St. Louis through the administrative support of the Women's Education Services Department of Women's and Children's Health Services. The AWARE program has one full-time staff member and many highly trained volunteers. In-person support and referral services are provided to battered women who are inpatients and non-ED outpatients in various clinic settings. Abused women using Barnes and Jewish Hospital's ED services receive telephone follow-up from AWARE staff. Domestic violence education and training of health care providers within the hospital and community are major foci of the program. AWARE staff routinely participate in statewide domestic violence training and prevention efforts and are building strong relationships within the criminal justice system to help train health care providers in better forensic documentation, including photographs, of abuse within health care records. Viewing domestic violence as a major women's health problem that exists beyond the ED is a major focus of the AWARE program. A philosophy of the AWARE program is to train health care workers to provide appropriate, thorough, minimal standards of domestic violence intervention and care and not have staff be dependent on a specialized domestic violence expert or team.

The Domestic Violence Program

In late 1994, St. Agnes Hospital in Fond du Lac, Wisconsin began its Domestic Violence Program (DVP) after a year of planning and community coalition building. Using part-time staff, services of the DVP include 24-hour crisis intervention to patients and staff, especially around issues of discharge safety planning. The DVP maintains a domestic violence resource library for patients and staff and provides violence identification and prevention training education to all hospital and clinic staff. Developing hospital-wide domestic violence treatment protocols and outreach and routine training of local police officers were early goals of the program.

Sample CDC-Funded Programs

Monies from federal government agencies such as the Centers for Disease Control (CDC) and other sources are presently funding a variety of model hospital and health care system-based programs in urban, suburban, and rural settings throughout the country. WomanKind is one such program as well as three hospital programs in Pennsylvania that partnered with member programs of the Pennsylvania Coalition Against Domestic Violence: (a) Mercy Hospital and the Women's Center and Shelter of Greater Pittsburgh (urban), (b) Abington Memorial Hospital and the Women's Center of Montgomery County (suburban), and (c) Wyoming Valley Health Care System and the Domestic Violence Service Center of Luzerne County (rural).

Services within these programs are similar to those described in many of the above programs; however, each program in Pennsylvania is trying to identify specific needs based on the size and location of health care services. Lessons learned from model programs from various population settings should prove helpful as DV programs continue to proliferate around the country.

Questions and Funding Issues

Defining Health Care System DV Programs

As more health care institutions formalize domestic violence services, many questions have arisen. For example, a basic question being addressed is what constitutes a health care system-based DV program? To be called a hospital-based DV program does the program have to have a nurse, social worker, or battered women's advocate whose primary responsibility it is to provide services to survivors? If a program provides only training and education to staff, does that constitute a health care system DV program? Some health care providers, such as Kaiser-Permanente Northwest Region, are not employing a specialized person or creating a special program. Rather, they have trained domestic violence response teams in all their clinics and hospitals. Team members have received many hours of specialized training in domestic violence intervention and documentation but provide these services, as needed, in addition to their regular health care duties. Should this model be included in discussions of DV programs?

The Role of Volunteers

Many programs rely heavily on volunteer domestic violence advocates to the point that direct care providers often do less history taking and documentation than if volunteers were not available. Are programs that rely heavily on volunteers adequate, because it is rare that volunteers are allowed to document in the medical record? Is potentially valuable forensic documentation lost if it is only shared with a volunteer and not the primary care staff?

The Need for Long-Term Funding

In addition to documentation issues, there are very real funding concerns. Many of newer hospital-based DV programs are being started with short-term seed monies obtained from community and government sources. Will health care agencies, which are continuously downsizing in a competitive managed care environment, prioritize allocating internal funding to maintain long-term domestic violence intervention and training services?

Although there is support from the guidelines published by the Joint Commission on the Accreditation of Healthcare Organizations (JCAHO; 1996) to maintain ongoing domestic violence training of all key personnel, that training is not dependent on maintaining a hospital-funded DV program. Health care system programs that are partnerships with community-based DV programs depend on the fiscal health of the community-based DV program, a prognosis that is tenuous at best as competition for dwindling community monies becomes more intense.

Insurance Industry Discrimination Against Battered Women

In theory, a steady flow of monies from the health insurance and HMO industry should be available because early identification, treatment, and referral of battered women decrease future domestic trauma and costs. However, the initial response of many insurance companies, major and minor, to thousands of battered women was to deny them insurance or reinsurance because they viewed women abuse as a preexisting condition. A woman's being beaten was cutting into profit margins, so instead of addressing the public health issue of domestic violence, these companies discriminated against a crime victim (Fromson & Durborow, 1997).

Future Program Questions

Among many questions yet to be answered include (a) Should health care-based DV programs exist to primarily train all health providers to give minimal standards of care to survivors? (b) Are specialized domestic violence experts or programming needed in all health care settings, especially because in-depth DV services in a health care setting can be time-prohibitive for most regular providers? and (c) Are the needs of health care DV programs in urban, suburban, and/or rural settings significantly different to develop separate program strategies?

Resources

Family Violence Prevention Fund

The San Francisco-based Family Violence Prevention Fund is an invaluable source of domestic violence health care information, including identification and treatment protocols. The fund is a national public policy and education institute that has numerous publications on justice, public education, and health issues of domestic violence. It receives federal funding to be the national clearinghouse for domestic violence health-related materials. The fund has a wealth of literature, public service, and public education materials that will be of benefit to any health care system DV program.

Nursing Organizations Address
Violence Against Women

To provide a forum for the necessary debate on these questions and countless others, the Nursing Network on Violence Against Women International (NNVAWI) created several years ago a Health Care System Domestic Violence Program Sub-Committee. The subcommittee has met almost yearly to discuss issues and to provide an opportunity for sharing program ideas, protocols, and experiences. Membership in this subcommittee is growing rapidly and is open to any interested agency or individual. Interested parties are encouraged to write NNVAWI, listed in the Resources at the end of this book. One of the major goals of the subcommittee is to coordinate a national conference on health care system DV programs.

The International Association of Forensic Nurses (IAFN) is rapidly expanding its forensic interests to domestic violence survivors. Those interested primarily in the forensic aspects of domestic violence are also encouraged to write the IAFN at the address in the Resources section.

Selected Hospital-Based Domestic Violence Project Contacts

Amanda Cosgrove
Domestic Violence Project
6308 8th Avenue
Kenosha, WI 53143

Susan Dersch
AWARE Program
Barnes Hospital
One Barnes Hospital Plaza
St. Louis, MO 63110

Nancy Durborow
Health Projects Coordinator
Pennsylvania Coalition Against Domestic Violence
6400 Flank Drive, Suite 1300
Harrisburg, PA 17112

Susan Hadley
WomanKind
Fairview Southdale Hospital
6401 France Avenue, South
Edina, MN 55435

Kim Riordan
Chicago Abused Women Coalition
Hospital Crisis Intervention Project
Cook County Hospital
P.O. Box 477916
Chicago, IL 60647

Jennifer Robertson
AWAKE/Children's Hospital
300 Longwood Avenue
Boston, MA 02115

Daniel J. Sheridan
Family Violence Consultant
Oregon Health Sciences University
School of Nursing
3181 SW Sam Jackson Park Road
Portland, OR 97201

Rene Firari Will, Coordinator
St. Agnes Hospital DV Program
430 East Division Street
Fond du Lac, WI 54935

3

Domestic Violence

Reconsideration of Ethical Issues in the Health Care System

Debra Gay Anderson
Barbara J. Limandri
Virginia P. Tilden

Domestic violence is a highly prevalent event in the United States, with approximately 3-4 million women being physically battered by their partners each year (American Medical Association, Council on Ethical and Judicial Affairs, 1992; Straus & Gelles, 1988). Health providers treat approximately 1.5 million abused women each year (Nechas & Foley, 1994); however, many do not routinely assess for family violence or suspect it even when the injuries seem fairly obvious (McFarlane, Parker, Soeken, & Bullock, 1992; Tilden & Shepherd, 1987b). Because abused women feel stigmatized by the violence, they are hesitant to volunteer the nature of their injuries. In 1990, the Joint Commission on the Accreditation of Healthcare Organizations (JCAHO; 1990, 1996), in recognition of the severity of the problem, added requirements for emergency and ambulatory care services to develop and use protocols for the identification of violence among patients. However, research indicates that health care professionals remain reluctant to assess for and intervene in family violence (Limandri & Tilden, 1996; Tilden et al., 1994).

AUTHORS' NOTE: This chapter was adapted from an ethics case prepared by Virginia P. Tilden, DNSc, RN, FAAN, for the Ethics Certificate Program, University of Washington, School of Medicine.

The nurse who is confronted with a situation of domestic violence faces several ethical and legal dilemmas. Ethically, nurses must balance concerns about fidelity (confidentiality) with the duty to warn. Nurses must follow the mandatory reporting laws of their states, which usually are limited to child and elder abuse cases and not adult intimate partner situations. However, when violence occurs in adult relationships, other vulnerable persons, such as children and incapacitated elders, often are involved. When violence is evident, health professionals are asked to predict the dangerousness of the situation in making decisions about interventions. Such predictions and their resultant interventions pose problems of liability for the professional.

This chapter uses two critical cases to illustrate some of the ethical and legal dilemmas faced by nurses in working with situations of family violence. These case studies include both the abuser and the victim as client. Issues of competing obligations to clients and to institutions often make health providers reluctant to get involved in family violence. In addition, the crisis nature of the situation sometimes complicates the nurse's ability to get a complete and accurate assessment. A common question is, who is the client? Is it the family, which includes both the victim and the abuser? Is it the individual, which excludes either the victim or the abuser? Finally, we address dilemmas in intervention. Mandatory reporting laws require reporting child and elder abuse but usually do not include adults in intimate relationships. Reporting may compromise the relationship with the client in such a way that the victim is in greater danger and without the support of the nurse.

Case Presentations

Michael, the Rejected Boyfriend

Michael, a 24-year-old graduate student, was asked to be seen at the counseling center of a large university. The mental health nurse practitioner saw him for three sessions. In the initial session, Michael described being depressed since an intimate relationship with his girlfriend had ended a month earlier. He recounted that his girlfriend had left him suddenly, with little explanation. Since then, he said he had been angry and withdrawn, had noticed deterioration in his school performance, had difficulty sleeping and eating, and had recurring feelings of rage and fantasies of murdering his ex-girlfriend. Michael had no history of psychiatric illness, suicidal ideation, violent behavior, or substance abuse.

The nurse's assessment was that Michael had an acute adjustment disorder and major depression. He was oriented to person, place, and time and denied hallucinations or delusions. He did not express his thoughts of harming the ex-girlfriend until the third therapy session. During that session, he spoke of fantasizing about buying a gun and following the woman, then shooting her when she jogged alone near a wooded area. He stated that he did not plan to actually do this and felt relieved at being able to tell the therapist, whom he felt he could trust. Michael stated that he wished to continue in therapy with the nurse practitioner. The nurse recommended a course of brief psychotherapy oriented toward resolution of a grief reaction and initiating therapy with an antidepressant medication. Michael agreed to this plan and seemed pleased that he could receive help. When Michael left the third session, the nurse questioned him again about the likelihood of his taking action on his fantasies and felt assured that he was not a threat to anyone, including his ex-girlfriend.

The nurse made careful notes in the record about Michael's statement and about the nurse's confidence that he had benefited from talking about his fantasies in such a way that he would not act on them. However, the next day at a clinical team conference when the nurse presented the case, other team members expressed concern about avoiding liability by warning the ex-girlfriend, calling the police, or perhaps admitting Michael to the hospital. The nurse worried about the issue of confidentiality, about what effect reporting would have on Michael and on the therapeutic relationship, and about her abilities to predict dangerousness. She asked for counsel from an attorney and an ethicist at the university. Should she report Michael's murderous fantasies and thereby protect herself from liability and protect the potential victim from possible harm, or should she maintain confidence for maximal therapeutic effect?

Clinical Analysis. The nurse searched Michael's history for prior episodes of violent fantasies or actions and found no evidence that he had ever been violent. Michael had never seen a therapist before, so there was no one to consult about a prior psychological profile. He said he had no police record and no previous violent behaviors or suicidal or homicidal ideations. He occasionally smoked marijuana and drank two to three beers on the weekends, but said he did not use hallucinogenic drugs or consume large quantities of alcohol. The issue of substance use and abuse is relevant because of the high correlation between recreational substance use and violent behavior (Bolton & Bolton, 1987).

When Michael mentioned his violent fantasies in the third session, the nurse questioned him closely in an effort to predict the degree of dangerousness. Monahan and Steadman (1996) proposed a risk assessment for use by mental health professionals in predicting violence. Tools such as these aid the health care provider; however, expert clinical judgment by the provider is the final determination. Risk assessments must be tailored to the variety of complex situations that prevail. How often did Michael think about hurting the woman? Had he ever shot a gun? Did he own a gun? Had he ever followed his ex-girlfriend without her knowing he was there? Michael admitted that he often thought about hurting the woman but said he had made no plans to obtain a weapon. He knew her schedule because they had been living together but said he had not stalked her.

He stated that he did not think he would act on his fantasies. The nurse judged the risk of dangerousness to be low, but worried about her own liability in case she were wrong. She was told by a colleague that the law since the California *Tarasoff* decisions (California Assembly Bill 1133 in 1985; *Tarasoff v. Regents of the University of California*, 1974, 1976) removed her clinical discretion and required her to warn the potential victim or alert the police. However, others said that the California law did not have jurisdiction in her state and she was free to use her clinical judgment to handle the situation.

Ethical Analysis. Confidentiality is the cornerstone of psychotherapy (Beauchamp & Childress, 1994). A dissenting opinion in the *Tarasoff* case said that assurance of confidentiality is fundamental for psychotherapy because it facilitates the seeking of help without stigma and fear of repercussions. It encourages the full disclosure needed for effective treatment, and it fosters trust in the therapist, "the very means by which treatment is affected" (*Tarasoff*, 1976). Psychotherapy is based on the proposition that verbalizing fantasies to a non-judgmental therapist is therapeutic and diminishes the need to act on fantasies. Because angry fantasies are a normal component of a grief reaction, the therapist encourages their expression as a matter of routine procedure (Feldmann, 1988).

In this case, Michael expressed relief at being able to talk about his violent fantasies and stated several times that he had no plans to act on them. We do not know his express wishes regarding whether he would want the nurse to maintain confidence about his fantasies or warn the potential victim (or police) that he might be dangerous. However, we can fairly safely assume that his strong preference, indeed his implicit assumption, is that what he tells the nurse is completely confidential. If confidentiality were to be broken, it is likely that he would be angry and might terminate therapy, the vehicle for resolving his grief and improving his emotional state. It is possible that Michael might sue the nurse for breach of professional contract or professional misconduct. He might argue that he was not informed that what he said could be told to others, despite having signed a general consent for treatment that stated the need to violate confidentiality under certain circumstances.

An issue in the field of mental health is the degree to which client preferences play a role in the resolution of an ethical dilemma. How autonomous can a person be when psychological distress impairs his or her reasoning capacity? More specific to this case, can a person in the midst of a major depression and acute adjustment disorder discern that his fantasies are only pure fantasy and that he definitely should not act on them? Is it possible that his psychological state impairs his judgment to such an extent that the nurse should overrule the client preference for confidentiality and warn the potential victim? This is a clinical judgment call, depending on the severity of diagnosis, the present mental status and ego functioning capacity, and the prior history of dangerous behavior or substance abuse.

Legal Analysis. The 1974 California *Tarasoff* decision established a therapist's duty to warn a third party who might be a victim of a client's violence. The American Psychological Association protested the ruling because of the anticipated adverse effects on the therapeutic relationship. As a result of the protest, the California Supreme Court reviewed the case. In *Tarasoff II* (1976), the court ruled that the therapist's duty was to protect, rather than to warn, the intended victim. In the ensuing years, many cases followed, not only in California but in a majority of other U.S. states, with some courts ruling that therapists have no duty to breach confidentiality, and other courts supporting the *Tarasoff* decisions (Egley & Ben-Ari, 1993; Monahan, 1993). A 1985 California Assembly law limits psychotherapists' liability and adds the new requirement that the intended victim and the police must be notified when a serious threat of physical violence has been made. Thus, although seeming to protect psychotherapists by limiting liability and reaffirming a duty to protect, the law encourages clinicians to respond in rote ways, rather than using expert clinical judgment and clinical interventions to prevent possible violence. Three cases in California expanded the legal scope of *Tarasoff* (see Leong, Eth, & Silva, 1992). In all three cases, once confidentiality was lost in one context, invoking the *Tarasoff* warning, it was lost completely. When a therapist chose to warn, all information leading to that decision and following it was permissible in court. The three cases described by Leong et al. (1992) occurred in California; however, these legal principles could easily be adjusted elsewhere as the original *Tarasoff* has been. Although the specific laws vary from state to state, the general sentiment among practicing therapists is that the safest course is to practice "defensive psychotherapy."

Psychotherapists are governed by two competing principles, that of fidelity, which directs the therapist to hold disclosures in confidence, and that of beneficence, which obligates a therapist to protect the public and promote community welfare. When a client reveals thoughts of harming other people, these two principles come into conflict for the therapist. The law in some states serves to reduce individual discretion by the therapist regarding resolution of the conflict and sways the argument in favor of protection of the public, as do similar laws that require reporting gunshot wounds and child abuse. However, these laws have been criticized for violating individuals' civil liberties, for encouraging therapists to be self-serving in their own protection, and for inhibiting the use of more creative clinical interventions in situations (Brown & Rayne, 1989; Mills, Sullivan, & Eth, 1987; Weinstock & Weinstock, 1988). The balance between the duty to protect the public and the duty to hold in confidence a client's disclosures is precarious and often tilted by the therapist's inclination to protect himself or herself. According to Pellegrino (1987), "Nothing more exposes a physician's true ethics than the way he or she balances his or her own interest against those of the patient" (p. 1939).

Case Recommendations. Significant features of this case include the following:

1. Michael's present emotional state includes features of depression and adjustment disorder.
2. He has named a specific person as a potential victim and has described a weapon and a plan.
3. Michael has no prior history of violence or substance abuse.
4. In the nurse's clinical judgment, he is not presently a danger to himself or another person.

The nurse is obligated to explore legal requirements of the state in which she practices. Thus, her consultation with the attorney should include the question of whether she is mandated to warn or whether she can use clinical judgment and discretion to determine the best action.

If she determines that she can use clinical judgment, she must decide a course of action. Because Michael named a specific intended victim and because he discussed buying a gun and a location for the fantasized act, the most prudent and conservative course would be to take some action to protect the potential victim from Michael and protect him from his current emotional crisis. However, simply telephoning the ex-girlfriend or the police, although maximally protective for the nurse with respect to any future liability, is likely to cause the patient the most distress and have the most negative effect on the therapeutic relationship. Because the nurse judges the risk of violence to be minimum to moderate, she can take the time to involve Michael in the process, which will have the effect of enhancing the therapeutic relationship because it likely will augment trust, rather than destroy it.

The nurse should telephone Michael and ask him to come in for an appointment within the next day. During the session, the nurse might explain that, on reflection, she has become concerned that his depression might lead him to act in some harmful way and that, after consultation with her team, she now recommends a short hospital stay. She can remind the client that antidepressant medication takes about 2 weeks before any therapeutic action occurs and that spending this time in the hospital is indicated.

If Michael objects, the nurse can explain that she would be able to allow him to refuse hospital admittance only if others are warned of his potential dangerousness, and thus he can choose the best course for him. She would emphasize that the hospital stay would be less stigmatizing than would warning others of the potential of danger and that she believes he will benefit from the intensive psychotherapy and careful monitoring of medications that will occur with a hospital stay.

Erica, the Fearful Girlfriend

Erica is a 30-year-old single mother of a 3-year-old girl who went to a Planned Parenthood Clinic for birth control pills. During the routine intake, Erica responded to the nurse's question about abusive relationships with "I'm not sure." She said she was currently in an intense relationship with a man she met at the cafeteria where she worked. Although she claimed he had never hit her, she felt intimidated by his anger and dependency. She said he was jealous of her relationship with her daughter because she was "getting all the attention." He got her daughter a kitten to occupy her, but in a sudden fit of rage, he kicked the kitten across the room, resulting in its death. The intake nurse thought the relationship sounded abusive and asked if Erica were interested in a follow-up appointment with the Women's Health Clinical Nurse Specialist. Erica agreed but noted, "This is silly. He's a good man and he hasn't hit me."

When Erica met with the clinical specialist the next week, she confided that she was afraid to leave her daughter alone with the boyfriend; however, 3 days of the week there was a 2-hour gap between her job starting and the day care opening. Her boyfriend had always been willing to watch the child and get her ready for day care. Erica noted that she had never seen the boyfriend hurt her child but noticed that the daughter cried much more when left with him.

Later during the session, Erica admitted that her boyfriend had forced her to have sex with him at times, but she did not identify it as rape because she felt she "was being selfish." She said her boyfriend was sexually aggressive at times, especially when he had many papers to write for school. She was worried that she would contract a sexually transmitted disease, especially AIDS, because the boyfriend was so sexually driven that, if Erica did not have sex with him, he would get it elsewhere.

Three months before she came to the Planned Parenthood Clinic, Erica went to the Employee Health Clinic after an especially prolonged argument in which her boyfriend prevented her from sleeping for 3 days because he wanted to "resolve the problem." The clinic physician prescribed benzodiazepines for anxiety and insomnia and advised her to "kiss and make up." No one asked about the extent of abuse beyond ascertaining that there was no physical violence occurring.

The nurse asked if Erica had considered leaving the boyfriend. She replied that she was afraid to break up with him because he had said several times that he could not live without her and would not let her live without him. She also was afraid that he would report to children's protective services (CPS) that she was abusive to and neglectful of her daughter. Because he was so persuasive, she was certain that CPS would believe him, rather than her. She said she could not afford an apartment of her own and had a poor relationship with her parents and could not move in with them. She said she had considered asking her mother to care for the child until she could ease herself away from this man.

The clinical specialist assessed that Erica was anxious and fearful about the relationship with her boyfriend. At this point, the nurse was concerned about Erica's minimization of the abuse and questioned the adequacy of Erica's judgment, especially with regard to the safety of her child. The nurse was uncertain if she had sufficient data to involve CPS and did not want to alienate Erica, which would prevent additional intervention. When the nurse shared her concerns with Erica, she burst into tears and begged the nurse not to contact CPS, because she thought that would only worsen the situation and her boyfriend might retaliate against her. The nurse had to struggle with the factors to be weighed in deciding the best action for protecting each member of this family and whether the conditions made it defensible *not* to report the situation.

Clinical Analysis. There are few physical health factors to be considered in this case because the case is composed overwhelmingly of complex psychosocial factors. However, the health factors that exist are important to clarify and address. The first consideration is the safety of family members, and in Erica's situation a careful physical assessment of Erica's daughter is foremost. Because of the time and cost involved, and without health insurance coverage, this probably has not been done. However, it is a prerequisite to the nurse's ability to intervene successfully in the psychosocial component of the problem.

Second, benzodiazepines have been prescribed for Erica in the past to lessen her symptoms of anxiety and insomnia. Abused women commonly are treated with tranquilizers in a "band-aid" approach to lessen the symptoms that accompany posttraumatic stress disorders (PTSDs) (Gelles & Straus, 1988; Nechas & Foley, 1994). The fallacy of this treatment is that it may erode the woman's ability to solve problems, advocate for herself, seek appropriate help, and make substantive changes in her social situation. It also gives a message of blaming the victim because it makes a statement that the problem is located within the individual and not within the situation.

Ethical Analysis. Battered women who remain in a chronically abusive relationship are caught by powerful forces, including traumatic bonding (Dutton & Painter, 1981); emotional dependency and low self-esteem; and economic necessity related to poverty, lack of child care, or other sources (Gelles & Straus, 1988). Characteristic of intimate partner abuse is the victim's simultaneous fear of disclosure (and its consequences). Stigmatization and fear of retaliation by the batterer often tip the scale in favor of nondisclosure (Limandri, 1989; Tilden, 1989).

Erica begged the nurse not to tell. As difficult as the situation was for her, Erica thought it was better than what it would become if outsiders got involved. She feared she would be in danger if her boyfriend were accused, she feared her daughter would be emotionally traumatized by an intervention by CPS, she feared CPS might remove her daughter, she feared she might lose her job if she had to miss work to deal with these problems, and she feared losing the boyfriend's income if he left. Erica said that from her perspective, things would only get worse if the nurse initiated action by the system.

How autonomous can Erica be when she is living in a chronically abusive, fear-inducing situation? Abused women justifiably can be diagnosed as having PTSD because of the powerful effects of intermittent personal violence. PTSD erodes judgment, depresses affect, and impairs decision making (American Psychiatric Association, 1994). Thus, how much weight should client preference be given in this case, because true autonomy likely is impaired by the situation? A certain amount of paternalism on the part of a health provider may be justified.

However, a person with PTSD is not psychotic, not cognitively impaired, and not lacking in social or civil liberties. Erica has the right to determine her lifestyle, her living situation, and her course of actions and behaviors. Clearly, she was functional to the extent that she held a job and understood her responsibilities as a parent to supervise and protect her daughter.

Erica stated her request for confidentiality. Does she have the right to expect it, or is the nurse obligated by law to report the suspected child abuse and neglect? Even if the nurse is not obligated to report the situation, which action by the nurse would most protect and least harm all family members? Is there a conflict among family members, such that an action best for one may be less beneficial or harmful for another? If that is true, whose best interest should be considered first, and how should a provider respond?

The overriding goal of all health care intervention is to improve patients' quality of life. According to Jonsen, Siegler, and Winslade (1986),

> Considerations of quality of life enter into decisions to act in accord with the principle of beneficence, that is, to do good and avoid harm. These considerations also arise in the utilitarian form of ethical deliberation, which involves, in part, the intention to affect a greater balance of pleasure over pain in the experiences of a person, of a population, or in the world. (pp. 101-102)

When factors that impair optimum quality of life are primarily psychosocial, as is true in this case, the problem of paternalism versus beneficence predominates. Who should judge the quality of life of a client who, in asking for birth control pills, reveals grave family factors that significantly erode quality of life for herself and her daughter? The client then requests nonintervention by the social service system as preferable to intervention by this well-meaning but largely inefficient helping system. When the social system demands to intervene to protect people (and thus improve quality of life), to what degree does its intervention result in improved quality of life versus additionally eroded quality of life? The dilemma for the health care professional arises when the outcome of one's expert clinical assessment results in a clinical judgment not to report, which may be in conflict with obligatory reporting laws. Should they be bound by the reporting laws, even if the probable consequence is an additionally reduced, rather than improved, quality of life?

Abused women tend to stay in unsatisfactory situations because the known, as bad as it is, often seems better than the unknown (Benton, 1986). If they are given enough support and protection to permanently leave a batterer or demand an abuse-free relationship with the batterer, they almost invariably report a greatly improved quality of life. However, considerable resources are needed to bring this about, including immediate safe housing, police protection, mental health and social service counseling, and social-psychological rehabilitation.

Erica maintained that she was coping with her situation and that despite the stress it had caused her, she preferred to continue with things as they were. However, the nurse believed that Erica's quality of life was suboptimal and would continue to be eroded by the chronicity of the stressors. This presents a situation of conflict between the *client's* quality of life as "the subjective satisfaction expressed or experienced by an individual in his or her physical, mental, and social situation (even though these may be deficient in some manner)" (Jonsen et al., 1986, p. 102) and the *nurse's* assessment of the client's quality of life, or "the subjective evaluation by an onlooker of another's subjective experiences of personal life" (Jonsen et al., 1986, p. 102).

Thus, one dilemma for the nurse is to decide whether Erica's opinion that her life is satisfactory is impaired by her stress and thus not fully autonomous. If the nurse decides Erica's response is not fully autonomous, the nurse may be justified in a paternalistic response, such as strongly urging Erica to contact an abused women's support group, and perhaps placing the call for Erica while she is in the office.

The nurse also must consider the quality of life of the daughter, who may be in danger. Thus, an additional factor in this case is the question of whose quality of life takes primary consideration? Ordinarily, it is the immediate client's, but in this case, concern for the daughter may take priority and justify paternalistic action by the nurse because the daughter is developmentally vulnerable. The daughter likely will have the greater losses if abuse or neglect is occurring than would the mother, who is an autonomous adult. Thus, if the nurse decides that Erica is fully competent and can decline intervention by a health professional for herself, is the nurse obligated to intervene against the mother's wishes to protect the daughter?

Legal Analysis. Legal definitions of child abuse vary by state, but abuse commonly is seen as any injury (physical or mental) or sexual abuse or sexual exploitation that has been caused by other than accidental means (Oregon Revised Statute 418.740). Throughout the United States, public and private officials are required to report a situation of any child with whom they have contact in an official capacity and who they have reasonable cause to believe is abused. Failure to report suspected abuse or neglect may be punishable by fines or other disciplinary action.

In the case of Erica, the nurse may choose to interpret the law conservatively (and thus maximally protect herself from liability) and report suspected abuse to the CPS on the basis of verbal information from a third party. However, the nurse may wonder whether reporting will lead to the best outcome for this child. Upsetting the child emotionally, enraging the perpetrator, removing the child from the home with all of the psychological and sometimes physical dangers that result are likely sequelae (Gelles & Straus, 1988). All may produce more harm than benefit.

Alternatively, the nurse may decide to interpret the law as allowing her some discretion because she has not had contact with the child or the suspected perpetrator. The nurse may decide that this mother is protecting the child adequately and that the nurse can benefit the family more by intervening herself than by involving CPS. If she chooses not to report, is she ethically and professionally obligated to take other steps to ensure the safety of this child? What are the consequences to the nurse of not reporting? Will she be subject to legal and professional disciplinary actions for failure to comply with a state law? If the nurse decides not to report immediately but waits for more data to support her decision to report, she risks negligence in the delay of reporting and thus may be in violation of the law. Such a prospect surely would encourage her to report to protect herself, even when in her clinical judgment she can best prevent harm and provide benefits by not reporting or by delaying her report until she can gather more data.

The nurse has clear data that current ongoing abuse of the woman is occurring. There is no law obligating her to report, and there is no agency, other than the police department, designated to receive such a report. The nurse can urge Erica to file a report with the police department and to initiate a temporary restraining order that would require the boyfriend to stay away from Erica's family. However, other than urging Erica to take these legal steps, there are no legal limits on the nurse's decision about handling the case.

Case Recommendations. The dilemma in this case is to decide action that will

1. Prevent harm while preserving confidentiality, trust, and a therapeutic alliance.
2. Provide benefits that do not simultaneously inflict harm.
3. Protect the vulnerable, even when they have not requested protection or consented to it.

In considering these three goals, it should be remembered that there are two clients to be considered: Erica and her daughter. The nurse's first duty is to respond therapeutically to Erica's immediate psychological distress. Characteristically, abused women, like victims of other types of abuse, have low self-esteem, believe they are somehow responsible for their misfortune, and believe that they are alone in having this kind of problem. The nurse's first intervention should be focused on reducing anxiety, increasing trust and self-esteem, decreasing a sense of isolation and helplessness, facilitating problem solving, and creating a therapeutic alliance as a base for future action (Tilden & Shepherd, 1987a).

The second action by the nurse should be to express grave concern about the daughter's safety. The nurse is obligated to collect much more information about the child's physical and emotional health. If there has been physical or psychological abuse, the nurse needs to establish its nature, recency, frequency, and likelihood of recurrence. It would be important to provide or refer the child for a general health assessment that includes a thorough assessment of her mental health. Given Erica's denial, it is unlikely that she is able to assess the degree of danger to the daughter and thus may be less likely to truly participate in a plan to ensure the daughter's safety.

Once this detailed history has been gathered, the nurse must make a decision about the severity of the abuse and Erica's capacity to protect the child. If the abuse is recent, current, frequent, or highly traumagenic, or Erica seems unable to advocate adequately for her daughter, the nurse should convince Erica that CPS must be involved. The immediate danger is that Erica will respond by terminating contact with the nurse. The nurse can lessen the likelihood of this happening by appealing to Erica's concern for her daughter and promising to stay involved in the case to help the family in a way that is ultimately helpful and not harmful.

The nurse should decide not to report *at present* if she is convinced that the danger is not immediate and not grave and if Erica seems genuinely able to provide protection. If the nurse decides not to report, she is obligated to continue to follow up the family to confirm that there is no present or future danger.

Conclusions

These two case presentations illustrate major ethical and legal issues confronting nurses and others working in the area of family violence. At the heart of both cases are two ethical principles in conflict: beneficence and fidelity. These principles underlie opposing duties for the nurse, that of doing good and protecting society (beneficence) versus that of maintaining the confidences of the client (fidelity). In addition, it is not simply a matter of whether to do good or be faithful to the implicit contract because there is no clear standard of what it means in these cases to do good.

When beneficence and confidentiality conflict, the balance generally tips in favor of confidentiality. The reason for this is that autonomy, which underlies confidentiality, is considered a greater good in a free society than is paternalism, which underlies beneficence (Veatch & Fry, 1987). However, selected violations of confidentiality are permitted when needed to prevent harm (Veatch & Fry, 1987). Nowhere is this clearer than in the state mandatory reporting laws for conditions such as communicable diseases, gunshot wounds, and child abuse. In such conditions, the benefits of protecting society by informing others outweigh the disadvantage of lost privacy to the individual.

Thus, violation of fidelity is permissible, even mandatory, when required by law. However, mandatory reporting laws lead to ethical dilemmas in situations in which a health care professional believes society and the individual can be better served by maintaining confidence than by complying with the law. Thus, as Veatch and Fry (1987) point out, health care professionals often find themselves in the bind of having made two contradictory promises: to protect confidential information and to obey the law that requires reporting. The conservative and defensive posture is to obey the letter of the law. The more reasoned posture may be to consider carefully the context and elements of the case, and adapt the law to the case, as was done in the counsel of the cases presented.

Limandri and Tilden (1996), in their report of research that explored factors that influence clinicians' choice to intervene in family violence, identified a "need for changes in institutional, legislative, and organizational policies that relate to family violence" (p. 252). Education in the area of family violence should be mandated in every school of nursing curriculum. This education should include ethical reasoning that focuses not only on individual cases but also on issues in the broader social and political contexts.

In conclusion, handling the complex environmental, emotional, and legal factors related to suspected family violence requires a good deal of therapeutic finesse by a nurse. There are burdens and benefits associated with any course of action, and they should be weighed in the context of each case to reach the approach that best upholds the intent of the law.

4

Woman Abuse

Educational Strategies to Change Nursing Practice

Josephine Ryan

M. Christine King

Nurses and other health care providers are ideal persons to intervene with women who are experiencing violence and abuse in their intimate relationships. All women are not assessed for this health care problem, partly because of lack of education on the part of their health care providers. This chapter presents principles and methods (with sample outlines and objectives) for education about women abuse to practicing nurses and students in graduate and undergraduate nursing programs. By redressing this lack of knowledge and skills, nurses can be empowered to provide clinical intervention and leadership in addressing this major health and social problem.

Within the past decade, violence and abuse have become recognized as important public health problems for women and children in the United States (U.S. Surgeon General, 1985). The U.S. Public Health Service, in response to the recommendations produced by the Surgeon General's Task Force on Violence, began to develop policies to address the critical health problem of violence against women. In 1990, these policies were formalized as a set of objectives on violent and abusive behavior and became part of the report *Healthy People 2000:*

National Health Promotion and Disease Prevention Objectives. The inclusion of these objectives demonstrates the urgency of this health problem for women. This report calls on health care workers to prevent, not just treat, illness. Although the report emphasizes that health promotion strategies related to individual lifestyle (personal choices that are made in a social context) offer the best opportunity to reduce the spiraling costs associated with treating illness and functional impairment, it also argues that the institution of legislation and social sanctions are critical to ensuring that the social environment becomes a healthier place (U.S. Department of Health and Human Services, 1990).

In addition, the Surgeon General's Task Force on Violence noted the need for the development of prevention and intervention programs to address the problem of spouse abuse and the development of spouse abuse protocols for use by health care professionals in all settings (U.S. Surgeon General, 1985). This directive has been echoed by the Joint Commission on the Accreditation of Healthcare Organizations (JCAHO; 1990, 1992, 1996) by the inclusion of standards intended to help emergency departments identify and address the needs of victims of abuse. These standards also dictate a plan for education of staff in identifying and intervening in woman abuse. This chapter presents responses to the need to develop educational programs aimed at preventing the adverse health effects of violence and abuse and the development of abuse protocols for use in health care settings.

Studies of women who have lived in abusive situations indicate that abused women have greater health problems than do nonabused women, including physical injuries, miscarriages, rape, chronic pain, stress and anxiety disorders, hypertension, hyperventilation, allergic reactions, anorexia, insomnia, depression, suicide attempts, and disturbed parent-child relationships (see Chapter 1 in this volume; see also Kerouac, Taggart, Lescop, & Fortin, 1986; Stark, Flitcraft, & Frazier, 1979). It is no surprise that the violence and abuse directed against women by male partners has been labeled a health care problem in disguise (Drake, 1972).

Although women who are experiencing violence in their lives are most likely to enter the health care system via the emergency department, there is a widespread lack of recognition of battering by health care personnel in emergency departments and other traditional health care settings (Kurz, 1987; McLeer & Anwar, 1989a). Abused women also are less likely to use primary health care services, with the important exception that childbearing women in the United States almost always come in contact with health care providers for perinatal care. Most women, from all cultural groups and every social class, have some contact with a nurse during prenatal, labor and delivery, or postpartum care.

Despite the high overall incidence and prevalence of battering that leads to physical and emotional health problems for women, health professionals fail to identify women experiencing violence in their lives, may use derogatory labeling, and generally are seen as judgmental and insensitive by abused women

(Drake, 1972; Goldberg & Tomlanovich, 1984) and less effective and helpful than other sources of help (Dobash & Dobash, 1988). This is especially unfortunate because it has been suggested that the quality of health care that an abused woman receives during contact with a health care provider often determines whether she follows through with referrals to legal, social service, and other health care agencies.

Nurses are ideally positioned to intervene with women who are in violent or abusive relationships. The lack of intervention by nurses is not evidence of a lack of concern for the health of abused women or their children but of a perceived lack of knowledge about effective approaches for intervening. Nurse graduates of most educational programs and those practicing in most clinical settings have not received the knowledge or skills to feel competent in intervening with women they know or suspect may be experiencing violence and abuse (Carbonell, Chez, & Hassler, 1995; King, 1988). The social construction of violence against women and the heavy mythology that surrounds the "causes" of violence and abuse may influence the response of nurses who encounter women suspected of being in abusive relationships. Nurses also report that they are unsure how to ask about violence directly and are reluctant to assess women for the presence of abuse in their relationships.

Nurses are aware that they have women in their practice who are experiencing abuse in their relationships. Although nurses are excellent interviewers, educators, and counselors, it is this perceived inadequacy and lack of education that limit their ability to assess and intervene for violence. Thus, it is important to redress this lack of knowledge and skills by presenting educational programs the will empower nurses to provide clinical intervention and leadership.

Educational Strategies

Well-constructed educational programs can be used to improve the identification of abused women and increase the likelihood of such women receiving effective intervention from the health care system. These include daylong programs for nurses working in specific settings, briefer in-service programs for practicing nurses, and curricular offerings in basic nursing education or clinical internship programs. In each setting, regardless of the length of the educational program, certain principles apply.

Principle 1. The presentation of information about violence and abuse in the lives of women is necessary but not sufficient to change practice. All change in behavior requires more than the provision of facts and clinical information: A personal belief system must be examined and altered so that new information may be incorporated into one's repertoire of behavior. Educational programs produce more change in behavior and beliefs if they incorporate instruction that assists participants to articulate and examine their personal values and beliefs concerning the abuse of women.

Principle 2. Nurses, and most members of this culture, have beliefs that may be erroneous about the extent, prevalence, and severity of violence and abuse experienced by women in the United States. It is imperative that statistical information be presented to inform participants of the significance of this health problem for their individual practice setting.

Principle 3. All practitioners make attributions about the cause of violence against women (King & Ryan, 1989). These attributions affect how, and under what circumstances, nurses offer help. Explorations of the attribution of violence against women must be an integral part of any educational program aimed at increasing identification of and intervention with abused women.

Principle 4. Structural variables within the practice setting enhance or hinder the identification of and intervention with women experiencing abuse. Thus, the education of individual nurses may not be sufficient to change practice within the setting. Nurses need setting-specific education and consultation to bring about institutional change. Providing the educational program in the institutional clinical setting, rather than in a conference setting, is advantageous. The impact of on-site education is greater because it includes a large number of nurses from the same institution. This results in a "critical mass" of nurses from a health facility who are likely to support each other in assessment and intervention for women experiencing violence. Such a strategy is more likely to generate an educated network and produce institutional, interdisciplinary task forces to create policies and protocols.

Principle 5. It is extremely difficult for individual nurses to carry the responsibility for the identification of and intervention with abused women. Educational offerings should include some provision for the encouragement of the formation of clinical interest groups or task forces to continue to develop policies and protocols for abuse and violence against women in the specific clinical setting. The providers of the educational programs must work with administration and practitioners in the development of educational opportunities and follow-up consultation and clinical management.

Principle 6. Language is an important medium for the provision of values in a culture. It is necessary to include some scrutiny and discussion of language when educating about violence against women. For instance, using the word *victim* when speaking about women experiencing violence and abuse has connotations of powerlessness and helplessness, indicating that the person is being acted on; this tends to elicit rescue fantasies on the part of nurses and other care providers. The terms *family violence* and *domestic violence* are to be avoided because they fail to convey that it is the woman, not the family, who is experiencing the violence and abuse. Because abused women may fail to identify with the harsh societal image embedded in the term *battered woman,* it is recommended that this term not be used extensively.

Principle 7. Although it generally is men who abuse their intimate partners, educators and practitioners should not forget that violence and abuse occur in lesbian relationships; women who live in these relationships need assessment and intervention.

Principle 8. Most health care providers are drawn from Anglo populations but serve a rapidly growing population of culturally diverse clients. This increase in diversity has not been attended by a change in the education of health care providers to meet the challenges of providing quality health care across cultures. Subtle and overt racial, ethnic, and cultural prejudice are inherent in this society and will operate in beliefs about violence directed at women. Explorations of racism and oppression should be initiated and discussed in any educational program purporting to discuss violence and abuse. Good literature exists regarding cultural sensitivity in nursing practice and cultural sensitivity in assessing and intervening with abused women (Campbell & Campbell, 1996; King et al., 1993; Torres, 1987, 1991).

Principle 9. When providing education about violence and abuse for health professionals, educators must remember that many of the participants or their friends or family have experienced such abuse. It is helpful to acknowledge this at the outset of the presentation so that participants recognize that personal experiences of abuse are represented in this group of people. If a participant discloses abuse, thank her for her courage in sharing her experience, provide supportive comments, and continue with the presentation. Use her example if it is helpful and comfortable for the woman and the group. Often these disclosures can be extremely powerful and serve to center the discussion and make it less academic and more real. Because some women in any group will be abused, this decreases the idea of "us" and "them" and helps all participants to see that woman abuse is a continuum, ranging from subtle belittling to overt violence and homicide.

Full-Day Educational Strategies

Two primary goals of continuing education in nursing are the bringing of new knowledge into the clinical setting and the developing of that knowledge to sustain change in practice. A third goal is to provide nurses the opportunity to participate in creating a learning community in which the complementary knowledge, skills, and experiences can be shared. In response to the need to educate practicing nurses about violence in women's lives and to provide them with prevention and intervention strategies for use in all practice settings, we developed and implemented a series of 8-hour educational programs designed to increase nurses' understanding of violence and nurses' ability to intervene with women experiencing violence and abuse (King, Perri, & Ryan, 1987). This program is used as an example of a curriculum that has been used frequently with success. There are many such programs, and a similar program can be developed to meet individual setting and educational needs.

The program is constructed in two parts: The first part explores common myths that surround the issue of violence and abuse, and the second part provides direction in assessment, intervention, referrals, documentation, and social policy. Two 4-hour sessions, offered on separate days, offer the optimum situation for learning, but the program is flexible and can be offered in 1 day or in four 2-hour sessions. The program has been formalized into a training manual that contains all of the necessary content, the experiential activities, teaching guidelines, and supplementary readings and research. This manual is designed so that any nurse who has been a participant in the workshop or has been prepared to implement training regarding abuse can use the manual to educate co-workers in any setting.

An advocacy protocol was developed as a useful adjunct to the workshop or for use in shorter in-service educational offerings in which time does not allow for the full program. The advocacy protocol answers nurses' most pressing need, "What do I do if the woman reveals abuse or violence?"

The first 4-hour segment introduces research on incidence, prevalence, and putative causes of battering. This material is initiated through a series of experiential group exercises designed for maximum participation by workshop members. First, the trainers establish a feeling of safety and comfort in the room and an emphasis on confidentiality. Then a newsprint exercise is used, during which participants are assisted in formulating a composite picture of the abused woman, the abuser, the circumstance of the abuse, and the kinds of help the woman may have sought or received. This exercise provides a group perspective on violence and tends to bring about a bond among participants and a feeling of safety and openness.

This exercise is followed by the main activity of the first 4 hours, which is a presentation of facts about battering. This is achieved by exploring with the participants the myths and societal beliefs that prevent nurses from recognizing and intervening with women clients who are experiencing violence and abuse. This aspect of the program, the exploration of current societal beliefs in the social construction of violence against women, is of great importance (King & Ryan, 1989). The aim of the workshop is to bring about change in the participants' belief systems that are more likely to bring about long-lasting changes in clinical practice.

Myths serve a powerful role in any society. Through our work with women and practicing nurses, we have identified 14 of the most powerful myths that serve to obfuscate and perpetuate violence. Examples of such myths are the following: violence happens only in problem families, alcohol causes battering, only a small proportion of women suffer violence, violence is greater in some ethnic groups, violence is a private matter, the abuse cannot be all that bad or the abused woman would leave the situation, and violence rarely escalates to homicide. These myths are a subtle convolution of the two most basic myths about violence against women: (a) The woman is responsible for the violence or abuse (i.e., she caused it), and (b) the man is ultimately not responsible for his actions (i.e., he was drunk, stressed, or out of control).

The ensuing discussion attempts to replace these various permutations of the two basic myths with a clear understanding that there is no excuse for violence or abuse directed at women and that individual men are responsible for their behaviors. These 14 myths are cast and recast to expose the subtle excusing of men and blaming of women that is so prevalent among society and nurses. For nurses to provide a visible role in responding to the health problems associated with abuse of women, it is imperative that a careful examination of the myths that hide this problem be conducted to produce interventions that are effective and helpful. By exposing these myths, we can raise a critical feminist consciousness needed to reframe issues of victimization into authentic health problems. Such reframing will make nurses more assured in the workplace, more confident in their practice with abused women, more active in the area of women's health, and more powerful practitioners and advocates for the health rights of women and children. Each myth and the way it is used to minimize violence or to allow the practitioner to be excused from asking about violence is discussed until time runs out or no additional discussion seems necessary. During this part of the program, the group is referred to the newsprint exercises (now taped on the walls) to highlight a myth or provide examples of how myths operate.

The first 4-hour segment is concluded by a videotape about woman abuse and nursing intervention. This serves as a break in the intensity of group process, and we have found that people are more likely to accept material when presented in the form of an "authoritative" source, such as video. Thus, the first session's work is reinforced from an "objective" formal source.

The second 4-hour segment begins with more experiential exercises asking participants to relate how they would ask a woman about abuse, what are the barriers to asking about abuse, and what they most fear if they ask about abuse. Through discussion, the group eventually is brought to the idea that unless a woman presents with obvious, intentional injuries, there is no way of deciding which women are experiencing abuse in their intimate relationships. The moral imperative is to assess for the possibility of abuse in all women because clinical indicators may be vague and it often is extremely difficult for women to voluntarily disclose abuse. The participants realize that all women should be asked specific questions about abuse. Finally, the abuse screening questions developed by the Nursing Research Consortium on Violence and Abuse (King et al., 1993) are introduced as useful and specific questions to identify abused women in clinical practice.

The training continues with a discussion of the difficulties perceived in asking the questions. The reasons practitioners most often cite for not asking questions of abuse fall into two categories: restraints imposed by the setting (not enough time, lack of privacy in the setting, fear of reprisals from physicians, or perceived inappropriateness given the health setting, e.g., postpartum, general adult medical or surgical, intensive care), and personal (not wanting to hear painful abuse stories, differences in age or ethnicity between the nurse and the client, subscribing to myths that assume only certain women are abused, and feeling inadequate to intervene should the woman respond positively). The feeling of inadequacy is the most frequently cited reason. The fears presented in the group are acknowledged, sometimes participants are referred to the myths and reminded how powerful and pervasive they are, and discussion about the fears is initiated.

After this discussion, the segment on nursing intervention is implemented. Nurses are provided with examples of statements they can use to respond to disclosures of physical, sexual, or emotional abuse. Intervention guidelines and client goals are identified. The advocacy protocol (King & Ryan, 1991) is presented and discussed. This protocol was developed for use in clinical agencies in which women are systematically assessed for violence and abuse. The protocol contains a section on approaches for acknowledgment to the disclosure of abuse; referral options to local shelters and social service agencies; the national hotline telephone number; legal options; a section on mobilizing social support; essential components of a safety plan; guidelines for effective documentation; and closing statements designed to validate, empower, and ensure continued health contact with abused women.

Using this tool, the participants are divided into pairs and provided with role-playing scripts. Each pair take turns playing the part of an abused woman or an intervening nurse. In the scripts, the women are either emotionally, sexually, or physically abused. This exercise is processed in the larger group with participants sharing their feelings and reactions about the role-play, discussing what it felt like to be asking about abuse, or how it felt to be an abused woman. This usually is an intense discussion and revelatory for many participants.

After this exercise, it often is helpful to bring in service providers from local battered women's agencies and shelters. Most agencies have someone who is experienced in discussing abuse and will be happy for the opportunity to interact with health care providers. They have a great deal of knowledge and experience about abuse and often a wealth of anecdotes drawn from experience. Bringing in shelter representatives serves to promote recognition of the reciprocal relationships between the community and the health care establishment and provides the opportunity for nurses to formally meet and interact with representatives of the resources in their community.

The program concludes with some kind of closing exercise designed to increase group resolve and decrease feelings of isolation. The trainers offer to provide additional assistance and consultation, and written feedback is obtained. This feedback is used in fine-tuning or reformulating the program. The program is outlined in Table 4.1.

This educational program has been offered more than 25 times to a variety of participants. Each workshop has been unique. Some have difficult moments, some have wonderful moments, but all are opportunities for learning.

In-Service Program

Although any opportunity to discuss violence and abuse of women is important, these shorter programs have special difficulties. In the 2 hours usually allotted to in-service programs, the aims and expected outcomes are quite different. In this short amount of time, it is unreasonable to be able to significantly improve assessment or intervention skills or to do what might be considered the necessary work of dispelling myths. Rather, these shorter sessions can provide only beginning content regarding the topic of woman abuse.

It often is useful to provide a list of the 14 myths and ask participants to select the one they would most like to discuss. In the discussion that follows, a great deal of content on incidence and prevalence can be delivered. An hour often is all that is available for this discussion. By allowing the group to dictate the discussion, one is able to deal with the group's most pressing issues, thus maximizing the efficiency of the presentation. The second hour is used to introduce the abuse screening questions and to distribute and highlight portions of the advocacy protocol. Use of local shelters for consultation and referral, mobilizing social support, and identification of a safety plan are emphasized. Short in-service programs always are concluded with an offer to provide additional in-service programs or to work with interested participants so that protocols and procedures can be developed for the particular clinical setting or health institution. An outline of this shorter program appears as Table 4.2.

Curricular Offerings

Nursing has unique opportunities for instituting assessment and management of health problems related to violence and abuse because nurses are the

Table 4.1 Outline of Full-Day Curricular Offering

First 4-hour session

Introductions, program overview and objectives, explanation of confidentiality.

Experimental exercises: Exercises designed to identify personal beliefs and attitudes about the battering of women.

Terms, definitions, and labels: Definitions of abuse and assault are contrasted, and related terms and definitions are presented and discussed. Discussion of the impact of language in hiding and minimizing violence against women.

Myths and reality: Exploration of current societal beliefs that influence the social construction of violence against women. Refutation of societal mythology through presentation of factual information and current research findings on violence and abuse.

Catalysts for change: Discussion of the reasons women stay in abusive relationships and strategies for empowering women.

Video: A video appropriate to the setting is viewed and discussed.

Closing exercise.

Second 4-hour session

Opening comments and discussion of morning discussion.

Health implications of violence against women and professional mandates.

Principles of nursing assessment for violence and abuse: Past history, pregnancy history, physical injuries, rape and sexual abuse, emotional indicators, environmental indicators.

Experimental exercise: Exercises designed to uncover individual and institutional barriers to assessment and intervention.

Abuse screening questions: These are distributed and discussed. Need for incorporation of questions into standardized assessment tools is discussed.

Nursing intervention: Advocacy protocol is distributed.

   Goals of nursing intervention: (a) identification; (b) empathy and affirmation;
   (c) privacy and safety; (d) treatment of health problems with care and sensitivity;
   (e) support, counseling, and education; (f) referral; (g) legal advocacy through
   accurate documentation; and (h) continued contact

   Client goals: (a) reestablish sense of power and control, (b) discuss abuse in concrete
   terms, (c) restore autonomy through setting goals and making decisions, (d) explore
   avenues of social support, and (e) gain knowledge of alternatives and options available

   Counseling intervention: (a) empathize and generalize, (b) provide information on
   battering, (c) provide supportive counseling and crisis intervention, (d) assess for
   suicide and homicide potential, (e) provide safety plan, and (f) form strategies for the
   future

   Referrals: (a) community services available for abused women, (b) shelters and their
   services, (c) legal rights and options, (d) counseling referrals, and (e) social services

Experiential exercise: Role-playing and group processing.

Documentation guidelines.

Panel of community resources and battered women shelter workers and survivors.

Evaluation of effectiveness of intervention.

Development of agency policies and protocols.

Closing exercise.

Table 4.2 Outline of Shorter In-Service Program

First hour

   Introduction, program overview and objectives, discussion of confidentiality.

   Myth list: Myth list is distributed, participants indicate whether they believe the myths or not, and the group is asked which myths they most want to discuss. Discussion of myths and presentation of research on abuse of women.

   Break

Second hour

   Abuse screening questions are distributed and discussed.

   Advocacy protocol is distributed, and sections of it are emphasized.

   Outreach is instituted for continued consultation and education.

---

largest work force in health care and are present in every health care setting. The best way to encourage nursing intervention in violence against women probably is to make content and related skills on violence against women an integral part of nursing curricula at the undergraduate and graduate levels. Programs in midwifery or clinical internship programs also are excellent opportunities for including content and clinical experiences in violence against women. Nursing students are responsive to this material because abuse is a significant woman's health issue, one that has received much national publicity and attention. Many of the students may have experienced violence or know friends or family members who are, or have been, abused.

Assessment for violence against women should be taught in the first nursing course in the undergraduate program or whenever assessment is first taught. Teaching students to ask specific questions about violence and abuse of women from the beginning of the nursing curriculum normalizes the questioning and places this activity in the context of routine nursing assessment of all women clients. From this point on, domestic violence and specifically, violence against women, should be included in every nursing course in the curriculum. Just as content regarding other health issues is incorporated in all nursing courses, building on each prior learning experience, so should content on abuse. It is not sufficient to introduce this material only once, because a change in behavior with regard to such a socially laden and hidden issue must come from repetition and advancement of knowledge and skills.

Ample opportunity exists in undergraduate programs for one- to three-credit elective courses or independent studies that focus on violence and abuse of women. These may be classroom courses or can be clinically focused. In such courses, undergraduates can be offered an opportunity to work with faculty on their research or on various clinical projects in the area of woman abuse, such as participating in educational offerings for nurses or lay groups in the community

Table 4.3 Sample Course Description and Objectives

Course description

This course is designed to allow students to develop a knowledge base concerning the nature and dynamics of woman abuse. It also is designed to enhance an understanding of the nursing and professional helping role with abused women in the primary health care setting.

Objectives

1. Understand the extent of the problem of woman abuse in the United States.

2. Gain knowledge concerning the nature and dynamics of woman abuse.

3. List and discuss one's personal attitudes and biases regarding woman abuse.

4. Examine common myths about woman abuse.

5. Gain a knowledge base in the areas of assessment, intervention, and referral for abused women.

6. Know the legal and social service resources available to abused women.

7. Appreciate the role and responsibility of the nurse and professional helper in advocating for abused women.

and clinical experiences in shelters for battered women. It is especially important from a learning point of view to get students actively involved in strategies that address the issues of abuse. A sample course description and objectives are presented in Table 4.3.

At the graduate level, woman abuse belongs in every clinical specialty. It obviously belongs in such clinical specialties as women's health, midwifery, and nurse practitioner programs but also should be included in administration, education, gerontology, child health, acute care, and psychiatric mental health nursing. Clinical specialists, nurse practitioners, educators, and administrators are in ideal positions to influence practice in institutions and to increase the identification of abuse and enhance intervention in every practice setting.

Shelters offer an ideal community health clinical setting in which students at every level can learn about women's health, children's health, health promotion, crisis intervention, self-help groups, community programs, and a wealth of community health concepts and interventions in practice with women residing in the shelters.

In addition to providing classroom and clinical experiences in the area of violence against women, nurses also are well suited to add to the development of new knowledge through clinically based research. Nursing researchers have conducted studies that incorporate a feminist viewpoint and a critical analysis that focuses on the experience of and responses to violence, rather than causation. This research provides a base from which nursing students can generate their research in this area. In honors theses, at the undergraduate level, and in master's theses or doctoral dissertations, nursing students are capable of excellent and useful investigation of many aspects of violence against women.

Summary

Violence against women has been identified as a serious health problem in the United States. The skills and knowledge of nurses can be focused on identifying abuse and intervening to promote health. Educational programs can be designed to explore the social construction of violence against women and provide for the acquisition of the knowledge and skills needed to improve the health of abused women. These all-day programs or shorter in-service programs, when combined with ongoing consultation for the institution of policies and protocols, can be enormously powerful in bringing about a beginning under-standing of the dynamics of abuse, abuse assessment, and the principles of intervention. Schools of nursing can easily include educational content, clinical experiences, and research opportunities in their curricula. All these activities are needed to empower nurses to meet the challenge of this important health problem for women and provide nursing leadership in addressing violence in the lives of women.

PART II

DYNAMICS OF
DOMESTIC VIOLENCE

5

Exploration of Women's Identity

Clinical Approaches With Abused Women

Kären M. Landenburger

T he purpose of this chapter is to delineate clinical approaches for caring for women who are in abusive relationships or those who recently have left such relationships. The process of entrapment in and recovering from an abusive relationship describes the experience of women in such relationships. Abuse is a continuous interactional process that takes place over time. The experiences also are affected by the culture in which we live and the demands made on women through ascribed roles of behavior. Thus, interventions must be phase specific and viewed within a sociocultural context. The clinical approaches developed were based on the results of two studies. The first study explored the experiences of women who were in abusive relationships or had left such relationships (Landenburger, 1988, 1989). The second study built on the previous research and explored the choices and struggles of women who had left abusive partners (Landenburger, 1991).

The first study described the experience of being abused within the context of a significant relationship and explained how the nature of the relationship influences a woman's choices over time. Thirty women who were in or had

AUTHOR'S NOTE: The author acknowledges the support of the Women's Health Nursing Research Training Grant, Center for Women's Health Research, University of Washington, Seattle.

recently left abusive relationships were interviewed using a semistructured, open-ended format to explore the experience of being abused. The transcribed interview texts of the women's reported experiences in the abusive relationship were analyzed using constant comparative analysis. A model of a process of entrapment in and recovering from an abusive relationship was identified. The process contained four phases: binding, enduring, disengaging, and recovering. The process was embedded in social context and the context of women's social and interpersonal attachments.

The purpose of the second study was to understand the process of leaving an abusive relationship and to determine factors that inhibit or enhance a woman's leaving such a relationship. Seventy women were recruited from a community shelter for battered women. Ten women participated in semistruc-tured, open-ended interviews that elicited information about past experiences of abuse with their partners and their recent decisions to come to the shelter. The interviews were recorded on audiotape and transcribed for data analysis. The women were followed over a period of 6 months and interviewed twice during this period at 3-month intervals. The follow-up interviews examined women's efforts to restructure their lives. A total sample of 70 women, including those who had participated in the open-ended interviews, took part in self-managed researcher-initiated focus groups. The focus groups consisted of an average of seven women per group and were conducted once a month for a period of 10 months. Data analysis using constant comparative analysis revealed a process of leaving an abusive relationship that is an integral part of the process of entrap-ment in and recovering from an abusive relationship. The model outlining a process of entrapment in and recovering from an abusive relationship was expanded on from the data analyses of the second study.

The Process of Entrapment in and Recovering From an Abusive Relationship

Abuse as examined in the literature usually is divided into two separate periods: the time spent in an abusive relationship and the time spent after having left the relationship. When an abusive relationship is examined in this manner, it is falsely identified as a distinct event, rather than as a continuous process that occurs over time. The experiences of women in abusive relationships must be viewed within a multilevel context, including the sociocultural context in which a woman lives; the context of the relationship as perceived by important others; and the perceptions of the woman about the relationship, the abuse, and her "self."

A woman who is abused lives in two conflicting realities. One reality encompasses the good aspects of the relationship with her partner. The other reality embodies the abusive aspects of her relationship. One reality is false but is supported by her partner and others around her. In the other reality, the abuse is real but unrecognized or denied. While in an abusive relationship, a woman tries to make sense of her skewed reality, and in the process loses a sense of who she is. She feels worthless as a person and loses hope that she can survive as an individual.

The process of entrapment and recovering from an abusive relationship describes how these conflicting realities inform and are informed by the multi-level context of a woman's life (Figure 5.1). Mills (1985), in an attempt to look at abuse as a process, interviewed women who recently had sought assistance in a shelter. The author found stages that are similar in scope to the process of entrapment and recovering. Although the names of the stages differ from the names of the phases, the meaning is ultimately the same. The process of entrapment and recovering is more extensive because women who were in and who had been out of abusive relationships were studied in addition to women who recently had left such relationships.

The process of entrapment and recovering is not linear. Pieces constantly weave together with the degree of behaviors, feelings, and thoughts changing in reaction to a cumulative experience. The phases of binding, enduring, disengaging, and recovering are not mutually exclusive. What happens in one phase triggers and carries over to some degree into the next phase. The abuse in the initial phase is a part of a woman's life. As a woman moves from the binding phase to the enduring phase, the abuse becomes more overwhelming and the woman begins to lose her identity. In the third phase (disengaging), the abuse remains overpowering, but the woman begins to identify inner strength and begins to make steps to leave the relationship. Because a woman's experiences and reality are constantly changing, the events in her life may take on new meaning. Choices made within the relationship are not always conscious. It is as if the subconscious takes over and ultimately permits a woman to leave a relationship. The recovering phase contains the period of initial readjustment after a woman has left her abusive partner until she gains a balance in her life. Although the woman has left the relationship, the abuse often continues in the form of harassment and direct intimidation and physical abuse.

The Binding Phase

The binding phase incorporates the initial development of a relationship and the beginnings of abuse within the relationship. A woman has a dream, a perception of what she wants in her life with her chosen partner, to fulfill, and the actual or perceived characteristics of the partner are seen within the framework of what she sees as a positive relationship. Warning signals such as characteristics of the man or events that are disconcerting to the woman are overlooked or passed over. Concentrated efforts are made to give the partner what he wants. The abuse is not labeled as such and is considered minor.

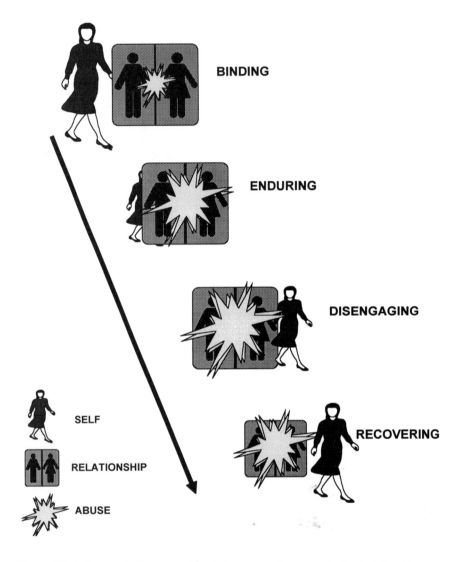

Figure 5.1. A Process of Entrapment in and Recovering From an Abusive Relationship

The Enduring Phase

As the abuse continues, it subsumes a larger part of the relationship. A woman endures the abuse while placing high value on the good aspects of the relationship. A woman continues to be willing to tolerate the abuse because she remains committed to the relationship. She feels as if she has invested so much in the relationship that she wants to believe her partner when he says, "It will never happen again." She feels responsible for the abuse and tries covering all signs of discordance between her and her partner. At the same time, she begins to feel "sucked dry" by the constant demands of her partner. She feels bad about herself, and her partner treats her as if she is an object or does not exist. She feels as if she cannot leave the relationship, but she will not survive if she does not leave. If she stays, he might kill her, or she might kill herself and/or her partner. It is this feeling of being trapped that moves her into a different level of awareness of her situation.

The Disengaging Phase

During the disengaging phase, the abuse has become representative of the relationship. An identity with other women in abusive situations begins to form. A woman struggles with feelings of loyalty toward her partner and feelings of an allegiance to the self if she is going to survive. At this time, a woman takes more risks to seek help and tries to find people who will support her instead of seeking support from those who blame or question her. She begins to realize that her life is meaningless if she stays and often thinks that she is better off dead than remaining in the relationship. The self begins to reemerge at different points in the relationship and often is pushed down or negated by the abused woman. Such women have renounced their feelings for so long that they are overwhelmed by these feelings of self reemerging.

The Recovering Phase

The recovering phase contains the period of initial readjustment after a woman has left her abusive partner until she gains a balance in her life. Her primary focus is survival. The abuse has overwhelmed and colored a woman's view of self, others, and the world in which she lives. Once she has made the definitive move to leave the relationship, the experiences slowly begin to coalesce into a woman's life experiences as she searches for meaning and tries to relinquish the relationship and the abuse.

Therapeutic Interventions

In all phases, there are specific approaches that health providers should use when assisting women in abusive relationships. It is important to help a woman to reframe her view of her situation. This reframing is essential for her to be able to come to terms with the conflicts that arise between her desires and the limitations ascribed to her by her abusive partner. In doing so, a woman will be able to make choices more clearly and regain or maintain some control over her life.

It is essential for those who work with women who are and have been abused to acknowledge a woman's feelings. This allows the woman to come to terms with how she is feeling and allows the health provider to validate the woman's feelings, instead of dismissing them as unreasonable or irrational.

Providers must accept where a woman is in understanding her situation. It is important to understand the woman's perspective of her situation, which is dependent on where she is in the process of entrapment and recovering from an abusive relationship.

Encourage the woman and give her opportunities for self-reflection and self-discovery. By asking open-ended questions that encourage the woman to think about how she is feeling, important issues may be raised for her self-reflection. The process of reflecting on certain issues may help the woman to reframe her perception of what is happening to her.

Resources for women and their children must be made available at all times. Although a woman may not be ready to use resources, knowing that they are available may help her to make choices.

Phase-Specific Interventions

Specific approaches for assisting women are discussed within the context of each phase of the process of entrapment and recovering from an abusive relationship. Approaches that are used in one phase should be carried over and applied in prospective phases.

Binding. It essential to look at the abuse within the context of a relationship. During the binding phase, abuse is a part of the relationship. The woman wants the abuse to end, not her relationship. Approaches with a woman at this time must be based on the assumption that the woman does not identify herself as abused. She must be assisted in examining what it is she wants from a relationship and whether she is having her needs met. Helping women to identify what it is they want out of life is helpful in the development of their ability to identify constraints placed on women by society and by individuals. She must be told that she is being abused. With assistance, women can identify and learn to value all parts of their selves (Miller, 1976, 1991). Regaining respect for self and learning to put her needs first are paramount. For a woman to be healthy, and thus have healthy relationships with others, she must know and love her self.

It is important to assist the woman in identifying abusive physical and psychological behavior. Before she can look at responsibility for hostile and antagonistic behaviors in her relationship with her partner, she must be able to identify abusive actions. In assisting her to identify abuse, she will also be assisted in identifying who owns the abusive behavior. It is the health provider's role to help a woman deal with the reality that the abuse is her partner's responsibility. She must be told that no one has the right to hurt her and that she has done nothing to incur the abuse she has sustained (Walker, 1985). She must be given some information about the cyclic nature of abuse. She may not be able to understand at this time that the abuse is not going to end, but she can understand and often will identify with the cycle of violence (Walker, 1984). A practical intervention that must be performed is the development of a safety plan. Because at this time it is unlikely that a woman will leave her partner, she must prepare for another abusive incident.

Enduring. During the enduring phase, the abuse often has gone on for a significant amount of time. Even if the physical abuse does not occur frequently, the psychological abuse has begun to take its toll on women's feelings about their selves. Many women talk about their selves being "annihilated" or "shrinking." All the good feelings a woman once had of self are being overcome by the abuser's perceptions of who she is. These feelings of worthlessness influence what alternatives a woman may think she has. She needs to understand that the abuse is not going to end. It must be reiterated that there is no flaw in her character or behavior that causes the abuse. Her partner is responsible for the abusive behavior and has no right to be abusive.

A woman often covers up the abuse because she feels stigmatized and ashamed of her situation. Although covering up may help her to present her relationship as normal, she needs to determine why she is covering up the abuse and what she gains from her behavior. It is important for her to understand that although she may feel she needs to protect her partner, she is the one in greater need of protection.

Disengaging. During this stage, a woman's overpowering feeling is fear. She must be helped in identifying the grip that her partner has on her. She needs to look at her beliefs about the relationship and her partner and identify that leaving her partner is not an insurmountable undertaking. She needs to assess for her safety and the possibility of her partner coming after her if she leaves the relationship. As in all the other phases, resources, especially a list of safe houses or shelters, must be discussed.

A woman needs to look within herself and identify who she really is and let go of the images from her partner that she has internalized. A woman may have alternate views of self. She may see herself as a qualified and successful professional person but may also see herself as worthless because she perceives herself as unable to fulfill her role as a partner. Regardless of a woman's perceptions of herself outside of the relationship, she needs to regain a positive image of self. Regaining positive images of self is a process, just as her declining sense of self was a process. For example, initial steps toward finding a new job or a place to live often are difficult for an abused woman. Succeeding in these responsibilities assists a woman initially in reclaiming her self.

Recovering. A woman's energy can be depleted in trying to justify to others why she has left the relationship. Others focus on their perception of the relationship, not on the abuse. Subsequently, she is blamed for the failure of the relationship and is stigmatized for her inability to fulfill her role as a woman. Comprehending why others blame her for the abuse and the failure of the relationship will help a woman to acquire the ability to uphold her convictions.

A woman should be assisted in focusing on what she might do to take control of her life. In assuming control over her life, learning that she is not alone in her experiences, and placing the abuse and the relationship in perspective, a woman can be helped in making a transition to disengage from the relationship. Constant reinforcement that she can depend on herself and her abilities is instrumental in her healing. The ability to learn that her efforts are effective is essential for the cultivation of a positive image of self and for the reduction of feelings of self-blame.

One goal of interventions is that a woman will be able to make sense of her experiences with her partner, especially the abusive aspects of the relationship. It may be important for a woman to receive help in directing her search for meaning outside of herself. The aversive experiences must be integrated into a woman's perceptions of personal vulnerability, her socialization as a woman, and her approval of and portrayal of self. Because significant others often blame a woman for the abuse or the disintegration of the relationship, and the responsibility for the abuse usually is assigned to the woman, the focus of blame is internal. A woman must be able to assign the blame for the abuse to her partner. But she must accept the abuse as part of an interactive relationship between two people. Examination of herself as an individual and in relation to others can assist in the development of a positive view of self and the knowledge that she can control decisions that affect her life.

A major step for a woman who has left an abusive relationship is the ability to recognize her partner as part of her past. A woman must grieve the loss of the relationship, the loss of roles that fit into that relationship, the loss of friends, and possibly the loss of the father of her children. If a woman can manage to reject in her mind the importance of her partner and place in its stead the importance of self, the power her partner has over her will diminish, and she will gain internal endorsement for who she is and her expression of self.

Many women fear returning to the abusive relationship or engaging in a similar relationship. It is important to assist women in identifying aspects of a healthy relationship. The abused woman needs to identify her behaviors and how some behaviors may attract abusive partners. Overwhelming feelings of self-doubt, worthlessness, and depression make a woman vulnerable, which in turn can result in the formation of unhealthy or overly dependent relationships. Identifying warning signals can help a woman avoid potentially abusive relationships.

Summary

The process of recovering and entrapment in an abusive relationship illuminates the meaning women attach to abuse, the relationship, and the reactions of others to her experience. In the beginning of the relationship, the woman seems to overlook the abuse because of the powerful intimacy factors in the relationship. The reality of her world contains aspects of abuse within an overall relationship. She attributes the conflict in the relationship to the beginning phase of any relationship in which people are getting to know each other. Initially, the abuse is psychological. For a woman in a physically abusive relationship, the denigration intensifies, and her belief in her self usually has diminished substantially by the time the first physically abusive incident occurs. Subsequently, she identifies something she has done, is, or has neglected as the reason for the abusive incident. As the relationship progresses, the woman is able to make little sense of what is happening to her because it is not validated by anyone. The lack of validation forces a woman to make sense of what is happening by looking within herself. To survive, she tries to make sense out of skewed reality, and in the process, almost diminishes her chances for survival. It is only when she receives some validation of what she is feeling and can develop a meaning that is shared by others that she is able to leave the relationship. The choice is not a matter of staying or leaving, but of survival.

The phenomenon of abuse is extremely complex. What happens to a woman is not linear and is full of contradictions. A woman's responses to the abuse, the feelings toward her partner, and her feelings about the self are never constant. A woman who is abused lives in two separate realities that are bound together by her shame. One reality encompasses the good aspects of the relationship and the other the abusive aspects.

Women in abusive relationships often feel isolated and powerless about their immediate situation and their lives. It may be difficult to assist a woman because of a lack of resources. Working with this population of women also may be frustrating. It is important to remember that although we as health providers may see clearly what is happening to her, a woman is confused by the conflicting messages she receives from her partner and from others. Assistance often takes the form of small steps taken one at a time. We may not see any change, but a woman may be beginning to identify her strengths and her situation with clarity. Our interventions may seem to go unheeded, but often a woman looks back at the assistance she has received and is spurred to take the step of leaving the abuse.

6

What Helped Most in Leaving Spouse Abuse

Implications for Interventions

Yvonne Campbell Ulrich

Women who are leaving abusive relationships rely on social support. However, their descriptions of the process of leaving, their reasons for leaving, and what helped them most in leaving relate to issues about the self as much as the availability of support. Clinicians who consider both of these resources can better support the decision making of women who are living in and leaving abusive male partners.

The general reaction of the public to knowing that many women are abused in the context of intimate relationships has been to ask why such women stay in the relationships. There have been many explanations of why women stay in an abusive relationship, but there has been little focus on how it is that women are able to leave such relationships. Women who leave or end the abuse present us with success stories. Nurses, other professionals, and women who are still in abusive relationships can learn from the women who were able to extract themselves from abuse. Their experience of what helped them most in leaving

AUTHOR'S NOTE: The comments of Dorothy Miller, Kansas Coalition Against Sexual and Domestic Violence, Pittsburg, Kansas, are greatly appreciated.

and knowledge of the factors within the environment associated with their leaving are tantalizing clues to understanding the women's process of leaving or ending the abuse.

Leaving Is a Process

Women may leave and go back to the relationship many times. Women's leaving patterns have been observed to look similar to wavelike excursions in and out of the relationship (Limandri, 1987). Different types of patterns in women's descriptions of their process of leaving are presented in Table 6.1.

The phases or stages in the process of leaving contain changes in women's awareness of themselves in the abusive relationship. The increased self-awareness may be the result of adaptive coping responses or of personal learning. Although each woman's reasons for leaving the abuse are specific to the individual and her situation, many women report leaving as a result of personal growth (Ulrich, 1991).

There are suggestions in the literature that some women who are seeking help may do so when they are feeling better about themselves (Limandri, 1987). If they are rebuffed or do not receive the help they need, they may manage their situation by purposively retreating, at least temporarily, to the relationship. The women who finally leave abusive situations are women who are and have been actively coping within the parameters of their particular environment. This kind of coping is a strength to be recognized and fostered by clinicians.

Nonsupportive Environment

The problem is that when the women contact relatives, friends, or professionals, they may encounter negative reactions (Limandri, 1987; McKenna, 1986; Ulrich, 1989a). The lack of support takes many forms. Women report that they have been told to go back home and stay there or to put up with the situation and be patient. They may be advised to hit him back or to ignore the beatings. Sometimes women experience a subtle form of blaming of the victim. They may be told to not provoke him or to find out what they can do to please him. In other instances, women may risk and reach out to others only to find that they are not believed. Another abusive attitude that women might experience was reported by a formerly abused woman. Her employer had begun to keep cosmetics for her at work so that she could make herself more presentable on the job after a beating (Ulrich, 1989b).

Table 6.1 Women's Descriptions of Self in the Process of Leaving Spouse
Abuse

	Changes in Self	*N*
Ferraro and Johnson (1983)	Women redefine the abuse as they become aware and angry about their own victimization	120
Mills (1985)	Women's restructuring of themselves represents stages in coping during the process of victimization and recovery	10
Landenburger (1989)	Meanings to women in the process of entrapment and recovering from abuse are phases of binding, enduring, disengaging, and recovering	30

Leaving

Women may retreat to the abusive relationship because of an environment that is not helpful to them in their struggle to end the abuse. However, in contradiction to the importance of social support to women being able to leave, most midwestern women who explained why they returned to the abusive relationship gave reasons that centered on the relationship; only 22% of them cited the lack of positive support (Ulrich, 1989a). It is evident that leaving and recovery is a complex process that takes place within women and may not be understood by the presence or absence of support alone. Nurses need to understand the complicated personal and environmental issues faced by women leaving abuse.

Social, Economic, and Relationship Factors and Reasons Associated With Leaving

Several investigators have measured the association between socioeconomic support and leaving and have found significant links. These factors are external to the women and say nothing about their views and experience of the leaving process. There also is evidence to support the importance to women of taking care of their relationship. This line of thinking points out the correlation between taking legal action, such as filing assault charges or obtaining restraint orders, and leaving the abusive male partner. Similarly, women may stay because of their investment in the relationship and their perception of their alternatives (Frisch & MacKenzie, 1991). (See Table 6.2.)

Table 6.2 Objective Factors (F) and Subjective Reasons (R) Associated With
              Leaving or Staying in Abusive Relationships

Leaving	Staying
Economic support (F) (Aguirre, 1985; Pfouts, 1978; Strube & Barbour, 1984)	Economic hardship (F) (Gondolf, Fisher, & McFerron, 1988; Kalmuss & Straus, 1984)
Support services (F) (Snyder & Scheer, 1981)	Traditional religions (F) (Pagelow, 1992; Ulrich, 1989a)
Relationship ties: Filing assault charges (F) (Strube & Barbour, 1984) or restraining orders; length of relationship (F) (Snyder & Scheer, 1981)	"Size of investments made in relationship . . . perceived quality of alternatives to abusive relationship" (R) (Frisch & MacKenzie, 1991, p. 342)
Previous separations (F); safety, personal growth, dependency (R) (Ulrich, 1991)	Love (R) (Strube & Barbour, 1984)

Changes in Self-Concept Are
Associated With Leaving

Several observers suggest that women change their self-concept as part of their process of leaving. The changing self has been described from more than one perspective. A woman may only gradually become aware of her victimization. This kind of self-awareness can lead women to experience feelings of anger that act as a catalyst to remove them from the relationship (Ferraro & Johnson, 1983).

A different perception of women's patterns is that victimization is a process that emanates more from societal roles than from women's psyches. In this view, women restructure themselves during their process of leaving to survive. This explanation holds that there are different stages of coping in the leaving process. These levels are experienced as women enter a violent relationship, manage the violence, experience a loss of self, reevaluate the relationship as violent, and leave (Mills, 1985). Landenburger (1989; see also Chapter 5) described women's pattern of leaving and recovery from the perspective of the abuse's meaning to the women. In this model, women's selves emerge and reemerge during their recovery from the abuse through phases of entrapment and recovering from the abuse (binding, enduring, disengaging, and recovering). Although these studies are from different fields, there are similarities in their descriptions. Both studies describe women as changing during the process of the abuse and getting out of the abuse. The results of these studies produce a picture of the process of leaving from the women's point of view. Women redefine what is happening to them to recognize their victimization. During the gradual process of victimization and then recovery, they restructure themselves to cope.

Table 6.3 Attributions of What Helped Most in Leaving Abusive Spouses: Releases

Self	*Social Support*
Lack of choice	Abuser let go
Relationship with abuser gone	Family affirmed her
Personal dreams	Friend(s) cared
Personal faith	Shelter/support group understood
Fear	Other professionals supported
Personal growth	

What Helps Most in Leaving Is Experienced as Release

Women were asked what helped them most in leaving abuse as part of an in-depth interview study (Ulrich, 1998). One woman used the term *release*. Release is defined by *Webster's* as "setting free from restraint, sorrow, or servitude." This definition is apt because it at once portrays two issues: the disengagement and what one is disengaging from, such as restraint, sorrow, or servitude. In other words, we cannot talk about women leaving or staying in abusive situations without understanding those situations from the view of the women.

Releases Show Women's Strengths

The releases, or what set the women free from the abuse, are listed in Table 6.3. The releases refer to something particular about the self or something about the social support that was available to the women. Women who attributed leaving to their own efforts seemed to understand and acknowledge their power and scored highest on a self-esteem questionnaire (Ulrich, 1998). Although support must be present in the community, it is the women who must be able to reach out to an unknown environment. Using an environment that is sometimes not friendly takes a great deal of coping and skill. Breaking away from the relationship also takes courage because in our society women often feel responsible for their relationships. The women's views of what helped most in leaving are indicators of the situation from their special point of view. Their view shows us the missing pieces that freed women to use their power to leave an intimate abusive relationship.

Releases Focus on the Women's Issues

The women's experiences of what helped them most in leaving, their releases, reveal the issue for them in leaving. Women who have left report changes in awareness about the situation, their abusive relationship, or themselves. The language of the women reflects personal growth and learning.

An example of how women can take responsibility for themselves was reported by Miller, a clinician who gives abused women an assignment of writing out an abuse history or a story of what happened in the relationship. Miller observed that women who responded to the assignment often were more able to remain out of the abusive relationship, even if the abuser attempted to regain the woman's affections. These women seemed to have a better idea of what was happening to them in the relationship. Miller says that many women have told her how useful this assignment was (D. Miller, personal communication, June 19, 1991).

The availability of positive social support was most important to many women. Women who tended to have lower self-esteem said the thing that helped them most was family, a friend, the shelter, or professionals. In some cases, it was the abuser's lack of getting better or the abuser's giving up on having a relationship with her that helped most.

Nurses can indicate their understanding of the woman's role in obtaining support. The nurse can assist the woman in identifying support that will be meaningful to her. A second step is to explore the potential avenues of obtaining the support that is accessible to each woman. This kind of approach that identifies the support accessibility from the woman's point of view can help her focus on the alternatives that are available when she is ready to use them. Clinicians who demonstrate their respect for the woman's experience of obtaining support point to and affirm the woman's efforts. The goal is to help her realize what it is like to do something for herself, which will increase her self-esteem.

Recognize and Respect
Women's Strengths

The women's point of view of what helped them most has implications for choosing interventions that will be meaningful and effective. Formerly abused women have described what helped them most in leaving or ending the abuse. Women with higher self-esteem attribute these releases to their own efforts, whereas women with lower self-esteem attribute the help as coming from the environment in the form of support from family, friends, or agencies.

Women Use Their Strengths to Leave

Women who attribute some responsibility for their situation to themselves have higher self-esteem than do those who blame totally either themselves or the abuser (Campbell, 1989a). Similarly, women who attribute leaving to their efforts tend to have higher self-esteem scores than do those who attribute their leaving to support from the environment (Ulrich, 1998). Although it is important to not blame women for their abuse, supporting their ability to take some control of their lives and to take credit (and responsibility) for their actions may help them raise their self-esteem.

Women Overcome Hidden Barriers to Contact Support

Nurses can use sensitivity and support to show an abused woman that they are listening to her story. Affirmation of the woman is critical to her, especially because many women have been or are in a relationship that is destructive to their "selves" (Landenburger, 1989; Mills, 1985). Affirmation of the woman is important so that she understands that the nurse is listening to her story and accepting her. Listening to the woman offers the caregiver the opportunity to understand the problem from the woman's point of view. Listening to what she wants will help the nurse identify the woman's issues. If the woman has left the abuse, listening to what has helped her in the past and what she wants offers insights into her coping skills (Nurius, Furrey, & Berliner, 1992). Listening and reflecting to the woman her process of thinking in a context of acceptance can allow her to increase awareness of herself (Rogers, 1951).

Examine Personal Attitudes

Subtle blaming of the woman is a problem that presents a barrier that may be hidden to women. Many nurses have responded to women's stories by asking themselves, if not the women, "What do you need to do so that he will not want to abuse you?" Focusing on women to change their behavior to get him to stop the abuse can be a way of making them responsible for the abuse. This may be a natural thing to do because, if one is able to explain the existence of the problem based on women's behavior, the world seems to be a safer place. People feel they have more control over what happens to them because they can simply explain that the abuse would not have happened if the victim had not behaved badly (Lerner & Simmons, 1966). Blaming the woman may serve to reinforce the blame that women may be experiencing from the abuser. Fostering women's self-blame makes it more difficult for them to leave.

Dependent Behavior May Not Be the Problem

Calling a woman dependent may not be useful to her recovery (Collins, 1993; Jack, 1991; Krestan & Bepko, 1990), and dismissing a woman's survival in an abusive relationship as dependent behavior is not adequate to explain the abused woman's behavior. Such a diagnosis can divert the practitioner's vision from women's coping skills. In this scene, the therapist in a hierarchical relationship may act to undermine a woman's sense of self. Women who are labeled dependent in this situation are told by sources outside themselves that they are at fault.

Making Themselves User Friendly

To rephrase the timely question that McKenna (1986, p. 89) asks, how often do abused women adapt to others who do not recognize within them the influence of having to cope with violence? Assessments and interventions that do not recognize, affirm, or use women's strengths place them in a situation in which their selves or their experiences are not validated (Merritt-Gray & Wuest, 1995). This time the undermining of self is stemming from those to whom they may be turning for help. Women who have managed to escape the violence sometimes express their dismay at a treatment system that requires them to adjust to others' conceptions and misconceptions of abusive relationships. Women speak of therapists who encourage their continued relationship with an abuser who has threatened to kill them. In one such instance, the therapist explained to the woman that the abuser wanted to change and that the woman just needed to be assertive with him (Ulrich, 1989b).

The problem for the woman who wants to leave an abusive relationship may become one of making herself user friendly to obtain support from the system. In other words, the woman may need to resist or to accept abusive attitudes from well-meaning professionals, such as therapists, school principals, and judges, to manage to obtain the support she needs to protect herself and her children.

Conclusion

Leaving abuse is a complex process. Women who describe themselves as changing during the process of leaving identify learning about themselves as being as important to their leaving the relationship as was the presence of social support. Women who score higher in self-esteem take credit for their role in leaving.

Nurses who recognize and affirm the women's strengths can help them overcome the abusive attitudes they may be encountering as they leave. Abused women are to be commended for their coping skills in using social support despite the stereotypic views of them that are held by some members of the community. Listening to the women to understand their situations from their point of view can help nurses understand the barriers women experience in leaving abuse. Progress will not be made until there is support and sensitivity to the issues as the women define them.

PART III

ABUSE AND PREGNANCY

7

The Dynamics of Battering During Pregnancy

Women's Explanations of Why

Jacquelyn C. Campbell
Catharine E. Oliver
Linda F. C. Bullock

Nursing and other discipline research has established abuse during pregnancy as a serious health problem needing assessment and intervention (Helton, McFarlane, & Anderson, 1987; McFarlane, Parker, Soeken, & Bullock, 1992). Both the pregnant woman and the unborn child are at risk (American College of Obstetricians and Gynecologists, 1989; Bullock & McFarlane, 1989; Parker, McFarlane, & Soeken, 1994). However, the image of a man physically hitting a woman pregnant with a child he helped create and usually professes to want continues to be a troubling one. Despite our awareness of violence toward women in intimate relationships, we find ourselves groping for useful explanations for this particularly distressing aspect of the problem. From clinical experience, we know that battered women are also seeking answers to why this would happen. This exploratory research study investigated reasons women used to explain their experiences of violence from their husbands or partners during pregnancy and also compared women battered during pregnancy with a group of women also abused with a history of pregnancy by the abuser but who were not battered during pregnancy.

Literature Review of Abuse During Pregnancy

Richard Gelles (1975) was the first to publish about the issue of abuse during pregnancy, seeking to call attention to the problem. His speculations about the reasons pregnant women might be abused included (a) male sexual frustration (pregnant women often refuse sex); (b) biochemical changes in the wife that result in mood swings; (c) family transition, stress, and strain; (d) prenatal child/fetal abuse; and (e) defenselessness of the wife. The first two seemed to suggest that normal female prenatal behaviors and responses were credible reasons for male partners abusing pregnant women. The current study also attempted to correct this reasoning.

Prevalence of Abuse During Pregnancy

Early retrospective studies described 40% to 60% of battered women reporting abuse during pregnancy (Fagan, Stewart, & Hansen, 1983; Walker, 1984). Current U.S. and Canadian studies address prevalence of abuse in women who are pregnant and find prevalence ranging from 2% to 17% during pregnancy and the most usual range between 3% and 9% (Gazmararian et al., 1996; Stewart & Cecutti, 1993). Prevalence rates varied according to how women were asked, who made the inquiry, and demographics of the sample. The highest prevalence in a large, ethnically heterogeneous sample was found by a study where the regular prenatal care nurse made a face-to-face oral inquiry at *each* prenatal care visit using the Abuse Assessment Screen (AAS), a four-question screen that asks separately about violent tactics, fear, and forced sex as well as emotional and physical abuse (McFarlane et al., 1992). The AAS is described in detail with its latest psychometric evaluations in Chapter 16 in this volume. The lowest prevalence of abuse during pregnancy was found in a private prenatal site in an affluent community, using two questions, both containing the term *abuse* as part of a longer, self-administered written questionnaire (Sampselle, Petersen, Murtland, & Oakley, 1992). However, in two other studies using both private and public patients, income level did not affect prevalence (Bullock & McFarlane, 1989; Helton et al., 1987). In a comparison of abuse during adolescent pregnancy with abuse during adult pregnancy, Parker, McFarlane, Soeken, Torres, and Campbell (1993) found a significantly higher prevalence of abuse for adolescents than adult women (20.7% vs. 15%).

Another purpose of the current study was to shed light on the prevalence-related question of whether pregnancy is a time of increased risk for abuse. Despite retrospective reports of many battered women saying that their first assault from their husband or partner was during pregnancy or that abuse became worse during pregnancy (e.g., Walker, 1984), analysis of national random survey data ($N = 6,002$) found that the 36% higher prevalence of abuse reported by pregnant women all but disappeared when analysis controlled for the age of the respondent (Gelles, 1988). However, the cross-sectional nature of the Gelles analysis makes it impossible to determine possible varying patterns of abuse during pregnancy.

Health Correlates and Outcomes

It is estimated that trauma is a complication in 6% to 7% of all pregnancies, and only 50% of those injuries are from automobile accidents (Stauffer, 1986), but it is unknown how much of trauma during pregnancy is related to abuse. However, because abuse is a primary cause of trauma to women in general in emergency rooms (Stark & Flitcraft, 1985), it is reasonable that a substantial proportion of trauma during pregnancy is similarly related. Women abused during pregnancy have described blows to the abdomen, breasts, and genitals accompanied by sexual assault when interviewed after the pregnancy (Dobash & Dobash, 1979). Battering during pregnancy has been associated with severity of abuse and has been identified as a risk factor for eventual homicide in battering relationships, suggesting that the man who beats his pregnant partner is an extremely dangerous man (Campbell, 1995; Fagan et al., 1983; see also Chapter 8 in this volume).

The literature review on pregnancy outcomes is presented in detail in Chapter 9, but for this overview, abuse during pregnancy has been associated with low birth weight (LBW) in some studies (Bullock & McFarlane, 1989; Parker et al., 1994; Schei, Samuelsen, & Bakketeig, 1991), although other studies do not show the same association (Amaro, Fried, Cabral, & Zuckerman, 1990; O'Campo, Gielen, Faden, & Kass, 1994). Other documented deleterious outcomes of abuse during pregnancy included miscarriage, substance abuse, smoking, inadequate weight gain, inadequate prenatal care, and anxiety and depression (Amaro et al., 1990; Campbell, Poland, Waller, & Ager, 1992; McFarlane, Parker, & Soeken, 1996b; Schei et al., 1991). No studies to date of postpartum depression specifically measured partner abuse, but many have identified lack of support from a partner as a risk factor. Given the association of battering and depression in other women, it is reasonable to assume that at least some women diagnosed with postpartum depression are experiencing abuse from an intimate partner. Gielen, O'Campo, Faden, Kass, and Xue (1994) found an increased prevalence (19% vs. 10%) of abuse during the postpartum period also alerting us to the necessity of considering abuse beginning or resuming after childbirth.

Battering during pregnancy, then, is a serious problem that affects a substantial number (by conservative estimate 150,000-330,000 per year) of women and their unborn children during the prenatal period (Gazmararian et al., 1996). Research has not established the risk factors for abuse during pregnancy, only for abuse before pregnancy. Most women abused during pregnancy say their husband or partner said he wanted the child. Why, then, would he abuse her?

Sample and Procedures

The sample for this study was taken from a larger sample of battered women ($N = 97$) recruited by newspaper advertisement and bulletin board postings from two demographically distinct cities for a study of women's responses to battering (Campbell, 1989a). Battered women were identified as such by their answers on the Conflict Tactics Scale (CTS), an instrument with established reliability and validity used extensively to measure frequency and severity of wife abuse (Straus & Gelles, 1990). The CTS was modified to take into account self-defense and to include women as battered who experienced sexual in addition to physical abuse from an intimate partner during the prior year, to operationalize the definition of battering, "repeated physical and/or sexual assault from an intimate partner or ex-partner within a context of coercive control" (Campbell & Humphreys, 1993, p. 69). Fifty-one of the women who had been pregnant by their abusive partner volunteered to take part in this additional aspect of the study.

Twenty-seven (53% of those pregnant by their abusive partner) women were not beaten during pregnancy although they were physically abused by that partner subsequent to (and in the majority of cases also prior to) the pregnancy. These women found pregnancy a protective period from abuse. One woman said, "I try to stay pregnant" so that her partner would not abuse her. However, one of the women not abused during pregnancy was battered the day she returned home from the hospital after delivery, "like he was saving it up." This subsample of women not beaten during pregnancy formed a comparison group for the study. The demographic characteristics at the time of interview of the women abused during pregnancy and the comparison group are presented in Table 7.1. The sample was fairly evenly divided between African American (47%) and European American (49%) women, with one Native American woman and one Puerto Rican woman.

Women who said they had been beaten during pregnancy were asked why they thought that had happened. Their answers were recorded verbatim in writing.

Results

A series of t tests was performed on the demographic variables and other study variables to determine if there were differences between those battered during pregnancy and those battered but not during pregnancy (Table 7.1). There were no significant differences in demographic variables between the two

Table 7.1 Comparison of Battered Women Abused and Not Abused During Pregnancy

Variable	Group	N	Mean	SD	Two-Tailed p
Woman's age	I	24	34.0833	6.704	.120
	II	27	30.4074	9.447	
Total family income	I	24	$18,688	$18,134	.979
	II	27	$18,824	$18,447	
Education	I	24	12.7500	2.625	.691
	II	27	12.4815	2.173	
Years together	I	24	9.0833	5.250	.155
	II	27	8.8519	7.059	
Violence severity/ frequency	I	24	297.0833	168.344	.007
	II	27	461.3333	238.861	
Severity of injury	I	24	2.1667	1.373	.022
	II	27	3.1111	1.476	

NOTE: I = abused but not while pregnant; II = abused while pregnant.

groups. Abuse during pregnancy was not significantly associated with ethnicity by chi-square analysis. However, there were two important differences. The women abused during pregnancy had experienced significantly more frequent and severe abuse as measured by the CTS throughout the course of the relationship. They also had been more severely injured by their abuser than had those not abused during pregnancy.

Responses to the open-ended question were coded by thematic analysis. Four basic themes emerged from the analysis: (a) jealousy of the unborn child ($n = 5$; 18.5%); (b) pregnancy-specific violence that was not directed toward the unborn child ($n = 4$; 14.8%); (c) anger toward the unborn child ($n = 4$; 14.8%); and (d) anger against the woman or "business as usual" ($n = 11$; 46%) (see Table 7.2).

The small group of the five women who said the partner was jealous of the unborn child clearly differentiated this emotion from him being angry at the unborn child. In these cases, the abused women felt the anger was directed at them because they were talking and thinking about the unborn child a great deal or doing things to prepare for the birth. As one woman put it, "I was not paying enough attention to him to suit him."

The four answers categorized under pregnancy specific represent a variety of responses not represented by the notions of anger against the woman or against the unborn child. One woman stated the abuse had started during pregnancy

Table 7.2 Themes of Women's Perceptions of Reasons for Abuse

Theme	Number of Women	Percentage
Jealousy of infant	5	18.5
Pregnancy specific (but not directed against infant)	4	14.8
Anger toward infant	4	14.8
"Business as usual"	11	46.0

precisely because she was committed to the relationship then, and he knew she could not get away. Another woman said the abuse had started during pregnancy because she was sick from the pregnancy and he did not like it because she could not "cater to him." Another woman said the abuse was because he did not like her when she was pregnant because she was "fat," but it was not directed against the unborn child; he wanted the child. The fourth woman talked about the battering as directed against her and the unborn child: The abuser was angry about the pregnancy and at her for becoming pregnant.

Anger directed at the unborn child was demonstrated by the man saying he was trying to cause a miscarriage or directing his blows specifically at the woman's abdomen. One woman said he tried to cause her to abort during her fourth and fifth pregnancies because he thought they had too many children. The other three said he was angry at the unborn child because he thought it was someone else's (they said it was not). One woman said the beatings caused her to miscarry, and another said a beating caused her water to break in the ninth month. The women who said he seemed to be angry at the unborn child experienced the most serious abuse during the pregnancy.

The largest single category ($n = 11$) had been beaten before pregnancy and continued to be beaten. One woman said, "He just hits me all the time," and another coined the phrase used to describe the category: "It was just business as usual." Another stated, "He was just mad at me," and a fourth woman said, "He's not out to hurt the baby, he's out to hurt *me*."

Discussion

This study was limited by its retrospective nature; in some cases, the interview took place many years after the pregnancy. It was also limited because it inquired only about women's perceptions of why they were abused during pregnancy. However, men's interpretations of their motivations for abuse generally are blaming of women (e.g., Gondolf, 1985) and could be expected to resemble Gelles's (1975) original speculations. The reasons the women gave for the abuse could be expected to be more useful to battered women who are seeking answers, and therefore more useful for designing appropriate interventions.

Among the important findings were no demographic differences between women battered during pregnancy and those who were not, a result also found by Helton et al. (1987). The greater severity and frequency of abuse for women battered during pregnancy supports other research finding that a man who beats a pregnant woman tends to be an extremely violent man.

Male jealousy as a reason for abuse is a theme that reverberates in the literature on woman abuse in general (e.g., Dobash & Dobash, 1979). The women in this sample often were hesitant as they advanced this thesis in terms of jealousy of the baby, finding it hard to imagine how a man could be jealous of a fetus. This kind of jealousy in abusers is a manifestation of the underlying needs for power and control, more encompassing than sexual jealousy (Gondolf, 1985; Okun, 1986). Thus, during pregnancy, the jealousy was expressed as resentment of the attention the woman is paying toward the unborn child as the pregnancy advances, and a normal developmental stage of pregnancy becomes a risk factor for women.

The second theme can also be seen as related to the desire for power and control. Pregnancy interfered with the woman performing roles and duties that the male partner saw as necessary. Rather than accommodating her pregnancy or negotiating alternate strategies for accomplishing tasks, the partner apparently thought he was justified in abusing the woman.

The theme of anger toward the unborn child is the one theme that resembles the Gelles (1975) reasons, that of prenatal child abuse. Strong associations between child abuse and wife abuse have been found in prior studies (Straus & Gelles, 1990). For one woman in this sample (and another in a second qualitative study by Campbell, Pugh, Campbell, & Visscher, 1995), the partner was insistent that the baby was someone else's, even though the woman maintained that this was not true. In families where there are children fathered by previous partners, Daly, Singh, and Wilson (1993) documented greater rates of fatal child abuse by stepfathers and mothers' boyfriends. This dynamic is an extremely dangerous one and needs to be assessed by clinicians.

The final theme of business as usual indicates that for most women, the underlying dynamics operating in their relationship were present whether or not they were pregnant. Although slightly more than half of the women saw their abuse as specific to the pregnancy, the largest single group did not. These results suggest varying patterns of abuse during pregnancy, with approximately 25% of the total sample of battered women being at higher risk during pregnancy (those identifying one of the first three themes), another 25% experiencing the same risk of abuse as when not pregnant, and approximately 50% finding pregnancy to be a protective period. Similarly, Hillard (1985) reported that 21% of the women abused during pregnancy reported an increase in violence during pregnancy, 36% reported a decrease, and 43% said the violence remained the same. Although battering tends to increase in severity and frequency throughout time, this trajectory can be exacerbated or interrupted during pregnancy. More research is needed to determine what factors are associated with which patterns. These variable patterns would explain Gelles's (1988) finding of no overall increased risk of abuse during pregnancy but indicate differential implications for health care system interventions.

Implications for Interventions

This study reinforces the need for assessment of all pregnant women for battering during the pregnancy and any prior abuse (Bohn, 1990; Helton et al., 1987; McFarlane et al., 1992). Women abused before pregnancy are at higher risk for abuse during pregnancy, as exemplified by the women in this study expressing the business-as-usual theme. In addition, the current study as well as that of Gielen and associates (1994) suggests that women abused before pregnancy may not be beaten during the prenatal period but will be abused after. This possibility needs to be explained to women and carefully assessed at postpartum and well-child appointments. Questions about abuse ideally are asked as part of the oral nursing history, with physical signs noted (March of Dimes, 1986b). Questions such as "Does your husband (partner) ever hit, kick, punch, or otherwise physically hurt you?" have been used successfully (see the AAS description in Chapter 16). Prior work also has suggested that abuse should be asked about in more than one way to elicit the greatest disclosure (Campbell et al., 1992). Finally, women should be assessed for battering at each prenatal visit, because the abuse may begin at any time during pregnancy.

In addition, the findings suggest assessing the woman's interpretation of why she is being abused. It is important to assess for self-blame, which has been associated with depression and low self-esteem (Campbell, 1989a), and to determine partner patterns that suggest particular danger for the woman and the child. In cases in which the woman thinks the abuser's anger is directed toward the unborn child, when the abuser seems jealous of the fetus, and especially when he suspects the baby is someone else's (even if it is not), the possibility of subsequent child abuse by the batterer is even more of a consideration. Such information must be shared with the woman and with nurses who will care for her and the infant in the future.

Abuse during pregnancy is a risk factor for both the woman's and the child's health serious enough to trigger at least one postpartum nursing home visit, as part of private childbirth insurance packages and as part of Medicaid, community health, Healthy Start, and/or family preservation initiatives for poor and otherwise at-risk families. That visit needs to include careful assessment for both woman and child abuse, assessment done in private with the mother. If privacy cannot be obtained in the home, the visiting nurse needs to make sure that assessment is done at the postpartum visit, at a WIC visit, and/or in a follow-up phone call arranged for privacy. Careful coordination between systems is absolutely critical in these cases.

Women battered during pregnancy may be even more invested in maintaining the relationship and hope that the abuse will end once the baby is born, especially if he has persisted in saying he wanted the baby. Women need to be warned that usually the abuse does not end, and should be told how to get help in the postpartum period if they need it. As detailed elsewhere (Bohn, 1990; Campbell & Humphreys, 1993; Helton, 1986; March of Dimes, 1986b; Chapters 5, 10, and 15 in this volume), any nursing or health care system intervention with abused women needs to include

1. A thorough assessment of the severity and frequency of abuse, including emotional and sexual abuse and risk of homicide
2. Accurate documentation, including history of injuries on a body map for potential future legal action
3. Sharing information about the abuse laws in the state, local legal and criminal justice resources, woman abuse shelter services including the national hotline number (1-800-799-SAFE), and batterer treatment programs
4. Brainstorming with the woman about her present and future options for action
5. Emotional support for the normalcy of her responses and her decisions
6. For pregnant women, follow-up at all subsequent prenatal appointments and at the hospital at delivery; and after birth, the family is followed for the risk of child and woman abuse

In summary, additional research into the reasons behind battering during pregnancy is needed, but this exploratory study suggests important possibilities for research and practice. Assessment for battering during pregnancy is an obvious necessity, but nursing care and other health care system interventions can be partially based on an additional assessment of the woman's interpretation of why she is being beaten.

8

Risk Factors for Femicide Among Pregnant and Nonpregnant Battered Women

Jacquelyn C. Campbell
Karen L. Soeken
Judith McFarlane
Barbara Parker

Femicide is terminology recently introduced and used in scholarly writings to refer specifically to the killing of women (Radford & Russell, 1992; Stout, 1991). Femicide is the leading cause of death in the United States for African American women aged 15-34 (Farley, 1986) and the seventh leading cause of premature death for women overall (U.S. Department of Health and Human Services, 1991a). Although rates of homicide within intimate heterosexual relationships is higher for African American than European American couples, they become comparable when socioeconomic status is controlled (Centerwall, 1984). Other female causes of death have been reduced since 1940, but death by femicide has increased for both European American and African American women (Farley, 1986). Femicide happens far less frequently to Hispanic women and has only

AUTHORS' NOTE: Research reported in this chapter was supported by the National Institute of Nursing Research, R29 No. NR01678 (J. Campbell, principal investigator), and the Centers for Disease Control, R49CCR No. 603514 (J. McFarlane and B. Parker, principal investigators).

been measured separately in the past few years, so that national rates over time are unavailable.

The risk of spousal homicide has decreased recently, especially for African American couples (Mercy & Saltzman, 1989; Rosenfeld, 1997). This may reflect African American couples' increasing tendency to neither live together constantly nor be married even though sexually and otherwise intimate. We can also hope that it reflects increasing resources for battered women.

Homicide involving women has different dynamics and risk factors from the more often studied phenomenon of male-to-male murders (Block, 1985; Mercy & Saltzman, 1989; Wilson & Daly, 1993). Ninety percent of women murdered are killed by men, men who are most often a family member, spouse, or ex-partner (Campbell, 1992; Stout, 1991; Wilbanks, 1986). Between 1976 and 1987, more than twice as many women were killed by a husband or sexual partner than by strangers (Kellermann & Mercy, 1992). Approximately two thirds of women murdered by intimate partners or ex-partners have been physically abused before they were killed (Campbell, 1981, 1992; Rasche, in press; Wallace, 1986). Homicide of a female partner or ex-partner followed by suicide is another form of homicide of women wherein a history of female battering is the most usual pattern (Humphrey, Hudson, & Cosgrove, 1981; Wallace, 1986). Thus, femicide is best understood as part of a configuration of abuse of female partners (Stark, 1990).

When women kill, they most often kill husbands, ex-husbands, and lovers, and again, there is a documented history of *wife* assault (Bernard, Vera, Vera, & Newman, 1982; Browne, 1987; Campbell, 1992). Less than 10% of women in various samples who were killed by a spouse precipitated that act by being the first to strike a blow or show a weapon (Campbell, 1992; Goetting, 1989; Jurik & Winn, 1990). In contrast, "victim precipitation" was common (56% to 79%) when a man was killed by his female partner (Campbell, 1992; Goetting, 1988; Mann, 1990). It has therefore been concluded that woman abuse is the primary risk factor for homicides involving women as victims or perpetrators and that femicide involves similar patterns of coercive control as other forms of battering (Stark, 1990).

From this information it is clear that one of the major ways to decrease femicide is to identify and intervene with battered women at risk (Campbell, 1995; Stark, 1990). The trajectory of severe abuse is generally an increase in severity and frequency over time (Straus & Gelles, 1990) that may culminate in a homicide if the woman does not leave or the man does not receive either treatment or incarceration. The majority of battered women do eventually leave the abuser, but they are probably most at risk for homicide after they have left the abuser or when they make it clear to him that they are leaving for good (J. C. Campbell, Miller, Cardwell, & Belknap, 1994; Hart, 1988; Wilson & Daly, 1993).

Recent studies of femicides in Chicago and New York City indicated that the leading cause of maternal death in those cities is now trauma, with homicide accounting for the largest percentage of those traumatic deaths and approximately one fourth of the total (Dannenberg et al., 1995; Fildes, Reed, Jones, Martin, & Barrett, 1992). Maternal death was defined as death occurring during pregnancy or within 90 days of the end of pregnancy. These are the first studies showing this alarming development. There is also some indication that battered women who have been abused during pregnancy are particularly at risk for eventual femicide and/or to kill their abuser (Browne, 1987; Campbell, 1986). Pregnancy also offers a "window of opportunity" wherein abused women are seen the most often by health care professionals and can receive a thorough abuse assessment and intervention. There has been very little research investigating the connections between abuse during pregnancy and femicide. The purpose of this study was to address this gap in our knowledge by investigating if risk factors associated with femicide are greater for battered women abused during pregnancy.

Development of an Instrument
to Assess Risk Factors for Femicide

In an attempt to help abused women realistically appraise their risk of homicide, the Danger Assessment (DA) was developed and has been tested in several different samples of battered women. (Campbell, 1995; McFarlane, Parker, & Soeken, 1996a). The instrument is a 15-item, yes/no format, listing of risk factors found in retrospective research to be present when abused women were killed by their batterer or killed him (Figure 8.1). Internal consistency has ranged from .60 to .71, reflecting relatively small sample sizes (ranging from 30 to 79), a dichotomous format, and the low item variability on some of the relatively rare but important risk factors (Campbell, 1995). Test-retest reliability over 1 to 3 weeks has ranged from .91 to .97. Support for construct validity has been found by moderately strong correlations in expected directions with instruments measuring frequency and severity of abuse such as the Conflict Tactics Scale (Straus, 1979) and degree of female injury (Campbell, 1986; Campbell & Stuart, 1989).

Fagan, Stewart, and Hansen (1983) found abuse during pregnancy to be a strong predictor of severity of abuse-related injury to women. In retrospective studies, women reported battering becoming more frequent and severe during the pregnancy (Walker, 1979, 1984). Browne (1987) also identified abuse during pregnancy as a factor differentiating abused women who kill their batterer from those who do not. Therefore, abuse during pregnancy was included as a risk factor for homicide on the DA. In prior research, this item was correlated with the total score at the .31 to .53 range. This item is usually considered retrospectively, that is, a battered woman answers yes if she was ever beaten by her present abuser

Several risk factors have been associated with homicides (murders) of both batterers and battered women in research conducted after the murders have taken place. We cannot predict what will happen in your case, but we would like you to be aware of the danger of homicide in situations of severe battering and for you to see how many of the risk factors apply to your situation. Using the calendar, please mark the approximate dates during the past year when you were beaten by your husband or partner. Write on that date how bad the incident was according to the following scale:

1. Slapping, pushing; no injuries and/or lasting pain.

2. Punching, kicking; bruises, cuts, and/or continuing pain.

3. "Beating up"; severe contusions, burns, broken bones.

4. Threats to use weapon; head injury, internal injury, permanent injury.

5. Use of a weapon; wounds from a weapon.

(If any of the descriptions from the higher number apply, use the higher number.)

Mark *yes* or *no* for each of the following. ("He" refers to your husband, partner, ex-husband, ex-partner, or whoever is currently hurting you.)

_____ 1. Has the physical violence increased in frequency over the past year?

_____ 2. Has the physical violence increased in severity during the past year and/or has a weapon or threat from a weapon ever been used?

_____ 3. Does he ever try to choke you?

_____ 4. Is there a gun in the house?

_____ 5. Has he ever forced you to have sex when you did not wish to do so?

_____ 6. Does he use drugs? (By drugs, I mean "uppers" or amphetamines, speed, angel dust, cocaine, crack, street drugs, heroin, or mixtures.)

_____ 7. Does he threaten to kill you, and/or do you believe he is capable of killing you?

_____ 8. Is he drunk every day, or almost every day? (In terms of quantity of alcohol.)

_____ 9. Does he control most or all of your daily activities? (For instance, does he tell you whom you can be friends with, how much money you can take with you shopping, or when you can take the car?)

(If he tries but you do not let him, check here _____.)

_____ 10. Have you ever been beaten by him while you were pregnant?

(If never pregnant by him, check here _____.)

_____ 11. Is he violently and constantly jealous of you? (For instance, does he say, "If I can't have you, no one can"?)

_____ 12. Have you ever threatened or tried to commit suicide?

_____ 13. Has he ever threatened or tried to commit suicide?

_____ 14. Is he violent toward your children?

_____ 15. Is he violent outside of the home?

_____ Total *yes* answers

Thank you. Please talk to your nurse, advocate, or counselor about what the Danger Assessment means in terms of your situation.

Figure 8.1. Danger Assessment
SOURCE: Copyright 1986 by Jacquelyn C. Campbell, RN, PhD.

during a pregnancy. In samples of abused women completing the DA, from 43% to 54% of women who had ever been pregnant by their abuser reported abuse during pregnancy (Campbell, 1986; Campbell & Stuart, 1989). This is considered to be a sign of a particularly violent man, because many abusers do not hit the partner during pregnancy although they beat them at other times (Chapter 7 in this volume; see also McFarlane et al., 1996a). It is not known if pregnant abused women are more or less at risk during pregnancy for femicide. National FBI statistics do not note if a woman was pregnant at the time of a homicide. None of the women in Campbell's (1992) review of 5 years of police records in one city for 65 femicides were pregnant when they were killed, but only approximately 3% of adult women are pregnant at any one time.

Methodology

This sample consisted of 381 women from the urban areas of Detroit ($n = 145$), Houston ($n = 83$), and Baltimore ($n = 153$) who reported being abused. One third (128) reported they had been beaten while pregnant. Mean age of the sample was 25.5 years with 87.6% reporting income below the poverty level and 47.1% reporting less than a high school education. Of the total, 185 (48.6%) were African American, 92 (24.1%) were Hispanic, and 92 (24.1%) were European American. There was a difference in age across ethnic groups. Mean age for African Americans was 27.6 years; European Americans, 24.2 years; and Hispanics, 21.5 years.

Instruments

The DA, described above, had an internal consistency reliability as measured by coefficient alpha of .68. The Index of Spouse Abuse (ISA; Hudson & McIntosh, 1981) is a 30-item, self-report scale measuring severity or magnitude of physical (ISA-P) and nonphysical (ISA-NP) abuse. Item weights are applied to reflect the various degrees of abuse represented by the items. Both the ISA-P and ISA-NP scores range from 0 to 100 where higher scores indicate greater abuse. In the current study, internal consistency was .95 for the instrument as a whole, .91 for the ISA-P subscale, and .94 for the ISA-NP subscale. Both the DA and the ISA were offered in English and Spanish.

Results

One third of the 381 surveyed women ($n = 128$) reported they had been beaten while pregnant by their male partner. Being beaten while pregnant was not related to age, income, ethnicity, or education. To compare DA scores for battered women abused during pregnancy with those not abused during pregnancy, the DA total score was computed without the abuse-during-pregnancy item. Given that age was positively correlated with all DA items except one (woman threatening/attempting suicide), age was controlled through analysis of covariance. Ethnicity was also included as an independent variable.

Overall, women reporting abuse during pregnancy scored significantly higher on the DA than abused women not reporting abuse during pregnancy (5.62 vs. 2.91, $F = 79.37$, $p < .001$), with no significant differences related to ethnicity or the interaction of ethnicity and abuse during pregnancy. Individual items on the DA also demonstrated significant ($p < .05$) differences related to abuse after adjusting for age (Table 8.1): A greater percentage of those beaten during pregnancy reported a yes on the items, with the exception of those having a gun in the house. A greater percentage of those not beaten during pregnancy reported a gun in the house than those abused during pregnancy. After adjusting for age, there were also some differences related to ethnicity (Table 8.2). Hispanic battered women reported the lowest incidence of choking; African American women reported a higher incidence of jealousy and lower incidence of being controlled in daily activities and threatening or attempting suicide. Some items on the DA were also related to income and education although the proportion of explained variance was less than 2%. Specifically, a higher proportion of those with income above the poverty level than those below reported increased incidence of choking ($r = .09$, $p < .01$), having a gun in the house ($r = .11$, $p < .01$), and a threat/belief that her partner would kill her ($r = .13$, $p < .01$). Increased education level was associated with increased violence in the past year ($r = .17$, $p < .01$), incidence of choking ($r = .11$, $p < .01$), and having a gun in the house ($r = .13$, $p < .01$).

Using multiple regression, all demographic variables were included in the prediction of DA scores, with dummy variables created to account for ethnicity. Controlling for the demographics of age, education, income, and ethnicity, those abused while pregnant had significantly higher scores on the DA than those not abused while pregnant ($t = 8.622$, $p < .001$). Although the demographic variables explained a significant amount of the variation in DA scores ($R^2 = .093$, $F = 6.68$, $df = 5.325$, $p < .001$), only age was significant by itself ($t = 5.16$, $p < .001$) with older women tending to have higher DA scores. Including the interaction between abuse status and ethnicity did not change the results. Thus, it appears that among women who are abused, older women beaten during pregnancy tend to report significantly higher DA scores.

Discussion

This study revealed that abused women reporting abuse during pregnancy report more risk factors associated with homicide. This was true across the three ethnic groups examined and across the three urban sites where women were

Table 8.1 Women Responding Yes to Danger Assessment (DA) Items by
Whether or Not Abused During Pregnancy, After Adjusting for Age

DA Item	Abused (%)	Not Abused (%)	F Ratio
Violence increased past year	44.7	18.1	28.30
Increase severity or with weapon	36.1	17.2	14.40
Tried to choke you	62.8	25.0	56.77
Gun in house	13.2	19.9	3.85
Forced sex	50.6	23.4	22.48
Drug usage	30.4	14.8	10.69
Threatened/believe he will kill you	56.2	23.3	44.98
Drunk daily or almost daily	30.4	14.5	12.14
He controls daily activities	50.8	31.3	13.25
Violent or jealous of you	74.7	46.7	31.03
You threatened or tried to commit suicide	34.2	23.8	4.57
He threatened or tried to commit suicide	33.7	17.1	12.45
Violent outside the home	46.5	21.7	22.12

NOTE: All differences are statistically significant.

interviewed. Ethnicity did not affect the number of factors associated with homicide, but women who were older had more factors.

Surprising in this research were the findings that increased education and increased income were associated with greater severity of physical and nonphysical abuse. However, the characteristics of the sample, the majority poor and with limited education, limit any interpretation of this finding.

From in-depth interviews with battered women, it is clear that the majority carefully weigh the pluses and minuses of the overall relationship, both in terms of their safety and well-being and that of their born and unborn children (J. C. Campbell, Miller, et al., 1994). However, the majority have not realistically appraised the potential for homicide. Even though many have thought about it, they may find it too frightening to dwell on. During pregnancy, women also tend to be idealistic about the pregnancy outcome and the beneficial effect the baby will have on the relationship. Discussion of homicide may have to be in the context of a contingency if the abuse continues after the baby is born. Thus, clinicians who work with abused women need to make sure women realize the potential of homicide in their situation without negating the hope they may have about the relationship. Giving them a way to realistically assess their risk of homicide on an ongoing basis is both an ethical and legal imperative (Campbell, 1995; Hart, 1988; Saunders & Browne, 1991). For health care professionals, there is some similarity to the risks of cancer given to smokers so that they can make their own decisions about actions to be taken. There are also some analogies to the appraisal done for risk of suicide by physical and mental health care

Table 8.2 Women Responding Yes to Danger Assessment (DA) Items for Which Differences Between Ethnic Groups Were Significant After Adjusting for Age (in percentages)

DA Item	Black	Hispanic	White
Tried to choke you	42.0	22.0	43.6
He controls daily activities	31.3	46.9	42.4
Violent or jealous of you	61.7	47.1	46.1
He threatened or tried to commit suicide	14.6	30.8	30.9

professionals wherein a clinical assessment is done, and if the risk considered great, action is taken to ensure the person's safety.

If a pregnant abused woman is discussing attempting to leave her abuser, professionals need to be sure she has a safe plan for doing so. Keeping in mind that the risk of homicide increases when abused women make clear that they are leaving for good, women should be warned that a polite discussion of her intentions is not a good idea. She will need to leave in secret. Additional detailed, specific recommendations for intervening for abuse during pregnancy are available (Campbell & Humphreys, 1993; McFarlane, 1989, 1991; Parker & McFarlane, 1991 and Chapters 7 and 10, this volume).

Even though ethnicity did not affect the risk of homicide for women abused during pregnancy, it is important to take into account the possible added barriers to safety for Hispanic women. The majority of the Hispanic women in this sample were first-generation Mexican Americans with many not speaking English and approximately 30% undocumented. A recent study of 400 undocumented immigrant women in the Bay Area conducted by the Coalition for Immigrant and Refugee Rights found 34% of 301 Latinas to be victims of domestic violence (Ramirez, 1991). Because of fear of detection and deportation, 64% of the women avoided using health and social services. A common belief for women in the Hispanic community is that "the system" is more harmful than abuse. Explicit questions may be considered too forward; private violence is often treated as an internal problem to be dealt with in the confines of the family for fear of bringing shame on the family. Working with Hispanic women requires a keen appreciation for language and immigration status as well as cultural beliefs (see Chapter 21).

In summary, a woman abused during pregnancy is being battered by a particularly dangerous man. Abused women are not only at risk for homicide from the partner during pregnancy but also after the pregnancy. It therefore becomes important to assess all battered women for abuse during pregnancy as a risk factor during pregnancy. It also becomes important to discuss potential long-term risk of homicide with women abused during pregnancy, even when their current abuse is not severe.

9

Stress Related to Domestic Violence During Pregnancy and Infant Birth Weight

Mary Ann Curry
S. Marie Harvey

As previously described in detail (Chapter 7), the assault of women during pregnancy occurs with sufficient frequency to pose a significant threat to the health of women and their children. Abuse during pregnancy may be understood as having direct or indirect causal relationships with negative health outcomes (Newberger et al., 1992). The direct relationship could operate through a variety of biological mechanisms, including blows to the abdomen, injuries to the breast and genitals, and sexual assault. The negative effects of physical assault involving abdominal trauma include, among others, placental separation; antepartum hemorrhage; fetal fractures; and rupture of the uterus, liver, or spleen (Gelles, 1988). In addition, trauma may cause uterine contractions, premature rupture of membranes, and infection leading to early onset of labor. Battered women are more likely to have one or more miscarriages (Stark et al., 1981), with 9% of the women of one study ($N = 1,000$) reporting miscarriage as a result of abuse (Bendtro & Bowker, 1989). Miscarriages and abuse-related abortions pose immediate and long-term health risks for the woman. Immediate risks include excessive blood loss, cervical or uterine trauma, infection, and disseminated intravascular coagulation (Hatcher et al., 1986; Whitley, 1985). Long-term risks include cervical incompetence, preterm birth, low birth weight (LBW), and placental problems (Berendes, 1977; Creasy & Heron, 1981; Gonik & Creasy, 1986).

In addition to the negative effects of direct abuse, a pregnant woman's health is also adversely influenced by indirect abuse effects. Studies have shown a higher prevalence of emotional problems in abused pregnant women compared with those who were not abused (Bergman & Brismar, 1991; Campbell, Poland, Waller, & Ager, 1992; Hillard, 1985; Martin, English, Andersen, Cilenti, & Kupper, 1996). The link between psychosocial factors and pregnancy outcomes has been studied both prospectively and retrospectively. Taken together, findings across studies document the negative effects of emotional conflict, anxiety, stress, and low self-esteem on pregnancy outcomes and the positive effects of social support and family functioning (Chalmers, 1983; Norbeck & Anderson, 1989; Norbeck & Tilden, 1983; Pagel, Smilkstein, Regen, & Montano, 1990).

Both physiological and behavioral pathways have been postulated as the mechanism by which psychosocial factors influence birth outcomes. Physiologically, it is hypothesized that stress increases catecholamine levels, which in turn decrease uterine blood flow, and this may result in contractions and/or lower birth weight babies. The behavioral mechanism proposes that psychosocial stress may influence health behaviors such as smoking, substance use, and prenatal care attendance.

Other indirect effects of abuse include isolation and lack of access to prenatal care and other health care services (Campbell et al., 1992). A study of 691 pregnant women found that abused women tended to enter prenatal care later in pregnancy compared with nonabused women (Parker, McFarlane, Soeken, Torres, & Campbell, 1993). The abuser may prevent the battered woman from seeking health care, or the woman herself may be reluctant to seek care. Women may be afraid of revealing their history of abuse to health care providers (Newberger et al., 1992). In addition, women who have undergone sexual abuse may find vaginal examinations to be painful and traumatic (Bohn & Parker, 1993).

Although it has been suggested that violence during pregnancy could lead to LBW, a review of relevant research concluded that the evidence is mixed (Petersen et al., 1997). In most studies, a direct relationship may be found, but it disappears when other risk factors for LBW are controlled. One of the few studies that found an effect even when controlling for other factors found a significant difference only for higher socioeconomic status women (Bullock & McFarlane, 1989). In their sample of 589 postpartum women at private and public hospitals, the overall percentage of battered women delivering LBW infants was 13% compared with 7% among nonbattered women. For women delivering in private hospitals, the percentage of battered women delivering LBW infants was 18% compared with 4% among the nonbattered women. The stronger association for middle-class women may be because there are so many other risk factors for LBW in the lives of poor women. The causal pathway between abuse and LBW may also be mediated through stress and/or the association of abuse with other risk factors for LBW such as smoking, substance abuse, less than optimal weight gain, and inadequate prenatal care (Campbell et al., 1992; McFarlane, Parker, & Soeken, 1996b). Abuse may also exacerbate chronic problems of the mother such as hypertension or diabetes (Newberger et al., 1992).

The overall goal of this study was to examine the relationship between domestic violence during pregnancy and adverse pregnancy outcomes. The specific aims were twofold: (a) to investigate the relationship between abuse during pregnancy and the psychosocial variables of stress, social support, and self-esteem; and (b) to examine the association between perceived stress related to domestic violence during pregnancy to infant birth weight.

Method

A prospective design was used. Women were interviewed once during pregnancy and information regarding their birth outcomes were retrieved from medical records and birth certificates after delivery.

Data were collected in two different settings during 1987-1988. One setting was an urban, university prenatal clinic that serves predominantly low-income women. After obtaining informed consent, women were interviewed at the time of a regularly scheduled prenatal visit. The other setting was a prenatal referral telephone "hotline" located in a semirural area. Women who called the hotline were asked if they would be willing to talk to a researcher. If they gave permission to be contacted, the researcher called them back and completed the interview over the telephone after obtaining informed consent.

Data from 403 participants ranging in age from 13 to 41 years, with a mean age of 24.7, were analyzed. The majority were Caucasian (88%), had completed 12 years of education (66%), and were living with a partner (70%). The mean family income per month was $887, with a standard deviation of $627. Nearly half of the women were primiparous.

Instruments

The Prenatal Psychosocial Profile (PPP) was used to measure women's perceptions of stress, support from partner, support from others, and self-esteem. The PPP is a brief, comprehensive measure of psychosocial risk during pregnancy (Curry, Campbell, & Christian, 1994). It is a composite of the Support Behaviors Inventory (Brown, 1986), the Rosenberg (1965) Self-Esteem Scale, and a newly developed measure of stress. The Support Behaviors Inventory and the Rosenberg Self-Esteem Scale have established validity and reliability. Construct and convergent validity of the stress subscale has been supported as well as test-retest reliability (Curry et al., 1994). The reliability coefficients for this study were .78 for the stress subscale, .90 for the partner and other support scales, and .84 for the self-esteem subscale.

Domestic violence was measured by 1 of the 11 stress items, which asks: "To what extent is current abuse, sexual, emotional, and/or physical, currently a stressor/hassle for you?" The response choices were as follows: *no stress, some stress, moderate stress,* and *severe stress,* scored on a 4-point, Likert-type scale ranging from 1 to 4. The 69 participants (17%) who responded they were experiencing some, moderate, or severe stress were coded as abused, and the remaining 334 were coded as nonabused.

Procedure

There was no attempt to control when during pregnancy the PPP was administered. The mean number of weeks gestation at administration was 14, and ranged from 5 to 36 weeks. At the university prenatal clinic, women were administered the PPP in person by a trained research assistant. This procedure took only 5 minutes and usually occurred in the examining room while the woman was waiting to be seen by a provider. A set of cards showing the response options for each subscale were handed to women to refer to while answering the questions, which were read by the research assistant. At the pregnancy hotline, women who agreed to be interviewed gave their telephone number to the hotline worker, and the researcher contacted her within a few days. The researcher asked women to write down the response options to refer to during the interview. No problems and no missing data were encountered with either method.

Findings

The sociodemographic characteristics of the women, infant's birth weights, and subscale scores of the abused and nonabused women were compared by *t* test. Predictors of mean birth weight were analyzed by multiple regression, and the odds ratio for delivering a LBW infant was calculated.

Sociodemographics. The sociodemographic characteristics of the two groups can be seen in Table 9.1. When compared by *t* test, the abused women reported significantly lower monthly incomes.

Birth Weight. The infants of abused women weighed significantly less ($M =$ 3,239 grams) than infants of nonabused women ($M =$ 3,486 grams), $t(2,70) =$ 81.6, $p < .008$. The LBW rate was 4.4% for the nonabused women and 8.2% for the abused women. The odds ratio for abused women having a LBW infant was 1.923.

Table 9.1 Characteristics of Abused and Nonabused Women

		Abused (n = 69)	Nonabused (n = 334)
Age	M	24.23	24.76
	SD	5.38	5.32
Monthly income	M	$706	$923*
	SD	$483	$617
Week first visit	M	11.69	13.08
	SD	6.85	7.15
Number of prenatal visits	M	11.2	11.7
	SD	7.40	4.57

*p < .05.

Table 9.2 Prenatal Psychosocial Profile Subscale Mean Scores of Abused and Nonabused Women

		Abused (n = 69)	Nonabused (n = 334)
Stress	M	27.65	19.82
	SD	5.22	4.75
Support from partner	M	45.50	54.71
	SD	14.61	10.29
Support from others	M	45.83	51.68
	SD	14.58	10.92
Self-esteem	M	32.25	35.44
	SD	5.53	4.63

NOTE: All ps < .0001.

Stress-Related Subscales. There were significant differences between the two groups on all four of the PPP subscales (see Table 9.2). Not surprisingly, the abused women reported more stress, less support from partner, less support from others, and lower self-esteem than the nonabused women. Furthermore, there were significant differences between all the items on the stress and partner support subscales, as shown in Tables 9.3 and 9.4.

Although the stress subscale item scores were significantly higher for the abused women, the ordering of the stressors was actually very similar for both groups. Women in each group ranked financial worries as the most stressful item. Nonabused women ranked other money worries as the second most stressful item, whereas abused women ranked family problems second. Both groups

Table 9.3 Stress Subscale Item Mean Scores of Abused and Nonabused Women

		Abused (n = 69)	Nonabused (n = 334)
Financial worries	M	3.27	2.54**
	SD	.74	.92
Other money worries	M	2.84	2.46*
	SD	1.02	1.03
Family problems	M	3.13	1.91**
	SD	.96	.93
Recent/future move	M	2.72	2.04**
	SD	1.18	1.09
Recent loss of a loved one	M	1.79	1.43*
	SD	1.14	.95
Current pregnancy	M	2.58	2.03**
	SD	.99	.82
Problems with alcohol/drugs	M	1.73	1.24**
	SD	.91	.63
Work problems	M	2.20	1.62**
	SD	1.24	.90
Problems with friends	M	1.66	1.35*
	SD	.85	.61
Feeling "overloaded"	M	2.94	2.15**
	SD	.95	.90

$*p < .01. **p < .001.$

ranked feeling "overloaded" as the third most stressful item. The ranking of the remaining items was nearly identical for both groups.

There were remarkable differences in the partner support subscale item scores, which asked women to rank how satisfied they were with their partners on a 6-point, Likert-type scale, where 0 = *very dissatisfied* and 6 = *very satisfied*. Abused women reported significantly less support from their partners compared with nonabused women.

The item with the highest score for both groups was "Lets me know that he will be around if I need assistance." Abused women ranked their partners lowest on the item "Says things that make my situation clearer and easier to understand," whereas the nonabused women ranked their partners lowest on the item "Shares similar experiences with me." There were also differences in the same direction between all the items on the other support subscale. Abused women rated their satisfaction with others significantly lower on all but two items. When the item scores of the two support subscales were compared, the nonabused women

Table 9.4 Partners' Support Scores: How Abused and Nonabused Women
Ranked Their Partners

		Abused (n = 69)	Nonabused (n = 334)
Shares similar experiences	M	3.89	4.64
	SD	1.47	1.34
Helps keep up morale	M	3.82	4.87
	SD	1.65	1.23
Helps out in a pinch	M	4.30	5.20
	SD	1.57	1.19
Interest in my activities and problems	M	4.00	4.83
	SD	1.68	1.34
Goes out of way for me	M	3.87	4.82
	SD	1.78	1.35
Allows to talk personal/private	M	4.39	5.34
	SD	1.75	1.09
Lets me know I'm appreciated	M	3.78	4.96
	SD	1.54	1.22
Tolerates ups and downs	M	3.94	4.80
	SD	1.57	1.28
Takes concerns seriously	M	4.08	5.11
	SD	1.57	1.13
Makes situation clearer	M	3.71	4.67
	SD	1.61	1.29
Around for assistance	M	4.67	5.44
	SD	1.67	1.11

NOTE: All $ps < .0001$.

ranked their partners as more supportive than others on every item. By contrast,
abused women ranked others as more supportive on 6 of the 11 items (see Table
9.5).

Although the total self-esteem subscale score was significantly lower for the
abused women compared with the nonabused women, only three items were
significantly lower. These were the items (a) wish you could have more respect
for yourself, (b) feel useless at times, and (c) at times think you are no good at
all.

Regression Analyses. Regression analyses were conducted to determine the
extent to which measured variables contributed to birth weight. First, correlation
coefficients were computed for age, education, income, and numbers of prenatal
visits because these variables have been associated with birth weight (Ketter-

Table 9.5 Others' Support Scores: How Abused and Nonabused Women Ranked Others

		Abused (n = 69)	Nonabused (n = 334)
Shares similar experiences	M	4.12	4.36
	SD	4.18	1.31
Helps keep up morale	M	4.18	4.66*
	SD	1.44	1.20
Helps out in a pinch	M	4.21	4.85**
	SD	4.21	1.24
Interest in my activities and problems	M	4.01	4.43
	SD	1.61	1.28
Goes out of way for me	M	3.66	4.47**
	SD	1.66	1.35
Allows to talk personal/private	M	4.34	4.66
	SD	1.78	1.43
Lets me know I'm appreciated	M	4.10	4.67**
	SD	1.59	1.30
Tolerates ups and downs	M	4.18	4.68*
	SD	1.60	1.35
Takes concerns seriously	M	4.39	4.94**
	SD	1.57	1.19
Makes situation clearer	M	3.97	4.61**
	SD	1.57	1.31
Around for assistance	M	4.63	5.31*
	SD	1.62	1.09

$*p < .01; **p < .005.$

linus, Henderson, & Lamb, 1990) and the four PPP subscales. All but income and support from partner were significantly correlated with birth weight in the expected directions. To determine the specific relationship between stress subscale items and birth weight, all items were correlated with birth weight. Eight of the 11 items were significantly correlated, including 4 that were highly correlated: recent loss of a loved one, the current pregnancy, problems with friends, and current abuse (see Table 9.6).

In the first analyses, age, education, and number of prenatal visits were entered first, resulting in an R^2 of .05. Then, the three PPP subscale scores were added. Only the stress subscale was significant, increasing the R^2 to .08. In the next analysis, age, education, and number of prenatal visits were forced into the model first, resulting in an R^2 of .05. Then, instead of entering the stress subscale

Table 9.6 Variables That Significantly Correlated With Birth Weight

Variable	Correlation	p
Age	.15	.004
Education	.14	.006
Number of prenatal visits	.17	.001
Stress subscale	−.18	.0006
Stress subscale items		
Financial worries	−.10	.03
Feeling "overloaded"	−.10	.04
Problems with family	−.12	.02
Problems with alcohol/drugs	−.12	.02
Recent loss of loved one	−.14	.005
Current pregnancy	−.14	.006
Current abuse	−.15	.003
Problems with friends	−.19	.0002
Other support subscale	.10	.04
Self-esteem subscale	.10	.04

score, the four subscale items that most highly correlated with birth weight were entered to determine their individual contribution. All but stress related to the current pregnancy entered the model. The current abuse item entered first, which increased the R^2 to .08. Next, recent loss of a loved one entered, followed by problems with friends. These increased the R^2 to .09 and .11, respectively (see Table 9.7).

In summary, compared with nonabused women, the abused women in this study had significantly lower incomes, more stress, less support from partner, less support from others, and lower self-esteem. They were also significantly more likely to have a LBW infant. Six variables emerged as significant predictors of birth weight: age, education, number of prenatal visits, stress due to abuse, stress due to recent loss of a loved one, and stress due to problems with friends.

Discussion

This study provides additional evidence of the relationship between psycho-social stress during pregnancy and infant birth weight. The data suggest that for these women, their current stress related to abuse, recent loss of a loved one, and problems with friends contributed the most to the variance in birth weight. In addition, the abused women in this study reported significantly more psycho-

Table 9.7 Regression Model

Variable	R^2	F	p
Age, education, no. of prenatal visits	.05	6.649	.0002
Current abuse	.08	7.235	.0000
Recent loss of a loved one	.09	7.124	.0000
Problems with friends	.11	6.847	.0000

social stress, which is consistent with the higher prevalence of emotional problems in abused pregnant women reported in the literature (Bergman & Brismar, 1991; Hillard, 1985). Thus, it seems plausible that both physiological and behavioral pathways may have contributed to lower infant birth weights.

Physiologically, the higher stress levels experienced by the abused women could theoretically have decreased uterine blood flow and contributed to lower birth weights. Behaviorally, these women did report more stress related to problems with drugs and alcohol (Table 9.3), although there was no difference in the timing or number of prenatal visits. This latter finding is inconsistent with other studies that reported abused women with inadequate prenatal care (Campbell et al., 1992; Parker et al., 1993). However, it does suggest that for the abused women in this study, receiving adequate prenatal care did not ameliorate the effects of abuse and psychosocial stress on their infants' birth weights.

These data also suggest the need to more carefully examine the impact of pregnant women's perceptions of support from partner and others. The abused women in this study reported significantly less support from partner and others. Furthermore, they were more likely to report they were satisfied with the support they received from others than the support they received from their partners. Although this comparison is not surprising, they also perceived support from others as less satisfying than the nonabused women. As will be recalled, support from others but not support from partners was significantly correlated with infant birth weight, although it did not enter the regression model.

The other two items on the stress scale that entered the regression model—recent loss of a loved one and problems with friends—merit consideration. Because no further information regarding these stressors was collected, it is not known who the loss was or what the nature of the problems was. It could be speculated that abused women responded to the loss item in terms of their abusive partner, particularly if they were permanently or temporarily separated from him. The problems with friends could also be related to problems with the partner because the majority of the women in the study were partnered, but not legally married, and thus may have interpreted the question as applying to their domestic partners. Alternatively, perhaps their friends wanted them to leave their abusive relationship and this conflict caused problems.

Strengths and Limitations of Study

The major strengths of this study included the prospective design and the use of the PPP. The PPP subscale and item mean scores provided a comprehensive contrast of the psychosocial stress of abused and nonabused women. The major limitation is the definition of abuse used in the study: current stress related to physical, sexual, and/or emotional abuse. It does not define the type or extent of abuse and is not consistent with the questions in common use today. Other limitations include the mainly Caucasian sample and absence of information about smoking and weight gain. The latter variables may have been useful in understanding the physiological pathways between abuse and infant birth weight.

Implications for Practice and Research

The 17% of the participants in this study who reported stress related to current abuse had infants that weighed significantly less than women who did not report abuse. It is not known if the abuse contributed to their perceptions of increased stress, lower self-esteem, and lower support from partner and others, but the relationship between these variables cannot be questioned. Clinically, this study strongly supports the importance of screening for current domestic violence, both for its potential relationship to birth weight and its relationship to other psychosocial factors related to women's health. For example, current abuse may be related to substance use and financial stress, both of which may also independently have an effect on health outcomes.

These findings point out the relevance of domestic violence as a health policy issue both at the primary and tertiary levels. The most obvious policy implication is eliminating the underlying societal factors that result in domestic violence, such as gender and economic inequality, victimization of women, and tolerance for violence. In the meantime, as a tertiary measure, more resources need to be allocated for comprehensive services for victims of domestic violence.

10

Nursing Interventions for Abused Women on Obstetrical Units

Linda F. C. Bullock

A ssessment interventions in the postpartum period are crucial for the future health and the quality of life of the mother and the infant. Nurses need to assess each woman for her ability to physically care for and nurture her newborn, but it also is crucial that they assess each woman for the number and types of stressors occurring in her life and her ability to adjust to the stressful situations that inevitably occur with the arrival of an infant. Women are on the obstetrical unit for an incredibly short time in relation to the amount of information the nursing staff needs to convey to each new mother. Most nurses ensure that mother is reasonably "safe" in handling the new infant and that she knows how to hold, feed, and clean the infant properly. What most nurses fail to assess is how "safe" the environment will be for the mother and infant after they leave the hospital.

Nurses who have worked in maternity units probably have seen indications that caused them to wonder about the circumstances of the client but did not pursue the significance of the indications. For example, a woman who was admitted to the labor and delivery unit in premature labor may say, during the investigation of possible causes for the premature labor, that she "fell down the stairs." Many nurses may be suspicious of such an answer but may accept the explanation because women are clumsy during pregnancy because of the gravid uterus. In a more extreme example, a patient admitted to the labor and delivery unit with premature labor said that her contractions started when the "refrigerator" fell on her while cleaning the kitchen. Many health care providers may not respond to this statement, even though it is highly implausible, because the provider may believe that one should not interfere with what goes on behind the doors of a person's home. By not addressing the plausibility of this kind of story, the provider has conveyed acceptance or ignorance of domestic violence.

Recent studies have shown that as many as one in six infants will be going home with mothers who were battered during pregnancy (McFarlane, Parker, Soeken, & Bullock, 1992), and approximately 2 million children in the United States are seriously injured by their parents every year (American Medical Association, 1992a, 1992b). Men who batter their wives are also likely to physically abuse their children (Straus & Gelles, 1990). In addition, it can be assumed that mothers who are subjected to the stress of battering must expend energy coping with the battering that could have been spent caring for the infant and any other children she may have.

Interventions Based on the
Neuman Health Care Systems Model

Nurses must realize that physical care of the newborn will be seen as a priority by most new mothers, but nurturing may be more difficult to achieve if the mother must cope with a multitude of stresses. Using the Betty Neuman health care systems model (Neuman & Young, 1972), nurses and other health care professionals can better understand the effect stress has on a woman's health and the resources available for her to nurture her infant. This model is appropriate because of its total-person approach and that person's response to stress. The Neuman model allows assessment of each woman as an individual and determination of how she will cope with new and existing stresses. The model also guides the level of intervention (primary, secondary, or tertiary) that would be appropriate for each individual.

Model Overview

Neuman's model (Neuman & Young, 1972) represents a person by using three concentric rings. The rings differ for each person because they include information from physiologic, psychologic, sociocultural, developmental, and spiritual attributes of the individual. The distance between the rings varies for each individual, but the greater the distance between each ring, the less likely the individual will be affected by any stressor penetrating and damaging, or ultimately destroying, the core. The interplay of balance and imbalance equals wellness or illness. The body will try to maintain an equilibrium while resisting stressors, but this requires energy. Over time, continuing disequilibrium will weaken the body's defenses, and illness will occur. If the stressor is left un-checked, the body's defenses could be weakened to the point that the stressor is able to penetrate the core, and the person may die.

The core of the individual is the inner ring of the three and is represented by a solid line indicating its stable nature. The core consists of the attributes for survival that are common to all of us, such as body temperature, but allows for the unique baseline of each individual based on that individual's genetic make-up, such as weakness and strengths of different body parts or organs.

The next concentric ring also is solid and is called the "normal line of defense." This ring represents what a person has become over time and will vary from person to person. The distance between this ring and the core will vary in each individual based on that person's stage of development. This ring would consist of physiologic and psychosocial attributes, such as level of health, self-esteem, coping mechanisms, social supports, education, job skills, and financial security.

The third ring is called the "flexible line of defense" and is represented by a broken line because it is dynamic and changing, varying in its distance from the core hour to hour. This line of defense for an individual is determined by factors such as the amount of sleep one has each night; nutritional status; exercise; health habits, such as drinking alcohol and smoking; and environmental factors and resources available that enable the person to better use his or her energy for preservation. As these factors change, so does the vulnerability of the person to a stressor.

When a stressor, which can be intrapersonal, interpersonal, or extrapersonal in nature, breaks through the flexible line of defense, the degree of reaction (or effect on health status) seen in the person will vary depending on the distance between the lines of defense and the resistant forces encountered. The resistant forces are termed "lines of resistance" and are the body's attempt to stabilize against the disequilibrium caused by the stressor. If the body does not support the basic structure against the disequilibrium, the structure will begin to collapse (concentric rings move closer together) and the person may die. Physiologically, a line of resistance would be the mobilization of leukocytes to the site of injury. Thus, the effect or degree of disequilibrium a stressor causes any one person (i.e., if a stressor affects one's health slightly vs. more serious health consequences) will be individualized.

The Neuman model can be used to plan nursing interventions at primary, secondary, and tertiary levels. Primary prevention includes identifying known or potential stressors and trying to reduce the possibility that the individual will encounter the stressor or at least reduce the degree of reaction of the stressor by strengthening the flexible and normal lines of defense. Secondary intervention is implemented once the stressor has broken through the flexible line of defense. This intervention includes early case finding and treatment of symptoms. The goal of the interventions is to strengthen the basic structure so that the effect of the stressor is minimized. Tertiary intervention focuses on maintaining or stabilizing a person's level of health to the highest level obtainable after encountering a stressor. The goals for this level of care are to reduce or prevent future occurrences with the stressor.

Obstetrical Clients in Relation
to Neuman's Model

Using the Neuman model, each patient can be assessed to determine the number and type of stressors occurring interpersonally, intrapersonally, and extrapersonally. The patient's physiologic, psychologic, sociocultural, developmental, and spiritual well-being can also be assessed to judge the amount of disequilibrium a new mother may experience when she takes her infant home. The level of intervention is determined by the degree the stressor has penetrated the flexible line of defense. However, before care goals are set, the nurse should discuss with the patient what goals should be set and negotiate expected outcomes. This assessment should be done in private with the woman. If the woman is being battered, a lack of privacy will prevent her from revealing the stress of being battered and may place the woman at risk for additional violence if her partner believes she has revealed abuse to the health provider.

Coping with the demands of a newborn and adjusting to changes in lifestyle can be stressful. A woman's flexible line of defense will be weakened with sleep interruptions because of nighttime feedings, the increased nutritional requirements of breast-feeding, a probable decrease in exercise because of the demands of the infant, and little time for herself. If the mother has other children at home, the flexible line of defense may be additionally challenged.

As noted in the model description, the second line of defense may prevent additional penetration of the stressor. If the new mother has adequate coping skills, a supportive partner who shares in the physical care of the infant, or other strong social supports including family and friends, the stresses brought about by the infant may cause little disequilibrium. Each new mother needs to be assessed for her individual strengths and weakness to determine the response she will have based on her particular lines of defense and resistance to the known and expected stressors. The Neuman model helps organize the strengths and weakness to give a picture of each new mother as an individual.

Obstetrical Clients Who Are Battered

For many women, the stress of the newborn infant may not be the only stress when the woman returns home. Although only one study has investigated abuse during the postpartum period, that research suggests that almost twice as many women are abused during that time as are abused during pregnancy (Gielen, O'Campo, Faden, Kass, & Xue, 1994). The first 6 weeks after delivery is when couples' coping skills are stretched to the limit in caring for the infant. It is time for nurses and other health care providers to take an active role in addressing violence before and after delivery. The issue must be addressed with every woman who seeks obstetrical care.

Health Needs of Abused Women

In a study by Dobbie and Tucker (1990) battered women residing in shelters were assessed for their perceived health needs. Although these women may or may not have been pregnant, the age range of the sample was 19 to 45 years, so many of the women were of childbearing age. More than 80% of the women never ate three meals a day, and 30% of the women had fewer than two servings a day of milk or milk products. Fewer than 40% of the women interviewed slept 6-8 hours at night, and only 12% said they awoke feeling fresh and relaxed. More than 60% of the women had no form of self-relaxation, and fewer than 30% said they knew how to handle stress. With regard to support from the extended family, only 25% of the women said they saw their family members on a regular basis, and many said they could not rely on them for support even if they did see them. Coping mechanisms for the women in the study seemed to revolve around the unhealthy practices of smoking (55%), drinking alcohol (70%), and the use of street drugs (43%). Nutrition, stress reduction, and stopping smoking were the three areas about which the women in the study desired more information.

Another study of women interviewed in the immediate postpartum period (Campbell, Poland, Waller, & Ager, 1992) found significant correlation between battering and anxiety, depression, and alcohol and drug use and inadequate prenatal care. If one applies these variables to the Neuman model, it is easy to see how a person's lines of defense are weakened by battering and the effect this has on the person's health. Depression usually causes a decrease in appetite and sleep, which additionally weakens the flexible line of defense. Depression may cause a decrease in self-esteem and feelings of helplessness and hopelessness, all of which weaken a person's second line of defense. Without adequate prenatal care, physiologic problems, such as hypertension or vitamin deficiencies, can develop; if these are untreated, they weaken the lines of defense and resistance. The depression, anxiety, substance abuse, and lack of prenatal care brought on by the battering weaken the structure to such an extent that the degree of disequilibrium caused by even a small stressor can have a major impact on the woman's health. For instance, battering may be the single most important cause of suicide in pregnant women (Stark & Flitcraft, 1995).

Assessing Women for Battering

Henderson and Ericksen (1994) point out that nurses are well suited in assessing for battering because of their focus on holistic health care and also because most nurses, especially on obstetrical units, are women. Before instituting a protocol for assessing all women for battering in the obstetrical unit, it is important to have in-service training with all of the nurses and staff in the unit. The updated March of Dimes Birth Defects Foundation's *Protocol of Care for the Battered Woman* (1986b) is an excellent resource to begin in-service training and can be obtained through a local March of Dimes chapter. Such training provides an excellent starting point for nurses to explore the resources available to battered women in their community and hospital and become familiar with the local laws and criminal justice system (see Chapter 4 in this volume).

Two hurdles may have to be overcome during in-service training. First, there may be staff members who have experienced battering and have never told anyone or may not have realized that they are battered women. Information about support and counseling must be available at all in-service programs to ensure the staff members get the care they may need, a list that also can be given to every woman assessed on the obstetrical unit. These resources can be printed on small cards with the unit's logo, which can be concealed by women who are being battered or kept for future use if they should be battered or have a friend being abused. The second hurdle is that the staff may be hesitant to address such a sensitive issue. To deal with this takes commitment from the leaders to help all health care providers understand the potential risk to every woman's health and the responsibility nurses have to provide health promotion.

A study of 600 postpartum women by Bullock (1987), in which women 24-72 hours after delivery were asked questions about battering during pregnancy, found most women expressing gratitude that someone was addressing the issue, regardless if they were battered or not. No one refused to participate in the study. Many of the women who were battered expressed relief that they were able to talk with someone about the problem. One woman in particular spoke about how difficult it was to tell what "really" happened when she went to the emergency department for treatment after being battered. She said it was like "tattling" on her husband, and she was taught as a child not to tattle. She went on to say that she purposefully made up ridiculous stories about how the injury occurred so that a health care provider would challenge the plausibility of the story and ask her directly if she had been battered. To her, this would not be tattling but truthfully answering a direct question and would open the way for her to discuss the problem she was experiencing. DeLahunta (1995) also reports that women expect health care providers to lead the discussion about battering.

Another woman interviewed 24 hours after a cesarean section for breech presentation (Bullock, 1987) told a more tragic story. The day of her "rescheduled" surgery, this woman presented with a black eye. The doctor asked, "What happened to you?" referring indirectly to the black eye. The patient said, "You really do not want to know," which she assumed must have been correct because the physician did not pursue the questioning. This avoidance by the health care provider was done with the knowledge that the woman was a "no show" for a scheduled cesarean section 2 days prior. When I asked the woman if her partner had hit her, she pulled down the bedcovers and revealed massive bruising on her chest, abdomen, and thighs. She said that the night before the original scheduled surgery, her husband had beat her with a boat oar and she was physically unable to come to the hospital the day of the surgery. When asked if a nurse or any other health care provider she had seen since admission to the hospital had talked to her about the bruises, she responded that no one had even mentioned them. This woman said she desperately wanted to talk to someone about the abuse and had no idea of the resources available. The social service agency was notified after the interview, and the woman received the information she required, but it is frightening to think she could have been sent home with an infant with no one taking the time to assess how she came to have massive bruising.

Protocol for Assessment

Obstetrical unit staff members should decide when is the best time to assess women for their safety. A nursing history usually is taken when a woman presents to the labor and delivery unit, and these questions could be incorporated into the psychosocial history. The labor and delivery unit may be where a pregnant woman comes immediately after a beating, and direct questioning about violence when it is suspected would be appropriate. However, active labor is not the best time to screen women for abuse and provide the health education that is required; it is much better to wait until the woman is on the postpartum unit. Before being discharged from the hospital, the mother and infant are assessed to see if they are physically able to go home. This may be the most appropriate time to assess whether the woman and infant will be safe when they go home. If the father, friends, or family members are in the room, they can be asked to leave for a specified time while the patient is assessed. It is not untypical for a man who batters to demand he be able to stay with his wife. He does this out of fear that the woman may reveal the abuse. Most men usually will leave, perhaps reluctantly, when it is explained it is hospital policy to assess all women in private. No matter how difficult it is to see the woman in private, the nurse must not abandon the abuse assessment. Research has not shown a profile that identifies battered woman by looking, and abuse cuts across all socioeconomic levels, so all women must be assessed.

The most important issue surrounding assessing for battering is the issue of trust. The woman must feel that the person she tells will keep the information confidential and also that the person will not act by expressing horror or minimization. Many battered women are afraid their partners will find out that they "told," and many others feel ashamed of the abuse or may feel they are to blame. If nurses have been properly instructed, they will be able to act in the supportive manner necessary and to assure the woman that she is not to blame.

Nurses must remember that the woman must choose what she will do, but if she does not have information about her legal rights and available resources, she cannot make an informed choice. Nurses should consider their intervention a success by providing all the information a woman needs to make her decision.

The March of Dimes *Protocol of Care for the Battered Woman* has guidelines for approaches and an assessment tool for screening all pregnant women. The Abuse Assessment Screen (AAS) is an abbreviated screen described by Soeken and colleagues in Chapter 16 in this volume. In a study of the AAS (McFarlane et al., 1992), it was found that Questions 2, 3, and 4 from the screen were able to detect a 17% prevalence rate of physical or sexual abuse during pregnancy. It has been the experience of these researchers that asking several abuse-focused questions is better than asking only one. Several questions seem to allow a woman time to decide whether she wants to reveal the abuse at this time and whether she can trust the person asking the question. Women want to make sure the person they reveal the abuse to is interested and concerned. One question about abuse can hardly convey interest and concern. Questions that are on a written questionnaire that is to be completed by the woman also do not elicit as much reporting of abuse (McFarlane, Christoffel, Bateman, Miller, & Bullock, 1991) probably because of the impersonal nature.

Primary Prevention Interventions

Nurses can use the AAS and the Neuman health care system model to decide at what level they must intervene. If a woman answers no to the questions on the AAS, the nurse must assess the number of stressors the woman has and how strong are her levels of defense. The main intervention for a nurse is to strengthen the woman's lines of defense through education and helping to increase the woman's self-esteem by positive role modeling. The nurse should ascertain how the woman plans to cope with the known stressors, where she will go if she has problems caring for her infant, and where she will go if she is battered. Educating all women about the cycle of violence can be seen as a means of preventing a public health problem (Elliott & Johnson, 1995).

Secondary Prevention Interventions

If the woman admits to being battered, the nurse should do a health assessment that includes a physical examination to determine the degree of injury the woman has sustained. The information obtained from the examination, including the location and extent of injuries, permanent damage from an injury, and the woman's statements of how the injury occurred, should be documented in the patient's chart. If it is possible to take pictures of current injuries, this should be done with the patient's permission. This information is useful in determining what immediate interventions are needed, and such documentation in medical records can be useful if the woman decides to bring charges against the batterer.

After the immediate medical problems have been addressed, the main goal of any intervention at this level is to prevent more abuse, especially because the abuse becomes more severe over time and could lead to the death of the woman or the child. If a woman admits to being abused, her risk for homicide should be assessed with the Danger Assessment (Campbell, 1986; see also Chapter 8). This instrument not only gives a score for potential risk of homicide but also is an effective way for the nurse to talk with the woman about a plan for her safety. This plan should include exploring with the woman how she will leave the house with the children, where she will go, items that she should bring, and her current and future options for action. The nurse should ensure that the woman has information about how to notify the police in an emergency, legal rights, counseling, and especially safe shelter. Some hospitals may have social workers available, but the woman should be informed and agree to reveal her information to additional people before the social work department is notified.

Tertiary Prevention Interventions

The main goal of tertiary intervention is reconstitution of the woman to an optimal level of health. Battered women may turn to drugs and alcohol as a means of coping with the battering. Education and appropriate referrals to resources dealing with substance abuse may be needed. Information about community programs dealing with stress management and assertiveness training should be given. These programs are useful in helping the woman to increase her self-esteem, coping skills, and problem-solving abilities. As in the interventions for secondary care, the nurse should do a thorough physical assessment to determine the extent of injuries and disabilities the woman may have sustained from the violence. Documentation in the medical records is essential.

Conclusion

Society usually thinks of the arrival of an infant as the "blessed event," but many pregnant women never experience this joy because their lives are in chaos. As many as one in every six pregnant women live in fear for their safety, and every woman is faced with stressors that can damage her health. With the use of the Neuman health care system model (Neuman & Young, 1972) and the AAS (McFarlane et al., 1992), every woman can be assessed and appropriate interventions planned and delivered by nurses working in obstetrical units. Showing concern for a woman's safety is a crucial role for nurses in maintaining optimal health for every woman.

PART IV

CHILDREN AND ADOLESCENTS

11

Helping Battered Women
Take Care of Their Children

Janice Humphreys

Children of battered women are at risk for a variety of emotional, cognitive, and behavioral difficulties. However, a growing body of research has described the important mediating effects on children of even one positive relationship with a significant person. Nurses and other health care professionals need to be aware of family violence and to assess every client and family for this problem. Early identification and interventions can stem detrimental effects and help mothers and children recover.

Mothers who are battered are subjected to repeated physical and verbal assaults. In addition, they have worries and fears about the direct and indirect effects of family violence on their children. Nurses and other professionals who work with battered women and their children have the opportunity to assist women in caring for their children. However, professionals must first be familiar with the nature of knowledge about children of battered women. Although little research has been directed at children, the frequently forgotten survivors of family violence, a beginning foundation of knowledge can guide nurses as they intervene to assist battered women and their children. This chapter highlights this knowledge about the problems and strengths of the children of battered women and suggests appropriate nursing interventions.

AUTHOR'S NOTE: Research conducted by the author was supported by the Department of Health and Human Services, National Research Service Award 1F31 NU-05708-01 from the Division of Nursing.

Scope of the Problem

The past two decades have been associated with ever more frequent reports in the scholarly and lay literature of family violence. Unlike children or adults who are directly subject to the shocking violence reported in the media, children of battered women are less well recognized survivors of family violence. Children of battered women have come to attention only when they too, generally inadvertently, became injured during a violent episode. The nature of their experience is less visible and perhaps more insidious than that of others who are directly abused on a regular basis. The scope and impact of family violence on the children of battered women has been examined only recently.

Estimates vary regarding the number of children exposed to the battering of their mothers. Davidson (1978) reported that children were present in 41% of the domestic disturbances in which police intervened. Carlson (1990) estimates (based on an average of two children in 55% of violent households) that at least 3.3 million children in the United States between the ages of 3 and 17 years are yearly at risk of exposure to parental violence.

Relationship to Other Types of Abuse

The impact on children of observing the abuse of their mothers is unclear. Research has described even young children's sensitivities to conflict and distress in their homes (Cummings, Pellegrini, Notarius, & Cummings, 1989; Zeanah, 1994). In addition, interviews with children revealed that children were much more aware of the violence in the home than parents believed.

Multiple authors have stated that children who come from violent homes are likely to experience violence in future relationships (Breslin, Riggs, O'Leary, & Arias, 1990; Davis & Carlson, 1987; Kalmuss & Straus, 1984). Most batterers have witnessed abusive behavior in their families of origin, and the rate of wife beating is dramatically higher for sons of batterers than for sons of nonviolent fathers (Straus, Gelles, & Steinmetz, 1980). However, not all sons growing up in violent homes become batterers, and in fact many siblings of batterers may live peacefully in nonviolent marriages (Dobash & Dobash, 1979). Stark and Flitcraft (1988) maintain that to conclude that violence in childhood produces violence in adult life is erroneous. In a reexamination of the data from the random 1980 study (Straus et al., 1980), Stark and Flitcraft (1988) concluded that although boys who experienced family violence as children were disproportionately violent as adults, 90% of all adults who were in violent homes as children and 80% from homes described as "most violent" did not abuse their wives.

For children who observe their mothers being abused and who are abused themselves, the consequences have been reported to be traumatic (Jaffe, Wolfe, & Wilson, 1990; Jaffe, Wolfe, Wilson, & Zak, 1986b), especially for young children (Hughes, 1988). Stark and Flitcraft (1988), in a feminist analysis of mothers of child abuse victims, conclude that battering is the most common context for child abuse and that the battering man is the typical child abuser. Thus, although a history of violence in the family of origin can seriously affect children and increases the risk of boys becoming adult batterers, exposure to violence does not automatically result in serious behavioral problems and a certainty of violence in future relationships.

Characteristics and Contributing Factors

Compared with the literature regarding child abuse and abuse of women, little has been published about the children of battered women. Early studies of shelters for battered women began to identify the needs of children who accompanied their mothers to safety. At least 70% of all battered women seeking shelter have children who accompany them, and 17% of the women bring along three or more children (MacLeod, 1989). Earliest reports were from battered women's shelters in which children were observed to demonstrate a variety of responses to the crises. These reports described a variety of stress-related symptoms in the children.

Children's responses to witnessing their mother being assaulted by their father have been reported to vary according to the age, gender, developmental stage, and role of the child in the family. Many other factors may play a role, such as the extent and frequency of the violence, the mother's response to the violence, repeated separations and moves, economic and social disadvantage, and special needs that a child may have independent of the violence. Some authors have equated children's responses to the abuse of their mothers with those of children who have been exposed to other types of trauma (Silvern & Kaersvang, 1989; Zeanah, 1994). Emery (1982) concluded that children in homes in which there is interparental conflict are at greater risk for a variety of problems than are children from intact or broken homes that are relatively free of conflict and that the amount and type of interparental conflict to which children are exposed are important determinants of the effect of conflict on the children. In this section, children's responses to the battering of their mothers are examined according to commonly reported classifications of those responses. These are cognitive and emotional responses and behavioral responses, including caring behaviors. Attention also is given to the role of factors that can mediate the long-term consequences of witnessing spouse abuse.

Cognitive and Emotional Responses

Much of the research on children of battered women has described them as demonstrating a variety of cognitive and emotional responses. The research findings have been somewhat contradictory, and this may be partially attributable to limitations in the methods used.

Early research suggested that the children of battered women demonstrated a variety of difficulties, including truancy, bullying, disturbed sleeping patterns, excessive screaming, clinging behaviors, failure to thrive, vomiting and diarrhea, headaches, bed-wetting, speech disorders, and cognitive difficulties including decreased verbal and quantitative abilities (Hilberman & Munson, 1978). However, this and other studies are limited in that the authors interviewed only the mothers and did not evaluate the children directly, an approach that is both problematic and persisting in current research.

Wolfe, Zak, Wilson, and Jaffe (1986), in a study of adjustment by children (ages 6-16 years), interviewed mothers (one half from shelters and one half from the community) about experiences with violence, maternal responses, and family stability. The researchers reported that the emotional and behavioral problems of the children were predicted on the basis of the amount and severity of wife abuse and the level of maternal stress. The researchers concluded that the degree of experience with violence and the mother's reaction to the violence significantly influenced children's responses.

Although Christopoulos et al. (1987) reported that 40 children in a battered women's shelter had scores higher than were expected on the emotional and behavioral subscales of the Child Behavior Checklist (adult's perception of child behavior problems) (Achenbach & Edelbrock, 1983), boys in the community comparison group also had elevated scores on the internalizing subscale. Christopoulos et al. concluded that the shared experience of low socioeconomic background may be the most significant factor contributing to the children's elevated emotional subscale scores.

I conducted a study that sought to describe the caring behaviors directed toward the prevention of hazards in mothers and their children who experience family violence (Humphreys, 1991). I proposed that in families in which violence is a common occurrence, mothers and their children experience worries. Children's worries varied from vague worries about their mothers, which is typical of children in general, to specific fears about their mothers' health. Not surprisingly, the greatest number (50%) of worries for children on behalf of their mothers had to do with battering. The violence inflicted on their mothers was the most mentioned source of worry for all of the children. For example:

Child 1:   I worry about my Mama and [the batterer]. One time I was in bed and they be fighting. I started to cry. I heard my Mama say, "She's awake," and he said, "No she isn't." So I cried louder, and he stopped [the hitting].

Child 2:   [Mother's boyfriend] grabbed her by her hair and dragged her up the top of the stairs. I was worried that my Mom would get hurt.

Nurse: What happened?

Child 2:   I hit him with a baseball bat.
Nurse: Was he hurt?
Child 2:   No. I didn't hit him hard enough.

I also found that there were no significant differences in the types of worries expressed by children of battered women based on selected demographic factors. I concluded that because of their exposure to violence, children experience more worries about violence, and these are less influenced by demographic factors.

Behavioral Responses

Much of the research on children of battered women has described them as demonstrating a variety of behavioral problems. Jaffe et al. (1990) noted that behavioral disturbances often are associated with child management problems, school problems, and lack of positive peer relations. Wolfe et al. (1986), in a study of battered women's shelter residents, former residents, and women who never experienced violence, found that although children recently exposed to family violence had fewer interests, social activities, and lower school perfor- mance, they were not significantly more likely to have behavior problems. In fact, although former shelter residents and their children obtained the highest scores on the Family Disadvantage Index, these mothers and children had no more behavioral or emotional symptoms than did the nonviolent community sample.

The contradictions in these studies of children of battered women make conclusions difficult. However, there appears to be some evidence that violence in the family is detrimental to many children under certain circumstances. In addition, the findings indicate that a child's gender and age, the frequency and severity of battering to the mother, and the mother's response may influence the child's reaction to family violence.

Caring Behaviors. Martin (1976), in one of the first and most influential books on battered women, described how her own 8-year-old grandchild was shaken by the violence he observed directed at his mother. However, the child became interested in developing strategies that he might use in the future should similar situations occur.

A small, but significant group of nursing research reports (Humphreys, 1989, 1990; Westra & Martin, 1981) were identified that addressed the caring behaviors of children for their battered mothers. At least one researcher who is not a nurse has suggested that the relationship between battered women and their children is a fertile area for study (Emery, 1982).

Monsma's (1984) study gives a better idea of what children think when their mothers are battered. She conducted in-depth, semistructured interviews with 12 children (6 boys and 6 girls) between the ages of 8 and 12. Monsma analyzed these interviews using content analysis and identified three major themes: (a) the destructiveness of the abuser during an assault on the child's mother, (b) the child's self-preservation strategies, and (c) the child protecting the real and imagined mother. Monsma reported that the children developed deliberate, creative ways of protecting their mothers. Often these caring behaviors required monitoring of the situation and anticipation on the part of the child to prevent the hazard. "Thad, a 10-year-old boy, claimed he knew when his mom was getting into trouble and so he and his siblings would try to prevent the assault on her" (Monsma, 1984, p. 41). At other times, the hazard of being battered could not be prevented; the child or children might seek to protect the mother by direct or indirect intervention with the hazard. One method identified by several of the children as a mechanism for protecting their mothers was to call the police.

Five children, three boys and two girls, mentioned they had called the police to stop an assault. This often involved the teamwork of siblings. Joan, for example, was a 10-year-old with four siblings. She told the researcher about various times when "Dee [her 13-year-old sister] would tell us to call the police. Lee [her 12-year-old brother] would stay home to help her and I would run to the corner to call the police" (p. 41).

Although children of battered women have been found to be aware of parental conflict and to take protective and supportive actions on the mother's behalf, the long-term consequences of growing up in a violent home cannot be viewed in any way as being beneficial to children. Much of the literature on children of battered women has examined the serious consequences for many children of witnessing and possibly directly experiencing family violence. However, there is growing literature that has described the strengths and resourcefulness of children of battered women.

Resilience and Other Factors

At first glance, it would seem that growing up in a violent home would be devastating to children. However, many children see their mothers battered on a regular basis and go on to have successful relationships. Only recently has attention been given to children of battered women who do not develop clinical pathology.

Jouriles, Murphy, and O'Leary (1989) note that 50% of the children in one study and approximately 70% in several others (Milner & Gold, 1986; Wolfe et al., 1986) from maritally aggressive homes were not evidencing problems at clinical levels, which suggests that for at least some children, negative factors in their home environments (violence and disorder) did not adversely affect them in clinically recognizable ways. Several authors (Emery, 1982; Milner, Robertson, & Rogers, 1990) concluded that a particularly warm relationship with one parent, adult, or caring friend can mitigate, but not eliminate, the effects of marital turmoil on children.

Garmezy (1983) has examined the role of resilience and other factors in children's responses to stressful life events. He defines these factors as "attributes of persons, environments, situations, and events that appear to temper predictions of psychopathology based upon an individual's at-risk status" (Garmezy, 1981, p. 73). His review of the literature consistently identifies three factors that seem to mediate the effects of even chronic stress on children. They are (a) dispositional attributes in the child (e.g., temperament, a positive mood, positive sense of self, cooperativeness); (b) family milieu (e.g., family warmth, support, orderliness); and (c) supportive environment (e.g., assistance with problems and school). It was important to note that "an intact family was *not* an identifiable consistent correlate" (Garmezy, 1981, p. 75).

According to Garmezy (1981), there was a striking lack of any consistent evidence in the studies reviewed that absence of the father had an adverse effect on children. However, the mother's style of coping with and compensating for an absent father had a powerful positive effect. "Significant adults provided for the children a representation of their efficacy and ability to exert control in the midst of upheaval" (Garmezy, 1981, p. 76). In multiple studies that used different methods with various groups, these factors have been shown to mediate the detrimental effects of stressful life on children (Garmezy, 1981; Simeonsson, 1994). Knowledge of these factors offers suggestions for nursing practice with battered women and their children.

Assessment

Every client should be assessed for family violence. All too often abuse in families goes unrecognized, even when the evidence is clearly present. Even if clients deny exposure to family violence, a nonjudgmental approach by nurses can indicate that violence is an acceptable topic for discussion. Well-child clinics easily lend themselves to nursing assessment for family violence. Nurses and other health care professionals can routinely inquire

Has anyone ever hurt you?
Has anyone ever forced you to do something that made you uncomfortable?
How are conflicts resolved at your house?
How do decisions get made at your house?

When assessing parent-child interactions, nurses may want to ask

How do you discipline [your child]?
How were you and your partner disciplined as children?
Who is the boss at your house?

If there is a major decision to be made, who has the last word at your house?

Nurses may want to ask parents about specific problem areas and get examples of how they are managed. For example:

What kinds of things does [your child] do that really get on your nerves?
If the baby is up all night or just won't stop crying, what happens? What do you or
    your partner do?

Such questions are attempts to understand how families manage while educating clients that problems in these areas are important. The nurse who never assesses for family violence is unlikely to ever "see" it in the clients served. Unfortunately, the violence will be there "unseen," and clients in need of nursing assistance will not receive it.

Mothers should be assessed for their perceptions of the children's involvement in and reactions to family violence. Assuming that the mothers are not so emotionally wrought and depressed that they are unable to experience the needs of their children, mothers may be unaware of children's perceptiveness of parental conflict. They also may lack knowledge of children's responses to conflict.

Interventions

Interventions with children of battered women cover a broad spectrum. The nurse is concerned about the inadvertently injured child of a battered woman and the adolescent who has questions about violence in adult relationships. The following discussion attempts to describe general areas of intervention according to the level of prevention. Particular attention is given to children in battered women's shelters because this group is the most obvious.

Primary Prevention

Primary prevention includes all interventions that prevent battering of women and child and family health promotion activities with well and at-risk populations. The type of intervention at this level varies with the location and nature of practice.

Societal Interventions. Abuse, in all its forms, of family members occurs in a society that condones violence within the context of the family. Implicit and explicit approval for the use of violence contribute to its occurrence within families. Thus, interventions at the societal level that diminish tolerance for violence serve as primary prevention for all types of violence. When violence against family members is no longer tolerated under any circumstances (including corporal punishment as discipline for children), much will have been accomplished toward diminishing the incidence of violence of all kinds.

Family life classes in schools provide schoolage children and adolescents with opportunities to experiment with various child-rearing and adult relationship dilemmas under the supervision of experienced nurses, counselors, and teachers. Involvement of parents is such programs additionally allows parents to become more knowledgeable and to guide their children toward greater understanding of the difficulties of adult relationships and parenting within "real life" settings.

Programs such as Big Brothers and Big Sisters can assist children in developing significant, supportive relationships outside their immediate families. When children lack frequent contact with one parent, usually fathers, Big Brothers and Big Sisters can provide positive experiences and role modeling that can enhance children's resilience to potential and actual stressors.

Education. Educational programs in the schools at all levels need to address family violence. Schools have an important role to play in educating children about violence and reinforcing values that contribute to ending it. The Surgeon General of the United States, in setting objectives for improving the health of the nation, has recognized the serious consequences of family violence (U.S. Department of Health and Human Services [DHHS], 1990). To decrease the overall occurrence of violence within the nation, the following objective was developed: "Increase to at least 50 percent the proportion of elementary and secondary schools that teach nonviolent conflict resolution skills, preferably as part of a quality school health education" (p. 101).

My Family and Me: Violence Free is a domestic violence prevention curriculum for kindergarten through third grade and fourth through sixth grade (Stavrou-Peterson & Gamache, 1988). This curriculum is designed to provide primary prevention of family violence. "However, by helping children to identify abusive actions, the curriculum can also promote early intervention with students who are being physically abused or are witnessing violence in their homes" (from a brochure about the curriculum by the Minnesota Coalition for Battered Women). The curriculum helps children, with the guidance of their teachers, gain a sense of their uniqueness and worth, learn assertiveness skills for nonviolent conflict resolution, and develop a personal safety plan to use in violence emergency situations.

Children need to learn that violence is only one way, albeit unacceptable, of dealing with anger and that other means are available. Helping children to face and deal with their anger and seeing that alternatives to violence are available can be addressed individually and in groups.

Some schools have peer patrol programs that offer nonviolent ways to resolve conflicts. At one Oak Park, Michigan elementary school the STOP (Students Talk Out Problems) program trains fourth- and fifth-grade students in conflict resolution (Kovanis, 1990). These red-vested patrol members team up during lunch and after school to break up fights and arguments. The principal reports one fourth the fights of previous years, and being on the STOP squad has become a status symbol. Such creative approaches help children learn nonviolent conflict resolution tactics.

Ever-increasing reports of violence in dating relationships support the need for education in schools. Adolescents need to learn that although they may have observed violence against women in their homes, battering is not a necessary part of intimate relationships. Classroom discussions with nurses or teachers and peers can be particularly influential with adolescents.

Little has been reported about education and primary prevention programs on violence with children. A notable exception is the work of Nibert, Cooper, Ford, Fitch, and Robinson (1989). These researchers report that even preschool children have the ability to learn basic prevention concepts for concrete, threatening situations.

The Child Assault Prevention (CAP) Project preschool model has been used with elementary school children in Columbus, Ohio since 1978. Children are taught assertiveness skills, physically moving away from the abusive situation, using a self-defense yell, using physical resistance techniques in the abduction situation, and telling trusted adults. The researchers found that although they studied two socially diverse groups of children (those in private preschool and those in the Head Start program), the children gave appropriate responses on three of the four scenarios. The findings indicate that even young children have the ability to learn basic prevention strategies when they are presented in clear and concrete context.

Secondary Prevention

When children are exposed to the abuse of their mothers, nursing interventions are termed *secondary prevention.* The goals of secondary prevention are early diagnosis and intervention to prevent recurrence. At the level of secondary prevention, battering has occurred, and interventions are aimed at limiting the impact of battering of mothers on their children.

Toward the goal of early identification and treatment of family violence, service and protection objectives have been established by the Surgeon General. These include the following objective: "Extend protocols for routinely identifying, treating, and properly referring suicide attempters, victims of sexual assault, and victims of spouse, elder, and child abuse to at least 90 percent of hospital emergency departments" (DHHS, 1990, p. 101). Nurses clearly have an important role in developing and implementing such protocols.

Direct interventions with children of battered women depend on the timing of the encounter, age and response of the child, and family circumstances. Even children in battered women's shelters require different interventions. If the child is returning to the violent home, interventions may need to focus on the most basic safety needs. If the family is relocating, the nurse may have the opportunity to help the mother and child to learn new ways of living and responding. Interventions that address a variety of potential times and experiences are presented.

Nursing research indicates that children of battered women have worries and need reassurance. Battered women use a variety of strategies to stop abuse, not the least of which is the temporary removal of their children and themselves from the violent home. Children of battered women need reassurance that their mothers will not leave them too. Children of battered women, like all children, need to express their worries and concerns, and nurses need to ask about them. With information about the children's worries regarding their mothers, nurses can help them deal with their expressed concerns. Nurses need to give information to these children, but they also need to help the children of battered women work through their feelings.

Adolescents who seek independence and self-control may need help in identifying the worries about their mothers that they cannot control. Nurses can help adolescents learn to deal with such worries. The nurse also can help children, with their permission, share their worries with their mothers. Mothers often are unaware of the children's experiences and perceptions during violent events. Discussions can address real or perceived responsibilities during the events and any feeling of blame children may be experiencing. The sharing process can be therapeutic for battered women and their children.

Battered Women's Shelters. Although variability exists, battered women's shelters usually are emergency shelters for women and their children. Women and children are provided temporary safe haven within a communal shelter setting. Battered women and their children are allowed to stay within the shelter for a relatively short period of time (usually a maximum of 60 days), during which they are given assistance to assess their situation, gain knowledge and insight regarding family violence, and obtain social services. Battered women and their children may leave the shelter to move in with family or friends or may move to a new residence. Many women and their children also return to their homes in the hope and belief that the act of leaving and their new information and insight will help to stop the violence. Battered women's shelters provide mothers and children safety, information, and opportunities for a short time. Many shelters also offer nonresidential group counseling and other services.

There is great variability in the services provided by battered women's shelters to children. Because of limited resources, many shelters can provide only occasional child care services; their scant funds are used to assist mothers with counseling, social, and potential relocation services. Ideally, services should be available for children of battered women, but helping mothers to cope with a recent crises is in the best interest of the children.

Concurrent with the development of a body of knowledge about the children of battered women is increased attention to the needs of the children while they are in shelters. Some battered women's shelters have always offered specialized services to children. Nurses who become involved with shelters can contribute to those services or assist in their development.

If the battered women's shelter is to be a positive experience for children, the children must be made to feel as welcome and comfortable as possible when they enter the environment. Children should be shown around the shelter, shown play areas, and introduced to other resident children. An individual assessment of each child should be conducted to identify his or her physical condition, experience, and responses. All of the health problems and needs seen by nurses in other settings may be present in the children of women in shelters.

Layzer, Goodson, and deLange (1985) recommend that all children admitted to battered women's shelters should have access to health screening and treatment. Involvement by the nurse as a health care provider can provide an excellent opportunity for clinical experiences for nursing students (Urbancic, Campbell, & Humphreys, 1993). As with all children, children in shelters need regular health screening. Mothers also need feedback regarding their children's growth, development, state of health, and anticipatory guidance. Mothers who are discharged from obstetrical units to shelters may need guidance in infant care, including bathing, feeding, and cord care. Clinical experience with battered women and their children in shelters has revealed that the provision of maternal-child care in such settings is similar to that required elsewhere. In addition, children of battered women may have difficulties that are unique to their experience. Some children have been physically injured in the attack on their mothers immediately preceding admission to the shelter. These traumatic injuries require the same attention as any other injury, with particular attention given to preventing infection, maintaining alignment of fractures, and facilitating suture removal.

Gross and Rosenberg (1987) have described the role of shelters as an underrecognized source of communicable disease transmission. Of the 73 full-time, government-funded shelters they surveyed in five geographic regions in 15 states, only 5% (4 of 73) had health care workers. In contrast, outbreaks of diarrheal illness involving more than 10 persons were reported by 12% (9 of 73) of shelter directors. Gross and Rosenberg recommend that even basic hygienic practices, such as strict hand washing and identification of groups of sick clients, may significantly reduce the transmission of a variety of communicable diseases. Experience has indicated that nurses can easily provide advice and assistance in establishing shelter guidelines in these areas. Mothers and staff usually are happy to comply but have had limited experience with communal living in large numbers. Nursing colleagues in the public health setting are obvious resources in establishing procedures for prevention of communicable disease.

Many children experience a variety of stress-related symptoms during their stay at shelters. Children may return to behaviors (such as bed-wetting, thumb-sucking, or bottle feeding) that they previously had stopped. Infants may respond to the dramatic changes in their mothers and in their environments associated with moving to shelters by becoming difficult to feed, irritable, or sleepless. Clinical experience has revealed that many children no longer demonstrate stress-related problems after admission to the shelter. Battered women have told me that while their children might have wet the bed or complained of stomachaches or other similar problems at home, upon settling in at the shelter, these symptoms and others disappeared. Nurses can assess children's stress and coping and discuss them with mothers. Mothers often lack knowledge of children's behaviors and are reassured to know that such behaviors are normal and generally disappear without attention once order has been established.

Battered women's shelters with children's services usually offer some structured programs for children. The form of these programs varies greatly. They generally include all or part of the following components: crisis intervention activities, academic program, daily program, therapy/counseling, parent-child program, and an advocacy program. Various approaches to these components have been reported and are presented.

Crisis Intervention. The difficulties that children often face as an accompaniment to family violence may be exacerbated for children who are brought to shelters for victims of domestic violence. Children in shelters are likely to have experienced a complete disruption in their social support systems, particularly with their school, friends, neighborhood, and usually the significant male adult in their lives.

Jaffe et al. (1990) have identified what they term *subtle symptoms* in children of battered women. They indicate that three areas require careful investigation, especially in children who do not have pronounced reactions to observations of abuse. They categorize these areas as (a) responses and attitudes about conflict resolution, (b) assigning responsibility for violence, and (c) knowledge and skills in dealing with violent incidents (p. 51). Jaffe et al. (1990) suggest that children often experience violence in ways that are not always readily apparent. Within the category of responses and attitudes they describe children who concluded that violent conflict resolution was acceptable behavior, children who learned to rationalize the violence, and children who blamed their mothers for causing the violence. Other children assigned blame for the violence to their fathers but pursued strategies for resolution of the violence (e.g., poisoning father) that were desperate. Some children described by Jaffe et al. accepted an exaggerated sense of responsibility for the violence in their families. This response was reported as typical of many young children. Finally, Jaffe et al. (1990) reported that children often failed to have basic knowledge and skills needed to handle emergency situations. Children in Jaffe et al.'s research did not have knowledge and skills of community and other resources to assist them with crises associated with the violence at home.

Silvern and Kaersvang (1989) concluded that adults were more willing, in regard to children, to leave "well enough alone." Adults were too eager to accept children's responses that "nothing was wrong." Although children (and adults) must be allowed the opportunity to share their feelings in their own way and time, a child's repeated assurance that he or she is "not bothered" by the events that led to admission to a shelter must be investigated. It is not helpful to assume that upsetting events are best left undisclosed. Nurses can use their therapeutic communication techniques to help children express themselves and discuss their experiences.

Daily Program. There is great variability in the routine daily programs for children in shelters. Such programs usually are structured to the extent that a similar schedule is followed most weekdays. Routine child care in shelters, at a minimum, allows mothers to attend to the many obligations associated with obtaining social services, apartment hunting, and employment. For children in women's shelters, structured time and activities provide organization and security in strange environments. If sufficiently qualified staff are available, routine play sessions can be used for additional educational and therapeutic group sessions that enhance individual counseling.

It is important for children of battered women to be exposed to male and female adults who respect each other and work together. Early in the women's shelter movement, men were rarely seen inside shelters. Fortunately, there are now many male staff members and volunteers who provide positive role models for children. Involvement of male and female nursing students in shelters is an excellent opportunity for children to observe positive role models and partnerships.

Therapy and Counseling. Children need to talk about their experiences and their feelings. Children of battered women may blame themselves for the violence in their homes, especially if abusive episodes were associated with parental conflicts regarding child rearing. This perception is not totally unfounded.

> Sex and money are widely believed to be the issues which cause the most trouble. But our data show that neither of these provoked the most violence. Rather, *it is conflict over children which is most likely to lead a couple to blows.* (Straus et al., 1980, p. 171)

Children also may perceive that they are responsible for the decision to leave the home, to return, or to get a divorce. As Elbow (1982) notes, what appears to be an egocentric perception by children of battered women may be reality. The best interests of children often are central to battered women's decisions about the future. A mother may stay in an abusive relationship because she believes that her children will benefit from the ongoing presence of a male adult. A battered woman also may make the decision to leave an abusive situation because of the impact the violence is having on her children. In either instance, children may feel responsible, not only for themselves but also for the entire family.

Children may have spent an inordinate amount of time trying to be "good" to prevent episodes of violence. For example, one child described past episodes of violence against his mother that began when his father returned home and found toys in the living room. In an effort to prevent episodes of battering of his mother, he convinced his younger sister to play with him in the bedroom closet. That way all the toys would be confined to the closet, and the home would appear tidy "like Daddy likes it."

If children intervened in attempts to stop violence between adults, they may have a false sense of confidence in their abilities to keep batterers from abusing again. If children were successful in stopping abuse on one occasion, they may feel personal failure if subsequent interventions are unsuccessful.

Many authors have described the valuable role of therapy for children having particular difficulty with recent events. Hughes (1982), in one of the earliest reports on children's services in battered women's shelters, recommends that therapy and counseling vary from Big Brother/Big Sister recreational approaches to longer, more intensive contacts that closely resemble traditional psychotherapy. The type of intervention used depends on the ages and needs of the children. Interventions need to be sensitive to children's developmental levels and needs, focus on children's attitudes about aggression and family behavior, and help children learn basic skills in resolving interpersonal problems. Individual counseling and therapy in peer, sibling, family, or multifamily groups may provide useful approaches. Play therapy can help very young children express their feelings. In instances when specific problems (such as substance abuse) affect children and mothers, special counseling with others with similar concerns should be devoted to those problems.

Parent-Child Program. Some shelters can provide services to battered women that help them to enhance their relationships with their children and, if necessary, learn nonviolent methods of child rearing. Shelters do not allow the use of violent conflict resolution tactics, including corporal punishment, by anyone. For some mothers, this necessitates learning different ways of disciplining their children. Although many mothers have heard of "time out" strategies for disciplining children, using these methods can be much more difficult. Some mothers have never experienced any disciplinary techniques other than hitting when they were children and use only the same techniques on their children. These mothers will need the most help to see alternatives in discipline. One of the most effective approaches is to have groups of mothers talk about their experiences, including their mistakes and successes. Such peer group discussions often provide a highly effective method of helping mothers who see corporal punishment as the only way to discipline. For example, I participated in such a peer group session on discipline at a shelter. When one mother stated that she had been spanked plenty of times as a child and that she turned out okay, another mother responded, "Imagine how much better you could have been if you hadn't been spanked."

Nurses can take an active role in helping mothers learn different approaches to discipline, considering the most appropriate approach for their children and circumstances, and role-modeling the use of the different strategies. Interventions with mothers in shelters have been shown to reduce subsequent episodes of violence directed toward children.

Advocacy Program. Finally, battered women and their children need follow-up services after they leave shelters. Funds for such services often are even more meager than those of the shelter. However, battered women and their children need knowledge of and access to community services, even after discharge from shelters. Nurses need to routinely make referrals and to collaborate with each other and other professionals. Nurses in shelters need to make contact with schools, preschools, and day care centers. Follow-up with families can be provided by school nurses to assure that resources and supports are maintained and that progress made by women and their children is not lost because of lack of assistance.

Tertiary Prevention

Ideally, battering of women is never allowed to progress to the tertiary prevention stage of intervention, yet all too often this is the case. Tertiary prevention is the level of intervention required when children of battered women have experienced irreversible effects from the violence. The goal of tertiary prevention is rehabilitation of the children to the maximum level of functioning possible with the limitations of disabilities.

When physical injuries have resulted in disability, women and their children may be eligible for additional social services. Referrals to public health and visiting nurse agencies can secure follow-up for those who are eligible.

Although most children of battered women are unlikely to be abused, research suggests that approximately 30% of children are abused. Nurses and others who assist battered women and their children need to continually assess for child abuse and work closely with children's protective services to assure early identification of suspected abuse and neglect. As Cummings and Mooney

(1988) point out, child protective service workers and battered women's advocates often find themselves at odds while trying to work with families. Both groups share an interest in stopping violence, yet their perspectives and approaches often are in conflict. Nurses are in an excellent position to collaborate with both groups of professionals and help all work toward a common goal.

Children of battered women often are victimized by prolonged legal disputes about which parent should have custody after separation or what kind of visitation schedule is reasonable. The legal battle is never one moment in time but rather a lengthy affair that occurs during the course of many years and often is associated with a history of threats and conflicts; many children discover that such conflicts continue after the separation and long after any court decisions.

Many battered women are threatened before the separation with the fact that their husbands will want custody of the children if the women decide to leave. Often this threat will be a central issue in keeping a woman prisoner in her home because she fears losing custody and other consequences (NiCarthy, 1982). Women who feel most vulnerable in these circumstances are the ones who believe that, because their husbands have never directly abused the children, the husbands would have a good opportunity to be awarded custody. Many of these women report that their husbands are better suited for the court battle because of the husband's ability to "charm and con selected important people for short-term interactions" required by this process (Walker & Edwall, 1987). Many of these fears are well founded. Nurses can help by documenting all episodes of violence that become known to them, reporting all suspected child abuse and neglect, and when appropriate, offering expert testimony on behalf of the battered women.

Evaluation

It is at the point of evaluation that the nurse reviews what changes have occurred based on the identified goals. The nurse must be realistic but hopeful in the evaluation of children of battered women. Evaluation is not the final step in the process of working with children from violent families. Evaluation is an ongoing process.

Information about children of battered women remains limited, and many children are seriously effected by the abuse directed toward their mothers. However, nurses also can be optimistic that for some children, the influence of even one significant person can make a great deal of difference. The challenge to nurses who work with battered women and their children is to assist them in forming significant, positive relationships.

12

Diverging Realities

Abused Women and Their Children

Janet R. Ericksen
Angela D. Henderson

There is a growing recognition in both the professional and lay literature of the impact violence has on its survivors. Nowhere is the impact more profound in its effect than when it occurs within the context of an intimate relationship. The sense of confusion and betrayed trust is intense when violence comes at the hand of a loved one.

It has long been recognized that the abuse of women within intimate relationships represents a major social and health problem within North American society (MacLeod, 1980, 1987). Research has also shown that growing up in a physically violent environment produces profound long-term effects in child witnesses including the possibility that, as adults, these children will repeat the pattern of violence by becoming either abusive or abused (Gage, 1990; Hershorn & Rosenbaum, 1985; Jaffe, Wolfe, Wilson, & Zak, 1986b, 1986c; Moore et al., 1990). Children can thus be considered abused by virtue of witnessing the abuse of their mothers.

There has also been recognition in the literature that parenting these children is a difficult and demanding task and would be so even if the mother herself were not in an emotionally vulnerable state (Henderson, 1993). Furthermore, mothers themselves report that dealing with their children is the most difficult aspect of the time following the separation from the abuser (Henderson, 1989, 1990).

The behavioral effects on children of witnessing marital violence are well documented (Ericksen & Henderson, 1992; Jouriles, Pfiffner, & O'Leary, 1988; Rosenbaum & O'Leary, 1981; Wolfe, Jaffe, Wilson, & Zak, 1985). However, although progress has been made toward addressing the needs of abused women and their children, a review of the literature revealed that a significant piece of information was missing—the children's perspective. Information about the children had generally been obtained through parental report or through observation by teachers, psychologists, or child care workers.

Two studies were undertaken to understand the experiences of child witnesses of violence in the home, during the time both prior to and following a move from the abuser. One study (Ericksen & Henderson, 1992) was intended to understand the experience of witnessing abuse of their mothers from the children's viewpoint. A second study (Henderson, 1993) was initially intended to expand on this understanding of the children's experience by requesting clarification from their mothers, but provided other insights as well. The diverging realities of mothers and children that are the thesis of this chapter are a result of analyzing the findings from these two studies. During analysis of the two sets of data, it became apparent that the reports of the children and their mothers diverged in several important ways. This chapter will expand on these differences and discuss several theoretical perspectives that can give direction to practitioners who work with abused mothers and their children.

Experiences of Children Accompanying
Their Mothers Leaving Abusive Relationships

The purpose of this study was to determine the needs of children aged 4-12 in the transition period as they accompany their mothers who are leaving violent relationships. Specific objectives of the study were (a) to describe the experiences of these children, (b) to identify factors that affect these experiences, and (c) to isolate aspects of the children's experience that affect program planning. The process of phenomenological analysis as described by Giorgi (1987) was used in an attempt to make a general statement that accurately explained the experiences of the children.

Phenomenology was chosen as the most appropriate research method because the perspective of the children was the focus. Phenomenology is a method that recognizes that human behavior is contingent on the meanings humans ascribe to their reality. The subjective views of the participants are elicited to understand the way they are making sense of their experiences. People act in ways that make sense to them based on their interpretation of the data available to them in their day-to-day lives. Because this is true, the kind of information generated by this approach is invaluable to nurses and other health care providers who work with child witnesses to abuse as they seek to understand their clients' experiences and to plan care based on that understanding.

A total of 13 children between the ages of 3 and 10 were interviewed. Children in the same family were all included provided that they fell within the age parameters. Views of the same events from children from different age groups in the same family provided another dimension to the study. The children were each interviewed three times. Examples of the questions used to guide the interviews are as follows: What do you remember about the time when you used to live in your old house with Dad? and What is different about your life now?

The children described their experience as having three components: living with violence, living in transition, and living with Mom. Each of these components had characteristic themes (see Table 12.1). Several findings are noteworthy. First, the children's acceptance of violence as a means of conflict resolution is alarming. The children not only perceived that violence is normal and acceptable but were unaware of alternative methods of handling anger and conflict other than through violence (e.g., hitting). Second, the sense of sadness that permeated these children's lives is disturbing. The children had difficulty describing this sadness but most attributed it to missing their fathers. Third, several of the coping behaviors used by the children are of concern: Most of the children felt powerless and used solitude, fantasy, disengagement, and avoidance as mechanisms to cope with their experience. Another clear implication of this study is the need to recognize that anyone who can communicate, in any way, is capable of contributing important and pertinent insights that have implications when planning their care. In this case, children younger than 4 years of age demonstrated their ability to understand and consider not only their own experiences and needs but also those of their mothers. In terms of feasibility, the only adjustment was to recognize the children's shorter attention span, to simplify the language, and to take into account their lack of recollection of dates and times.

Abused Women's Perceptions of Their Children's Experiences

This phenomenological study examined abused women's perceptions of their children's experiences while living with their mothers during and after leaving an abusive relationship. Ten women who had left abusive relationships within the past year were interviewed. All had at least one child between the ages of 3 and 10 who was involved in the children's study.

All the women were in contact with their abusers—in most cases because the father had court-mandated access to the children and, in the other cases, because the abusers were continuing to harass the women. It was clear that

Table 12.1 Children's Themes

Living With Violence	Living in Transition	Living With Mom
Witnessing the violence	Relief	Sadness
Fear	Pleasure	Protectiveness
Vigilance	Protectiveness	Uncertainty
Powerlessness		Acceptance of violence
Coping		Coping

although the women had left the abuser, they were in no way free of abuse; their lives continued to be incredibly stressful and uncertain.

In relation to their children's experiences, women described themselves as being inadequately prepared to meet what they described as their children's enormous unmet needs. They described themselves as being too tired, stressed, and overwhelmed to deal with their children and found it very difficult to communicate with them. In addition, although concerned on an intellectual level about what effect living in an abusive environment might have on their children in the future, they were unable to focus on the reality of their children's experiences either in the past or the present.

Diverging Realities

For the most part, the children and their mothers in these studies agreed with each other about the chronology of events and the realities of life as it was presently being lived. In several major areas, however, the perceptions of the children and their mothers diverged (see Table 12.2). These differences in perception have implications for understanding the needs of mothers and children as well as for program delivery to meet these needs.

Perceptions of the Violence

The children were able to give clear and explicit reports of the incidents they witnessed, even remembering details of pieces of furniture that had been broken. One child said: "He started to hit my mom and pull her hair, and the kitchen table, he threw it down. That's when we first got it. I phoned the police, but my dad had already left."

The children reported being sent away and told not to come out when there was fighting, but they rarely went far enough away to avoid knowing what was happening. One girl said: "And he always said: 'Go upstairs!' We used to sneak

Table 12.2 Diverging Realities

Component	Mothers	Children
Perceptions of the violence	Minimized/vague descriptions	Clear/explicit descriptions
Perceptions of the need for help	Want outside resources for their children	Seek mothers as resources
Moving on	Ready to move on, but tied to the past	Coping with the changes in the present, but uncertain of the future
Perceptions of the abuser/Dad	Trying to disengage from abuser, but tied to him through the children	Miss their dad and have good times with him
Emotional reactions	Numbed exhaustion	Overwhelming sadness

and look what they were doing. . . . I really hated that when we needed to go to the bathroom."

However, the mothers were very vague and often contradictory when talking about the degree of violence to which their children had been exposed. In some cases, this was apparently because the women were vague and contradictory about the degree of violence they themselves had experienced. This seemed to be due to their own need to minimize what they had been through. One woman, for example, said: "Actually, he didn't do any physical violence; it was all just mental." Moments later, when discussing a particular evening, she said: "He was cornering me, hitting me in the corner and then not letting me out."

Even when women were able to be quite accurate about the violence they had experienced, they found it hard to admit that their children had witnessed any of the incidents. This resulted in a startling discrepancy between the accounts of the mothers and those of the children and the disturbing realization on the part of the researchers that the children's accounts and insights appeared to be more accurate. Remarks like "Most of the worst things happened when he was either asleep or away with his dad" were common. Interestingly, when it was reported to one of the women who said that her child had not actually witnessed any abuse that her son had indeed reported a violent incident in great detail, she said "Oh yes, I guess he was there" and immediately went on to talk about something else. Variations on this reaction were not uncommon.

From the reports of the mothers it seemed that they were, understandably, too preoccupied with their own survival to do more than try to ensure that their children were not actually in the room during violent incidents. This, coupled with their tendency to minimize or deny the extent of the abuse, left the mothers with little appreciation for their children's experiences.

Perceptions of Need for Help

Children felt physically separated from their fathers and emotionally separated from their mothers. They wanted to talk about their experiences and shared them willingly with the interviewer, but were sometimes told by their mothers not to talk to anyone else about their family situation. This left them feeling powerless, because they did not know how to cope without help. One small child said, for example: "I can't do anything if I was little."

Children wanted to be able to talk with their mothers, but their feelings of protectiveness toward their mothers prevented them from doing so. A 5-year-old quite poignantly said:

Child: I always cry when I go to sleep, about my dad. Sometimes my mom doesn't know because I don't let her know. I don't yell or scream. I just let my tears down.
Interviewer: So you don't want Mom to know that you are crying?
Child: No, because I want Mom to have a different thing.

One child summed up the feelings of all the children about the help they needed. Talking about himself in the third person, he said:

Child: You know, he needs love because he doesn't have any love.
Interviewer: Who is he going to get this love from?
Child: His mommy.

Mothers recognized that their children required some form of help. On an emotional level, however, they were simply unable to deal with any more than the absolute necessities and were, therefore, emotionally unavailable to the children. This lack of availability involved an inability to attend to the emotional or behavioral problems that the child was presently showing. One woman whose sister and brother-in-law had been shot by her husband was asked what changes she had noticed in her son. She replied:

I don't really notice too much. It's usually friends who tell me, and my family notice a lot of difference [in him]. Especially after the shooting. He was talking baby talk, and I didn't even notice that until my parents pointed it out. Then the school counselor called and said, "He's extremely unhappy, all he talks about is the shooting." But I was so stressed out myself. I was in my own little world.

So while the mothers were concerned with the pragmatic business of day-to-day survival, the emotional needs of the children were being overlooked. On a cognitive level, they were painfully aware that their children couldn't talk to them about feelings nor they to their children. They made comments like the following:

> I know she was unhappy with the last visit, but she won't talk about it. She'll talk to someone else but not to me.

> He won't talk about it. He doesn't ask any questions either. I just have to try to think of what to discuss with him. I didn't know what to ask him. He doesn't tell me what bothers him. He just acts hysterical.

The mothers wanted to do the best for their children, but they were unlikely to see themselves as the appropriate ones to handle the children's needs. Almost all the mothers said that the reason they had volunteered to be in the study was to find resources to help their children. One mother expressed the general feeling of all of them: "*She's* got to get some counseling [for her 3 years, 10 months old child]. I can't do it, OK? I'm too tired. I was trying but it was too hard. I just couldn't handle it."

Mothers need help, and children know that their mothers need help, but children need mothers. Mothers want outside resources to take over the emotional care of their children, but children want their mothers. One of the most encouraging findings of these studies is that both mothers and children are highly motivated. Both groups want help for themselves and each other. As well, mothers are highly motivated to do what's best for their children, because they fear for their children's future mental health. One mother said: "I don't want him to become angry and start taking it out on garbage cans and other kids at school and getting into trouble, becoming a bully. I could see that happening."

Moving On

Mothers were, for the most part, ready to move on to a life without their abusers. They still felt enormous anger toward their ex-partners and were somewhat enmeshed with them through the children. One woman described her son's message from his father after a visit: "[Son] says that Daddy says he sits around the house and cries. I don't think its probably all the time. I don't think he does that continuously, but I think it's in the evening."

At the same time, women were making sense of their own experiences during the relationship and resolving them as best they could. Although they still had difficulty acknowledging the degree of abuse they had endured, they had a realistic understanding of its effect on their present lives. One woman talked about leaving as being the best thing she ever did: "I've grown so much, I've got independent. He broke me so low that I had to grow again. I've changed so much,

I'm happy. I look at him and he is so miserable still. I don't think he'll ever change."

The children represented an important influence on women's planning for the future. On one hand, the children were a drain on them; mothers could not do whatever they wanted. They needed to consider their children and plan for their care and support. Women with no money needed to, as a condition of government subsidization, continue to pursue their husbands for child support even though such pursuit exposes them to his retaliation. On the other hand, children also had a positive influence on the mother's planning. Women who might not ordinarily have had the energy to change themselves worried about the example they were providing to their children.

> One of my things is that I want to feel independent emotionally as well as financially. I don't want to become dependent on anyone again, you know, and do for myself. I want to be strong, and hopefully that will be reflected in the girls so that they can be strong.

For the most part, the children moved on and attempted to cope with their many changes in school, living accommodations, and friends.

> My mom wanted to move in faster because she wants me to start school whatever school I am supposed to go to, to go in the middle. I am going to be going to school in [name of town] then. I am going to spend 1 month at my school here and I guess I am going to spend the rest of the year in [name of town].

The future for them was, however, tinged with uncertainty. As one child said: "My mom and dad will be divorced, and I don't know what will happen to my sister and brother and me." This uncertainty, combined with their inability to talk about it with their parents, left them sad.

Perceptions of the Abuser

It is important to recognize that for the children, the abuser was still their father. For most of the children, their times with their father since the separation were enjoyable because their fathers took them to fun places: "It's fun. He takes us to the *Jungle Book,* to *Ghostbusters.*"

The children desperately missed their fathers when they weren't with them and were acutely aware that their fathers wanted to be with them and missed them. "Well, yesterday I called him and today two times I called him. I called him a lot of times. Cause I miss him so much you know," said a little girl. One boy expressed concern about his dad: "I don't want my dad unhappy; he always wants his boy."

The mothers' perceptions of the fathers were different, however. Because of court-mandated access orders, mothers needed to be in contact with their abusers through child visits. The fathers continued to exert control over the women through the children. The mothers felt that they needed to be vigilant as to the father's mood and potential dangerousness to determine whether or not it was safe to be around him. As well, they needed to negotiate the day-to-day problems created by this access. As a result, mothers were angry at the fathers—at their obvious manipulation of the children, which they saw as a transparent attempt to "suck up."

> He comes over, and I'll be in the kitchen. He comes in, insults me up and down, goes back in the living room, plays all nicey-poo with the kid, comes back and insults me again—how do you deal with that?

The tone of their anger implied that they felt helpless and unable to deal with ongoing difficulties with their ex-partners; however, they expressed confidence that sooner or later the fathers would get what was coming to them—through the kids. "He's just putting on an act but what will he do when S. is 6 or 7? He's not going to be able to fool him anymore."

Emotional Reactions

There were marked differences in the predominant emotions displayed by the children and the mothers. The children all expressed great sadness—primarily a longing for their fathers. A 5-year-old said: (Drawing a picture of a heart that is split in two) "I'm drawing something big, and it's broke because my dad's gone and I miss him so much."

Although their sadness was primarily because they missed their fathers, many were sad as well because of the many losses they had experienced in moving from their homes. Children missed their toys and friends and schools and the familiarity of what they were accustomed to. For several children, their sadness was compounded by their lack of understanding of the reasons for their separation from their father. "The morning that we woke up and we left our house, my sister didn't understand it, she still doesn't understand. I don't really either," said one child. The children's feelings of protectiveness toward both their mothers and their fathers limited their ability to express and manage their sadness. This, combined with the mother's emotional unavailability, left them feeling even more sad.

Sadness was not the predominant emotion expressed by their mothers, however. Mothers seemed to be expressing a mixture of exhaustion, dull anger toward the ex-partners, and regret for their children. Talking about being tired, one woman spoke for them all: "I was just always tired. I could barely . . . I just sit here. To me a holiday is to just sit home and read. I don't go out or do things other people consider normal."

Compounding the mothers' weariness was a recognition of being caught in an insoluble dilemma regarding their children and the children's fathers. They were worried about the message that they gave their children and upset when their children got the wrong message.

> She may know of my apprehension letting them [the children] go to him, and then she gets torn. Not that she wants to, she doesn't want to hurt him so she gets right in the middle. She just wouldn't listen to me. She just hated me. She thought I was trying to stop her seeing her dad.

Women's feelings at this point in their lives were a complex mixture of tiredness, anger, and regret—all complicated by the fact that they wanted to move on but were tied to the past by the necessity for ongoing contact with the abuser.

Discussion

Theoretical Perspectives

Various theoretical insights into the reality of leaving abusive relationships may provide direction for intervention with these women and their children. It is clear, however, that some perspectives are more useful than others and that some are only useful under certain circumstances. Some theories, for example, work well to explain the women's responses but do not explain the children's experiences. Others may be of use to certain professions but not to others. For instance, the biological theories of violent behavior represent an interesting opportunity for research by physicians or biochemists but provide little direction for research or intervention by nurses and other clinicians. One way to classify theories that explain responses to an abusive relationship in a way that is useful to direct service providers is to divide them into theories that attempt to explain the reality of women or children from a more or less pathologizing perspective. Examples of the more pathological perspectives include those that label the woman as suffering from learned helplessness or posttraumatic stress disorder. The other theoretical approach, which will be used here, is more in keeping with a feminist perspective in that it seeks to explain women's and children's reactions as reasonable responses to the entirely unreasonable things that have been done to them. An example of this theoretical approach is Landenburger's (1989) entrapment and recovery process (see Chapter 5). A feminist perspective gives direction to examine the experience of abused women and their children in the context of their lives in the larger society and directs the practitioner away from pathologizing, labeling, and medicalizing the experience.

Posttraumatic Stress

Posttraumatic stress theory suggests that some traumatic life experiences are so overwhelming for certain individuals that they cannot assimilate them and thus are psychologically harmed by them (Johnson, 1993). This psychological harm is characterized by a cluster of symptoms (anxiety, hyperarousal/ hypervigilance, intrusiveness or reliving of the event, avoidance of stimuli associated with the event, and numbing of general responsiveness) known as posttraumatic stress disorder (PTSD). Traumatic events that are thought to precipitate PTSD include natural disasters; accidental humanmade disasters; and intentional humanmade disasters such as combat, sexual assault, and prolonged physical and psychological abuse (Horowitz, 1986). Suggested interventions to resolve the disorder include the development of trust within the therapeutic relationship, education regarding the recovery process, stress management, and helping these individuals to reexperience the trauma and to integrate it into their lives and identities (Mejo, 1990). Posttraumatic stress theory has been applied to both abused women and their children.

Although this perspective beneficially reconceptualizes abuse as trauma, it is of limited usefulness for practitioners working with abused women, for several reasons. First and foremost, labeling a woman with PTSD labels a woman's experience as pathology, thus putting the onus for change on her. In a sense, it continues to blame the victim. Also, although living in an abusive relationship is indeed traumatic, the event for abused women is not an isolated one but is an ongoing experience. The experience of abuse continues for abused women even after leaving the relationship. Women report they must continue to deal with the controlling and violent behavior of the abusers (through harassment and continued violence, custody and access hassles, etc.) even after they are no longer living together. Consequently, it does not seem possible to assimilate this experience into one's identity and life as easily as posttraumatic stress theory implies. Neither does this theory fully explain many of the other troublesome symptoms that abused women demonstrate—depression, low self-esteem, and self-blame (Campbell, 1993).

Viewing the traumatic event as the exposure of children to the perceived or actual harm of their mothers (Eth & Pinoos, 1985), intervention programs have been developed for child witnesses based on posttraumatic stress theory. Childhood recovery from trauma is thought to be facilitated by education on domestic violence; help in identifying and talking about feelings; learning about coping, safety, and self-protection; and enhancing self-esteem (Koranda, 1993). As Humphreys (1993) suggests, however, this theory may be useful in helping children during the immediate crisis phase, but it may be of limited usefulness in working with all the children of abused mothers over time. This is a result of (a) developmental and other differences in children's ability to assimilate information and experience, and (b) the ongoing nature of the violence to which children of abused women are exposed.

Complex Posttraumatic Stress

In an attempt to account for some of the differences seen in abused women in response to trauma, Herman (1992) describes a phenomenon she calls complex posttraumatic stress disorder, which arises in response to a history of subjection to prolonged totalitarian control. According to this theory, individuals who have been exposed to ongoing trauma such as prolonged childhood sexual abuse or prolonged psychological/physical woman abuse develop more complex and characteristic personality changes such as alterations in affect, consciousness, self-perception, relationships, and perception of perpetrator. According to Herman, these changes are not so easily overcome as the harms associated with (simple) PTSD and should be addressed differently. In this theory, there are three stages of recovery from the disorder: safety, remembrance and mourning, and reconnection. Each stage builds on the previous one and entails different therapeutic tasks and foci. Essential in all stages is a focus on empowerment. Although it has been used to explain the responses of women to prolonged abuse and to provide direction to helping them, this theory has not yet been applied to children.

This theory builds on (simple) posttraumatic stress theory in that it accounts for the profound and complex influence of abuse on women, acknowledges the differing needs of abused women at different stages of their experience, and stresses the needs of abused women for empowerment and control. Although useful in providing direction to, especially, group work with this population, complex posttraumatic stress theory continues, however, to pathologize these women as suffering from a disorder that should be cured.

Although this theory has not yet been applied to children, it holds some promise in that it allows for individual differences and recognizes the needs of children for grieving and ongoing support.

Grief

Turner and Shapiro (1986) relate the physical and the emotional losses that abused women experience at the end of the relationship to grief theory. These authors describe women as needing to "mourn the death" of the relationship (p. 374). They describe the process as being the same as mourning any death and point out that such a process needs to be worked through. Society, however, does not perceive the end of an abusive relationship as a situation to be mourned and, therefore, a woman who needs to mourn the end of an abusive relationship is likely to find herself with no one to talk to. As a result, the process is unresolved. The need for children to grieve is more readily recognizable. In other words, those who are potential sources of support for mothers and/or children may find it easier to understand the child's need to mourn the loss of her or his father than they do the mother's need to mourn the loss of her relationship. This may help to explain why women who have left the abusive situation seem to have so many unresolved issues (Ericksen & Henderson, 1992).

This theoretical perspective normalizes the experience of abuse. It places the experience of abused women in the context of an entirely reasonable emotional response to a situation that was not of her making.

Entrapment

It is important to point out that the process of resolving an abusive relationship involves more than mourning its ending. It also involves coming to terms with all the emotions and questions that such an experience engenders. Landenburger (Chapter 5) describes a four-stage process of entrapment in and recovery from an abusive relationship. The final two stages, disengaging and recovering, are particularly important and relevant to women who have left. Disengaging involves the emotional separation from the abuser, which may begin the process of physically leaving the relationship. Recovery involves three components: grieving the end of the relationship, struggling for survival, and searching for meaning. The need to grieve such a loss has already been addressed. Struggling for survival includes learning all the practical tips about finances, dealing with the courts, custody and access issues, and learning the most effective ways to deal with children. Searching for meaning involves coming to terms with all that has happened; that, for these women, includes looking at their own part in the process. This theoretical explanation of women's experience is one of the most useful yet to be developed. It places the woman's experience in a social context by recognizing how family members, friends, and service providers can influence a woman's process of recovery. This influence can be either positive or negative. The theory importantly makes explicit the influence that the larger society has in either helping or hindering a woman in her search for a violence-free existence.

Resilience

Although witnessing abuse is certainly associated with future behavioral and psychological problems (Gage, 1990; Hershorn & Rosenbaum, 1985; Jaffe et al., 1986b, 1986c; Moore et al., 1990), studies on woman abuse reveal that not all children who grow up in violent homes are negatively affected. Garmezy (1983), in discussing the role of resilience and other factors in children's responses to stressful experiences, identifies three categories of factors that seem to mediate the effects of stress on children: (a) characteristics of the child, such as temperament; (b) nature of the family environment, such as warmth and organization; and (c) presence of environmental supports, such as significant peers and adults. Others have shown that the presence of a supportive relationship with at least one warm, caring person (parent, friend, other caring adult) can mediate the effects of witnessing or experiencing violence (Emery, 1982; Milner, Robertson, & Rogers, 1990). Such theories lend further support to the need for caring and supportive relationships in helping women and their children overcome the effects of living with violence. As well, helping abused mothers to provide more support and warmth to their children may offset the effects of witnessing violence.

Feminism

It is impossible to conclude an examination of theoretical perspectives relevant to work with abused women and their children without discussing feminism. Although not a theory as such, a feminist perspective is almost a prerequisite "way of being" in working with this population. As outlined by Yllö and Bograd (1988):

> All feminist researchers, clinicians and activists address a primary question: "why do men beat their wives?" . . . Feminists seek answers to their question at the social or group level. . . . Feminists seek to understand why men in general use physical force against their partners and what functions this serves for a given society in a specific historical context. (p. 13)

One of the most important aspects of working from this perspective is a commitment to validating women's experiences. Specifically, this commitment includes verbal recognition that many of the ways society responds to abused women come from a victim-blaming stance. It also involves recognition that because all women are at risk of violence and abuse by virtue of living in a society that views men's experience as the norm, there can be no hierarchy (a them and us stance) between abused and not-yet-abused women if work to end violence is to be successful.

Work conducted from a feminist perspective includes believing women, validating their experiences, reminding them that—under impossible circumstances—they did their best, and advocating for them on request. Underlying everything else is a belief that each individual woman is the expert on her own life and therefore the only one qualified to make decisions for her. Others may offer alternate views or suggest alternative actions, but the abused woman must be supported in her final decision. To do anything else would be to perpetuate the disempowering process with which she has lived. It is, thus, taken as a given in the following discussion that all theories are being discussed from a feminist philosophical stance and that their implementation would be consistent with feminist principles.

Interrelationships Between Themes in the Literature and the Findings of the Studies

Children in the research study expressed a deeply felt need for someone with whom to share their thoughts and emotions. They were sad, torn between their mothers and their fathers. At the same time, they clearly felt a degree of responsibility for meeting the emotional needs of both their parents. They demonstrated an ability to see things accurately from their parents' perspective, which exceeded that of their mothers (and presumably their fathers). This can be a threat given what is known about resiliency. It may be difficult, given the hidden nature of abuse and the probability that women need to move frequently, for children to build a supportive relationship with anyone other than their mothers. Also, under conditions such as the ones experienced by these families, it is clearly difficult for mothers to provide a family atmosphere of warmth and organization. Any child will benefit from the support of a caring relationship with another person but such support is crucial for the child who does not have the type of temperament to withstand the stresses inherent in an abusive situation. It is important to remember that the person from whom children want warmth, caring, and support is the mother. There is, however, one exception. No matter how supportive the mother, children may find it difficult to talk to their moms about their dads. These are remarkable children with remarkable strength and insight. They are too concerned about the mothers' feelings to be able to freely express their emotions to them. Programs need to be aimed at improving the fit between children's needs and maternal parenting approaches. Two facets of such programs are required. The first involves providing mothers with support and space to continue working on resolving their own issues. The other involves providing help for these women with their parenting.

Social support has been demonstrated to be an important factor contributing to increased coping abilities in both women and their children. Mothers who are themselves stressed may find it virtually impossible to provide their children with the needed emotional support without some support for themselves. Although it is possible to gain social support through close ongoing contact with either supportive family and friends or with a counselor, women who have recently left an abusive relationship may find it difficult to link up with friends who are understanding, and ongoing counseling usually involves prohibitive costs. Support groups can provide acceptable alternatives for both women and children to find concrete and emotional help. Within a group of women who have all experienced similar events in their relationships, women can at last find a place where it is acceptable to grieve their loss. Other abused women can understand the conflicting emotions that arise as well as the conflicting responses that are evoked by the emotions. In an atmosphere of trust and acceptance, women can feel safe to explore and move toward resolution of their issues. With this type of support available to them, women may find it easier to gain understanding of their children and to respond to their needs.

Children's groups can provide an important alternative source of support for the children. A group can provide children with a safe setting in which to explore their sadness and discuss their feelings about the losses in their lives. Mom is often in no emotional state to recognize the impact of moving away from Dad, perhaps changing schools and thereby losing friends, leaving behind house, toys, and all that is familiar. Children can benefit from discussions about these feelings as well as issues such as acceptance of violence, conflict resolution, and safety. Alternative ways of dealing with problems can be explored in an atmosphere of acceptance where children need not worry about hurting anyone's feelings. Also, a group provides a perfect opportunity for a regular check-in with children about ongoing issues that may arise during contact with their fathers. Children can be exposed to a great deal of pressure when mothers and fathers are engaged in disputes about custody and access or when mothers are being subjected to the ongoing harassment generated by their partners' attempts to get them back.

There are a number of issues and concrete tasks that can be addressed in a group setting for women. Abused women consistently worry about their children and about their own ability to parent. In part this is due to their own low energy levels and self-esteem and, in part, this is because children who have witnessed abuse frequently have behavioral disturbances that are often associated with child management problems (Jaffe, Wolfe, & Wilson, 1990). These are not easy children to parent, particularly for women who are themselves in a fragile emotional state. Other concerns overlap—housing, finances, contact with ex-partners all have an impact. Women's own issues also intrude—their tiredness, and their anger and frustration at partners and children. In a group setting women meet other women who are at different stages in the process of recovery. Women who have already dealt with a particular issue can assist with concrete suggestions as well as encouragement: "I survived, and so will you. A year ago I felt just like you do now—I can't believe how much better I feel now and so will you." Women who are further behind in the process can provide proof to a woman that she has come a long way. When a woman is enmeshed in the situation, it is hard for her to realize that progress is being made. Meeting someone who is 6 months behind her can be extremely empowering. Thus, a group can be the perfect setting in which to acknowledge that women have different needs at different times. One woman, for example, might be grieving the loss of her relationship, another might be terrified by the prospect of having to confront her partner in court during a custody hearing, and a third might be angry because her children are acting out after each visit to their father. Each woman's experience can inform and affect the others.

Acknowledging that people have differing needs at different times might mean that for a particular woman or child a group setting might not be the strategy of choice. Whether working with women and children in a group setting or on an individual basis, empowerment should be a central aim. Empowerment is a concept that is central to feminist work. Inherent in the concept are several important ideas. Empowerment is, for example, positively linked to increasing self-esteem and is accomplished through "understand[ing] what types of actions are their responsibilities and which are not, as well as the difference between what they can control and change and what they cannot" (Hughes & Marshall, 1995, p. 123). When abused women and their children are encouraged to recognize the large areas of their lives with their partners/parents over which they had no control, it becomes easier to recognize that some of the resulting difficulties with parenting or with resolving the past or with being confident about the future are not surprising, not their fault, and not insurmountable.

Another important idea is that empowerment is closely linked with advocacy. Feminist advocates not only advocate on behalf of women but also teach women to be able to employ the same skills on their own behalf (Hughes & Marshall, 1995). Child advocates do the same for children. Empowered people are the ones who are clear, not only on what are their problems and what are not but also on what are their responsibilities and what are not. Empowered mothers are able to give up on much of the guilt inherent in leaving an abusive relationship "in a culture which clearly affixes blame onto them" and to gain confidence in their ability to parent (Bilinkoff, 1995, p. 99).

Advocacy, empowerment, and feminism are inextricably linked, as they must be if work with abused women and their children is to be successful on both an individual and a societal level. Theories pertaining to work with this population must be used from a position that recognizes this interrelationship. Women must be recognized as the experts in their lives, and practitioners working with them and their children must always guard against doing anything to perpetuate the oppression under which they have been living. As well, a balance must be maintained between the need for an individualized approach with specific women and children and the need to address issues of violence in the broader social context.

Conclusions

Children, as demonstrated by this research, are well aware of the reality of their situation and are frequently torn between love and fear in dealings with their father as well as between conflicting loyalties to both parents. The predominant effect of the high level of tension in the family is that because mothers are preoccupied with unresolved issues from the past and with the pressures of day-to-day living, the children are trying to watch over their mothers, often at the expense of their own mental well-being. Because the differences in perceptions are so great, an approach is needed that will help to make the worldviews of these mothers and children more congruent.

Women from abusive relations are a population with unique support needs. They usually have fewer social resources because of their need to lead hidden lives, they may continue to experience both harassment and abuse, they may be inexperienced in social interactions because of partner-imposed social isolations, and they may have difficulty trusting others (Henderson, 1989). Additionally, they may well have come from a violent family of origin and may not have any experience of positive parental models.

Children from abusive relationships, through no fault of their own, are caught in an environment clearly not conducive to mental health. It is of vital importance that this population of children is helped to achieve mental health if the transmission of violence through generations is to be stopped. This may be achieved by providing their mothers with a supportive environment that will, in turn, help them to provide a supportive environment for their children—an environment where violence is unacceptable and the quality of parent-child interactions is enhanced.

It is recognized that those who live with violence as children are likely to repeat it as adults. Children themselves have told us that it is their mothers that they need to help them to make sense of their experiences; mothers have told us that they are unequal to the task without our help. These children are like time bombs set to go off in a predictable way if no action is taken to "defuse" them. Accordingly, the authors have developed a parent support program and are implementing a study do determine its effect on (a) mothers' stress related to parenting and perceived level of social support, and (b) the stress, anxiety, and coping strategies of their children.

13

The Struggles of Runaway Youth

Violence and Abuse

Faye Annette Gary
Doris Williams Campbell

Youth who run away are at risk. These youth are more likely to perform poorly in school, drop out of school, and become members of community gangs. When this happens, the potential for crime, incarceration, and a blighted future is almost certain. Culturally specific interventions, based on the values of the youth in certain communities, need to be developed for schools and communities. Parental involvement is essential, along with the help of other caring and committed adults. It becomes essential to evaluate the life experiences of children and youth who live in violent environments and to recognize that they often react to violence through a variety of means such as running away, using drugs and alcohol, engaging in unsafe sex, reproducing too soon, or committing acts of violence or aggression.

What Is a Runaway Youth?

From a worldwide perspective, there are more than 100 million youth, all younger than age 18, who are usually referred to collectively as street children. The majority of these youth are in developing countries. About 40 million live in Latin America, 25-35 million in Asia, and more than 10 million in Africa. But millions of marginal or disenfranchised youth also live in America. Box 13.1 provides a profile of troubled youth within the United States. Definitions vary, but for purposes of this chapter, a runaway youth is an individual who is away from home for more than 24 hours without adult supervision, or who was away from home and refused to return. This definition includes all of those youth who may be labeled as street children, homeless, runaways, throwaways, and pushaways, as well as the neglected. In most instances, these youth also have been abused (Gary, Moorhead, & Warren, 1996; Kennedy, 1991; Lopez & Gary, 1996; Rotheram-Borus, 1991; Rotheram-Borus, Koopman, & Ehrhardt, 1991; U.S. General Accounting Office, 1989). These at-risk youth have no particular profile. They represent all socioeconomic and ethnic groups, religious orientations, and geographic locales within this nation (Bass, 1992).

After they leave home, the lives of runaways seldom improve. In terms of health status, runaway youth tend to suffer from skin diseases, poor personal hygiene, drug and alcohol abuse, sexually transmitted diseases (STDs), and inadequate nutrition (Shaffer & Canton, 1984; Yates, MacKenzie, Pennbridge, & Cohen, 1988). They are also at risk for depression and suicide (Rotheram-Borus, 1993). While on the run, they seldom receive help for these maladies.

This chapter will present characteristics of runaway youth and detail those conditions that precipitate running away behaviors. It will discuss what happens to youth once they run away. Then, attention will be given to concerns about preventing run away behaviors, assisting those youth who have run away and recommendations for action, taking violence issues into account. Violence is both a precipitant to youth's decisions to leave home and frequently the fate that these

---

Parental and family abduction

354,400 children per year

Stranger/nonfamily abduction

3,200-4,600 children per year

Runaway youth

450,700 per year

Throwaway youth

127,100 per year

Otherwise missing

438,200 youth

Homeless youth

2,000,000 (estimate)

Box 13.1
SOURCE: Adapted from Finkelhor, Hotaling, and Sedlack (1991).

youth encounter, once on the streets. Hence, violence is an antecedent and a consequence.

Violence-Related Trends

Among America's youth, there are some troublesome patterns, among which are increases in the numbers of youth who are incarcerated (Justice Research and Statistics Association, 1996), attempt suicide (U.S. Department of Health and Human Services [DHHS], 1990), or run away from home. In fact, many youths, by age 16, have experienced all three of these phenomena. In America, juvenile crimes are the fastest growing area of crime. The number of youth cases processed by juvenile courts increased 41% in one year to approximately 1,500,200 cases or 56.1 per 1,000 youth (Butts, Snyder, Finnegan, Aughenbaugh, & Poole, 1994). By 2010, it is predicted that juvenile arrests for violent crimes will double (see Figure 13.1).

Suicide is the second leading cause of death among males, and it is increasing. EuroAmerican males are most likely to commit suicide, with those between 20 to 24 years at highest risk, and those between 15 to 19 increasing in risk. Suicide is decreasing among older males but increasing among younger males (DHHS, 1990). Females tend to have lower suicide rates than their male counterparts. However, females attempt suicide about three times more frequently than do males (DHHS, 1990).

Homicide is the second leading cause of death among all youth. However, it ranks first among African American youth. Between 1984 and 1987, homicide among African Americans increased by 40%, or 87 per 100,000. Socioeconomic status tends to be the key factor that influences this pattern (DHHS, 1990).

The Nature and Nurture Proposition

To develop interventions that take into account the effects of violence in the lives of youth, it is important to understand the paradigms that can be used to understand the phenomenon. A foundation of this chapter is the belief that children and youth are complex beings who respond to a variety of stimuli. The environment within which they live is very influential, and ranges from simple stimuli to complex levels of organizations (Horowitz & O'Brien, 1989). There is a risk that crime, youth violence, and child abuse will be viewed from a paradigm of only genetic and biological propositions. Runaway youth, if viewed primarily from a genetic perspective, could too easily be cast as "bad," or youth who could not change without psychopharmacologic or other biological interventions. A position of pure genetic determinism can be used for social controls and undermines an empowerment perspective. Instead, all youth must be understood in terms of the interaction of the genetic endowments and the environments to which they are exposed.

Juvenile population growth foreshadows increases in violent crimes by juveniles

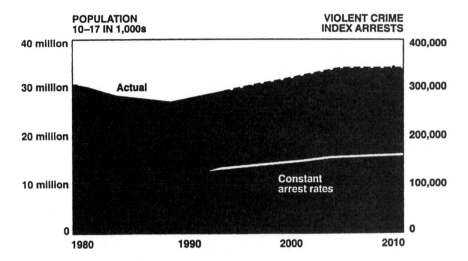

Figure 13.1. Juvenile Population Growth Foreshadows Increases in Violent Crimes by Juveniles
SOURCE: Snyder, Sickmund, and Poe-Yamagata (1996). This analysis is based on Uniform Crime Reports arrest data and Census Bureau estimates and projections.

For years, scientists and clinicians have debated nature (biology) versus nurture (environment) issues. From the nature side, we learn that biology is a basic behavioral determinant and will influence what manifest behaviors emerge over time. The genetic makeup is the essence of individuality. Humans as genetically determined have the capacity to acquire language, specific thought processes, and so on that are universal to all humans, and particular to the individual. On the other hand, the environment is critical. It has the power to affect the biological substrate and influence the "constitutional" tendencies that might affect genetic outcomes, but are not necessarily genetic in derivation (Horowitz & O'Brien, 1989).

Because individual measurements or empirical referents are more developed and available, the data about individual human behavior are more accessible. The environment and the factors that influence behaviors and development are not understood as well. The functional environment, its mechanisms of action, and how it influences individuals over time need more research and theoretical attention. The interaction between the environment and the individual, the experiences within the environment, and the genetic and constitutional elements are critical components for the development of a future social and scientific agenda that addresses health and mental health problems (Horowitz & O'Brien, 1989) and social issues (Gary-Hopps, Penderhughes, & Shunkar, 1995).

The best researchers and theoreticians carefully examine the mechanisms of action between the individual and the environment (Horowitz & O'Brien, 1989; Stanton et al., 1994; Tuma, 1989). Because environmental risk factors seldom occur in isolation, we are compelled to examine broad risk factors such as low socioeconomic status. Other profoundly influential variables are ethnicity, race, and culture (Gary, Campbell, & Serlin, 1996; Saylor-Buggs, 1996; Tuma, 1989). Much of the knowledge related to human functioning is based on an in-depth understanding of the social context, the social expectations, and the cultural context within our environment (Horowitz & O'Brien, 1989).

Diverse Cultural Communities

We must more clearly understand cultural influences and their impact on the development of children and youth. Culture and lifestyles also influence educational attainments, health beliefs and habits, and the experiences of pleasure and pain. In the future, health providers, policy makers, researchers, and theoreticians will need to recognize what is known and not known about culture. The entire language system used to discuss, describe, and categorize *ethnic* will be reevaluated. For example, the terms *Hispanic* and *Asian* do not capture the diverse cultural dimensions inherent in these populations. These terms do not have biological creditability, vary drastically depending on the classifier, and are used as political and social phenomena. Moreover, the term *minority* is beginning to be perceived by ethnic people as pejorative or derogatory (Davis, 1995; Sorofman, 1986; Takeuchi & Uehara, 1996; Wilson, 1989).

Health care providers should focus on the impact of the culture's organizing influence on the environment, recognize that it is pervasive and exists among all people, and learn to respect it. We must be responsive to the culture that is reflected in all individuals' worldview, their expressed values, their patterns of behavior, and the character of emotional responses (Gary, 1991). Culture also influences the nature of interactions between the individual and societal institutions (Gary-Hopps et al., 1995; Horowitz & O'Brien, 1989).

Culture within the context of "nurture" must be more clearly understood as we grapple with these complex factors that are associated with runaway behaviors and their consequences. Perhaps, with further examination, running away could be associated with subculture issues that are not yet identified. Young males may be without role models, and they may not sufficiently learn adequate problem-solving skills or how to negotiate with words and emotions without the physical expressions that often lead to violence and abuse. On the other hand, some subcultures encourage their family members to seek refuge within the family structure only. Examples of the latter are some African American and Hispanic families. It is also present among recent immigrant families who think that they must reveal "model behaviors" as potentially good citizens. In other instances, many of these families do not know how to seek help. In more than 1 million families in America, no one in the household older than 14 years of age speaks English (Institute of Medicine, 1994). Youth often serve as the interpreters of culture, and they influence many parameters of decision making within their homes.

Runaway Youth and Family Violence

In the United States, more than 2 million children run away from home each year. Several characteristics of the backgrounds of runaway youth distinguish them from the general population of teenagers: family violence and a variety of forms of child abuse, including sexual, physical, emotional abuse and neglect. As shown in a report on youth in a shelter in a rural community in north-central Florida (Table 13.1), the whole gamut of abuse is experienced by runaways. These youth indicated that abuse with their families was a major factor in their decisions to leave home.

It is important to clarify that a process or pattern of runaway behaviors can be identified. In fact, many youth usually leave home numerous times, and travel various distances over a period of years, before they actually "run away" (Lopez & Gary, 1996; Rotheram-Borus, 1991; Shaffer & Canton, 1984; Yates, 1987). Garcia is an example.

Tensions, fighting, and other forms of violence between Garcia's mother and father were evident in their home. Garcia is a 14-year-old male who began running away from home at about age 10 and refused to return at his parents' request. He would travel to a cousin's house or the home of a friend, in the next town, about 10 miles away. Garcia frequently "stayed over" with his cousin or his friend, and then returned home. Over a period of 4 years, Garcia continued to leave and return. He would go farther, and remain gone longer. By age 14, he was living on the streets, where he remained until he became ill and was taken to an emergency department at a community hospital. Hence, for Garcia, running away was a process and not a single event.

The Family as a Unit of Violence

The term *violence* denotes any act of power that causes people pain or harm or violates them in some other way (Emery, 1989). Violence has many roots, such as sexism, class bias, poverty, and racism. In this chapter, the term violence is considered to be broader than, but may be used interchangeably with, aggression and abuse.

We can conceptualize violence within the family system as having three components. First, the conflict between family members serves as a noxious

Table 13.1 Types of Abuse Reported by Runaway Youth in a Shelter
            ($N = 43$)

Type	No.	Percentage
Physical	20	46.5
Sexual	10	23.3
Emotional	12	29.9
All types	1	2.3

SOURCE: Gary, Moorhead, and Warren (1996).

stimulus that creates distress in the child. Second, the child reacts emotionally or instrumentally in an attempt to alleviate the distress. Third, the child's reactions that serve to reduce the conflict will be maintained because of its effect on the entire family system. The child's maladaptive behaviors can actually defuse some family tensions. In fact, researchers posit that children as young as 1 year of age have responded (e.g., by crying or withdrawing) to episodes of anger not directed at them, but occurring within their environment (Emery, 1982, 1989).

When there is conflict within the family, the child may be influenced to take sides with one parent against the other, or one sibling against another. The child's maladaptive response can be reinforced if it serves some conflict-diffusing purpose for the family system. This child, or some other family member, could become a scapegoat, and serve as a mutual force around which the parents unite their anger against the child. In such instances, these children are vulnerable and carry the burden of stabilizing their families. Such burdens can become overwhelming for the child (Emery, 1989; Greydanus, Farrell, Sladkin, et al., 1990; Lopez & Gary, 1996) and compromise his or her development (Earl & Smith, 1991).

One in 3 females and 1 in 11 males are sexually abused by the age of 18, with about 95% of all sexually abused children being females. The perpetrator, more than 90% of the time, is someone the youth knows: father, stepfather, sibling, grandfather, uncle, neighbor, or friend (Emery, 1989). These families tend to be isolated, alienated, and disconnected from other extended family and community support systems, including friendship networks for the children (Earl & Smith, 1991; Osofsky, Wewens, Hann, & Fick, 1993). Often neglected in the depictions of family violence is sibling abuse, including sexual abuse of females by their brothers (Emery, 1989). Sexual abuse is one of the most powerful variables that lead to the youth's decisions to run away (Gary et al., 1996; Lopez & Gary, 1996).

The family scene is not complete without a discussion about the influence of drug and alcohol use. Parents who consume large amounts of alcohol place their children at risk because of their altered decision making, general unavailability, mood swings, and temper tantrums. They therefore predispose these children to faulty problem-solving and coping skills. Substance use and abuse assure trouble for the youth. The traditional sexual constraints may be relaxed, and youth could become victims of seduction. Such instances are not uncommon experiences for maturing females. Physical aggression can accompany sexual aggression.

How Aggression Is Learned:
Antecedents and Consequences

Among youth who run away, aggression is a dominant antecedent and a likely consequence. When there is violence within the family, the youth learns this method of settling differences, displaying power, or gaining control over others. When this behavior is integrated into his or her repertoire of behaviors, these behaviors become a component of the expressed behaviors. They could be reinforced; if environments are not facilitative and psychologically and physically safe, the youth is more prone to respond in extreme ways. These youth may move toward individuals in an aggressive and threatening manner. Or, others withdraw. Some youth will decide to run away in search of a safer haven. Understanding how aggression is learned and maintained is essential for prevention and treatment programs for these youth.

Gary and Lopez (1995) conducted focus groups with police and deputy sheriffs in a small semirural community in the southern United States. The purpose of the focus groups was to gain insight into law enforcement officers' views on the antecedents of manifest aggression among youth between 13 and 17 years of age, and how the officers' perceptions compared with the perceptions of teachers and parents regarding how youth learn aggression.

One major theme that occurred throughout the focus group discussions was clear: The officers were convinced that families headed by women, with male children, were at particularly high risk. When there are no role models or no one to assist the mother in setting limits and teaching the youth basic rules of good family and societal citizenship, aggression is more likely. There was consensus among the officers that when one of these male children is about 8 years of age, he is out of the mother's control and vulnerable to peer pressure and gang involvement. Because the mother begins to have difficulty controlling the child as he gets older, simply because of limited strength, she does not, or cannot, enforce her own household rules. Once the young male child falls to the influence of older males (14, 15, 16 years of age), he gains acceptance into these peer groups through antisocial behaviors, sexual exploits, and "tough strutting." Given their sense of invincibility, they do not fear their mother or parents, the law, school authorities, or anyone else. Thus, they are indeed vulnerable, perhaps especially to gangs. In general, youth are attracted to the structure, the clear roles and obligations, and the overt system of sanctions and rewards of gangs (Berland, Homlish, & Blotcky, 1989; Earl & Smith, 1991; Hartup, 1989).

In typical family research, outcomes such as mental health status are usually explored using a dichotomous independent variable, such as intact or nonintact family or father absent or present in the home. This type of dichotomy does not take into account the many other types of families that exist, because of illegitimacy or divorce or desertion (Herzog & Sudia, 1973). Other studies have shown that mother alone and mother/stepfather families have high risks of psychological and behavioral problems among children, whereas mother/father and mother/grandmother families have the lowest risk. Mother/aunt families were also very effective and mirrored the outcomes of mother/grandmother-headed families. The aloneness of the mother with children tends to be the variable that is most powerful and far more significant than the absence of the father (Kellam, Ensminger, & Turner, 1977).

All kinds of families can provide male authority figures for youth. The males could be family members (uncles, cousins, fictive kin) or men in the community such as coaches, teachers, big brothers, ministers, neighbors, and friends. These bonds do not develop quickly, and occur too infrequently. If the male child does not have responsible role models, he is prone to acting out: stay out too late, become involved in drugs and alcohol, get introduced to sexual activity too soon, become truant from school, and disregard his mother's rules about curfews and other safety concerns. Some consequences of this scenario are runaway behaviors, delinquency and gangs, and exposure to HIV/AIDS infections and other STDs (Committee on Health Care for Homeless People, 1988; Lopez & Gary, 1996).

A Major Public Health Problem: HIV/AIDS

Although there is not yet definitive evidence that runaway youth are more likely to be infected with HIV/AIDS, it is a known fact that these youth are overexposed to the risk factors (Yates et al., 1988). The youth have dangerous ideas about their abilities to protect themselves. The invincible attitudes that are evident during adolescence are exaggerated in runaways. Some myths associated with HIV/AIDS and other STDs that occur among runaway youth who are also labeled as delinquents follow. These comments were gleaned from youths' focus groups regarding safer sex practices (Gary, 1995):

A person can look at another and tell if he or she (usually she) has HIV/AIDS by assessing the amount of "butter" (plaque) on her teeth.

Chlamydia is the name of a flower that grows in the South.

If a female holds her breath during sex, she will not get HIV/AIDS, and will probably not get pregnant.

Drugs and alcohol have no influence on a young person's behaviors because he or she can "hold stuff."

These types of grandiose, inaccurate, and self-defeating behaviors can be devastating to youth, and when they are on the run, their lives are in even greater jeopardy. The case of Ivy, a 15-year-old female who ran away from home because of her stepfather's continuous sexual assaults, is instructive. Ivy was doing well in school and had a dream of becoming an attorney and working for the United Nations one day. When she reached the age of 14, her stepfather began to sexually abuse her and forced her to participate in sexual acts with him. She was sworn to secrecy, and the stepfather threatened her by saying, "Your mother would not believe you anyway, even if you decided to tell her about us. Furthermore, if you tell, you might cause me to go to prison, and then you would be sad for the rest of your life. . . . You and your mother will have to give up the house, and all of the other pleasant things that I provide for you and your siblings."

She ran away. Another young female, Ivy's best friend, was having similar experiences in her own home. They frequently shared these experiences and kept each other's secrets, for they were convinced that their mothers, the teachers, the clergy could not believe their life circumstances. Still, others would think that they were bad girls, not believe them, and reject them. They planned to "catch rides" to the west coast where they thought they could get help and change their lives. During their trip to the coast, they were picked up by men who sexually exploited them in exchange for food, shelter, and the ride. Once on the coast, they found the streets to be mean, filled with violence and drugs. They eventually were picked up by the police and taken to a shelter for runaway youth. At the shelter, the two girls told their story. Each had been diagnosed with pelvic inflammatory disease, skin rashes, foot problems, and gastrointestinal distress. Ivy also had sores in her mouth, and she was beginning to show signs of depression. She cried frequently, refused to eat, and had difficulty sleeping. At the shelter she remained in bed for 12-15 hours a day.

Rotheram-Borus and colleagues (1991) have written that sexual exploits that occur among these youth may not be the usual type of sexual acting-out behaviors. Instead, they participate in sex as a matter of human survival; they describe it as "survival sex." With no money, limited skills, and no immediate support system, the female youth have few assets that would appeal to the mean streets. These girls are overexposed to opportunities for HIV/AIDS and other STDs.

On the other hand, when youth run away, many of them are never found. In American, more than 5,000 youth are buried in unmarked graves each year. The fact that these two youth, Ivy and her friend, did find shelter and help is one positive outcome of this event.

The Developmental Model for Antisocial Behavior

Continuous exposure to mean streets, uncaring adults, and systems that are unresponsive to their needs sets a background for antisocial behavior. Among many youth who run away, some have not had adequate attachments with parents and societal values regarding work, responsibility, and conformity, which leaves a deficit in the development of the youths' internal mechanisms of control. When the child is exposed to early antisocial behavior from parents or peer groups, they will probably learn these habits and behaviors. When behaviors become manifest, the child could be denied access to helping interpersonal and socialization experiences within the school, the community, and other more positive peer groups. Academic failure and rejection by peers are two powerful factors that serve to reinforce negativism among these youth (Emery, 1989; Patterson, DeBaryshe, & Ramsey, 1989). A developmental model for antisocial behavior is presented in Figure 13.2. It depicts the factors that influence delinquency in early childhood, middle childhood, and through adolescence (Emery, 1989).

Many youth who run away can easily become classified as delinquent, even though they may not be. However, when a youth is away from home, and on the streets, the chances of having negative contacts with law enforcement officers increase (Maxson, Little, & Klein, 1988).

Responding to Runaway Youth

Prevention programs are necessary to stop the growing numbers of at-risk youth in our society. These programs should focus on parent training and on social skills and academic skills acquisition for the youth (Patterson et al., 1989). Programs also need to assess for family violence. Many youth in juvenile detention centers have suspicious backgrounds that could point to abuse.

Mixed reviews characterize the outcome evaluations of intervention programs with at-risk adolescents. Usually, it is thought that most intervention programs produce short-term results, with limited discernible differences after about 1 year. Yet prevention must remain as the cornerstone for at-risk youth. The cost of housing a youth in a detention center is approximately $4,000 per year (Moone, 1994). The difference depends on the amount of services (tutoring, counseling, mental health and physical assessment and treatment, etc.) that the child receives. Without some type of intervention, these youth are likely to remain in institutional systems, be nonproductive, and probably have children who are not adequately parented, lack social skills, and experience school failure. This cycle must be broken with sound prevention strategies that expose the youth

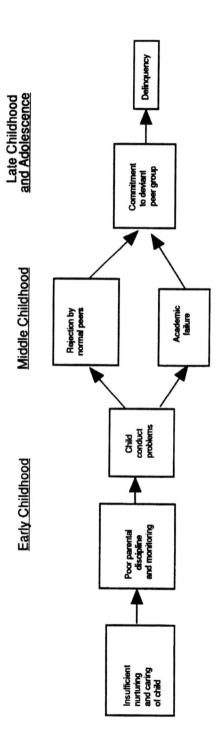

Figure 13.2. A Developmental Progression for Antisocial Behavior
SOURCE: Adapted from Patterson, DeBaryshe, and Ramsey (1989).

to a different type of value system, galvanize social responsibility, and encourage contributions to the society through their productivity.

Although debates continue about the efficacy of intervention programs for troubled at-risk youth, professionals must continue to work toward solutions. Interventions addressing factors such as substance use and abuse, poor school achievement, early sexual experiences, and involvement in antisocial behaviors such as gang-related activities and other infractions against people or property can all help troubled youth either before or after they leave home.

Substance Abuse. Among runaway youth, the incidence of substance abuse is very high. In fact, it is very difficult for youth to avoid substance use when they are on the run. Substances tend to be in their environment, in some form, most of the time (DHHS, 1990, 1995; Newcomb & Bentler, 1989). These youth sell, buy, trade, barter, deliver, and consume substances. The influence of substances deserve greater attention in programs.

The case of Dakkota serves as an example of a young runaway male who was pushed out or thrown out of his home because of drug use, among other reasons. Dakkota was 14 when he ran away from home. He was physically abused by his stepfather and sometimes by his mother. He was also deprived of food and the other comforts of home that most children take for granted. They yelled at him, called him names, and reminded him that he looked like his "no-good father," who had deserted him and his mother years ago for a younger woman. Dakkota began to withdraw to his room while at home. Over a period of time, he stayed away from home for long hours and just "hung out." During the time on the streets, he was introduced to drugs, a little marijuana, mostly. Then, he was invited to house parties on the weekends. At the parties, he learned about sex, and the possibility of joining a gang. Dakkota decided to take some "weed" home to smoke to get mellow and distracted from the tensions within the home. He did. His stepfather caught Dakkota smoking weed in his room late at night, and on the spot, put him out. He left the home, and went to the streets with his "friends." The friends accepted him, gave him more drugs, paired him up with an older woman who would teach him about "good loving" (sex) and more drug and alcohol tricks. Later, Dakkota was welcomed into the gang. He was initiated into the gang: He was beaten mercilessly as a part of the initiation ceremony, and he pledged to be loyal to all of its members, forever. Then, he was branded with the gang symbol. Within a 6-week period, Dakkota was charged with strong-arm robbery and disorderly conduct while under the influence of drugs. He was detained at a youth facility, along with several other gang members, awaiting his trial. He comments: "They are my brothers, they will always love me, and we will be together for life." At this time, Dakkota thinks that the gang is forever, but not the family. His commitment to the gang is strikingly strong.

In this instance, several behaviors could be viewed as warning signs:

- Tension existed between the parents and between the parents and Dakkota
- His presence in the home was a noxious stimulus for the stepfather
- The need for nurturance, support, guidance, and love was not satisfied within his home
- Emotional and physical isolation
- The introduction of drugs occurred when he was experiencing aloneness, the desire to be wanted, and the need to experiment
- Rejection by both parents
- No resources or adult guidance/no identified adult role models
- Dependence on peers who are gang members, and the continuous use of substances that influenced his decision to participate in the robbery

Gang Membership. Many youth who are runaways are vulnerable to gang membership. The case of Dakkota makes it clear that youth need additional safety nets in times of trouble. Because gangs are perceived by youth as an alternative, it is instructive to learn something about their basic characteristics. The most recent estimate indicates that in 1991, there were 4,881 gangs with a total membership of 249,324 members, predominantly males, although the number of females is increasing. Until the 1950s, the majority of gangs in America were white. In the 1970s, gang membership also comprised large numbers of African American and Hispanic youth. Currently, in the 1990s, Asian gangs are emerging rapidly. There are some continuing trends, however, in gang membership: Members tend to be recent migrants and representative of the lower socio-economic classes (Office of Juvenile Justice and Delinquency Prevention [OJJDP], 1994).

Gangs are in the schools, the neighborhoods, and communities. They are a close-knit group of youth who are at risk for acts of delinquency, sexual risk-taking behaviors, substance abuse, school failure, and a blighted future. To prevent gangs, the following risk factors must be addressed (OJJDP, 1994):

- Strained relationships among youth and adults
- Social disorganization, poverty, access to drugs, and low neighborhood attachment
- Family disorganization, violence within the family, and inadequate family management
- School failure, limited vocational aspirations, and labeling by teachers and other peers
- High level of tolerance for criminal activity within the individual

Responsible Sexual Behaviors

Teaching responsible sexual behaviors must be a component of any prevention program, and this teaching can be interwoven into many other health teaching opportunities. Nurses and other researchers, however, must unravel the complexities associated with sexual behaviors as expressed among youth, and go beyond exploring pregnancy, age of first intercourse, and contraceptive use. These foci are related to contraceptive issues and are of vital importance. But it is also of extreme importance to understand what sexuality means to youth, and how it relates to their lives within the context of their values, communities, social class status, age, gender, ethnicity, and culture (Brooks-Gunn & Furstenberg, 1989; Lopez & Gary, 1996).

When youth begin to mature, they start requesting more freedom from their parents regarding dating, sleeping over with friends, and later curfews. Maturing girls are more likely to have older friends, which might predispose them to early intercourse, substance use and abuse, and truancy from school, which can lead to poor academic performance and early pregnancies (Brooks-Gunn & Furstenberg, 1989; Warren, Gary, & Moorhead, 1995; Williams, 1983). As reported in *Healthy People 2000* (DHHS, 1990), it is estimated that 78% of all adolescent girls and 86% of all adolescent males have become sexually active by age 20. The risks that follow are unintended and unwanted pregnancy and infection with STDs such as HIV/AIDS and syphilis. More than 1.1 million females between the ages of 15 and 19 become pregnant, and less than 84% of this population intended to get pregnant. When an adolescent female becomes a parent, she is at greater risk to experience poverty, to not complete high school, be unemployed, to have low birth weight babies, and to lack parental skills (Williams, 1983). After birth, she may be further rejected and abused, and emotionally damaging parent-child interactions ensue. Over generations the effects of such relationships are evident as youth from these environments have children of their own and produce similar situations in their own families. Such scenarios are also the breeding grounds for problems between the youth and adults who are caught in these situations.

Once a runaway, a youth experiences a double bind: abuse at home and more abuse on the streets. These youth are indeed vulnerable to any malady. Once on the streets, life gets tougher and the possibility for more sexual exploitation occurs.

The Case of Anna Maria. Anna Maria was 13 when her uncle seduced her while she was baby-sitting in his home. She was frightened, confused, and devastated. She did not tell her father and mother, and she convinced herself that it would not happen again. But it did—again and again. The abuse continued for 2 years during which time she began to run away for brief periods of time. After the 25th run, Anna Maria decided to leave her home in Michigan and hitch to Florida. She was befriended by an older man who promised to take her with him to Florida and drop her off at a cousin's home. During the 3-day trip, Anna Maria stated that the man requested sex with her several times. He, like her uncle, refused to wear condoms, and he became physically aggressive when she mentioned safer sex behaviors and the threat of HIV/AIDS. She was fearful of becoming pregnant, of getting HIV/AIDS, or maybe some other sexual disease. When Anna Maria got to Florida, she went to a convenience store that had the "Safe Place" sign. The personnel at the store befriended her and took her to a shelter for runaways. A physical examination revealed that Anna Maria had become infected with chlamydia and gonorrhea. It was at the shelter that she shared this experience.

Anna Maria's experience and millions like hers must be confronted by responsible professionals, parents, and other community members. The prevention of such circumstances needs to be focused on primary prevention, responsible sexuality, adequate and culturally relevant sex education and counseling programs, and access to health care for male and female youth (Lopez & Gary, 1996). More needs to be known about how sexuality relates to youth who run away. The complexities and interrelationships of economic status, social factors, and family factors need to be unraveled so that effective intervention programs can be implemented. Parental involvement and the support of other responsible adults in role-modeling capacities are essential elements of effective sexual responsibility programs (DHHS, 1990).

Alternative Living Arrangements for Runaway Youth

Because the youth not only run away from their family homes but also leave group homes, foster homes, therapeutic homes, or the homes of relatives, more attention needs to be given to alternative living arrangements that are provided for these youth. Systems youth, according to Rotheram-Borus (1993), can sometimes be shunted from one facility or family to another. They may be as unhappy and distressed in the system as they were in their "prerun" environments.

However, for many the runaway youth shelters are a haven, as demonstrated in Kahalia's story. Kahalia, a 15-year-old talented musician, describes herself as an unwanted child. She was born when her mother was a junior in high school. Her father, an unemployed skilled craftsman, was 10 years older than her mother. Even though the father promised to marry Kahalia's mother and take care of them, he never did.

Kahalia ran away from home when she began to think that she was a burden to her mother and new boyfriend. Tensions developed in the home; the mother and her new boyfriend began to fight about Kahalia's presence in the home. Because the new boyfriend and her mother consumed increasingly larger quantities of substances, "partied," and participated in adult entertainment activities, there was no place or time in their home for Kahalia. At times, other adults would join Kahalia's parents in their home, for drug and alcohol parties. Kahalia was perceived as an intrusion and a barrier to their lifestyles. Kahalia began to sleep over with her friends. But that was not enough. Kahalia became more disconnected from her mother. She spent long hours alone in her room, at the school practicing her music, and with friends.

As the relationship continued to develop between Kahalia's mother and her new boyfriend, Kahalia determined that her mother had emotionally abandoned her. Kahalia left home and went to a nearby shelter for youth and requested a place to stay. At this point, Kahalia had admitted herself to the system for nurturance, shelter, food, and guidance.

Conclusion

Adults and other responsible youth must be taught to identify youth on the streets and assist them with attaining the needed services. The national program Safe Place is an excellent example of a community effort to help runaway youth find a haven from their struggles. Nurses and other health care professionals, policy makers, legislators, economists, and so forth must also intensify their actions to better understand and more effectively prevent and treat the antecedents to runaway behaviors. An action list follows (Butts et al., 1994; Institute of Medicine, 1994):

- Community leaders must develop self-assessment plans to determine the needs of the youth in their communities and develop a profile and work plan for each community.
- Agents must work together to coordinate services among law enforcement, schools, health care providers, the courts, child protective services, juvenile justice, parents and guardians, and nonprofit agencies.
- Communities will need to develop a plan that protect youth from familial violence and exploitation, and disseminate this plan.
- Community members should provide clear guidelines and procedures for responding to familial violence and abuse against youth; sanctions must be clear and individuals held accountable for their actions.
- School counselors, in addition to nurses, physicians, social workers, psychologists, and others, must be well trained in the areas of prevention, treatment, and rehabilitation of child abuse and family violence.
- Communities can now be connected to the Internet or World Wide Web and receive or share information about methods and strategies to protect youth from family violence and abuse and to assist with locating them and providing them a safe environment.
- Educational and training information must be disseminated to all individuals who have contact with youth, including, for example, police, parents, teachers, nurses, and other service personnel.
- The assessment of violence in families, and abuse of youth, should be an integral component of all comprehensive assessment processes.

- Greater emphasis must be placed on the prevention of trauma or abuse of any nature: research, advanced practice, and policy promulgation that focus on youth at risk and their families must be a major component of the health and social agenda.
- The environmental factors that act as antecedents to a youth's decision to run away must be perceived in a framework of prevention, and prompt and efficient treatment that involves the youth, the family, and the community should be implemented.

PART V

CLINICAL APPLICATIONS AND INTERVENTIONS

14

Changing Women's Lives

The Primary Prevention of Violence Against Women

M. Christine King

As has been detailed in previous chapters, significant numbers of women in the United States experience violence and abuse in their intimate relationships that compromise the health and safety of the women and their children. This chapter discusses the problem of violence against women and outlines strategies for responding to violence and abuse in the primary care setting. Nurses and primary care physicians can play a vital role in the primary prevention of abuse by implementing abuse screening and education on the issue of violence against women. This chapter presents strategies for the primary prevention of abuse and guidelines for mobilizing support for women. Collective prevention strategies aimed at eliminating violence against women at the institutional, community, professional, and political level are highlighted.

Violence and abuse experienced by women in intimate relationships is a health concern that affects a significant number of women in the United States. Conservative estimates indicate that 20% to 30% of all women in the United States experience physical abuse from their husbands or partners at least once, with 2-4 million women each year being physically battered by partners, including husbands, former husbands, boyfriends, and lovers (Straus & Gelles, 1990). These studies present an incidence of violence and abuse that is remarkably higher than official crime statistics, national health reports, or clinical experience indications, suggesting that violence against women is epidemic in the United States (Carmen, Rieker, & Mills, 1984; Koss, Gidycz, & Wisniewski, 1987).

Battering and abuse of women are rooted in historic and societal contexts and reflect a pattern of coercive control that one person exercises over another (Schechter, 1987). The abuse directed at women by male partners includes physical and sexual violence, intimidation and threats, emotional insults, isolation, and economic deprivation. These forms of violence and abuse most often occur within the context of the family, an institution that has been defined socially as nonviolent and nurturing. This social definition of the family as a unit of love and harmony, coupled with the enforced secrecy and denial that is perpetuated by abusers, "causes a perceptual blackout" of the violence that exists in "normal" families (Gelles, 1974).

Despite the overall lack of recognition of the widespread nature of violence against women, studies indicate that abuse results in physical and emotional problems that adversely affect the health of women and severely compromise their ability to participate in health promotion or health maintenance activities (Campbell & Humphreys, 1993; Helton, McFarlane, & Anderson, 1987; Kerouac, Taggart, Lescop, & Fortin, 1986; McLeer & Anwar, 1989a; Ryan & King, 1989; Stark, Flitcraft, & Frazier, 1979). Abused women also are less likely to seek primary health care because issues of survival take precedence, and abusers systematically limit women's access to outside resources (Ryan & King, 1989).

Dynamics of Violence and Abuse

Physical violence includes acts such as hitting, slapping, kicking, punching, shoving, choking, and using weapons. Acts of violence cause not only immediate injury but also may result in chronic pain, disfigurement, physical limitations, miscarriages, and stress and anxiety disorders, such as hypertension, hyperventilation, insomnia, and gastrointestinal and eating disorders. As a means of coping with the abuse and the resultant health problems, women may resort to drug and alcohol use. Some women are coerced into substance abuse by their abusers, providing another vehicle for abusers to maintain control over their partners.

Sexual abuse is experienced by many abused women but may not be easily disclosed because of intense feelings of embarrassment and shame. Women report being raped by their partners, asked to perform sex acts against their will, and physically harmed while engaging in sex. They may be treated as sexual objects, forced to view pornography, and in some situations, forced to have sex with others. Their abusers may be sexually promiscuous, placing the woman at risk for sexually transmitted diseases and HIV infection. Many abusive men refuse to use condoms. Some men, after receiving a diagnosis of a sexually transmitted disease or HIV infection, do not inform their female sex partners.

Emotional abuse is characteristic of most abusive relationships and often predates and precedes the use of physical violence. Displays of emotional abuse include yelling, screaming, name-calling, insulting comments, harassment, and public humiliation. Abusers systematically degrade a woman's sense of self-worth, making her feel unattractive, incompetent, and crazy. An abuser also may physically confine a woman and destroy her and her children's belongings, causing additional emotional pain. Emotional abuse can result in feelings of low self-esteem, anxiety, depression, disturbed parent-child relationships, symptoms of paranoia and chaos, and sometimes suicide.

Maintaining economic power over women is another form of abuse that binds women in violent relationships. Women may be prevented from getting a job or securing a higher-paying job. Abusive men may limit a woman's access to family money and resources, take her paychecks, and provide her with only a small allowance each week. Such men often control ownership of the home and transportation. This makes it difficult for women to acquire enough money or resources to feel they can survive alone and financially support a home and children. Societal discrimination in the workplace reinforces this reality because many women in the United States earn only minimum wage, with a small percentage earning more than $25,000 a year; in addition, many men fail to pay child support.

Making threats is another method of maintaining control over the woman and thwarting her attempts at leaving. Abusers may threaten to physically harm or kill her or her children, threaten to take the children away, or threaten to kill themselves. Threats also are used to make women anxious about their ability to live independently and obtain custody of the children. Abusers threaten to report damaging information about her to her family and friends, her employer, the courts, and social agencies. Whether this information is true, and whether it is in fact damaging, is irrelevant because it serves to immobilize the woman from taking action. For undocumented immigrant women and women who do not speak English, these threats are particularly effective.

Abusive men also control women through the use of emotional manipulation. Abusive incidents often are followed by statements of sorrow, promises not to abuse again, gift giving, and other displays of contrite and loving behavior. This pattern of behavior makes women question the severity of the abuse and reinforces their hope that the abuse will stop. Finally, abusers gradually isolate their partners from all avenues of support and outside help. This begins by controlling her relationships with family and friends, monitoring and restricting her conversations and friendships, and finally alienating her from all social support. Isolation also occurs as the abuser progressively limits her contacts with outside sources of help, such as health and social service agencies. This is accomplished by telling her there is no money or insurance coverage or simply threatening to harm her if she seeks outside professional care for herself or her children.

"Why do women stay?" probably is the most frequently asked question about women experiencing violence and abuse from intimate partners. External forces limit a woman's ability to leave an abusive relationship; these forces include a fear of greater physical harm or emotional damage to themselves or their children, economic dependency, social stigmatization for being a victim of abuse, social isolation, religious and cultural restraints, inadequate or withheld financial resources, lack of education or job skills, fear of losing custody of the children or becoming involved in the court process, and little information concerning the availability of resources and alternatives. Internal forces restrict women's behavior as they face insecurities about their ability to live independently, experience guilt over the failed relationship, are afraid of loneliness and lack of emotional support, are concerned about their ability to parent children alone, and are ambivalent and fearful about making significant and difficult life changes. These same factors may make it difficult for women to avoid or stay free of abusive relationships.

These external and internal forces exist within a context of a society and a community that is minimally supportive of abused women. Abused women face major barriers to change. These barriers stem from societal attitudes and tolerance of woman abuse, sex role stereotyping for women, women's position in the home and family, lack of social and community support, and legal system ineffectiveness. Given these barriers, it is remarkable that women are able to stay free of abusive relationships or to take actions designed to decrease the abuse or end the relationship. A question more relevant than "Why does she stay?" is "What resources help women stay free of or leave abusive relationships?"

Responding to Violence and Abuse in the Primary Care Setting

The primary care setting is an ideal setting for acknowledging violence and abuse as a significant health problem for women. By acknowledging this health issue, measures can be instituted to aid in prevention and intervention of woman abuse. Only by incorporating abuse assessment and intervention into the primary health care of all women will the problem of abuse be uncovered and ameliorated.

Nurses, nurse practitioners, nurse-midwives, and other health care professionals working in primary care settings can be instrumental in providing comprehensive and repeated assessment and intervention for the problem of abuse in intimate relationships. Primary care settings afford a unique opportunity for assessment of violence and abuse in the lives of all female clients. Women seek primary health care for a variety of routine health issues, such as gynecologic and women's health care, birth control, prenatal care, and health care for their children. In these settings, women are seen for episodic health care and often return for periodic health management and routine screenings, thus providing the nurse with continued contacts with these clients.

Abuse Assessment

Assessing for violence and abuse in the lives of women is the first step in the process of intervention, and it also serves as a vehicle for primary prevention of abuse for all women. By asking abuse screening questions of all women, nurses are acknowledging the enormous nature of abuse, which counters society's blatant denial of this health problem. When nurses identify abuse as a health concern that affects all women, they are able to provide education and anticipatory guidance before cycles of abuse begin. For women who are experiencing abuse, nursing assessment is crucial for helping women disclose this abuse so that intervention may follow.

Just as in the case of screening questions for other sensitive health issues, such as substance abuse, depression, breast masses, and sexually transmitted diseases, it is helpful to generalize and empathize before asking questions about abuse. Many abused women feel ashamed and responsible for their victimization and are embarrassed to voluntarily disclose abuse. For these women and for women not experiencing abuse, this approach conveys the message that screening for abuse is part of the routine health assessment. Nurses can use statements such as, "I am now going to ask you some questions I ask all women in my practice, questions concerning the possibility of violence and abuse in your personal relationships." This can be followed by a statement that indicates that you are aware that battering and abuse affect many women and that you consider abuse to be a health problem that you are able to address. It also is useful to inform women that you do not believe that women are responsible for their abuse and that you realize how difficult this issue is to discuss.

The Nursing Research Consortium on Violence and Abuse has designed five screening questions that can be used after these introductory remarks (King et al., 1993; Chapter 16 in this volume). Given that many women are reluctant to voluntarily disclose abuse, the questions are direct and specifically ask about the various forms of abuse. These questions elicit information concerning the possibility of physical, sexual, and emotional abuse and the issue of control and fear.

1. Do you feel emotionally abused by your partner?
2. Has your partner ever hit, slapped, kicked, or otherwise physically hurt you?
3. Are you afraid of your partner?
4. Do you feel your partner tries to control you?
5. Has your partner ever forced you into sex that you did not wish to participate in?

It is important to ask these screening questions in a private setting, away from the woman's partner and family or friends, assuring confidentiality and support. A woman will not feel safe disclosing abuse when her partner is present. Many abusive men intimidate women and threaten to harm them or their children if they disclose the abuse to anyone, effectively isolating women from all sources of help and support. If such women are asked abuse questions in their partners' presence, most will deny abuse and subsequently see the practitioner as insensitive and someone not to be trusted with this information.

Asking abuse questions in the presence of family and friends is similarly ineffective because women may be embarrassed or fearful of public disclosure. A woman may be unknowingly placed at risk for future violence from the partner if friends or family members report that she has discussed her abusive relationship with a health care provider. An abuser may manipulate or intimidate others into reporting the details of the health visit or bribe others into letting him know if their relationship was mentioned. Friends and family also may have an investment in the woman maintaining silence because they may be embarrassed or intent on the woman remaining in the relationship despite the abuse. In these situations, women will not feel safe in discussing the abuse unless privacy and confidentiality are assured.

It is not sufficient to screen for abuse only in the initial visit. Because of the shame and myths that surround abuse and the fear and control exerted by the abuser, it often is difficult for women to feel safe and comfortable in disclosing abuse to a health care provider. Thus, it is important to assess women for abuse at subsequent health visits. This can be accomplished by preceding the abuse screening questions with a statement informing women that you again will be asking a series of questions concerning the possibility of abuse in their intimate relationship. Women can be told that although these questions may have been asked before, you feel that this health issue is significant enough to be raised again and that their replies may differ from what they previously have told you or others. This encourages women to reveal abuse that they may have denied at a past health visit or to disclose abuse that has occurred recently.

Abuse Intervention

Some women will have positive responses to one or all of the abuse screening questions. An initial intervention is to enable women to discuss their abuse in concrete and specific terms. This can be facilitated by creating an environment in which the woman will feel comfortable in discussing her life situation and asking for help. It is useful to ask direct questions that help women re-create the forms of abuse they experience, the frequency and severity of that abuse, and any efforts they may have taken to seek help or assistance. The nurse can serve as a catalyst for change by highlighting the level of violence, providing an external definition of the relationship as abusive, providing supportive counseling, and assisting the woman in determining a strategy for the immediate future. Specific goals include helping women to reestablish a feeling of control and power in their lives and gain a sense of autonomy and personal empowerment by setting their goals and making their decisions (King, Perri, & Ryan, 1987).

Intervention entails helping abused women identify a personal support system and a safety plan in the event that the abuse escalates and providing information and referrals to shelter services and other community and legal resources. It is crucial to provide accurate and complete documentation of the woman's abuse history. This includes a statement identifying the abuser and the nature of the relationship the woman has with him. Descriptions of physical, emotional, and sexual abuse should be included, as should photographs taken for objective evidence. This documentation improves the woman's health care and serves as legal protection and evidence in the event of future court proceedings.

It is important to conclude all intervention contacts with abused women with a statement that reinforces the health care provider's belief that women do not deserve to be abused, that surviving abuse takes much courage, and that regardless of a woman's immediate decisions, she can always return for health care and assistance in the future. Detailed intervention strategies are outlined in other chapters in this volume. This chapter details strategies to be used in the prevention of woman abuse.

Primary Prevention

Many women will respond negatively to the abuse screening questions, reporting that they are not experiencing abuse from their partners. Some women may be in an abusive relationship but do not feel safe or emotionally ready to disclose this abuse. In either situation, it is helpful to inform the woman that many women experience abuse and that if this happens to her in the future, she should come and talk with you or another health care provider.

This is an ideal opportunity to discuss the problem of abuse with women and to provide education about the nature and dynamics of woman abuse. Prevention entails highlighting the incidence of violence in women's lives and exposing the forms that abuse takes, providing examples of the behaviors that men use to abuse and control their partners. As a result of societal denial of the problem of violence against women, many women have not discussed this issue with anyone. Mothers, other family members, and friends often are silent on the issue, not wanting to paint negative pictures of intimate relationships. Little if any information on abuse is presented in high school or college classes. This leaves women unaware of how common abuse is and prevents them from recognizing their potential vulnerability. If they are involved in an abusive relationship at a future time, they may be reluctant to discuss this with anyone, believing that they are the only ones who are experiencing this type of abuse and control.

Women may need assistance in sorting out male behaviors, hearing from others what are inappropriate and harmful actions, and obtaining validation for an objective view of behaviors that are abusive and controlling. Women often receive potent societal messages in the home and in the media that portray male violence and control as a normal part of intimate relationships. Discussions with health care providers about male behavior and relationship dynamics provide outside validation that abuse and control should not be a part of caring relationships.

Prevention also includes a discussion of the common myths people hold in our society about woman abuse. These myths keep women and men from understanding the societal underpinnings of abusive behavior and perpetuate the view that the woman who is being abused is responsible for her victimization, thereby absolving the abuser and society at large of responsibility. Myths originate from our attempts to explain the battering of women and serve the purpose of protecting ourselves from thinking that we may someday experience abuse or relieving our own feelings of helplessness when we are unable to stop the abuse (King & Ryan, 1989). When these myths are internalized, they make it difficult for women to acknowledge abuse in their lives or to feel capable of disclosing this abuse. These myths immobilize abused women from seeking assistance because they trap women into feeling guilty, isolated, ashamed, and confused. Believing these myths often renders women unable to contemplate that they may someday be involved in an abusive and controlling relationship; this blinds them to the possibility of victimization and allows them to ignore or minimize early signs of emotional abuse and control.

Common Woman Abuse Myths

Myths can provide a framework for discussing the issue of violence and abuse with female clients. Discussion of these myths often enables women to talk about their situations or the abuse of family and friends and helps them to share their feelings and concerns. The common myths are as follows.

1. Battering affects only a small percentage of the population or occurs only in certain ethnic groups or social classes.
2. Battering occurs only in "problem" families.
3. Violence in families is a private matter, one that should not be discussed with others.
4. Strong, protective men engage in some forms of abuse and control; it is part of the "male role," and it demonstrates their love and concern; this is especially true of jealousy.
5. Only men with "psychological problems" or men who are under stress abuse women.

6. Alcohol and drugs cause men to abuse; once free of substances, he will not act abusively.

7. Women who are abused ask for it, they are not performing their "woman/partner role" appropriately, or they have low self-esteem and are helpless.

8. Women would leave the relationship if the abuse was really that bad; women can "control the abuse" by placating their partners.

9. Men will not abuse pregnant women.

10. Only people who come from families in which abuse existed end up in abusive relationships.

Primary Prevention Strategies

Prevention of violence and abuse in women's lives necessitates a concerted effort on the part of all segments of society. The philosophy of primary prevention is one of exposing potential health problems, identifying people at risk for these problems, and using screening and education as primary prevention strategies. Women are clearly at considerable risk for violence and abuse from intimate partners, with this abuse resulting in health problems for significant numbers of women. The health problems of hypertension, diabetes, breast cancer, HIV, and sexually transmitted diseases require screening and education, and the health problem of violence against women should be similarly addressed. Nurses and other health care providers can play a vital role in preventing woman abuse by implementing abuse screening and providing education on the issue of violence against women. Exploration of the common woman abuse myths, coupled with a discussion of behaviors that are typical of abusive and controlling men, are important educational strategies to be used with individual women. Discussing these myths is a key to consciousness-raising and demythologizing for all women. Disseminating this information to one woman often has a wider impact because she shares this information with others, which epitomizes the spirit and principles of primary prevention at the community level.

When these discussions occur with women who are experiencing abuse but who have not disclosed that abuse in response to the screening questions, it serves to normalize the abuse, and aids in changing the mythologies that effectively isolate and immobilize abused women. This discussion may help women articulate their abuse at this time or at a future health visit.

It is not uncommon for women to report that a friend, neighbor, or family member is involved in a troubled or abusive relationship. The strategies outlined can help others understand the complex dynamics of abuse and provide validation of their perception that this relationship may be abusive. Interventions that enable friends and family members to better understand the abusive situation they see and to feel more effective in rendering support are useful. People outside of the abusive relationship need help in understanding that although they can provide support, only the abused woman knows what decisions are best for her and at what time. This may be frustrating for friends and family members as they strive to support a woman in extricating herself from a troubled or violent relationship, a process that often takes considerable time and repeated attempts at leaving and seeking of help. It is important that others listen, offer nonjudgmental support, and provide tangible offers of help.

Enhancing the ability of others to provide support to women in troubled or abusive relationships is another primary prevention strategy. The following guidelines are helpful to discuss with friends and family.

Guidelines for Mobilizing Support

If one suspects that a woman is involved in a relationship in which she is abused, controlled, or afraid, one should voice concern. A friend can offer to listen to her story, let her know that you believe her, which validates her perception of the abuse she is experiencing. If you are concerned for her safety, inform her. Help her to overcome feelings of shame and isolation by letting her know that many women experience abuse, that you do not blame her, and that no one deserves to be treated this way. Acknowledge how difficult this issue is for her to discuss and how major life decisions are not easily made. If she does not acknowledge the abuse, provide her with the number of a local hotline or resource if she ever needs it or knows someone else who does.

It is essential to be discrete and mindful of her safety. Do not discuss her abuse with others unless she gives you permission. If you seek advice from others, do not use her name or other possibly identifying information. Never discuss her situation in a setting in which others may overhear. Her safety may be jeopardized if others, known or unknown to you, report your conversation to her abuser or the abuser's supporters.

Assist her in feeling more powerful and self-assured. Comment on her courage and strength of survival. Help her identify her strengths, pointing out the areas in which she is competent and successful. Provide support and respect for the decisions she makes, remembering that she is the best judge of her safety. Do not encourage her to confront her abuser or take actions that may place her in danger. If she chooses to leave her abuser, advise her not to inform him, the children, or unsupportive friends and family because this may result in her harm.

Offer to be a resource and follow through with all offers of assistance. Provide her with the telephone numbers of agencies that assist abused women, including shelters and legal system options and advocates. Abused women may need help in obtaining access to resources, particularly if their freedom is controlled or they feel vulnerable and unsure of taking independent actions.

Be clear about the types of assistance you can personally offer, such as money, child care, transportation, housing, and advocacy in obtaining professional assistance. Do not offer assistance you will not be able to provide; help her identify other sources of support. And finally, let her know that regardless of the decisions she makes, she can always discuss her situation with you.

Collective Prevention Strategies

In addition to the efforts undertaken with individual women, it is important to institute collective prevention strategies at the institutional, community, professional, and political level to eliminate violence against women. It is only when strategies are institutionalized that prevention will reach the full community of women we serve.

Within the health care setting, nurses can engage in actions that expose the societal problem of woman abuse and raise the personal consciousness of women clients and health care providers. Posters, pamphlets, and other literature regarding violence and abuse of women can be made available in all primary care facilities, in highly visible places, such as waiting rooms and near entrances and elevators, and in discrete places, such as bathrooms and examining rooms. Information can be obtained from national organizations, such as the National Coalition Against Domestic Violence, the Family Violence Prevention Fund, and the March of Dimes; flyers and brochures can be obtained from local agencies that serve abused women. Books, journal articles, and videos on battering and abuse can be made available for staff and clients. Activities can be planned and instituted during October, which is Domestic Violence Awareness Month.

Efforts aimed at changing the nursing and health care practices of the primary care setting are crucial. It is essential that health care providers continually examine their feelings and reactions to the myths of violence against women. Confronting myths and biases is an ongoing process that necessitates group interaction and clinical supervision. Working with abused women can be a draining and frustrating process as we struggle to help women feel more powerful and courageous in confronting their abuse and the societal institutions that reinforce women's victimization, discrimination, and poverty. Staff support groups, client case conferences, and in-service education programs are useful. It is important that time be allocated for working on activities, projects, and research. Violence task forces or clinical interest groups can be developed to enable nurses and other health care providers to work collectively to institute educational sessions, protocols, and culturally relevant intervention approaches for women. Protocols are extremely important because they provide an accessible outline for intervention in the clinical setting (King & Ryan, 1991). Domestic violence programs and services can be developed within hospitals and agencies, managed by a clinical experts, and linked to existing community services. Support groups for women in troubled relationships can be facilitated in health agencies with linkages to battered women's service agencies.

Nurses can be instrumental in helping the community expose and address the health issue of violence against women, serving as knowledgeable resources and advocates. Community prevention efforts should be as exhaustive as those designed to address other community health problems, such as hypertension screening and education, cancer awareness, smoking cessation, and nutritional awareness. Nurses can participate in primary prevention by developing and teaching community education programs on violence against women. It is beneficial to present these programs in collaboration with representatives of local women's service agencies or shelters for abused women. Programs can be offered in a variety of settings, including hospitals and clinics, health centers, schools, day care centers, prenatal classes, community agencies, churches, and women's groups. Violence against women can be included as a topic at community health fairs, with nurses in conjunction with the staff from shelters for battered women operating an informational booth. Public service announcements on television and radio and posters displayed on buses and other public arenas can highlight the health ramifications of violence and abuse.

On a professional level, nurses can take an active role in addressing this health problem by developing task forces and interest groups on this topic in a variety of nursing organizations that focus on the health of women. The Nursing Network on Violence Against Women, established in 1985, is a national organization committed to eradicating violence in women's lives. This organization provides informed nursing opinion and policy, professional education, and clinical consultation to health agencies and organizations. It provides a way for nurses interested in violence and abuse to exchange knowledge and ideas and gain support for their work. This organization holds national conferences every 18 months and publishes a column in the journal *Response*. Nurses can play a vital role in educating other health and social service professionals by using a feminist-oriented approach that assists these professionals in applying an empowerment model of intervention. Nurses also can conduct research on all aspects of violence against women, generating new knowledge and changing the ways abused women are helped.

Political strategies are fundamental to changing the societal context that perpetuates violence against women and limits women's autonomy. Political activism includes advocating for a decrease in the portrayal of violence in the media, supporting legislative efforts at the state and national level, and petitioning for legal remedies designed to protect women. Public policy also must be influenced with regard to issues relevant to women, such as adequate funding for battered women's shelters, universal health care, affordable and quality housing, education and job opportunities, comparable worth, an improved welfare structure, and comprehensive child care.

The battering and abuse of women by intimate partners is a health concern that threatens the lives and safety of women and their children. Violence and abuse result in physical injury and acute and chronic health conditions and compromise a woman's ability to maintain her health and that of her children. It is the responsibility of nurses, collectively and individually, to identify violence against women as a primary health care problem and to assist in the eradication of violence from women's lives.

15

Screening for Abuse in the Clinical Setting

Kathleen K. Furniss

P hysical examinations can be positive patient experiences, providing reassurance, education, and case finding. However, examinations also can be extremely anxiety provoking because of feelings of shame and embarrassment about visible injuries from an abuser. They also may provoke flashbacks related to incest, child sexual abuse, and rape. Nurses involved in clinical assessment of any kind need to be aware that a patient's history often affects her response to clinical evaluation. Asking a patient about abuse before evaluation is respectful and empowering and often establishes a valuable opportunity for intervention.

Child Abuse

Victims of child abuse, incest, or sexual abuse often are frequent users of health care. Incest is the most common form of child sexual abuse and is defined by Hendricks-Matthews (1991) as "the sexual exploitation of a child by another person in the family, who stands toward them in a parental role, or in a relationship invested with significant intimacy and authority" (p. 299). According to Bachman, Moeller, and Benett (1988), women who are abused as children have more health problems and operations as adults than do those who were never victimized. In one study, victims of child sexual abuse had more chronic depression, morbid obesity, marital instability, high use of medical care, gastrointestinal problems, and headaches. Some patients have had repeated laparoscopies for chronic pelvic pain, without any diagnostic findings, but have never been asked about a history of abuse. Because it is estimated that 15% to 20% of adults have been sexually abused as children, more than one in five women are adult incest survivors. Between 30 and 40 million adult Americans have been abused as children; such abuse often results in feelings of worthlessness, guilt, and vulnerability. Memories often are repressed and surface only later in life. The victims often are needy and grieving and may make a conscious or unconscious decision to repress the trauma to maintain the family as a unit. Often, the closer the perpetrator, the deeper the denial. Boundaries have been violated, leaving the individual unclear about self-rights. Repression of painful memories is demanding and can leave little energy for other developmental tasks. Psychological growth, intimacy, and self-fulfillment often are compromised.

Some women recall repressed trauma in young adulthood if they again experience trauma. Other women do not remember until midlife. Potential reasons cited for recall at this age are a sense of physical safety, a sense of emotional health, and a relationship with someone who can understand. Flashbacks may occur during dental work, gynecologic examinations, and after car accidents or operations, which may simulate aspects of earlier trauma.

Flashbacks can be sensory, including experiencing feelings, hearing voices, or remembering wallpaper or other environmental cues relating to the trauma. Pounding headaches, neck pain, and rigid behavior may emerge as other signs of childhood trauma. Other potential clues to victimization include shame, addiction, workaholism, self-abuse, chronic pain, multiple accidents, frequent gynecologic problems, and hyperawareness. One study (Zierler et al., 1991) states that victims are more prone to risky sexual practices and thus more prone to risk of HIV infection and other sexually transmitted diseases.

A patient experiencing anxiety or flashbacks during any clinical assessment needs reassurance and empathy. Experts advise avoiding touching during a flashback because this may increase anxiety. Because touch is a common nursing response when a patient is anxious, clinicians need to be aware that there are times when touch will not be helpful or therapeutic. Resolution of feelings related to incest or child sexual abuse may involve as much as 2 years of therapy to deal with grief and anger.

Screening all women before a clinical examination for a history of abuse is essential. Many women have never been asked about abuse. Some women will respond negatively but reintroduce the topic later when a trust or comfort level has been reached. If a woman responds affirmatively to queries about sexual abuse as a child, the clinician must be prepared to offer information and referral. Because this type of counseling involves specific expertise, local resources must be investigated regarding training and experience. Counseling often is refused. In this case, self-help literature, such as *The Courage to Heal* (Bass & Davis, 1990), can be suggested. Numbers and locations of local self-help groups can be provided (see Resources). Patients who initially reject a counseling referral subsequently may request it after reading about victimization and realizing that they are not alone.

Dating Violence

Because one in eight adolescents will be involved in some form of dating violence and the incidence in college-age women (those 18-22 years of age) is even higher (Makepeace, 1981), all young women should be routinely questioned during any health encounter. Questioning teenagers about jealous or possessive partners in a family planning clinic, emergency department, or pediatric setting may provide clues. The power and control issues that are hallmarks of violent relationships often begin with jealousy that seems flattering to the teenager who is just beginning a serious relationship. Adolescents often are reluctant to share their worries about an abusive dating relationship with parents because they fear that criticism or some form of parental action may ensue. The developmental task of separation and need for independence also can hinder disclosure. Teenagers often are uncomfortable disclosing violence to a health care provider and may present with headaches, weight loss, or other somatic clues that may signal distress. Depression and suicidal ideation also may occur.

Nurses need to be aware of the services provided by the battered women's shelter in their locality for teenagers or locate a counselor skilled in dating violence. According to Prato and Braham (1991), resolution often involves teamwork by shelter staff, care provider, school, parents, and the teenager. Literature on dating violence should be present in all health care settings for adolescents and can be obtained from a variety of sources (see Resources).

Domestic Violence

Because it is estimated that 1 of 4 to 1 of 10 women has been or currently is in a violent relationship, all women should be screened in a safe and private environment (i.e., where no one can overhear a conversation). Failure to do so can result in continued victimization, frequent returns to the health care setting with vague medical complaints, severe injury, rape, or death. An abused woman often first shares her trauma and fear with a trusted care provider. Asking about abuse implies caring and knowledge. An initial question may not induce a battered woman to disclose her dilemma but opens the door for future discussion.

Obstetric nurses' awareness of the prevalence of violence in pregnancy may aid early case finding and prevention of subsequent complications. McFarlane, Parker, Soeken, and Bullock (1992) found a 17% prevalence rate of physical or sexual abuse in pregnancy with screening questions from the Abuse Assessment Screen (see Chapter 16). Because abuse often begins or worsens in pregnancy, screening is crucial in prenatal settings. Pregnancy loss, preterm labor, low birth weight, and fetal injury and death have been associated with abuse during gestation.

Two or three questions significantly increase detection of abuse. Varying the query is effective and essential. The clinician can ask, "Is anyone physically hurting you?" "Has anyone ever hurt you physically?" and "Are you ever afraid of your partner?"

If a positive response is elicited, the use of a simple mnemonic tool may be helpful to the clinician. Developed by Holtz and Furniss (1993), this simple tool provides quick recall of all essential aspects of proper treatment.

A—Reassure the woman that she is not *alone*. Such women often are isolated and denigrated by their abusers and need reassurance that this has happened to many other women. The abused woman also needs to know that she has shared her situation with care providers who can help. Knowing that assistance and support are available may be the first step in envisioning a life without violence.

B—Express the *belief* that violence is not acceptable, no matter what she has been told by the batterer. Women often have heard that the violence is their fault or that it occurred only because the batterer was stressed. When a care provider says that the abused woman should never be physically hurt, she may begin self-protection and may gain a clearer perception of boundaries.

C—Women need to be reassured that what they share is *confidential*. Let the woman know that her disclosure is private but will be documented on her medical record in case she ever needs it for legal purposes. (Child abuse must be reported.)

D—*Documentation* includes a statement by the patient about the abuse that avoids long descriptions that deviate from the abuse or subjective data that may be used against the patient (e.g., "It was my fault that he hit me"). Clear descriptions of all injuries and a history of the first, worst, and most recent incident of abuse are important. Saving evidence and photographs of injury with patient consent must be done per protocol, available from various sources, including the Jersey Battered Women's Service, New Jersey Division on Women, and March of Dimes (see Resources).

E—*Education* regarding the cycle of violence and likely escalation of abuse is essential. Women need to be made aware that violence is not a one-time occurrence that will disappear when the abuser's job is better or when dinner is on the table on time. Information about options must be provided. Returning home with shelter information and hotline telephone numbers or admittance to a battered women's shelter or another safe haven are choices that are explored. Literature about the local shelter should be provided. A brief description of services is helpful because women often are not aware that assistance with housing, jobs, legal issues, and crisis are offered. If the woman chooses to return to her abuser, safety is an issue. Telephone numbers for the local shelter and police must be provided. Discussion of a safety plan for a quick escape is important. A bag packed with important personal belongings can be hidden or left with a neighbor or friend. All legal options should be explored and explained (i.e., restraining orders or orders of protection). Again, a protocol is helpful and essential in all settings. A patient may choose not to take any action, but if a shelter hotline telephone number is provided, the patient may opt for counseling or assistance later. She should feel safer after her health care encounter than before it.

Health care providers need to be aware that leaving an unsafe situation is a process that requires time. Women often hope that things will change if they try once more. They often have been threatened with death or loss of the children if they do not return to the abuser. Any type of judgmental attitude on the part of the health care provider if the woman chooses to return to the abuser will lessen trust and increase her isolation.

Because leaving often is the most dangerous time for a woman, it needs to be her decision, not one that has been imposed by others. Good health care has been provided if education about options is given before discharge. Empowerment is allowing the abused woman to make her own choices.

Unfortunately, women can become victims at any stage of life, from childhood to old age. Questioning all women about abuse during health care encounters can result in saved lives, decreased violence, more efficient resolution of serious life problems, and more effective health care. Nurses who routinely screen all women will find that the teaching and interventions involved are not time-consuming or difficult.

Nurses who are aware of potential victimization in all patients will be aware of clues during physical assessment. Anxiety that seems more acute than would be expected during a routine physical assessment, embarrassment, fear, bruises in various stages of healing, rape, vague somatic complaints, multiple or recurrent sexually transmitted diseases, addiction, excessive concerns about fetal well-being, headaches, and weight loss are just a few of the symptoms, signs, and conditions that may occur.

Until society becomes liberated from patriarchal beliefs that result in a less-than-equal status for women and until all individuals become nonviolent and nonabusive, nurses need to be alert to the possibility of violence and abuse in the lives of every patient during every health encounter. Detection and appropriate treatment may be just as life-saving as effective cardiopulmonary resuscitation.

16

The Abuse Assessment Screen

A Clinical Instrument to Measure Frequency, Severity, and Perpetrator of Abuse Against Women

Karen L. Soeken
Judith McFarlane
Barbara Parker
Mary Carter Lominack

Physical and sexual abuse of women is at epidemic levels in America. An estimated 8-12 million women in the United States are at risk for abuse, meaning they will be abused by a current or former partner some time during their lives (Flitcraft, Hadley, Hendricks-Matthews, McLeer, & Warshaw, 1992). Studies conservatively indicate that each year 2 million women are assaulted by their partners, and national experts agree that the true incidence of battering of women is at least twice that figure (Suggs & Inui, 1992).

AUTHORS' NOTE: This study was supported by Grant R49/CCR603514-01 from the Division of Injury Epidemiology and Injury Control, Centers for Disease Control, Atlanta, Georgia.

Intentional injury is expensive. Following heart disease, injury is the leading cause of hospitalization (excluding childbirth deliveries). According to *Cost of Injury in the United States,* during 1987, 1 of 10 discharges and 1 of 12 days of care were injury related (Rice & MacKenzie, 1989). Frequently, the injury is abuse of women. Emergency department records document that 30% of women seen are victims of physical abuse (McLeer & Anwar, 1989b). In 1991, the Joint Commission on the Accreditation of Healthcare Organizations (JCAHO; 1992) called for standards for health care staff training on identification of and procedures for handling possible abuse victims.

To identify abused women, a clinical assessment instrument is required. This chapter presents the reliability and validity testing of the Abuse Assessment Screen (AAS), a clinical instrument developed to measure the frequency, severity, and perpetrator of abuse against women. A protocol for use of the AAS is discussed.

Method

The Nursing Research Consortium on Violence and Abuse designed the AAS (Parker & McFarlane, 1991). (See Figure 16.1.) The AAS consists of questions to determine the frequency, severity, perpetrator, and body site of injury that occur within a stated period of time. The AAS was developed for both pregnant and nonpregnant women with the pregnancy question (Item 3) to be included or deleted as needed. (If the woman is not pregnant, the body map and severity scale are moved to follow Question 2.) The AAS was developed on the premise that assessment for abuse must be straightforward and direct. Content validity was established for the five-question AAS with a panel of 12 nurse researchers of Anglo, African American, and Hispanic ethnicities working in the area of abuse of women.

To test the effectiveness of the AAS for identification of abuse during pregnancy, an ethnically stratified sample of 1,203 pregnant women in public prenatal clinics were asked the five-question screen. The AAS detected an abuse rate during pregnancy of 20.6% for teens and 14.2% for adult women (Parker, McFarlane, & Soeken, 1994). This prevalence rate was more than double all previous reports. Previous reports of abuse during pregnancy varied from 3% to 8% depending on the population surveyed and the number of questions asked (Amaro, Fried, Cabral, & Zuckerman, 1990; Berenson, Stiglich, Wilkinson, & Anderson, 1991; Campbell, Poland, Waller, & Ager, 1992; Helton, McFarlane, & Anderson, 1987; Hillard, 1985; Schei & Bakketeig, 1989).

This chapter reports on the reliability and criterion-related validity of the AAS. Because no total score is computed for the AAS, responses to individual items were compared with scores from other scales, namely, the Conflict Tactics Scale (CTS; Straus, 1979), Index of Spouse Abuse (ISA; Hudson & McIntosh, 1981), and the Danger Assessment (DA; Campbell, 1986) that have demonstrated

(Circle Yes or No for each question)

1. Have you *ever* been emotionally or physically abused by your partner or someone important to you?   Yes   No

2. *Within the last year,* have you been hit, slapped, kicked or otherwise physically hurt by someone?   Yes   No

    If Yes, by whom (circle all that apply)

        Husband   Ex-husband   Boyfriend   Stranger   Other   Multiple

        Total number of times _____

3. *Since you've been pregnant,* have you been hit, slapped, kicked or otherwise physically hurt by someone?   Yes   No

    If Yes, by whom (circle all that apply)

    Husband   Ex-husband   Boyfriend   Stranger   Other   Multiple

    Total number of times _____

    Mark the area of injury on the body map [Refer to Chapter 18 in this volume for diagram of body map]

    Score each incident according to the following scale: [If any of the descriptions for the higher number apply, use the higher number]

        1 = Threats of abuse including use of a weapon   Score _____

        2 = Slapping, pushing; no injuries and/or lasting pain   Score _____

        3 = Punching, kicking, bruises, cuts and/or continuing pain   Score _____

        4 = Beating up, severe contusions, burns, broken bones   Score _____

        5 = Head injury, internal injury, permanent injury   Score _____

        6 = Use of weapon; wound from weapon   Score _____

4. *Within the last year,* has anyone forced you to have sexual activities?   Yes   No

    If Yes, by whom (circle all that apply)

    Husband   Ex-husband   Boyfriend   Stranger   Other   Multiple

    Total number of times _____

5. Are you afraid of your partner or anyone you listed above?   Yes   No

Name of person completing form _____

Figure 16.1. Abuse Assessment Screen

reliability and validity and that have been used in research about violence within the family. For reliability purposes, a test-retest approach was used.

Sample

Data were extracted from a larger study of 1,203 women that examined the incidence and prevalence of abuse during pregnancy (Parker, McFarlane, Soeken, Torres, & Campbell, 1993). Of this number, 280 reported on the AAS during the first prenatal visit that they had been abused during the past year and/or since becoming pregnant. Abuse was defined as having been hit, slapped, kicked, or otherwise physically hurt by someone. For validity assessment, a random sample of 280 women not reporting abuse on the AAS was then selected as a comparison group. The resulting sample was 35.8% Afro American, 30.7% Hispanic, and 33.5% Caucasian. Almost all (95.3%) were below the poverty level and most (66.8%) were multips. There were no differences between the abuse groups on these three variables.

Criterion Measures

Three measures administered concurrently were used for validity analysis. Both the CTS (Straus, 1979) and the ISA (Hudson & McIntosh, 1981) were administered to all women. The DA (Campbell, 1986) was administered primarily to women reporting abuse on the AAS, although there was a subsample of nonabused women who also responded to the scale.

The CTS is a 19-item scale that measures the use of "reasoning, verbal aggression and violence" tactics to settle differences between spouses and partners within the past year. Items are weighted in accord with the frequencies indicated by the response categories presented to the respondent, and four frequencies weighted subscale scores are computed: Reasoning, Verbal Aggression, Minor Violence, and Severe Violence. Overall internal consistency reliability for this sample was $\alpha = .79$.

The ISA is a 30-item summated scale designed for use in clinical settings to assess the degree or severity of physical and nonphysical abuse. Prior to summation, items are weighted to reflect the severity of the abuse. The instructions specifically refer to the relationship with the partner, but give no time reference for the abuse. For this sample, internal consistency reliability of the ISA was $\alpha = .89$ for the Physical subscale and $\alpha = .93$ for the Nonphysical subscale.

The third measure, the DA, contains 14 dichotomous items and assesses the potential danger of homicide within the relationship with one's partner. No time reference is given in the instructions, although some items specifically refer to the past year. Internal consistency reliability for this sample was $\alpha = .84$.

Results

Reliability Assessment

Given the nature of the AAS, test-retest reliability was considered the most appropriate method of assessment. Of the original sample of 1,203 women, 48 were queried twice within the same trimester using the AAS. Agreement across the two times was 83%. Because it was possible that the abuse had occurred between the two assessments, a second sample of 40 women from another prenatal clinic was queried twice within the same trimester using the AAS. When asked about abuse within the year before becoming pregnant, the agreement was 97.5%. When asked about abuse since becoming pregnant, the responses of one woman did not agree. However, she indicated that the abuse had occurred between the two visits. Thus, the agreement was 100%.

Validity Assessment

A hypothesis-testing approach was used to assess the validity of the AAS. First, it was hypothesized that those reporting abuse on the AAS within the past year (Question 2) and/or since becoming pregnant (Question 3) would have higher scores on the DA, CTS, and ISA as compared to those not reporting abuse. Significant differences ($p < .001$) were found on the DA and the ISA and on all subscales of the CTS except for the Reasoning subscale (Table 16.1). In each instance, the mean score was higher for those reporting abuse. The lack of a significant difference between the abuse groups on Reasoning may reflect that the AAS defines abuse as physical (hit, slapped, kicked, or otherwise physically hurt). Also, use of Reasoning may have contributed to the absence of abuse.

A second hypothesis was that the severity of abuse during pregnancy as reported on the AAS would be positively related to scores on the DA, CTS, and ISA. Each incidence of abuse was scored for severity on the AAS on a scale from 1 (*threats of abuse including use of a weapon*) to 6 (*use of weapon; wound from weapon*), but only the most severe incident was assigned to each woman. The AAS also asks for the relationship with the perpetrator of the abuse. For this analysis, only those who reported they were abused by husband/ex-husband/ boyfriend were used so as to correspond with the reference to husband/ex-husband/partner on the other scales. Significant positive relationships ($p < .01$) were found with the DA ($r = .358$) and the ISA ($r = .355$ for Physical and $r = .297$ for Nonphysical). Those reporting a more severe episode of abuse on the AAS tended to report increased severity of abuse as measured by the ISA, increased use of conflict tactics, and increased danger of homicide. As expected, the relationship was stronger between the AAS and the ISA Physical subscale than between AAS and ISA Nonphysical subscale given that the severity of abuse on the AAS refers to physical abuse. When relationships to the CTS subscales were examined, only the Severe Violence subscale demonstrated a positive relationship ($r = .278$, $p < .01$) with severity of abuse as reported on the AAS. Perhaps this reflects the scoring of the AAS in that only the most severe episode was assigned to each woman.

It was also hypothesized that the frequency of abuse during the past year as reported on the AAS would correlate positively with scores on the DA, CTS, and ISA. Significant positive correlations were found with Verbal Aggression ($r =$

Table 16.1 Mean Scores on the Danger Assessment (DA), Conflict Tactics
Scale (CTS), and Index of Spouse Abuse (ISA) by Abuse Status

	Abuse Status		
Scale	Abused	Not Abused	t Value
DA	3.4	0.6	11.94*
CTS: Reason	16.5	14.6	1.21
CTS: Verbal Aggression	39.4	11.7	9.95*
CTS: Minor Violence	11.7	0.8	9.55*
CTS: Severe Violence	8.0	0.2	6.92*
ISA: Physical	16.9	2.3	11.59*
ISA: Nonphysical	25.1	6.6	12.08*

*$p < .001$.

.13), Minor Violence ($r = .26$), Severe Violence ($r = .37$), ISA Physical ($r = .29$),
ISA Nonphysical ($r = .20$), and DA ($r = .21$); the correlation with Reasoning was
not significant. Again, the correlation with the Physical subscale was stronger
than that with the Nonphysical subscale and the correlation with Severe Violence
was stronger than that with Minor Violence and Verbal Aggression.

The final analysis was based on a comparison of responses to Question 3 on
the AAS (Since you've been pregnant, have you been hit, slapped, kicked or
otherwise physically hurt by someone?) and one item on the DA (Have you ever
been beaten while you were pregnant?). Only primips were used for this analysis
so that the current pregnancy became the point of reference. Data were available
for 101 women on both the DA and AAS. Seventeen women responded yes on
the AAS and no on the DA. Although they indicated they were "physically hurt"
(the wording on the AAS), they may not have perceived themselves as having
been "beaten" (the wording on the DA). When the severity of abuse indicated by
these 17 were examined, only 1 indicated on the AAS that the most severe episode
was "beating up, severe contusions, burns, broken bones." The rest characterized
the severity as threats, slapping, punching, or kicking. Another 3 women responded no on the AAS and yes on the DA, an obvious inconsistency. Thus, only
4 women (4%) appear to have responded inconsistently to the AAS and the DA,
resulting in 96% agreement between the two measures.

Discussion

Violent and abusive behavior is a major threat to the physical, emotional,
social, and financial health of women in the United States. As noted in *Healthy
People 2000* (U.S. Department of Health and Human Services [DHHS], 1990),

"Child abuse, spouse abuse and other forms of family violence continue to threaten the health of thousands of American families." A national health objective for the year 2000 is for at least 90% of hospital emergency departments to have protocols for routinely identifying, treating, and referring victims of sexual assault and spouse abuse. *Setting the National Agenda for Injury Control in the 1990s* (DHHS, 1991b) also states the need to improve the identification and referral of high-risk individuals. A recent study of California emergency departments revealed that most nurses and doctors receive no training on the identification and treatment of battered adults. As a result, abused women seeking health care in emergency departments are not identified (McLoughlin, Lee, Letellier, & Salber, 1993).

Homicides between intimates are often preceded by a history of physical and emotional abuse directed at the woman; prevention of homicide is directly linked to the prevention of abuse of women (Browne, 1987). Dannenberg (personal communication, 1994) reviewed medical examiner records of 2,351 women aged 15-44 in New York City and found homicide to be the largest single cause of injury-related death among pregnant and nonpregnant women, with the proportion of deaths due to homicide higher for pregnant women. A related study in Cook County, Illinois found homicide to be the leading cause of injury death for pregnant women (Fildes, Reed, Jones, Martin, & Barrett, 1992). The importance of interviewing to assess for abuse has been discussed in a related article where approximately 8% of women self-reported abuse on a standard medical history intake form, but when asked the same abuse assessment questions by a health care provider, 29% of the women reported abuse (McFarlane, Christoffel, Bateman, Miller, & Bullock, 1991).

Healthy People 2000 (DHHS, 1990) notes that families living in poverty are particularly vulnerable to violence. The document calls for preventive interventions directed toward all persons living in poverty. The objectives also call for a reduction in physical abuse directed at women by male partners and notes that many women are battered by their partners during pregnancy.

In 1985, the *Surgeon General's Workshop on Violence and Public Health* (U.S. Surgeon General, 1985) recommended:

> Questions concerning possible spouse abuse should be included on prenatal history forms and be routinely asked during medical, nursing, and social work assessment of pregnant women. A physically or sexually abused pregnant woman should be identified as having a high-risk pregnancy and be eligible for high-risk prenatal care.

Once identified, it is essential the abused woman be offered education, advocacy, and community referral information. Recommended strategies for intervening for abuse during pregnancy have been developed (McFarlane & Parker, 1994a, 1994b).

Conclusion

Before violence and abuse of women can be interrupted and interventions applied, identification is required. For population surveillance, a reliable and valid straightforward instrument is essential. The AAS has been tested on an ethnically stratified cohort of women and found effective in detection of abuse. A protocol for clinical use of the AAS is presented in Figure 16.2. To protect the health and safety of women and prevent trauma and disability, routine clinical use of the AAS is recommended for all women.

---

1. *Provide a private and confidential setting for assessment.*
   a. Assess all women for abuse apart from the male partner and any children. (Children as young as two years may report back to the male partner or family members that mother discussed the abuse.)
   b. Assure confidentiality by telling the woman that the information she provides will not be shared with other family members or her male partner.

NOTE: Some states have mandatory reporting for spouse abuse. If your state has such a law, find out how the institution informs women of the law and specifics about the reporting procedure. In a state without a mandatory reporting law, assure the woman that the abuse will not be reported to the police unless she wants it reported. Your offer to report the abuse to the police could be a useful option for the woman if it is a seriously abusive situation. A health care provider calling the police may both increase her credibility with law enforcement and take the responsibility of reporting away from her. However, a report to law enforcement may increase her danger from the abuser. The pros and cons of reporting must be carefully discussed with the woman. (In some states, regardless of age, pregnant women receiving health care are emancipated and not subject to abuse reporting laws for minors. The provider needs to know the criteria for emancipation in her state.)

2. *Tell each woman that all women are assessed for abuse.*
   Approach the topic of abuse assessment as done when assessing for other health risks.

3. *Read the Abuse Assessment questions to the woman.*
   Research has demonstrated the importance of direct, face-to-face assessment for abuse. Since there is great reluctance to add questions to the medical record, providers and administrators may decide to have women self-report abuse.

   When self-report for abuse was measured against primary provider assessment, 8% of women self-reported abuse on a standard medical history intake form.

Figure 16.2. A Protocol for Use of the Abuse Assessment Screen

When asked the same abuse assessment questions by a health care provider as part of a regular oral history, 29% of the women report abuse (McFarlane, Christoffel, Bateman, Miller, & Bullock, 1991).

4. Record the abuse.

If the woman reports abuse, hand the pencil or pen to the woman and ask her to mark the areas of abuse on the body map.

Together score each abuse incident using the 6-point scale.

Maintain eye contact when assessing women for abuse and always thank the woman for sharing the information.

If the woman hesitates when asked to answer "yes" or "no" to abuse, offer the option of "sometimes." The word "sometimes" offers the woman an opportunity to answer affirmatively but without the absoluteness of the word "yes."

5. *Respect the woman's response.*

The woman will choose when and with whom she will share her history of abuse. Being accepting of a negative response (even if you feel the woman is abused) conveys respect for her response and builds trust. Abused women have been controlled by their male partner, and your respect for her negative response may be one of the few choices she has without fear of retribution.

6. *Documentation.*

If no history or threat of abuse exists as recorded on the AAS, make a statement of no abuse, note any community resources, phone numbers, and educational materials offered. If positive for abuse, record the frequency and severity of present and past abuse. Describe location and extent of injuries, including pain reported and any disability days from work due to the assault. Describe any treatments and interventions provided including handouts, educational materials, and phone numbers for shelter and police. For each abused woman, note that a plan of escape was discussed and if shelter assistance was declined at this time *or* if shelter should be or was contacted per client's request. Specify any potential long-term damage or need for follow-up. Record all follow-up care such as X-rays, surgery, consultations, and referrals. When describing the abuse, use direct quotes from the woman as much as possible. If physical evidence of abuse remains, including scars, bruises, or cuts, seek written permission to photograph the injuries and document any refusals. Include the name, position, and agency for each referral made.

7. *Intervention.*

Assessing for abuse carries the responsibility for intervention following a positive response. At a minimum, all agencies should have referral sources available as well as information on available legal and criminal options. Intervention protocols that include safety assessment, legal, shelter, and social services referral have been described (McFarlane & Parker, 1994a, 1994b).

Figure 16.2. Continued

17

Assessing Physical and Nonphysical Abuse Against Women in a Hospital Setting

Deborah Page-Adams
Susan Dersch

In response to the obvious threats posed by abuse to women's health and well-being, numerous studies have been undertaken in various health care settings including family practice and outpatient services (Hamberger, Saunders, & Hovey, 1992; Rath, Jarratt, & Leonardson, 1989), chronic pain clinics (Haber, 1985), and emergency departments (Goldberg & Tomlanovich, 1984; McLeer & Anwar, 1989b; Stark, Flitcraft, & Frazier, 1979; Tilden & Shepard, 1987b). There has also been previous research on abuse against women seeking health care services during pregnancy (Helton, McFarlane, & Anderson, 1987; Hillard, 1985; McFarlane, Parker, Soeken, & Bullock, 1992; Parker, 1993; see also Chapters 7-10 in this volume), as well as research addressing abuse against women receiving psychiatric and chemical dependency services (Bergman, Larsson, Brismar, & Klang, 1989; Herman, 1986; Mills, Rieker, & Carmen, 1984).

Research in health care settings has been helpful in documenting abuse against women patients (see Chapter 1 for a review). However, previous studies have been limited to women seeking services in the types of specialized settings described above. Much of the earlier research has also been based on nonrandom samples. Furthermore, most earlier studies in health care settings have focused exclusively on physical abuse. Information about nonphysical abuse in the lives of female patients is essential in building our knowledge base about the complex patterns of coercive control, stress, social isolation, and feelings of entrapment experienced by women who are physically abused and at risk for such abuse (Stark, 1994). This chapter describes a random sample study of physical and nonphysical abuse by intimate partners of women who were patients in a general hospital setting.

Description of the Study

This study was conducted in March 1994 in a large, metropolitan hospital in the Midwest serving a socioeconomically and racially diverse population. The authors were interested in helping to establish hospital-based services for victims of domestic violence. Key hospital administrators were supportive of the idea, but wanted to know how many women in their own patient population were abused. This information was seen as being vital for program planning purposes and for resource development to fund the program. The authors worked with both nursing and social work departments to plan a random sample study assessing abuse against women patients by their intimate partners.

To be included in the study, women had to be 18 years of age or older and in satisfactory condition on their admission to the hospital. Physicians had to give consent for their patients to participate. During the data collection period, the hospital's medical records department generated lists of women admitted each day who met these eligibility criteria. Using a table of random numbers, the authors selected 149 women for initial visits.

During the initial visits, women were excluded from participating in the study if they suffered from dementia (16) or did not speak and read English (1). Of the 132 women who met all of the eligibility criteria, 1 woman died and 8 women were discharged before they could be asked to participate. Another 8 women refused to participate. This resulted in a sample of 115 women, or 87% of those patients who were eligible to participate. The patients in our sample were a diverse group of women. Demographic characteristics of the sample are in Table 17.1.

Procedures and Measures

Each selected patient was visited in her room, given a brief description of the study, and invited to participate. Women were assured of the confidential nature of the study and written consent was obtained. In addition, emotional support was available through the social work department for women who

Table 17.1 Demographic Characteristics of the Total Sample of Women
              Patients ($N = 115$)

Characteristic	n	Percentage
Age[a]		
19-29 years	16	13.9
30-39 years	21	18.3
40-49 years	14	12.2
50-59 years	23	20.0
60-69 years	23	20.0
70-79 years	15	13.0
80+ years	3	2.6
Race		
White	62	53.9
African American	53	46.1
Marital status		
Single	24	20.9
Married	48	41.7
Separated/divorced	23	20.0
Widowed	20	17.4
Relationship status		
Has intimate partner	77	67.0
No intimate partner	38	33.0
Employment status[b]		
Employed	40	35.4
Not employed	73	64.6
Home ownership[c]		
Owns home	62	57.4
Does not own home	46	42.6
Number of children		
None	64	55.7
1-2	38	33.0
3 or more	13	11.3

NOTES:
a. Mean age = 50.91 years; SD = 17.21; range = 19-82.
b. Two respondents did not answer the employment question.
c. Seven respondents did not answer the homeownership question.

experienced distress as a result of participating in the research. None of the
participants requested such support.

  Self-administered questionnaire packets that included the Index of Spouse
Abuse (ISA: Hudson & McIntosh, 1981), the Abuse Assessment Screen (AAS;

Parker & McFarlane, 1991), and demographic questions were given to the women. The ISA is a 30-item, self-report instrument that measures the presence and the severity of physical (ISA-P) and nonphysical (ISA-NP) abuse by male partners as perceived by female respondents. The ISA was used to assess physical and nonphysical abuse against the women by their current partners. The AAS was used to measure abuse against the women by former partners. The AAS includes four items designed to help clinicians assess the presence of physical, nonphysical, and sexual abuse as well as a woman's fear of her partner or former partner (see Chapter 16).

Abuse Against Women by Current and Former Partners

Six women (5.2%) had been physically abused by their current partners as indicated by scores of 10 or more on the ISA-P. This is the score that Hudson and McIntosh (1981) recommend using as a clinical cutting score for physical abuse. In addition, 29 women (25.2%) had lower ISA-P scores but were considered to be at risk because their current partners had used at least one behavior indicative of physical abuse against them. Altogether, 35 of the 115 women (30.4%) had either been physically abused by their current partners or were considered to be at risk for physical abuse.

The median ISA-P score was 2.75 for the 35 women in our sample who reported any indicators of physical abuse. Most of the women with scores near the median had been punched with a fist by their partners. Women with ISA-P scores near the mean (6.46) typically reported that their partners had used three or four different behaviors indicative of physical abuse.

The percentages of women with current partners who reported each of the indicators of physical abuse are detailed in Figure 17.1. More than 10% of the women with current partners reported abuse in the context of their partners' drinking. Nine percent reported that their partners frightened them. More than 6% of the women said that their partners had made them perform sex acts that they did not enjoy or like. Six percent also reported that their partners had acted as though they would like to kill them, and one woman had been threatened with a weapon. Another woman reported that her partner had punched her with his fists, slapped her around the head and face, made her perform sex acts, became abusive when he drank, and acted as though he would like to kill her. Her score was *not* the highest ISA-P score in the study.

None of the abused or at-risk women reported injury as the primary reason for hospitalization. About three fourths of these 35 women gave one of five reasons for their hospitalizations: childbirth or pregnancy related (8), cancer (6), depression (5), surgery (4), and heart problems (3). These reasons for hospitalization paralleled the top five reasons given by women who reported no indicators of abuse.

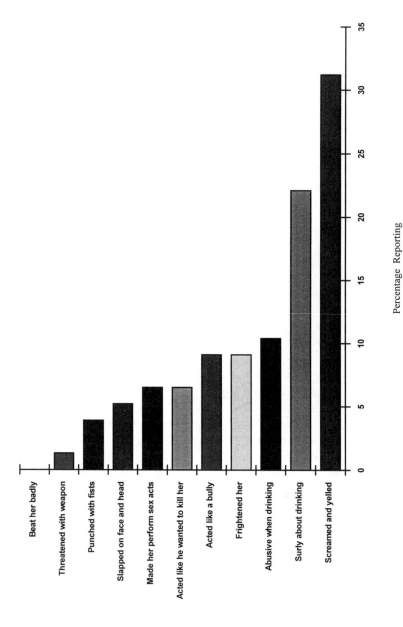

Figure 17.1. Percentage of Women With Current Partners Reporting Behaviors Indicative of Physical Abuse ($n = 77$)

Thirty of the 35 women who reported indicators of physical abuse by current partners also reported indicators of nonphysical abuse. In addition, 13 women (11.3%) reported no indicators of physical abuse but at least one indicator of nonphysical abuse by current partners. The percentage of women reporting each of the indicators of nonphysical abuse by current partners is detailed in Figure 17.2

Typically, women who reported indicators of nonphysical abuse had partners who belittled them, treated them like servants, became angry if the women disagreed with their point of view, and were stingy in providing enough money to run their homes. The woman in our sample who reported the highest level of nonphysical abuse, but no physical abuse, from her current partner had experienced all of these behaviors. In addition, she reported that her partner had used four other behaviors indicative of nonphysical abuse against her, including demanding sex whether she wanted it or not.

In addition to assessing abuse against women by current partners, we used the AAS to ask women about abuse by former partners. Twenty-two of the 115 women in our sample (19.1%) reported that they had been physically or non-physically abused in the context of an intimate adult relationship. Six of these women further specified that the abuse they had suffered at the hands of former partners had been physical in nature. For some of these women, the abuse was neither long ago nor far away. In fact, three of the women had been physically hurt or sexually assaulted by a former partner within the past year. Four of the women reported that they were still afraid of their former partners at the time of the study.

To summarize, 6 of the 115 women in our sample (5.2%) had been physically abused by their current partners as evidenced by high scores on the ISA-P. An additional 29 women (25.2%) had lower scores on the ISA-P but were considered at risk because their current partners had used at least one behavior indicative of physical abuse against them. Another 13 women (11.3%) reported that their current partners had not been physically abusive but had used at least one behavior indicative of nonphysical abuse against them. Turning to abuse in the context of previous relationships, 22 women (19.1%) had been physically or nonphysically abused by former partners. Of the 115 women in our sample, 45 (39.1%) reported no physical or nonphysical abuse in any intimate adult relationship. These findings are presented in Figure 17.3.

Demographic Differences

In addition to assessing abuse, we explored demographic differences between women who reported indicators of physical abuse in any adult relationship and those who did not. The major finding from these analyses was that women who reported indicators of physical abuse differed very little in terms of demo-

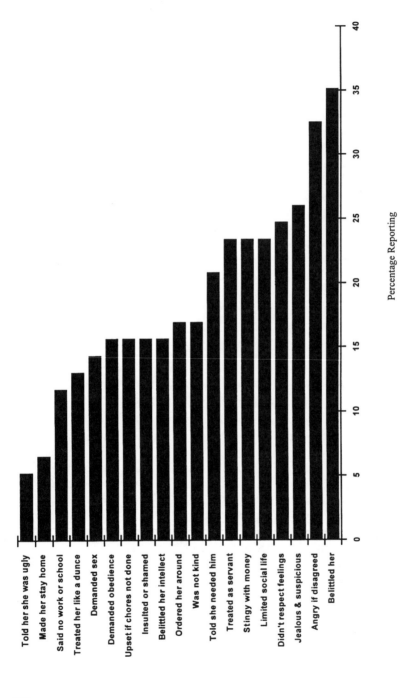

Figure 17.2. Percentage of Women With Current Partners Reporting Behaviors Indicative of Nonphysical Abuse (*n* = 77)

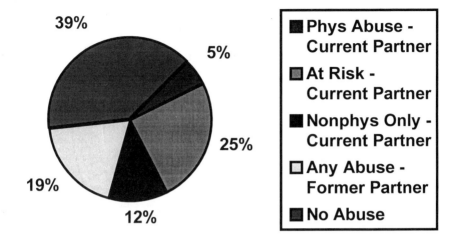

Figure 17.3. Approximate Percentage of Women in Total Sample Reporting Physical and Nonphysical Abuse (*N* = 115)

graphics from those who reported no indication of physical abuse. There were no statistically significant age, race, employment, or homeownership differences between the two groups of women. In addition, there were no significant differences in terms of either the presence of children or the number of children in the women's households.

In fact, the only statistically significant demographic differences between women who reported indicators of physical abuse in any intimate adult relationship and those who did not involved marital and relationship status. Married women were significantly more likely than nonmarried women to report such abuse (χ^2 = 5.4, *df* = 1, *p* < .05). Indicators of physical abuse in any adult relationship were significantly less likely to be reported by women who were widowed (χ^2 = 9.9, *df* = 1, *p* < .01). Women in our sample who had a current intimate partner were significantly more likely than other women to have been physically abused in the context of an intimate adult relationship (χ^2 = 12.5, *df* = 1, *p* < .001).

Discussion and Implications

The main purposes of this study were to (a) assess physical and nonphysical abuse by intimate partners against randomly selected women patients in a general hospital setting, and (b) explore demographic differences between women who reported indicators of physical abuse and those who did not. Our findings indicate that 30.4% of the 115 women in our sample had experienced at least one behavior indicative of physical abuse by their current partners. This rate is consistent with the findings of researchers who have studied physical abuse among women in specialized health care settings, often using nonrandom samples. The primary implication of this consistency is that the high rates of physical abuse against female patients reported on the basis of earlier studies are not likely to be mere artifacts of either sampling strategies or setting limitations.

In this study, we also found the experience of nonphysical abuse to be quite common among the women in our sample. Women who reported indicators of physical abuse by a current partner almost always reported indicators of nonphysical abuse as well. In addition, 11.3% of women reported indicators of nonphysical abuse in the absence of physical abuse by their current partners. Typically, patterns of nonphysical abuse involved several different behaviors by partners that are likely to lead to stress, social isolation, and low self-esteem for women.

Assessing for abuse with questions that ask about a broad range of nonphysical as well as physical behaviors may be a particularly useful approach for health care providers. As Stark (1994) notes, there are many health and mental health consequences that are associated with patterns of coercive control in abusive relationships.

An exclusive focus on physical violence or, worse yet, on severe physical violence may lead to identification of only the most seriously abused women in a patient population. By way of example, if we had considered only the women in this study who had IDA-P scores of 10 or more, we would have identified only those women needing remedial services. Such a focus unnecessarily limits the prevention and early intervention efforts of health care providers.

Our findings regarding minimal demographic differences between women who reported physical abuse in any adult relationship and those who did not are consistent with earlier health care setting studies of woman abuse (Helton et al., 1987; Saunders, Hamberger, & Hovey, 1993). We did find some marital status and relationship status differences between the two groups of women. Married women were more likely than nonmarried women to report such abuse. Women who had current intimate partners were more likely than women who were not partnered to report abuse. Most likely, these marital and relationship status differences simply reflect the fact that having had at least one intimate partner is a necessary condition for having experienced abuse in the context of an intimate relationship.

We also found that widows were significantly less likely than women who had not been widowed to report physical abuse in any adult relationship. This is somewhat unexpected given the minimal change in national marital violence rates over time (Straus & Gelles, 1986). Saunders and his colleagues (1993), who found that older women reported low lifetime victimization rates, suggested that women may suppress memories of abuse as they age. Because of the high correlation between age and widowhood, this suggestion may help to explain our findings. It is also possible that women who have been widowed are reluctant to "speak ill of the dead."

Both our finding of high rates of physical and nonphysical abuse and our finding of minimal differences between women who reported physical abuse and those who did not have important practical implications for health care providers. In addition, none of the women reported injury as a primary reason for hospitalization. These findings suggest that many women receiving health care services are abused, have a history of abuse, or are at risk for abuse and that health care providers are unlikely to be able to identify these women unless they ask.

The Joint Commission on the Accreditation of Healthcare Organizations (JCAHO; 1992) has guidelines requiring routine abuse assessment in emergency and ambulatory care settings. Health care providers working to implement such guidelines may be encouraged by our low refusal rate and our experience with participants' reactions to the study. Very few women declined to answer questions about abuse by intimate adult partners. Furthermore, none of the women requested emotional support because of distress as a result of their participation. Several participants thanked us for focusing on abuse in this study. With adequate attention to the sensitive nature of such assessment, our experience suggests that women are open to being asked about abuse by health care providers. For many women, being asked about abuse may not cause as much distress as being abused and having no one ask.

18

Domestic Violence

A Practical Guide to the Use of Forensic Evaluation in Clinical Examination and Documentation of Injuries

Diane M. Brockmeyer
Daniel J. Sheridan

Health care providers are often among the first people outside of a violent home to recognize and assist survivors of adult intimate partner abuse. At least 4 million women are physically assaulted by their male partner each year (Novella, 1992). In addition, thousands of men are battered by women and unknown numbers of gays and lesbians are abused by their intimate partners.

Although there are increasing efforts to train health professionals in the identification, treatment, and referral of battered patients (Campbell & Sheridan, 1989; Chiodo, Tilden, Limandri, & Schmidt, 1994; Flitcraft, Hadley, Hendricks-Matthews, McLeer, & Warshaw, 1992; McLeer, Anwar, Herman, & Maquiling, 1989; Sassetti, 1993), there has been only limited recognition of the health provider's opportunity to provide clinical forensic examination and documentation to survivors of family violence.

This chapter discusses the science of clinical forensics (forensic means simply "medicine pertaining to the law"). We include a detailed description of how to assess and document physical findings in patients with known or suspected assaultive injuries. Focused history taking, danger assessment, and photographic documentation are discussed.

The techniques described here can be critical in delivering comprehensive medical care; in addition, they can play a crucial role by providing a powerful tool in legal and court proceedings (i.e., restraining/protective orders and criminal prosecutions) that may help break cycles of violent behavior (Lynch, 1991; Sheridan, 1993, 1996).

Forensics

The science of forensic pathology (forensics of the dead) has been growing for over 100 years. With the recognition of the battered child syndrome (Kempe et al., 1962), forensic principles began to be applied to investigating injuries in child abuse survivors. In the early 1970s, women's advocates demonstrated to the medical-legal community the inconsistencies in the evaluation and evidence-gathering practices in the treatment of rape survivors. In response, sexual assault treatment protocols for emergency departments were developed and are now in common use throughout the country (Ledray, 1992a, 1992b, 1993; Young, Bracken, Goddard, & Matheson, 1992). These protocols include systematized use of evidence collection kits designed to increase the ability of medical exams to provide evidence that can aid in the prosecution of sexual assault perpetrators.

The authors advocate that the principles and techniques of clinical forensics (written history of the assault; findings of the injuries on physical exam; assessment of the pattern, age, and type of injuries; photographic documentation; and evidence preservation) be routinely applied to diagnosing and documenting all episodes or histories of domestic violence revealed to or suspected by the health care provider.

Currently, in many cases where intimate partner abuse has occurred and is known, the diagnosis and history are omitted from the medical record (Bergman & Brismar, 1990). Clear and detailed description of the specifics of the assault, the history of violence, and the pattern of injuries are of tremendous clinical value. Knowledge of the details of the attack guides diagnosis and treatment, and may be important in detecting seemingly unrelated direct medical sequelae months later (Thomas & Lowitt, 1995). Thorough documentation makes it more likely that the problem of domestic violence, often chronic, is called to the attention of future medical providers. The medical and psychiatric sequelae of assault and abuse are myriad (Berrios & Grady, 1991; Plichta, 1992; Rapkin, Kames, Darke, Stampler, & Naliboff, 1990; Schei, Samuelsen, & Bakketeig, 1991); many injuries might be diagnosed earlier or even prevented if health care personnel routinely assessed for abuse and included adequate documentation in the medical record.

In addition to the medical benefits of documenting domestic violence, clear records, including photographs of visible injuries, may greatly assist the patient in future judicial and/or legal proceedings. In many cases, legal or criminal consequences of abusive behavior may be the only effective deterrent. Except in those states that require health professionals to contact police in cases of domestic assault (i.e., California and Kentucky), the patient must be the one to make any decision regarding filing a complaint with the police or obtaining court protection.

Detailed documentation of injuries can make obtaining a restraining/ protective order much easier. If criminal charges are filed, a clearly written, legible, near verbatim history of the patient's account of the violence, if consistent with well-documented injuries, can considerably strengthen prosecution's case and help the patient to obtain adequate protection from further abuse. Even if the patient chooses not to use the legal system at the time of the assault, a careful and comprehensive medical record may be invaluable at a later date. Such a record may support the patient in leaving safely when finally ready to do so; in less fortunate cases, it may also be useful in future serious assault and even murder trials. This type of documentation is a strong step in holding batterers accountable for their abusive and criminal behavior.

History and Documentation

A written history of an assault should begin with a basic description of the events of the attack. Who does the patient name as the attacker? What happened? Exactly how many blows were there, and to what areas of the body? Were any objects or weapons used? Did the attacker use an open hand or a closed fist? If kicked, was the attacker wearing steel-toed boots or tennis shoes? Were any threats made? When and where did the attack occur? Were there any witnesses? Were the children, if any, near? Were they threatened or hurt? Was there also a sexual assault?

This type of assessment and documentation of the answers is much more useful medically and legally than the common, shorter descriptions most often found in current medical records (e.g., "patient struck multiple times to torso with baseball bat" or "patient with multiple facial trauma, struck to face by known assailant"). Patients are often afraid of further abuse and may be very embarrassed and reluctant to divulge to health providers the full extent of the attacks. The health provider must ask specifically and directly about exactly what happened, as this makes it much easier to provide appropriate medical care.

The patient's report of the abuse should always be documented specifically in the medical record. Statements made "in the course of receiving medical care" have been viewed by the courts as evidence rather than hearsay, as the U.S. Supreme Court reaffirmed in 1992 (*White v. Illinois,* 1992). In addition, a statement made in a "moment of excitement" carries more weight legally than a similar statement made in a courtroom. Police investigators often refer to such spontaneous statements as "excited utterances." Moreover, statements made in the course of procuring medical services are often deemed to carry "special guarantees of credibility" in the eyes of the court. These evidentiary rules make medical documentation of abuse, especially when corroborated by physical findings, quite valuable in a related, subsequent court proceeding.

Unfortunately, in practice, intimate partner abuse reported to health care providers is grossly underdocumented, or worse, not even mentioned as abuse in the medical record. Sometimes, what the health care provider writes contains pejorative (biased) statements. It is critical to avoid writing phrases such as "patient refuses to talk with the police or call the shelter," "patient is noncompliant with treatment plan of being admitted to the hospital," or "patient allegedly was beaten by her boyfriend." Instead, words such as *chooses, declines,* and *patient states or said* are nonpejorative, nonbiased descriptors of patient behavior. Jurors may interpret the word *alleged* to mean that the person was being less then truthful (Sheridan, 1996); simply describing what the patient reports is more direct and less potentially damaging. An assessment of the concordance (or discordance) of the history with the injuries should be included in the record. Details on analyzing injuries are presented below. Table 18.1 contains a sample of typical inappropriate charting and an example of forensically sound medical documentation.

In the event of a subsequent criminal prosecution, the health care provider is often subpoenaed to testify in person about events that occurred months or years prior. Comprehensive, nonbiased written and photographic documentation make such testimony much more reliable, credible, and valuable. In fact, it has been our experience that comprehensive documentation of domestic abuse in the medical record increases the likelihood that the medical record can be introduced as evidence. This may actually decrease the likelihood that the provider would need to appear in court personally.

Danger Assessment

It is important to obtain a history of the seriousness of the violence in the relationship, with the goal of assessing the immediate and future safety of the patient (Campbell, 1995). The questions in the Danger Assessment have been demonstrated to correlate with increased risk for severe or potentially lethal violence. (Please refer to Chapter 8, Figure 8.1, for the Danger Assessment.)

Clinical Forensic Physical Examination

In assessing and documenting any injury for clinical forensic purposes, it is important to evaluate three features of the wound: pattern, age, and the presence of any foreign material. The pattern of an injury is its shape, size, texture, and

Table 18.1 Sample Progress Notes

Inappropriate Documentation:

22 y/o white female allegedly assaulted by boyfriend. Positive ETOH (alcohol) on breath. Multiple, superficial lacerations and abrasions to head, superficial injuries to extremities. Wounds cleansed and bandaged. Refuses to talk to police or shelters. Visibly upset and angry. Disruptive to unit. Social worker called.

Recommended Documentation:

Patient arrived to clinic ambulatory at approximately 5 p.m. States that while driving to the store around 9 p.m. yesterday (12-21-96) her boyfriend, Ron Schumann (DOB 2-16-72), "beat me up really bad. He said he was going to kill me. He wouldn't let me out of the car for hours." States Mr. Schumann was driving and was mad at her for forgetting to bring an umbrella with them. She said that Mr. Schumann punched her about 6 or 7 times to her left upper arm, two or three times to her left face and head, then slammed her head into the passenger side window while threatening to drive the car off the road. She stated, "Ron was acting crazy. He kept saying that if I ever tried to leave him he'd kill me and bury me where nobody would ever find the body." Patient states that around midnight "he stopped for cigarettes at a gas station and when he went to the bathroom, I jumped out and hid in some bushes until he got tired of looking for me." She reports there was no loss of consciousness, and no sexual assault.

Patient reports a two-year, progressively more physically and emotionally violent and controlling relationship with Mr. Schumann. Reports about five violent episodes during the past two months, each accompanied by accusations of infidelity and death threats. Denies any abuse to her two year old son who was with maternal grandmother last night and today. States she had a few mixed drinks prior to coming to clinic.

Objective:

General: Tearful woman, alert and oriented.

HEENT: Pupils equal, round, and reactive to light. Fundi normal, without hemorrhage or papilledema. Four shallow, curved lacerations above right ear, each about 4 cm long. Tender, slightly swollen area to right temple area above the hairline. Left face and jaw slightly swollen and painful on palpation. No bony step-offs. Tympanic membranes intact bilaterally. No otorrhea, no clear rhinorrhea, and no septal hematoma. No Battle's sign.

Neck: Full range of motion, without evidence of injury.

CV: Regular rate and rhythm, no murmurs.

Lung clear to auscultation bilaterally.

Abdomen: Soft, non-tender. Liver and spleen non-palpable. No external evidence of injury.

Extremities: Left deltoid region markedly swollen and tender, with two circular bluish-red circular punch-like contusions 5 cm × 6 cm. Left ulnar area with three smaller, punch-like, circular, red contusions 2 cm × 2 cm. Full range of motion without pain to wrists, elbows, and shoulders.

Neuro: Cranial nerves 2-12 grossly intact. Motor: 5/5 strength in all extremities. DTRs 2+ throughout. Sensory grossly intact. Gait normal. Finger to nose intact.

Left forearm series: no fractures.

Assessment:

Patient's injuries are consistent with history given. The left arm trauma is consistent with punch and defensive posturing. The left face and jaw injuries are consistent with punch blunt trauma. The

Table 18.1 Continued

---

right head lacerations and swelling are consistent with blunt force trauma of history of being forcibly pushed into passenger door/window area of car.

Per her history, patient is involved in a progressively worsening abusive intimate relationship. She is verbalizing significant fear of further abuse and is choosing to not talk with police until she picks up her baby from grandmother's care.

Plan:

Lacerations too superficial for suturing; cleaned and bandaged. Told to return if she develops confusion, lethargy, worsening headache, nausea, or vomiting.

Patient is not sure where Mr. Schumann is at present. She does not want to see him if he shows up in treatment area. Hospital security notified and given following description—24 y/o white male, (DOB—2-16-72) 5′ 10″, 160 lbs, thin-framed, wears glasses, medium length, blond curly hair, usually wears jeans, gym shoes, dress shirt and a navy blue rain coat. Per history normally does not carry a weapon. Social services with patient now completing Danger Assessment form. Nursing staff to photograph injuries. Will discharge to grandmother's after safety planning and clearance by social service. Police notification deferred until patient has baby in her possession. Women's hotline and shelter services referral card given. Follow up in clinic in 48 hours or prn. Tylenol for pain, prn.

---

any other features that might indicate the mechanism of injury. Several patterns seen in common domestic violence injuries are discussed below. For injuries with an obvious pattern, photographs are critical.

The age of an injury may be grossly estimated from its appearance, but is usually difficult to pinpoint with accuracy. There is such variation in healing time between individuals that it is impossible, even for experts in forensics, to accurately date wounds (Langlois & Gresham, 1991; Wilson, 1977). It is best simply to describe features that are indicative of age (color of contusion, scab present or absent, infection present or absent, etc.). An assessment can be made as to approximate age (acute, recent, healed), and this should be described as either consistent or inconsistent with the history given. In addition, it is possible to assess relative ages of multiple injuries seen in the same individual, that is, a "pattern of injuries" inflicted over time. This can be used to substantiate that a patient has suffered repeated assaults over time.

Finally, it is necessary to look for foreign material (trace evidence) in and around injuries. Splinters of wood in a laceration or gravel and dirt in an abrasion should be described and, if possible, saved as evidence. Such small items can be invaluable, legally, in substantiating the details of an assault. Labeled specimen jars may be used to save this evidence, or sexual assault kits themselves may be used to collect evidence. Torn, cut, or bloodied clothing should be air-dried and saved in a paper, not plastic, bag. This bag should be stapled closed and labeled with the patient's name. All evidence should be stored in a locked location until it can be picked up by police. Guidelines published by the Joint Commission on the Accreditation of Healthcare Organizations (JCAHO) stipulate that hospitals and clinics have a protocol in place for maintaining a "chain of evidence."

Accidental Versus Intentional Injuries

It is common for adults assaulted by partners or family members to attribute their injuries to some accidental cause. Many patients, out of embarrassment or fear, will give an explanation such as bumping into something or falling. It is critical that the clinician be able to assess the likelihood that the proposed mechanism caused the patient's injuries. Intentional trauma can often be distinguished from accidental trauma by analyzing the location and type of wounds.

Accidental trauma tends to be peripheral, involving the extremities and bony prominences. Elbows, knees, hands, and feet are commonly involved. For example, if a patient has fallen, there are frequently abrasions to the palms. Accidental head trauma is often to the occiput, forehead, or chin, as these surfaces are easily injured by bumping into objects or by falling (Campbell & Sheridan, 1989; Sheridan, 1993, 1996).

Intentionally inflicted trauma is more often proximal trauma, with injuries to the upper arms, head (especially face), neck, thorax, abdomen, back, upper lateral and medial thighs, and to the rectal and perineal regions. While accidents tend to injure one area or side of the body, assaults often result in multiple injuries involving more than one plane of the body. Sexual areas may be targeted, and purposeful attacks are sometimes carried out in such a way that the injuries can be hidden by clothing. Delay in seeking treatment often occurs (Campbell & Sheridan, 1989; Sheridan, 1993, 1996), because the controlling and abusive partner is frequently unwilling to allow the abused person to contact medical help or anyone else following the attack.

Types of Injuries

A classification of common visible injuries is given below. For more detail, refer to a textbook of forensic medicine (DiMaio & DiMaio, 1989; Gordon, Shapiro, & Berson, 1988), or contact the local medical examiner.

Abrasions. An abrasion is a superficial scraping injury of the epidermis caused by friction against an object or surface. These typically form scabs and heal without scarring within about 2 weeks. Common abrasions seen in intimate abuse are fingernail scratches, abrasions seen at the margins of blunt-impact injuries, and linear abrasions caused when the person is pushed against or dragged along a rough surface. Length, shape, and pattern of an abrasion should be noted. Fingernail scratches are commonly multiple parallel abrasions, often on the neck or arms. If a patient describes scratching the assailant during the assault, fingernail scrapings may be obtained as evidence, just as they are routinely in sexual assault examinations. A distinctive circular, semicircular, or horseshoe-shaped abrasion can be seen in the middle of a larger area of bruising in cases where the patient has been punched by someone wearing a raised ring that has a stone setting.

Contusions. A contusion, bruise, or ecchymosis is a region of soft tissue hemorrhage due to blunt impact or trauma caused by sustained pressure. Size, shape, and color should be noted. Healing times between individuals vary enough to make accurate dating of bruises by color almost impossible, even for experts (Langlois & Gresham, 1991; Wilson, 1977). As noted above, however, if there are multiple bruises on the same individual, an assessment can be made as to their relative ages. Thus, if the patient has multiple contusions of distinctly different colors, it may be possible to say that a patient was probably assaulted on multiple occasions. This finding may help confirm the history given, even if the specific dates of injury cannot be determined with accuracy.

Typical patterned contusions seen in domestic abuse are the following:

1. Fingertip pressure bruises: These are usually about the size of a dime, nickel, or penny. They are commonly seen on the upper arms in the case of grabbing and shaking injuries, on the neck in the case of choking, and to the medial thighs in the case of forced sex.
2. Punch injuries: These are usually round to oval, and are somewhat larger than the area of impact, because there is spreading of the extravasated blood to surrounding soft tissues. Punch injuries are common to the upper lateral arms, face and head, torso, and ulnar surface of the forearm. These forearm bruises are the result of defensive posturing by the patient during the attack, that is, raising the arms above the head to ward off a blow. They are commonly small and multiple, indicating a sustained attack.
3. Open-hand slap injuries: These are two to four linear bruises in parallel, often on the face, back, or buttocks area. These bruise lines are usually thinner than a finger, because the vessels rupture between the fingers of the slapping hand. Slap injuries to the side of the head may be delivered with sufficient force to rupture the tympanic membrane.
4. Kick injuries: These are common to the lower legs if the patient was standing, or the thighs, back, or head if the patient was pushed or fell down. Sometimes, there is a clear, patterned shoe or boot heel mark.

Lacerations. A laceration is the splitting or tearing of soft tissues due to blunt impact, such as a forceful punch, a blow with an object or weapon, or a fall. They are commonly found in the skin over bony prominences. Internal organs can be lacerated as well. Lacerations of the skin often have irregular margins, commonly with abrasions and contusions at the edges. Small nerves and vessels may remain intact in the deeper parts of the laceration, even though the surrounding tissues are torn. These bridges across the wound are proof that the injury was blunt rather than sharp. If an object was used to deliver the blow, the surrounding contusion or abrasion may closely match its shape.

Cuts and Stab Wounds. Incisions with a blade, or other pointed or sharp objects, are often deeper than they are wide, with no strands of tissue bridging the gap. Weapons used are often household items, such as kitchen knives, forks, skewers, scissors, and screwdrivers. The margins of these wounds are often, but not necessarily, sharp, clean, and free of contusions and abrasions. The cut may be straight, but can be jagged if a serrated weapon was used, or Y-shaped if a struggle was involved. Most stab wounds reflect homicidal intent.

Firearm Wounds. Firearm (pistol, rifle, or shotgun) wounds are challenging to evaluate forensically in the acute clinical setting, because they usually represent a medical emergency. It is difficult to differentiate entrance from exit wounds. In one study, physicians determined the course of the bullet incorrectly about half the time (Randall, 1993). In all firearm injuries, note the presence or absence of powder residue, and its spread, around each hole, before these regions are washed. Photographs of all bullet holes taken prior to any cleansing or surgery in the area are very useful, but may not be realistically obtained in the emergency setting. Obviously, any bullets or pellets must be retained as evidence.

Bite Marks. Bite marks may be found in any area, but when inflicted during domestic violence, are commonly in sexual areas of the patient's body. In one series of human bite marks (Vale & Noguchi, 1983), women were most commonly bitten on the breasts, followed by the arms and legs. As a patterned injury, such marks can sometimes be matched to the teeth of the perpetrator with near absolute certainty. Even identical twins will have different tooth patterns (Rawson, Ommen, Kinard, Johnson, & Yontis, 1984; Sogannaes, Rawson, Gratt, & Nouyer, 1982). There are published guidelines for collecting and analyzing bite mark evidence (American Board of Forensic Odontology, 1986). Documentation should always include close-up photographs, which can later be compared with models of the suspect's teeth. Impressions and tracings are also used (Benson, Cottone, Bomberg, & Sperber, 1988). If adequately documented, bite marks can provide excellent forensic evidence (Beckstead, Rawson, & Giles, 1979; Furniss, 1981; Gold, Roenigk, Smith, & Pierce, 1989).

Sexual Assault. A full sexual assault/evidentiary exam should be offered to every patient who reports a sexual assault within the previous 72 hours. These usually include oral, vaginal, and/or anal swabs, as indicated; an external genitalia and speculum exam; a colposcopic vaginal exam by a trained sexual assault examiner; combing for foreign pubic hairs; and a body surface exam for sperm using a Wood's (ultraviolet) lamp. Published protocols are available (Young et al., 1992).

Photographs and Body Maps

Taking photographs of a battered patient may be the single most valuable part of forensic documentation. Photographs speak volumes about the extent and pattern of injuries, and they can be invaluable in legal proceedings. Pictures should always be taken of patterned bruises and patterns of injuries. Whenever possible, photographs should be taken before and after the wounds are cleaned. Because wound cleansing is often delegated to the registered nurse, he or she must initiate forensic photographic documentation as soon as possible. It is impractical to wait for the police to arrive in the treatment area with a camera. Therefore, health care system cameras need to be immediately accessible.

Pictures of a patient's condition following an assault, accompanied by knowledgeable assessment of the injuries, can be more convincing to a judge or jury than the most comprehensive of written records alone. If a camera is unavailable or if the patient declines to be photographed, a detailed body map of injuries should be completed (see Figures 18.1 and 18.2).

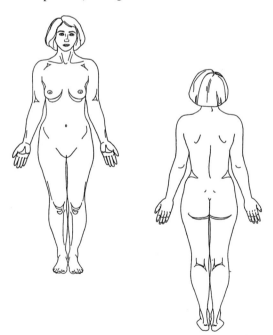

Figure 18.1. Sample Injury Map—Female

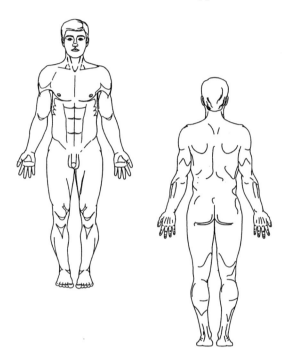

Figure 18.2. Sample Injury Map—Male

The following are recommended guidelines for forensic photography:

1. Always obtain a signed informed consent to photograph.
2. Use adequate lighting and ISO 100 or 200 color print film. Do not overlight the injury site by using high-powered spot or surgical lights. Too much light will ruin the photograph.
3. Use a separate roll of film for each patient. For a 35 mm camera, rolls of 12-exposure film are most cost-effective. If the patient has extensive injuries, use additional rolls of film.
4. Start the series of photographs with a picture of the patient's face and body or clothed full-body picture, just to identify the patient. Also, photograph the signed consent form, so that this document remains in the negatives.
5. Photograph each area of injury separately, starting with a more distant shot of the wound, then taking progressively more close-up photographs.
6. Always include a size scale, such as a ruler or coin, in photographs of injuries. Quality camera supply shops sell gray scale or color reference rulers. If the

A person who is in or trying to leave an abusive relationship interacts with multiple helping systems: health care, police, courts, clergy, social service agencies, and/or women's or shelter services. Advocacy by health care providers is greatly enhanced by understanding the roles and services provided by these other systems. Below are a few tips for learning about and building bridges with others who can help people break out of cycles of abuse:

1. Know if there are mandatory reporting statutes in your state for domestic violence or other crime victims. Ask your hospital's legal counsel or prosecuting attorney for more information.
2. Local prosecuting attorneys and criminal investigators can provide valuable training on medical-legal documentation of abuse cases.
3. Be familiar with how, when, and where one would obtain local restraining/protective and/or antistalking orders.
4. Inform all abused patients that domestic violence is a crime and explore their willingness to talk further with the police. Share with patients that police involvement has been shown in multiple studies to be an effective deterrent when coupled with good safety planning.
5. Contact a local shelter and women's resources for training and retraining on safety planning.
6. Keep a list of all current emergency hotline and shelter services in the treatment area and consider placing hotline cards in all women's restrooms.

Box 18.1. Interfacing With Other Agencies

scale will cover part of the patient's skin, take an additional photograph without the scale to demonstrate that the scale hides nothing.

7. Have the film developed with double prints, at a hospital in-house photo lab if available. Request that the film be handled by as few people as possible.
8. Label the back of every photograph with the patient's name, medical record number, date of birth, date of injury, date photo taken, and the name of the photographer. This can be expedited by using computer-printed mailing labels.
9. Place one set of the prints in the patient's medical record. Give the other to the patient (mail only to a safe address), or with permission, send the photo set with the other medical records to the police or prosecuting attorney.
10. Although 35 mm print film is recommended, Polaroid or other instant prints, even though inferior in resolution and color quality, are convenient, confidential, and better than no photographs.

Adult Maltreatment Syndrome

Discharge diagnoses should not only include the specific trauma-related descriptors but also *adult maltreatment syndrome,* which is code 995.81 from the ICDM-9 diagnostic code book. Routine use of the diagnosis of adult maltreatment syndrome can greatly enhance efforts to monitor prevalence, recidivism, and facilitate rapid chart retrieval if a provider or institution is asked to produce domestic violence charts for review by JCAHO site survey reviewers. Adult maltreatment syndrome diagnosis can also be used with patients without acute injury where domestic violence is a part of their current history.

Summary

Routine assessment, in-depth history taking, and thorough, unbiased, non-pejorative written and photographic documentation of patients who have injuries from intimate partner abuse is invaluable in medical-legal treatment. As survivors of intimate partner abuse struggle with the process of leaving violent relationships, the forensic clinical evaluation and documentation of their injuries may help prevent further abuse.

PART VI

CULTURALLY SPECIFIC CLINICAL INTERVENTIONS

19

Providing Effective Interventions for African American Battered Women

Afrocentric Perspectives

Doris Williams Campbell
Faye Annette Gary

The focus of this chapter is on prominent Eurocentric beliefs, attitudes, and behaviors that may prevent African American battered women from receiving effective intervention by health care professionals and other providers. Afrocentric perspectives are presented to provide an alternative context for understanding the traditions, beliefs, and behaviors that should be considered when providing care for African American battered women. These perspectives are integrated into discussions of suspected contributions to the incidence of violence in the lives of African American women. They also are incorporated into suggested interventions and a case study exploring considerations that may be unique to providing effective health care for African American battered women.

The purpose of this chapter is to assist health care providers to better understand, and thus provide culturally specific interventions with, African American battered women in health care and other community settings. Our basic premise is that applications of Eurocentric interpretations of behavior and values in health assessments and interventions may lead to inappropriate assessments and intervention activities with African American battered women.

A Eurocentric model of behavior presents a European American view of behavior, primarily an Anglo male-dominated view of the world (Asante, 1990; Asbury, 1987). The Eurocentric model often is used in psychology and the behavioral sciences and asserts that human behavior is universal and thus can be explained by universal theories of behavior. These "universals" are presumed to transcend differences related to race, gender, class, and sexual orientation. Unfortunately, such an approach negates, devalues, and misinterprets the psychological importance attached to experiences of persons who differ from the "norm." Families who vary from this model are viewed as deviant, dysfunctional, or unhealthy. African American women are one group of individuals whose behavior and experiences are likely to be misinterpreted by health professionals whose orientation is solely Eurocentric. An Afrocentric model for understanding the experiences of African American women should lead to more culturally competent and sensitive care for African American battered women.

An Afrocentric model emphasizes prominent African traditions and values that are the roots of African American culture. These include the notion of unity among human beings, nature, and the spiritual world (Asante, 1990; Baldwin, 1986). Individuals are viewed as an integral part of the "larger African American society" and are collectively responsible for one another (McNair, 1992). Central to this worldview is the belief that the individual cannot and does not exist alone. Thus, the social context in which many African American women exist supports social connectedness and interrelatedness as opposed to autonomy and individuation.

Contributors to Violence in the
Lives of African American Women

African American women have not been included in much of the mainstream research on spouse abuse. As a result, it is difficult to address their needs on the basis of knowledge available from the mainstream literature. Mainstream spouse abuse research suggests that traditional sex role socialization is associated with high levels of family violence. However, the strict sex role socialization found in European American families is less typical of African American families (Lewis, 1975). Lewis (1975) also suggests that in keeping with their African roots, African American families typically demonstrate more unity and role synthesis and flexibility in how the family functions. For example, economic and child-rearing responsibilities usually are shared by the partners.

An analysis by Roy (1982) suggests that economic difficulty may be a major factor triggering violent episodes in African American families. Compared with African American women and European American women and men, African

American men are much more likely to be the victims of psychological, social, and economic suppression. Racial discrimination frequently is a factor in preventing African American men from fulfilling the traditional male role of head of household and provider. Thus, to the extent that African American men internalize mainstream standards for appropriate masculine roles, they experience conflict between who they are and what they have been led to believe they should be (Asbury, 1987).

Cazenave and Straus (1979) also suggest a positive relationship between abuse and income level. They reported that in general, the higher the level of family income, the lower the level of abuse reported. The participation of African American wives in the labor force also appeared to affect how they were treated and influenced their tolerance for, or rejection of, abuse. The rate of abuse was lower for employed wives in middle-income families than for unemployed wives in middle-income families.

Among African Americans, being embedded in family, neighborhood, and organizational networks was found to be associated with lower levels of reported spousal abuse. However, spouses who were isolated or minimally involved reported a high incident of spousal slapping (Cazenave & Straus, 1979).

Carlson (1977) maintained that financial and interpersonal stresses, rather than intrapsychic causes, lead to domestic violence. In Carlson's view, the primary basis for spousal violence was environmental stress related to limited social and economic resources. Carlson additionally contended that within the environmental setting, violence tended to occur when the husband's role was not traditional (lower than wife's) and if accompanied by structural stress and a history of learned violence. Other behaviors strongly associated with environmental stress are alcohol and drug abuse. During the current "crack cocaine" epidemic, many African American women who are partners of crack abusers report being beaten if they do not provide the partner with money for drugs.

Incidence of Violence in the Lives of African American Women

African American women appear to be at multiple jeopardy for experiencing violence in their lives. Family violence occurs in all levels of society but is believed to be more prevalent in some groups than others because of socioeconomic factors. Many African Americans live in dire socioeconomic straits. They often are confronted with racism in addition to the usual stressful events of everyday life and live under continuous and varying stress because of oppression. Multiple sources of stress for many African American families include poor employment prospects, ranging from unemployment to underemployment, and inadequate educational opportunities (Myers, 1987). Unfortunately, many studies have viewed African American families as deviant and problem prone while ignoring the behaviors, attitudes, and coping mechanisms required to survive within the context of what Chester Pierce, a noted black psychiatrist, views as living in "a mundane, extreme environment" (as quoted in Myers, 1987, p. 237). Such an environment is described as one in which "racism and subtle oppression are ubiquitous, constant, continuing and mundane, rather than an occasional misfortune" (as quoted in Myers, 1987, p. 237).

Each year in the United States, 3-4 million women are assaulted in their homes by their husbands, ex-husbands, boyfriends, or ex-boyfriends. This includes approximately 1.8 million women living with a man and an equal number who are single, legally separated, or divorced. Another 3-4 million women have been beaten in the past and remain in abusive relationships (Rosenberg, Stark, & Zahn, 1986). It is unclear whether African American women are at greater risk for experiencing abuse than are white women. Although population surveys indicate that battering is two to three times more common among blacks than whites, among groups with similar incomes, blacks are less likely than whites to experience spousal violence. Surveys also report higher rates of abuse among poor, unemployed, or working-class groups. However, the difference between low-income and middle-income women may be small, and extensive abuse has been identified in relatively affluent communities (Stark & Flitcraft, 1992). Lockart (1985) concluded that there is insufficient evidence on the extent of wife abuse in the various racial and ethnic groups. When careful procedures in cross-cultural research are used, results show no significant differences between the races.

Reported racial or ethnic differences in the incidence of violence may be attributable to African American women being more likely to report their abuse than white women. Studies linking battering to conventional indicators of social class tend to be inconclusive, with some reporting far higher rates among low-income groups and others reporting alarmingly high rates among the middle class. The risk of battering has been found to be greatest in situations in which the woman has a higher educational status than her partner or where the man is unemployed or consistently underemployed. These kinds of social situations often are found in African American male-female relationships. Although poor, minority women may appear to be at greater risk, battering is neither confined to, nor explained by, poverty or race.

Community Violence and Homicide

The most frightening type of violence confronted by African American women in many urban communities is homicide. African American women in inner-city urban areas and their children are at greater jeopardy than are their female counterparts in other environments for witnessing the homicide of their adolescent sons, spouses, other family members, and friends. They also may be at higher risk for battering and homicide by a spouse or male partner than are women in other settings.

Homicides usually are categorized by the nature of the victim-offender relationship: family, friend, acquaintance, or stranger. The overall male-female homicide-victim ratio is approximately 3.5:1 (Rosenberg et al., 1986). Men are at higher risk for each category of victim offender relationship. Black and other minority men have the highest death rates in each relationship category. However, black and other minority women, when compared with white women, consistently have higher death rates attributable to homicide. The rates for black and other minority women for homicide by a family member or friend are higher than the rates for white men (Rosenberg et al., 1986). We conclude that although it is difficult to disentangle the contribution of race from socioeconomic status in explaining the high homicide rates among black men, several studies suggest that socioeconomic status is the more important determinant. In the study by Rosenberg et al. (1986), for young people (15-34 years old) who were black or members of other minorities, homicide was the leading cause of death. A dominant factor associated with homicide is poverty. Poverty appears to be more strongly associated with murders of family members and friends than murders of acquaintances. Spouse homicides tend to be associated with a belief in male dominance. Other factors associated with homicide of all types, except child homicide, are the consumption of alcohol, abuse of illicit drugs (Rosenberg et al., 1986), and the presence of a gun in the home. Whether one is considering violence in the home, community, or workplace, the male is most likely the initiator and women or children, the victims (Tomes, 1995).

The few available studies on women homicide offenders reviewed by Mann (1987) report that African American women are the most frequently arrested female offenders in cleared murder cases, and they also make up the largest proportion of women incarcerated for criminal homicide. The primary victims of female homicides are husbands or lovers. Family members, friends, or acquaintances also are victims but less frequently. The most common causes of homicide by African Americans seem to be psychological or emotional (including anger and revenge). The second most frequent motive is self-defense or "self-preservation." A literature review by Uzzell and Peebles-Wilkins (1989) showed that African American women are more likely to strike back at their abusive husbands, whereas husbands are more likely to assault wives and cause bodily harm. They also reported that wives were more likely to kill abusive husbands after years of assault. Most of the homicides are committed at home, with a gun as a weapon. This is contrary to the commonly held notion that black female homicide offenders are more likely to use knives or other cutting instruments as murder weapons. Once convicted, black women tend to receive harsher sentences than do white women who commit the same crime (Mann, 1987).

Although it is clear that the problem of interpersonal violence is not unique to African American communities, homicide is a major health problem for many black communities because of black-on-black murders. This problem has not been dealt with by the health care system, primarily because of the common misconception that violence in the black community is connected only with crime and thus is considered a legal, rather than a health, problem. This view is supported by a large body of social-psychological literature documenting the prevalence of racial stereotypes about blacks. Among these racial or cultural stereotypes is the belief that blacks are more aggressive and violent than are whites. One consequence of such racial prejudice is the differential treatment of black and white youths. A study that matched black youths with white youths on their level of psychopathology and violent behavior reported that black youths were more frequently sent to correctional institutions, whereas white youths were sent to mental health facilities (Lewis, Shanok, Cohen, Kligfeld, & Frisone, 1980). Lewis et al. (1980) concluded that although there seems to be an awareness that violent behavior can underlie emotional or mental health problems, in the case of black youth, such judgments seem to be overridden by cultural stereotypes.

The impact of family and community violence on children has not been studied as intensively as has direct child abuse. Recent studies of children exposed to abusive parental relationships have indicated that such children may be at greater risk for emotional and behavioral difficulties than are their counterparts in nonviolent homes (Gage, 1990; Holden & Ritchie, 1991). Evidence also exists to link child abuse with wife beating (Straus, Gelles, & Steinmetz, 1980) and indicates that spouses who hit each other also tend to hit their children (Gelles, 1980; Straus et al., 1980).

White (1985) describes silence as the typical response of the black community to violence committed against its most vulnerable members: women and children. White states that the silence does not stem from acceptance of violence as a black cultural norm (a view the media perpetuates and many whites believe), but rather from shame, fear, and an understandable, but nonetheless detrimental, sense of racial loyalty. Internal and external forces have prevented the African American community from addressing the multiple issues of violence as they are manifested through rape, incest, and domestic violence.

Afrocentric Perspectives on Intervention

A large proportion of interpersonal violence among African Americans, as with other groups, occurs within the context of the family. Thus, it would appear that intervention at the family level would be logical. However, many ideological barriers need to be confronted and discarded before rates of family violence among African Americans will be lowered (Hawkins, 1987). Hawkins argues that three major ideological barriers must be confronted to successfully intervene with African American families in the area of domestic violence. The first barrier stems from the noninterventionist model traditionally associated with family violence in the United States. The strength of the belief that one should not intervene in family matters has been diminishing in recent years but persists. Hawkins also states that despite increasing public concern and legislation requiring intervention in domestic disputes, the prevention of family violence among African Americans faces other race-specific ideological barriers. The second of these barriers derives from the historical devaluation of black life in the United States. A third barrier is a product of stereotypical views that suggest that violence among blacks is normal (Hawkins, 1987).

The devalued status of the black victim and the view that violence is normal among blacks are reflected in a pattern of unequal legal response to black and white victims of violence. Hawkins (1987) suggests that the devalued status of the black victim affects the actions of a wide range of other officials who respond to violent behavior or other crime, including health care workers, prosecutors, judges, and juries. The status of the black victim has relevance for understanding the attitude of public officials toward family violence among blacks. The literature on the devalued status of the black victim indicates that among black and white domestic violence murders, blacks receive less punishment than do their white counterparts. This makes it difficult for the African American woman to readily seek assistance from the police in her community. She may have observed police brutality against blacks and have a strong sense of community loyalty that causes her to hesitate to "betray" the race by calling the police. In fact, Joseph (1997) found that white battered women were twice as likely as African American women to request a restraining order against their partners from the criminal justice system.

An alternative resource for safety that may be more available to African American women than to women of other cultures includes the extended family. The black woman may choose to notify relatives and friends in the community of her situation. Her parents or the abuser's parents may be accessible to her, considering the long-standing tradition of extended families and social support in African American communities. This kind of support may be more immediately accessible than the nearest community shelter. It is common in the African American community for individuals in the community to be willing to provide temporary shelter for the woman and her children. Joseph (1997) found white battered women four times as likely to use a shelter as African American battered women.

The unequal treatment by police, judicial officials, and others is not only evidence of the devalued status of the black victim of violence but also may contribute to additional violence (Bachman & Coker, 1995). To the extent that commonly occurring acts of minor violence are not investigated and major acts of intraracial violence go unpunished, patterns of vigilantism may emerge among blacks (Hawkins, 1987). Some evidence suggests that this may be a factor contributing to the high rates of violence in the black community.

The idea that violence is more or less normal, and thus inevitable, within the black community may affect the behavior of many potential interveners outside the legal arena. If social service personnel, public health officials, counselors, and others share this view of black criminality, they may believe that their intervention efforts are futile and instead aim their work at the middle class and whites, rather than blacks in the lower economic class.

The belief that a high rate of violence among blacks is inevitable and normal is partly grounded in a racial stereotype. It also is a product of observations made by Eurocentric social scientists, who have sought to explain disproportionate levels of violence within the black community. Historically, black women and children have been afforded less protection from abuse within the family than any other groups within American society. White women and children also have been underprotected, but much less so than blacks. Unless persisting ideological constraints are confronted and challenged, increasing official intervention in domestic violence will merely result in an unequal race-of-victim pattern of intervention similar to that found in the handling of nonfamily criminal violence. That is, black and poor victims of family violence may be ignored, and most prevention efforts targeted at the white middle class.

Case Study and Implications
for Health Care Providers

The following case study and discussion demonstrates an Afrocentric approach to assisting an African American battered woman and her family. It includes patterns of speech sometimes used by poorly educated African American women to describe violence in their lives. It also suggests considerations related to the unique experiences of African American women that will assist health care professionals to provide the abused black woman with more sensitive and competent care.

Case Report

Charles and Mary Crawford, both age 28, live in a neighborhood of primarily African American families. Family income in this census tract averages approximately $20,000, and in most families the male and female partners both work. However, unemployment rates are high, especially among the men. This makes it difficult for many families to keep current on mortgage payments on the small block homes they are trying to buy in a community vacated during the past two decades by white families. The homes are fairly well kept and the lawns neatly manicured. During the past year, the neighbors organized a "Drug Watch" and with the help of the local police were able to drive persons who were dealing drugs out of the community.

Charles and Mary married shortly after graduating from high school. They lived with Mary's parents during the early years of their marriage but eventually were able to make a down payment on the small home where they have lived for several years with their three children, Dionne (10 years of age), Damien (7 years), and Tameka (4 years). Charles has always been emotionally and financially supportive of Mary and the children, working fairly consistently as a longshoreman with his father. Help from both sets of parents with afterschool child care provided Mary with an opportunity to complete a computer course offered by the local Urban League. She has worked for the past 3 years as a computer operator with the local telephone company.

Tameka was born after Charles and Mary moved into their home. Tameka has sickle-cell disease. The other two children have no health problems and do well in school. Charles continued to work steadily as a longshoreman on the docks with his father until he was laid off 9 months ago. Child care for Tameka usually is provided by the next-door neighbor while the other children are in school. However, Mary frequently misses work when Tameka becomes ill.

The home health nurse made a visit to the home of the Crawfords to assess Tameka after a recent hospital stay for sickle-cell crisis. At the time of the visit, Mary had been home from work for several days caring for Tameka. The nurse found Tameka to be making satisfactory progress at this time, with only mild joint tenderness.

However, the nurse observed that Mary's lips were swollen and bruised, which made it difficult for her to talk. She had swelling under the left eye and cheek area and bruise marks around her throat. She also had bruises on her arms. When asked what happened, Mary stated that she fell down the back stairs while taking out the garbage. Upon additional questioning by the nurse, who asked Mary if someone had tried to hurt her, Mary began to cry. She stated that her husband had come home earlier in the day after going to the "union hall trying to catch a job" and then to the Job Services agency. She stated that he made his "daily rounds" looking for a job and felt that he had been passed over for several good jobs as a laborer. He had a few drinks and started arguing with Mary about not having dinner ready. He accused her of not taking good care of Tameka and of being responsible for her having to be admitted to the hospital so often. Mary stated that things just "got out of hand and I called him a 'good for nothing.' " She stated that he then "jumped on me and starting fighting me." She explained that he "hit me upside my head and busted my lips." He also "wrang my arm and tried to choke me." Tameka ran next door to the baby-sitter, who called the police. Mary stated that when the police finally came, they took Charles to jail, "even though everything was cool when they arrived." She continued crying and said, "I just wanted them to tell him to leave me alone. Go cool off. . . . I didn't want to cause trouble in the neighborhood. . . . Charles really is a good person; he might drink but he don't do drugs. . . . I guess he just gets frustrated at the system and not being able to find a job. He's really been dogging me around in the last few months. . . . Now, I don't know what I'm going to do about posting bail to get him out."

Discussion

Asbury (1987) states that to help a battered woman, help must be available and the woman must know that it is available and how to gain access to it. She also must know how to use it and must decide to use it. However, other factors must be considered when assisting many African American women: The health care provider should be aware that the response time of the police to her call for assistance may be unduly slow and that with the arrival of the police, the batterer may be treated less harshly than the batterer of a white woman.

Public services often are in short supply in African American communities. However, the emergency needs of the African American woman are met in the same manner as for any other woman. Because there was no hospital or clinic nearby, the nurse in this case assisted Mary to contact her mother-in-law, who, although upset that her son was in jail, accompanied Mary to the hospital for emergency evaluation and treatment and documentation of her injuries. Mary's mother took care of Tameka. The nurse in the trauma center at the hospital provided Mary with a private setting in which to additionally inquire about patterns of abuse in her life. (Useful questions to screen for abuse are described in Chapters 14, 15, and 16 in this volume.) In addition, the nurse or other health care provider should inquire about Mary's continued safety and explore safety plans with her before she leaves the hospital. Mary decided not to contact a domestic violence shelter because she did not believe that she was in any immediate danger. Even so, the nurse was aware that the nearest domestic violence shelter was located across town in another community. Because African American women live in a society dominated by European Americans, they may feel that they will not be understood or even welcomed at shelters outside their immediate community (Asbury, 1987), so there is a tendency for African American women not to seek shelter outside their neighborhoods.

Mary decided that she and the children would move in with her parents for a while, just in case "Charles was let go and started acting up again." One concern of health care providers in such situations is that although it was helpful for Mary to be able to seek support and guidance from her family, family members, because of their closeness to the persons involved, may not be able to objectively provide the battered woman with alternatives. They also lack the professional training that might be needed to handle a crisis. Thus, as the nurse and social worker helped Mary plan for the next few days, they provided her with written information about resources available to her. The social worker discussed Mary's legal options and local counseling and crisis intervention services available in her community and provided her with telephone numbers.

Asbury (1987) states that whether or not appropriate help is available, the woman must choose to take advantage of the help. The African American woman's special experience results in different considerations in making that choice.

An African American woman's decision to seek help may be influenced by her feelings about her abuser. Although studies have shown that battered women of all ethnic backgrounds may be reluctant to reveal their abuse out of concern for their abusers (Walker, 1979), this may be an even greater consideration among African American women. Cazenave (1981) and Hare (1979) suggest that African American men are in a more vulnerable position than other men relative to the dominant culture. Being aware of the suppression, as Hare describes it, may make African American women reluctant to expose the men to more ridicule. However, White (1985) asserts that the woman should not take her partner's abuse lightly and should recognize it as a serious crime despite the problematic relationship between the police and the black community. White also stresses that the African American woman, although sensitive to the effects of racism and the victimization of black men, should not feel she has to tolerate abusive behavior from her partner because the bank did not give him a loan or he cannot find a job. The poet Pat Parker writes:

> *Brother/I don't want to hear/about how my real enemy/is the*
> *system.*
> */i'm no genius, /but i do know/that system/you hit me with*
> */is called /a fist.* (as quoted in White, 1985, p. 25)

All health care providers must be cognizant that no woman deserves to be beaten and should encourage the woman to take the abuse seriously.

An African American woman also may be more reluctant to bring attention to her situation if she has internalized common stereotypes about African American women. These stereotypes, common in the media and in popular literature, portray these women

> as everything from sexual temptresses to ugly mammies, from the
> sturdy bridges who hold together the race (and therefore the community) to emasculating matriarchs who are responsible for the instability of the family (and therefore the community) because they drive
> away their men with their domination. (Asbury, 1987, pp. 100-101)

Although many African American women have had to demonstrate strength and independence to survive, this image may be problematic for women who find themselves in violent relationships. The woman who believes that being strong and independent means she "should be able to handle it" may be prohibited from calling attention to her situation and seeking help and other resources (Asbury, 1987).

Finally, consideration should be given to the unique aspects of the African American experience in attempts to change the battered woman's situation. Mainstream literature on this question focuses primarily on ways to induce the woman to end the relationship. This may be the only alternative. However, the African American woman who has been led to believe that it is her responsibility to maintain the family, regardless of costs to herself, may be more likely to remain and do nothing (White, 1985). She also may be more interested than women of other ethnic groups in working with a professional toward modifying her abuser's behavior. These important differences should be considered when planning therapeutic interventions from an Afrocentric perspective with African American women.

When the community health nurse visited Mary 2 weeks later, she learned that Mary had moved back into her home with the children. Charles's parents had posted bail to get him out of jail. After his hearing, he was ordered to attend a counseling program for men who batter their partners. Focusing intervention on male batterers is proving to be an effective educational intervention for domestic violence. Most batterers treatment programs are based on the notion that violence is a learned behavior, and as such, it can be changed (Dennis, Key, Kirk, & Smith, 1995). Charles is living with his parents and visits with Mary and the children once a week. He believes that he is learning to handle anger at his current life circumstances in ways that are less self-destructive to him and his family. He and Mary say they feel strongly that physical and emotional abuse is not acceptable in their relationship and believe that at some time in the future they may be able to live together again as a family.

Conclusion

Health care providers can better meet the health care needs of African American battered women with an increased understanding of prominent Afrocentric and Eurocentric views and how these views influence interventions. Although much empirical work remains to be done, health care providers in clinical settings can begin to address many of the unique issues and care considerations when working with African American battered women.

20

Clinical Interventions
With Native American
Battered Women

Diane K. Bohn

$\mathbf{A}$ dearth of empirical evidence exists regarding rates of abuse in Native
American communities. It is difficult to obtain access to study abuse among
Native Americans. Those who do often do not publish the results of their studies.
However, many believe that the problem is widespread (Gunn Allen, 1985) and
that incest, sexual abuse, and domestic abuse may be the norm rather than the
exception in many Native populations (Wolk, 1982). The physical and sexual
abuse of women and children within some Native American and Canadian
aboriginal populations occurs at rates far in excess of other North American
groups. In three studies, 77% to 90% of Native women reported a history of abuse
(Bohn, 1993; Bohn, Jones, & Jene, 1995; Ontario Native Women's Association,
1989). The endemic nature of violence in Native American communities is
reflected in the high mortality rates from homicide and suicide experienced by
Native American teens and adult women and men in the United States (Indian
Health Service, 1995; Jacobson, 1994; Old Dog Cross & Hunter, 1990).

Within-group interpersonal violence is a relatively new phenomenon in
Native American and Canadian aboriginal cultures and is attributed to the cultural
disintegration and sense of powerlessness that has accompanied 400 years of
oppression. In traditional Native American cultures, cruelty to women and
children resulted in ostracism, loss of honor, and public humiliation for the
abuser. To abuse a woman was seen as tantamount to abusing life itself (Chester,

Robin, Koss, Lopez, & Goldman, 1994; Columbus, Day-Garcia, Wallace, & Walt, 1980; Gunn Allen, 1985; McIntire, 1988; Warren, 1982; Wolk, 1982).

Lack of self-determination, disenfranchisement, poverty, isolation, racism, and high rates of alcoholism and substance abuse have perpetuated the problem of violence in Indian country. Health professionals who work with Native American battered women should have at least a basic understanding of the history of the white-Indian relations that have led to the current problems within Native communities. As with other social and public health problems, violence against women viewed from an ahistorical perspective cannot be adequately understood or resolved. A historical awareness may also prompt health care providers to reexamine the prejudices and biases they may hold, as well as directing intervention efforts to draw from the strengths of Native American cultures.

There is danger, however, in focusing too narrowly on history and traditional culture. To assist Native American battered women, health care providers must not forget that each woman is an individual and that all Native American women are not the same (Warren, 1982). Battered women of all ethnic and cultural origins feel similar pain and have similar issues and needs (Sorenson, 1996).

Health care providers may be the only contact some Native American battered women have with someone who can assist them in ending the cycle of violence in their lives. Abuse is a public health problem that many health professionals have difficulty addressing with their clients. This discomfort is often the result of a lack of knowledge and a fear of responding inappropriately or offending. The same skills that allow clinicians to address complex issues such as death and dying and HIV/AIDS can be used effectively to help survivors of domestic abuse.

Homicide and Suicide Mortality
Among Native Americans

U.S. mortality statistics for American Indians and Alaskan Natives reflect the high rates of both other-inflicted and self-inflicted violence among these groups (see Table 20.1). Suicide and homicide rates vary greatly by region (Grossman, Milligan, & Deyo, 1991; Indian Health Service, 1993; Old Dog Cross & Hunter, 1990). Alcohol abuse, which is a form of self-abuse, also accounts for a significant number of deaths in Indian country. Deaths due to alcohol abuse (e.g., chronic liver disease, accidents) are much higher among Native Americans than among other groups. Age-adjusted alcoholism mortality rates for 1987-1989 among Native Americans in Indian Health Service areas were 634% higher than rates for the general population (Indian Health Service, 1993). Alcohol abuse is also a major risk factor for suicide (Old Dog Cross & Hunter, 1990).

Table 20.1 U.S. Age-Adjusted Homicide and Suicide Mortality Rates[a] for
Native Americans (NA)[b] and Other Races

Cause of Death	NA	All Races	White	Ratio NA to All Races	Ratio NA to White
Homicide	14.6	10.9	6.2	1.3	2.4
Suicide	16.2	11.4	12.1	1.4	1.3

SOURCE: Adapted from Indian Health Service (1995).
NOTE: 1990-1992 data.
a. Rate per 100,000 population.
b. American Indian and Alaska Native.

Suicide and homicide rates, when examined by sex and selected age groups (see Tables 20.2 and 20.3), are generally higher for Native American females and males, as well as both sexes combined, when compared with rates for whites or all races. In the older age groups, suicide rates are comparatively lower and homicide rates higher among Native Americans when compared with other races (Indian Health Service, 1995). Increased rates of homicide and suicide have also been found among Canadian aboriginals in British Columbia (Hislop, Threfall, Gallagher, & Band, 1987). Native American suicide and homicide mortality rates in the United States have steadily decreased since 1973. Although there is a general trend toward decreased homicide and suicide mortality rates among whites and all races, rates for Native Americans have decreased more dramatically and at a faster rate than for other groups (Hisnanick, 1994; Indian Health Service, 1995).

Abuse and Suicide Attempts

Empirical evidence of child and adult physical and sexual abuse and suicide attempts among Native Americans is limited. Studies that have examined these problems, with the exception of the recent national study of American Indian and Alaska Native youth (Blum, Harmon, Harris, Bergeison, & Resnick, 1992), have been limited to specific geographic areas or tribes. Studies have often been limited to children or adults receiving mental health or social services. These individuals may have abuse histories that differ from the general population of Native Americans.

Child Abuse and Neglect

Prevalence rates of child abuse and neglect are difficult to determine for any population. Data on abuse and neglect among Native American children are

Table 20.2 U.S. Suicide Mortality Rates[a] by Age, Sex, and Race

Age	Gender	NA[b]	All Races	White
5-14	Female	0.5	0.0	0.4
	Male	2.4	1.1	1.2
	Both	1.5	0.7	0.8
15-24	Female	9.0	3.8	4.2
	Male	60.8	21.9	23.1
	Both	35.4	13.1	13.9
25-34	Female	8.4	5.4	5.8
	Male	45.9	25.1	26.1
	Both	26.8	15.2	16.0
35-44	Female	4.9	6.5	7.2
	Male	34.7	23.1	24.7
	Both	19.3	14.7	16.0
45-54	Female	6.5	7.7	8.4
	Male	17.1	23.8	25.4
	Both	11.6	15.5	16.8

SOURCE: Adapted from Indian Health Service (1995).
NOTE: 1990-1992 data.
a. Rate per 100,000 population.
b. American Indian and Alaska Native.

difficult to interpret because of the methodology and limited geographical scope of most studies. Prevalence rates of child abuse and neglect, from both primary and secondary sources, vary widely. Secondary sources report prevalence rates of 5.7-26 per 1,000 children per year (DeBruyn, Hymbaugh, & Valdez, 1988; Fischler, 1985). In their study of 1,155 children identified as being abused or neglected or in need of mental health services, Piasecki and associates (1989) found 67% were abused or neglected. Ashby, Gilchrist, and Miramontez (1987) reported as many as one third of Indian women enrolling for social work services in one state report a history of sexual abuse, but did not specify whether the abuse occurred during childhood. Lujan, DeBruyn, May, and Bird (1989) studied 53 Native American families in the Southwest that had been identified as experiencing child abuse and/or neglect. They concluded that child abuse and neglect are often found in multiproblem families that frequently report multigenerational alcohol abuse and domestic violence.

Abuse, Violence, and Suicide Risk
Among Native American Teens

A recent national study examined the health of 13,454 American Indian and Alaska Native 7th- through 12th-grade youth (Blum et al., 1992). Among other

Table 20.3 U.S. Homicide Mortality Rates[a] by Age, Sex, and Race

Age	Sex	NA[b]	All Races	White
5-14	Female	1.0	1.0	0.7
	Male	3.3	1.8	1.2
	Both	2.1	1.4	1.0
15-24	Female	6.7	7.0	4.4
	Male	35.8	37.4	17.0
	Both	20.9	22.4	10.9
25-34	Female	10.6	7.5	4.4
	Male	41.1	29.1	15.6
	Both	24.8	18.2	10.1
35-44	Female	8.4	5.1	3.5
	Male	33.4	18.5	11.2
	Both	20.0	11.6	7.3
45-54	Female	4.7	3.8	3.0
	Male	24.9	12.9	8.8
	Both	14.0	8.2	5.9

SOURCE: Adapted from Indian Health Service (1995).
NOTE: 1990-1992 data.
a. Rate per 100,000 population.
b. American Indian and Alaska Native.

variables, the investigators examined interpersonal violence, suicide attempts, and substance use. Eighteen percent of the students reported having experienced some form of abuse. Ten percent of participants reported a history of physical abuse, and 13% reported sexual abuse. The rates were highest among girls, with 17% overall, and 23.9% of 12th-grade girls reporting a history of physical abuse. Nineteen percent overall and 21.6% of 12th-grade girls reported sexual abuse. Rates of physical abuse among Indian students was nearly twice that of non-Indian youth in rural Minnesota. The prevalence of problems in the Native American youth may have been artificially low because of the self-administered nature of the questionnaire, the high rate of absenteeism from school, and the high drop-out rate of Native American youth (60%, Jacobson, 1994).

In terms of outcomes, 16.9% of the adolescents had attempted suicide in the past, two thirds of them in the past year (Blum et al., 1992). More females than males reported attempting suicide (21.6% and 11.8%, respectively). Participants who had a family member who had killed himself or herself were more likely to attempt suicide (30.3%) than those without a family history of suicide (13.2%). Participants who were considered to be at high risk for suicide were more likely to have a history of sexual abuse (20.1% vs. 8.2%) or physical abuse (26.5% vs. 10.8%).

Using a subset of the larger survey, Grossman et al. (1991) used multiple logistic regression modeling to identify the following risk factors for suicide attempts: history of mental health problems, alienation from community and family, having a friend or family member attempt suicide, alcohol abuse, poor general health, past physical or sexual abuse, and female gender. Interactions between gender and abuse were found, with risk of suicide attempts being increased for males who had been sexually abused and for physically abused females.

Battered Native American Women

Abuse of Native American women has received little attention in the literature despite a recognition that the problem is widespread (Chester et al., 1994; Columbus et al., 1980; Gunn Allen, 1985; Lussier, 1982; Martin & Pence, 1988; Wolk, 1982). Few empirical studies have been published. In their study of Canadian Aboriginal women, the Ontario Native Women's Association (1989) obtained abuse-focused information from 271 women living on reserves, in urban centers, in rural settings and in isolated communities. Eighty percent of the women reported they had personally experienced family violence. Seventy-eight percent said more than one family member was a victim of regular abuse. Sixty percent reported that more than one person was involved in the abuse of women and children in their family. Twenty-four percent of the women personally knew of individuals who had died as a result of family violence.

The Native American Abuse
During Pregnancy Study

Bohn (1993) conducted a combined retrospective-prospective study of 30 pregnant, urban Native American women in Minnesota. Study participants included three fourths of the women obtaining prenatal care at one Native American clinic in a 4-month period. The study focused on the prevalence of past and current abuse and the health effects of abuse.

Ninety percent ($n = 27$) of the women in this study had experienced some type of abuse in their lifetime. One of these women reported only nonphysical abuse. Sixty percent ($n = 18$) were involved with a physically abusive partner at the time of the study, and 33% ($n = 10$) reported abuse during the current pregnancy (Bohn, 1993). Twenty-seven percent ($n = 8$) of study participants had experienced physical abuse as a child. Forty percent ($n = 12$) had experienced sexual abuse as children. Forty-seven percent ($n = 14$) had experienced either physical or sexual abuse as children, and 20% ($n = 6$) had experienced both.

All the women abused as children were also abused as adults. The majority of women (66%) had two or more abusive partners as adults, with two women reporting six abusive partners. Seventeen percent ($n = 5$) had been sexually abused as adults. Cumulative lifetime abuses or abuse events were significantly related to a number of variables. Abuse events were defined as the sum of the total number of abuses the woman has experienced, with child physical abuse, child sexual abuse, adult sexual abuse, and each emotionally and/or physically abusive partner counting as one event (Bohn, 1993).

Half of the women in the study had a history of substance abuse. A third had received chemical dependency treatment. Chemical dependency was significantly related to child abuse, total abuse events, and abuse events that occurred in adulthood. Nine women (30%) had attempted suicide at least once. Eight women made their first or only attempts during adolescence. Seven of these nine women had experienced some form of abuse prior to their suicide attempts (Bohn, 1993).

Other Research on Violence Against
Native American Women

In a recent retrospective study of 230 women receiving care from a certified nurse-midwife at an urban community health center in the Midwest (Bohn et al., 1995), 60% of women reported having experienced physical and/or sexual abuse in their lifetime. When the 43 Native American women in the study were examined separately, a prevalence rate of 77% was found compared with 56% among women of other races.

Norton and Manson (1995) interviewed 16 Native American women seeking counseling for domestic violence at an urban Indian health center. Frequently reported characteristics of the partner-perpetrated abuse included rape (38%) and attempted rape (12%) and injuries severe enough to require medical attention (38%). All the women in this study reported they were more depressed or stressed since they were abused by their partners. Nearly one third reported suicidal thoughts in the past year. Thirty-one percent felt their general health was much worse, and 38% stated their abuse of substances had increased since the abuse. In addition, over half of the women reported being physically abused as children, and 56% were aware of domestic violence between their parents.

The rates of lifetime abuses experienced by Native American women in these studies (Bohn, 1993; Bohn et al., 1995; Ontario Native Women's Association, 1989) are higher than the estimated U.S. prevalence rates of one third (Straus & Gelles, 1990). However, research on violence against women in all populations has generally focused on specific types of abuse (incest, child abuse, rape, domestic violence) rather than lifetime abuses, making comparison difficult. During personal communication with two Native American women who work with abuse in the Native community, both women stated they did not personally know any Native women who had not experienced abuse. As with other battered women, these experiences of abuse are manifested in an array of health problems, including suicide attempts, substance abuse, and depression.

The Native American Experience:
A Historical Perspective

Women in Traditional Cultures

Prior to European contact, Native American tribal groups were based on a communal economy, with little or no class distinction. Harmony with and respect for nature and all living things, sharing, and cooperation were the basis of spirituality and morality. Interdependence of the sexes was viewed as desirable and necessary for survival of the group. Although some activities were gender specific, the contributions of each individual was highly valued. Many activities were shared by men and women. In many groups, traditional male roles, such as those of warrior and hunter, were frequently assumed by women (Albers & Medicine, 1983; Buffalohead, 1985; Columbus et al., 1980; Danziger, 1978; Gridley, 1974; Hickerson, 1971; Kohl, 1985; Niethammer, 1977; Wolk, 1982).

Many indigenous American cultures were matrilineal, matrilocal, and/or matriarchal, meaning bloodlines, place of residence after marriage, and family decisions were determined by women. Some Native American nations were governed by women. Women were often spiritual leaders and healers. Creation myths often involved simultaneous creation of males and females by a gender-neutral or female creator. Women's voices were influential in tribal decision making, and women also had property ownership and distribution rights (Buffalohead, 1985; Columbus et al., 1980; Gridley, 1974; Kehoe, 1983; Maxwell, 1978; Wolk, 1982).

Influences of European Contact
and the U.S. Government

The early contact experiences of the various Indian nations with European explorers, traders, missionaries, colonists, government agents, and the militia varied based on geographical location and the purpose or circumstances of the contact. It is not the intent of this chapter to define these experiences. Interested readers are encouraged to visit their local libraries, historical societies, and museums. Readers are encouraged to keep in mind that early historians and ethnographers were often missionaries, government agents, and gentlemen of the late Victorian era whose agendas and biases colored what they observed and recorded concerning traditional Indian cultures. In many cases, ethnographies were written after 200 years of European-Native American contact had significantly changed the cultures they attempted to define. The events of the early years of European-Indian contact, exemplified by the history books of American schoolchildren, are also distorted by ethnocentric bias. This discussion will be limited to only a few of the many ways in which Native American life was influenced by early contact, Christianity, and the policies of the U.S. government.

At the time the first Europeans landed in the New World, over 300 separate tribal groups, now known collectively as Native Americans or American Indians, populated the area that is now the United States (Columbus et al., 1980). By the 1920s, decimated by disease, poverty, and violent campaigns of eradication and control, the U.S. Native population totaled 245,000 individuals. Several entire nations (tribal groups) of native people, their languages, and their cultures had ceased to exist (Maxwell, 1978).

With few exceptions, from the first days of European contact Native Americans were defined as uncivilized, savage, barbaric, and intellectually, biologically, and spiritually inferior. The general policy of the early days was to exploit and destroy them. Later, expansionist tactics were to "civilize" them by destroying their cultures. Many means were employed over the years to accomplish this.

From the time of Columbus, through the early years with the Pilgrims, and continuing even after the enslavement of African Americans was abolished, North and South American Indians were used and sold as slaves. The sale of Indian slaves helped finance the expeditions of early explorers. The Pilgrims used Indian slaves for domestic work and sold them in a lucrative foreign market. The profit helped finance further westward expansion. Native American slaves, being cheaper than those from Africa, were used by early colonists for plantation labor. Slavery was also practiced by the Spaniards in the south, including the missionaries of what is now California. The United States outlawed the enslavement of Native Americans in the Southwest in 1868 (Weatherford, 1991).

Mass killing and enslavement were only two of the tactics used to acquire Native American land prior to the use of treaties. Alcohol, widely used in trade and coercive practices, created another kind of enslavement. "Tactics also included placing strychnine-soaked biscuits and small-pox infested blankets where the Indians would find them" (Wolk, 1982, p. 16). Death, disease, enslavement, and the displacement of Indian nations to the west, in front of westward colonial expansion, forced tremendous change in all facets of Native life. Wars broke out between displaced nations and those whose traditional lands they were forced to occupy. Customary values and institutions broke down in the face of the upheaval.

Tremendous change was also brought about by missionaries and Christianity. For many Native Americans, missionaries were among the first Europeans with whom they had contact. The conversion to Christianity did not come quickly or easily. A number of Christian and biblical teachings were contrary to the social practices and religious beliefs of Native American peoples. The creation story of a male god creating Adam first, then Eve from Adam's rib, was contrary to more egalitarian creation myths. Exclusive male religious leadership was a new concept. The principle that man was to have authority over women and children and the teachings of early missionaries that violence (punishment) was a legitimate and sometimes necessary means to assert that authority were also foreign concepts. Control and punishment of women for infidelity or refusing to live with their husbands (the equivalent of divorce in many tribes) was also advocated by early missionaries, in keeping with the European practices of the time. For many Native American people, the first within-group or intrafamily violence they experienced or witnessed was in this context (Gunn Allen, 1985; Leacock, 1981; Wolk, 1982). Beyond changes in religious beliefs and practices, gender roles and authority, Christian conversion had other effects. Leacock (1981) states, "Punitiveness toward self and others . . . accompanied the often tormented attempt on the part of converts to reject a familiar set of values and replace it with another" (p. 58).

In the early years of American independence, as military tactics became too costly and European pressure for more humane treatment of Native Americans mounted, treaties became the means to acquire land. The Northwest Ordinance of 1787 stated that Indian lands were to be purchased rather than taken. However, the treaties that were signed were often misunderstood or obtained under considerable duress. Government agents sometimes tricked or bribed a tribal member to sign the treaty by promising to confer on them the title of Chief (Maxwell, 1978; Wolk, 1982).

After the War of 1812, there was increasing pressure to remove Native Americans from many of the lands that they occupied (Danziger, 1978). In 1830, Andrew Jackson signed into law a bill to relocate all Indians to areas west of the Mississippi River. By the 1850s, Native peoples throughout the country were forced onto reservations, leaving them with a total of 140 million acres of land. Many tribes were hundreds of miles from their traditional lands. Without the mobility necessary to obtain food by traditional means, and devastated by disease and starvation, the once self-sufficient nations became totally reliant on the federal government for subsistence (Danziger, 1978; League of Women Voters, 1971; Maxwell, 1978; Wolk, 1982).

U.S. governmental policy in the early reservation period was to "civilize" the Native American people and replace traditional cultures with white culture. They were forbidden to practice their traditional religions. From 1890 to 1920, and much later in some areas, children were removed from the reservations to attend government boarding schools, often many miles away. Threats of withheld rations were sometimes used to force parents to send their children, sometimes as young as 3 years old, to these schools. Children were often away from home for at least 9 months, and sometimes many years. In many cases, their parents were not allowed to visit them. At the boarding schools, which were places of military discipline and complete regimentation, children were punished for speaking their native language or practicing traditional religions or customs and for many lessor offenses. Many children had their first experience with corporal punishment in these schools (League of Women Voters, 1971; Martin & Pence, 1988; Wolk, 1982). Many middle-aged and elderly Native Americans are products of these boarding schools.

In 1887, the Allotment Act broke up tribal lands to give each family 160 acres. The intent was for Native Americans to become farmers and for the tribal unit to be replaced by isolated nuclear families. The 90 million acres of land left over after the allotment was absorbed by the government. Over time the original 160 acres were split up between family members. Land that was inherited often consisted of small plots on different parts of the reservation. Both the size and the quality of these lands made them unsuitable for farming. Many plots were sold through tax default or to settle debts arising from excessive credits that were eagerly afforded to land-holding Indians. A total of 90 million acres were sold, and many more acres were leased by the Bureau of Indian Affairs (BIA), who in turn leased the land to white farmers and ranchers (Maxwell, 1978; Wolk, 1982).

In 1934, after the government realized that its attempts to assimilate Native American people had failed miserably, the Indian Reorganization Act (Howard-Wheeler Act) was signed by Franklin D. Roosevelt. This act ended land allotment and permitted, for the first time, tribal self-government. It also set aside $2 million for the purchase of Indian land to be held in trust. The act was never fully implemented. Some of the trust funds were diverted during World War II, and the BIA continued to control many Native American affairs. The Johnson-O'Malley Act of 1934 gave responsibility for administration of federally funded programs such as education, welfare, medical, and agricultural assistance to the state (Maxwell, 1978; Wolk, 1982).

In the 1950s, acts to terminate reservations and cut off financial and administrative support were passed by the Congress, but never fully implemented. In 1975, the Indian Self-Determination and Education Act was passed after much lobbying and pressure from the Native American community. This act allowed Native Americans, for the first time, to take over the responsibility for their own affairs including education and the management and use of funds. Self-government and development of reservation resources were to be encouraged (Maxwell, 1978; Wolk, 1982).

After 120 years of reservation life, and the forced assimilation and eradication policies that preceded reservation life, Native Americans were given the right to govern their own affairs. But the years and the influences of government policies, boarding schools, alcohol, prejudice, poverty, and the loss of traditional ways had taken a toll, and the prejudice remained. The lack of self-determination and oppression resulted in limited options and decreased self-esteem (Gunn Allen, 1985) or cultural learned helplessness (Wolk, 1982). The violence that was a learned expression of frustration and anger is directed from men to themselves, women, children, and other men, and from women to themselves, their children, and other women. "Suicide, alcoholism, child abuse and neglect—all are part of this terrible escalation of violence in Indian country as Native Americans take on the qualities ascribed to them for centuries by the society around them" (Gunn Allen, 1985).

Since the 1970s, Indian nations have used their new chance at self-determination to develop schools, businesses, and a variety of health and other programs specific to the needs of their communities. However, attention to the problem of violence has been limited. Of the few programs nationwide that focus on the needs of battered Native American women, most have come from the grassroots efforts of Native American women, rather than from tribal sources. There are many reasons for this, including the male-dominated leadership of most tribes, the enormity of the needs of many groups, and the difficulty in addressing issues that carry with them the pain and shame that abuse does. Lussier (1982) states there is also concern that calling attention to issues such as violence will reinforce negative stereotypes.

Clinical Care of Native American Battered Women

Identification

Health care providers knowingly or unknowingly encounter battered women wherever they work with women. Those who work with Native American women also encounter battered women. The first responsibility of the clinician is to identify women who are being abused. This is best accomplished by direct questioning in a private setting. It may take time for a Native American woman to develop the trust she needs to divulge a history of abuse. If she is approached in a respectful way and given time to talk, she will open up to questions regarding abuse.

A review of the woman's chart may reveal a number of health problems that should alert the health care provider to the possibility of abuse. These include a history of injuries, substance abuse, depression, suicide attempts, unexplained somatic symptoms, eating disorders, sexually transmitted diseases, miscarriages, and pregnancy complications such as preterm birth and low birth weight. A review of the woman's history may provide an entry point to abuse-focused questions.

Eye contact and body language are very important in communication with a Native American woman. As with most minority group members, she is adept at picking up nonverbal cues. Any biases the clinician has about Native Americans may be communicated by posture, tone of voice, eye contact, and communication style. A sincere, caring style and an open posture with good eye contact speak volumes. Joking is an important part of communication among Native Americans. If the provider can share laughter with the women, it may help break the ice and develop trust (Warren, 1982; Wolk, 1982).

When communicating with a Native American woman, the health care provider should slow down and lower her or his voice, although this does not mean speaking to the woman like a child. Rapid or loud speech may make the woman uncomfortable. Watch for and respect her nonverbal cues. The clinician may learn more about the woman's comfort and trust levels through her posture and gestures than her words. Use open questions, rather than forced-choice questions. If the Native American woman feels cornered, she may say what she thinks the clinician wants to hear, rather than what she is thinking or feeling. The provider must also learn to be comfortable with periods of silence when communicating with Native American women (Wolk, 1982). Physical contact and embraces should be avoided until a trusting relationship is well established, and may not be welcome even then (Columbus et al., 1980).

Assessment

The second role of the health care provider is to assess the severity of the abuse and the effect the abuse has had on the woman's health. Ask her about injuries, physical symptoms or problems, pregnancy problems, depression, substance use, and suicide attempts. Many of these health problems may be related to abuse (Bohn, 1993). Discuss the types and severity of abuse she has experienced, including the use of weapons and sexual abuse. Equally important are the nonphysical types of abuse she has experienced. According to Georgia Mayotte (personal communication, November 1992) of the Eagles Nest shelter in Minnesota, common tactics may include belittling, being noncommunicative, or her partner leaving and staying away without contact for long periods. Other forms of nonphysical abuse include economic abuse, coercion, threats, intimidation, blaming, isolation, and using children as leverage (Domestic Abuse Intervention Project, 1990).

Intervention

After assessing abuse, the clinician's role is to intervene by providing information, exploring options, and supporting the woman in her decisions. In doing this, it may be necessary for the health care professional to sublimate her or his own cultural standards and expectations and try to understand the woman's individual perspective. It is important to listen to the woman's own needs and desires. The role of the clinician is to facilitate choices, not to give answers (Wolk, 1982). Information should be offered rather than waiting for the women to ask for it (Columbus et al., 1980).

Whenever possible, the discussions of options should focus on Native American resources for battered women, because these are most likely to be sensitive to her needs and her culture. Most of the Native American resources focus on traditional spirituality and culture as a part of the healing process and a way to reclaim one's identity and strength. The health care provider should have knowledge of local resources for both battered Native American women and abusive men. If only non-Indian resources are available, the clinician should seek information regarding the experience of Native Americans with these agencies.

A number of variables need to be taken into account when discussing abuse and options with a Native American woman. What the health care provider may see as an intolerable situation may, in fact, be the most desirable option to the woman. The variables that need to be considered include the woman's support system, the racism and sexism she may encounter in her attempts to get help, her personal and cultural value system, and her financial situation.

Native Americans traditionally rely heavily on an extended family support system. This is particularly true of those who live on reservations or in Native American communities. In many cases, the families of the woman and her abuser live in the same community. Abuse is often expected to be taken care of by and within the family. A Native American woman most often uses family and friends as her first resources to help with an abusive situation. If the woman goes outside the family and community for help, such as calling the police or going to a shelter, she may be ostracized by both families. She may fear being reprimanded by the abuser's family. For a woman to end the abuse, she may have to leave her community, family, and support system. The isolation, relocation, and economic hardship involved in leaving may be financially, physically, and/or emotionally prohibitive (Columbus et al., 1980; Warren, 1982; Wolk, 1982).

The institutions and agencies that may be enlisted to help battered women or women with financial or other needs may not be viewed with favor or optimism by Native American women. At government and social service agencies, she faces the double burdens of racism and sexism. The forms of racism she may have to endure include rudeness and value judgments. She may be equally hesitant to use local shelters or support groups. These organizations are often founded on the feminist beliefs that empowerment of women is key in ending abuse and that assertiveness and independence are part of empowerment. Native American women are traditionally quiet and may appear passive. They may have difficulty speaking in support or shelter groups. In contrast to feminist philosophy, they may see raising their children as more important than career training or advancement. In addition to a cultural value system that may be out of synch with the standards of success set forth by feminist organizations, Native American women may experience more outward expressions of racism by individual shelter staff or other residents (Columbus et al., 1980; McIntire, 1988; Wolk, 1982).

A Native American woman may also avoid involving the police and the court system, where she again faces sexism and racism. She may wish to not only protect herself from these institutions but her partner as well. She knows that he will be treated differently, in many cases, because he is Indian. Racism may be a larger issue than the violence (Columbus et al., 1980; Wolk, 1982). Police involvement may also result in children being removed from the home, especially if both the woman and man are arrested for assault or taken to a detoxification center. The children may be scattered in several foster homes. If the woman is unable to visit, which may occur if she has no car, her parental rights may be terminated. On reservations, the police may be friends or relatives of the woman or her partner.

It is considered a virtue, in the Native American community, for a woman to stay with her man no matter what. The woman's family may have told her that she should just accept the abuse (Ontario Native Women's Association, 1989). Traditional women who were married by a medicine man or woman may be more likely to stay in an abusive relationship. According to Wolk (1982), "In general . . . an Indian woman's choice to stay in a violent relationship is more likely to be based on loyalty to her companion because he is an Indian rather than because he is a man" (p. 49).

A Native American woman may be so battered and drained by years of racism, abuse, and poverty that she does not have the energy or feel the empowerment necessary to fight for change in her life. She may have tried to leave before, only to find that no one would rent an apartment to an Indian woman with children. She may have reached out for help in the past and been turned down or further shamed, humiliated, or belittled. She may be so involved with the caregiver role, taking care of everyone else, that she doesn't even know how she feels about the abuse or her partner. She may have lived with so much abuse that it seems normal.

The support that the health care professional provides to the Native American woman may be key in helping to stop the cycle of violence. The woman needs to know that the clinician does care what happens to her. She needs to be told that she is a worthwhile person. It is important to focus on her strengths, such as her mothering ability or her sense of humor, or whatever skills she may have. If she is determined to continue her relationship with her partner, she needs to believe that there is hope for both of them to heal.

Plan

After discussing the available options, or referring that task to an on-site domestic violence advocate, the clinician's role is to assure that the woman receives the appropriate referrals. Regardless of whether the woman chooses to leave or go home to her partner, she should be given telephone numbers of shelters and advocacy services. She should also receive referrals for domestic violence counseling or groups for herself and her partner. If there are Native American resources or shelters in the region, even if they are some distance away, she should be given their phone numbers. Transportation for the woman may be arranged by these facilities. Her children may also be in need of counseling. If the woman is referred to social services, it should not be assumed that the woman will receive domestic violence referrals from that source.

If chemical abuse or dependency is an issue for the woman or her partner, the clinician should provide referrals for in- or outpatient treatment. Often, abuse issues cannot be adequately dealt with until the substance abuse is addressed. It should not be assumed that chemical dependency services will deal with abuse issues or that domestic abuse will stop when the woman or her partner achieve sobriety.

If the woman decides to leave her partner, she should be encouraged to use battered women's services to help with the transition. Some agencies will provide advocates to accompany her to various agencies to assure she is treated fairly. Temporary shelter; relocation; counseling for the woman and her children; assistance in arranging housing, job training, or other education; legal advocacy; and financial assistance are often provided or arranged by shelters and advocacy projects.

Whether the woman chooses to stay with her partner or leave to stay with friends or relatives, safety issues should be addressed. Battered women's advocates can provide this information if they are available. The health care provider should discuss with the woman what she plans to do if she is in danger. The plan should include where to go and whom to call. If the woman does need to leave quickly, it will be helpful to her to have household receipts and birth certificates for her children, a change of clothes, and money stored in a safe place. Some of these items are critical to obtain housing or enroll children in school. If at all possible, she should take her children with her if she hopes to retain custody.

The abuse information the Native American woman shares with the clinician must be confidential. Relatives and friends of the woman or her partner may be employed at reservation or rural hospitals and clinics. A breach of confidence could result in further harm for the woman and will certainly destroy any trust the clinician has established with her. In their study of Canadian women, the Ontario Native Women's Association (1989) found that 54% of the women interviewed knew of cases where a woman who needed medical attention for abuse injuries did not seek medical help out of fear or shame. It is vital that battered Native American women view their local health care providers as trustworthy and compassionate.

Community Response

Public awareness and sensitivity is necessary for abuse to be properly addressed in the Native American community. Family violence affects the whole community on spiritual, social, mental, and physical levels. Family violence is inherited by sons and daughters who witness and are themselves victims of abuse. These children then grow up to abuse and to be further victimized. At a tender age, they begin a course of self-destruction that includes alcohol, suicide attempts, and violence. It is essential that the community response be directed toward men, women, and children alike (Ontario Native Women's Association, 1989; Wolk, 1982).

At a community level, violence must be deemed unacceptable. Women must be permitted and encouraged to confront the issue of abuse, to bring it out into the open without shame, and to assert their rights. Men need to be held accountable for their violence by other men, tribal elders, and tribal courts. Men and women alike need to be strengthened and healed. Abused children need to be identified and counseled before they learn to accept violence as a way of life. The use of elders as healers, teachers, and counselors; relearning traditional spirituality and values such as respect and dignity; healing lodges and dance; and the development of Native American substance and domestic abuse programs are among the community responses that are needed to combat domestic abuse (Martin & Pence, 1988; Ontario Native Women's Association, 1989; Wolk, 1982).

The health care professional may also play an important role in dealing with the issue of abuse on a community level. It is important that clinicians ally themselves with existing Native American resources. If health care professionals are sensitive and respectful with Native American people, and especially if they are Native American, they can help to develop or expand existing programs. Health care professionals can provide education in a variety of forums from grade schools to tribal governments to heighten awareness that abuse is a serious public health issue. They can sensitize and educate other health professionals to recognize and address abuse in the health care setting.

Conclusions

Native American nations and peoples have suffered hundreds of years of oppression, forced assimilation, and concerted efforts to destroy their cultures. The years of prejudice, poverty, humiliation, and pain are evident in the high rates of alcoholism, suicide, homicide, and domestic violence. These symptoms of cultural erosion perpetuate one another in a cyclic fashion. The abused become abusers of both themselves and others. Lack of self-determination as a people has bred decreased self-esteem in individuals.

Not all Native American people are abused or abusive, alcoholic, or suicidal, but these social and public health problems touch each individual. The Native American community is addressing alcohol abuse and many have found sobriety and healing in traditional spirituality and values. The same practice of drawing from the strengths of traditional culture, with an emphasis on dignity and respect for self and one another, is needed to address the issue of domestic violence.

Health care professionals who work with Native American populations have important roles to play in ending the cycle of oppression and abuse at both individual and community levels. Abuse must be addressed as a significant public health problem. Respectful and culturally sensitive care, with attention to confidentiality, are key in health care settings. Health professionals should take time to learn the history and traditions of the Native American people they serve. They should also familiarize themselves and become involved with Native American programs and resources. Programs to address abuse that come from within the Indian community are most likely to be successful.

21

Intervening With Battered
Hispanic Pregnant Women

Sara Torres

Culturally specific interventions that target Hispanic women are needed if we are to effectively combat the problem of woman abuse in this population. The role that culture plays in battered Hispanic women's access to health care services and the provision of services must be more clearly understood. The ways that different cultures view health and illness are frequently unknown to health care providers of other cultural backgrounds. Cultures also have their own ways of viewing pregnancy, their own definition of woman abuse, and their own mechanisms for coping with the problem of abuse. Health care professions should make efforts to learn to provide quality care to those of all cultural groups, including Hispanic women. By delivering care in a culturally sensitive manner, the providers are best able to respond appropriately to the needs of Hispanic women. This chapter will focus on the cultural, socioeconomic, and health factors that should be considered in caring for battered Hispanic pregnant women and makes recommendations for culturally relevant interventions to respond to their needs.

Sociodemographic Characteristics of the
Hispanic Population in the United States

To understand the reality of women's health and deliver culturally appropriate care, health care providers need to have a thorough understanding of the sociodemographic characteristics and health care practices of Hispanics in the United States. Hispanics are the second largest minority group in the United States and constitute 36% of the U.S. minority population. From 1980 to 1990, the Hispanic population increased by 53%—five times as fast as the total population. Today, there are 22.4 million Hispanics in the United States, 9% of the total population (U.S. Bureau of the Census, 1991). Several estimates indicate that there are close to an additional 5 million living illegally in the United States.

Approximately 1 in 11 Americans is Hispanic. An additional 3 million Hispanics live in Puerto Rico. It is projected that by the year 2000, the Hispanic population will increase to 47 million and will account for 14% of the population, thus making Hispanics the largest minority group in the United States. Most Hispanics in the United States are of Mexican origin (60%), followed by Puerto Rican (14%), Cuban (7%), and the remainder (19%) originating from other countries, mainly Central and South American (see Table 21.1).

Hispanics have varied backgrounds and originate from 22 different countries. This diversity has created debate about whether *Hispanic* or *Latino* is the most appropriate identifier. *Hispanic* will be used in this chapter.

Contrary to popular belief, 71% of Hispanics in this country were born in the United States and only 29% were foreign born. Most Hispanics have migrated to the United States for either political or economic reasons. The migration pattern of Hispanic groups to the United States varies and influences their access to maternal health care and their health care status.

Hispanics live in every part of the United States, but are heavily concentrated in a few states. More than half the Hispanic population resides in California (34%) and Texas (19%). Other states with large numbers of Hispanics are New York (10%), Florida (7%), Illinois (4%), New Jersey (3%), Arizona (3%), New Mexico (3%), and Colorado (2%). Specific Hispanic groups are concentrated in particular states. Mexican Americans are mainly concentrated in the five southwestern states of California, Texas, Arizona, Colorado, and New Mexico; Puerto Ricans in New York, the surrounding states, and the Midwest; Cuban Americans in Florida and northern New Jersey; and Central and South Americans in the eastern states and in the Washington, D.C. area.

The great majority of Hispanics live in urban areas. A larger percentage of Hispanics (91.8%) compared with non-Hispanics (72.8%) are urban residents. There are some differences in the Hispanic subgroups: 90.5% of Mexican Americans live in urban areas compared with 95.2% of Puerto Ricans, 95.7% of Cuban Americans, and 97.0% of Central and South Americans.

To a degree, Hispanics share a commonality of culture, traditions, religion, and language. However, variations do exist among individuals of any Hispanic group, even among those who come from the same country, and even from the same region (Poma, 1987). Other sociodemographic characteristics of the Hispanic population that influence pregnant women's health care are the following: median income and health insurance, employment, educational status, household size, and age.

Hispanic males and females are most often employed in relatively low-paying jobs. Hispanic workers have earnings far below those of non-Hispanics. In 1990, the median annual earnings of Hispanic women were $10,099 compared with $12,464 for non-Hispanic women. Hispanics save for a better future in the

Table 21.1 Regional Distribution of Hispanics in the United States

Ethnicity	Percentage	Region
Mexican Americans	69	Southwestern states
Puerto Ricans	14	New York, mid-Atlantic states, Midwest
Cuban Americans	7	Florida, northern New Jersey
Central and South Americans	19	Eastern states, Washington, D.C.

"old" country, sometimes traveling back and forth attempting to improve their quality of life (Poma, 1987). Hispanics are people in transition, and their occupations are usually seasonal migrant work, service work, or factory work.

Hispanics have less education on average than whites, and they have a smaller proportion of two-career households. Only about half of Hispanic adults are high school graduates, and fewer than 1 in 10 graduate from college. Twelve percent of Hispanics have fewer than 5 years of schooling, compared with 5% for African Americans and 2% for whites (Aguirre-Molina & Molina, 1994).

Hispanics also tend to have larger households, often consisting of many children, extended family, and friends. It has been noted that the Hispanic population is the youngest group in the United States, with a median age of 26.1 compared with 33.8 for non-Hispanics. There are major subgroup differences, with Mexican Americans being the youngest with a median age of 24.3 years, compared with 26.7 for Puerto Ricans, 28.9 for Central and South Americans, and 39.3 for Cuban Americans.

In summary, compared with non-Hispanic groups, Hispanics experience a shortage of relevant and accessible health care services, have a higher incidence of poverty, higher school drop-out rates, higher unemployment rates, and larger households, all of which have the potential to create stress-producing situations. They also have higher morbidity rates (Herrell, 1993), attend inadequate schools (Rodriguez, 1996), face substandard housing (Lazere & Leonard, 1989; Wilk, 1993), and have poor nutrition (Murphy, Castillo, Martorell, & Mendoza, 1990).

Factors Affecting Access to Health
Care for Hispanic Women

Several barriers limit Hispanic women's access to health care. One barrier is that Hispanics are far more likely to be uninsured than other Americans. Thirty-two percent of Hispanics compared with 13% of whites lack health insurance. Education is another important factor contributing to Hispanics' decreased use of health services. According to Anderson, Giachello, and Aday

(1986), low levels of education are related to traditional health beliefs and practices, high levels of distrust of modern medicine and doctors, informational gaps about available services, willingness to be hospitalized, and low rates of preventive examinations (i.e., breast self-exam, mammography, and Pap smears). At best, these preventive measures are minimally employed by Hispanic women. Perhaps this accounts for the incidence of cervical cancer being at least twice as high among Hispanic women (Poma, 1987).

Lack of knowledge also contributes to noncompliance, a problem often encountered by physicians and health care providers. Prescriptions are frequently not filled or medication is suspended soon after the patient feels better. Many will wait for their seasonal return to the old country to take care of their medical needs. This obviously indicates that they trust their country's health care system and physicians more, most likely because of the familiarity with them. This frequent contact with the old country, however, prevents a speedy acculturation.

In addition, characteristics of the health care delivery system itself present barriers to the use of maternal health care services by Hispanics. Some of these are (a) long traveling times to the source of care, (b) long waiting times in the doctor's office for a brief visit with the physician or the health care providers, and (c) the assignment of different doctors to patients on follow-up appointments.

Another barrier affecting the access and quality of health care for Hispanics is that few health professionals and paraprofessionals speak Spanish. The language barrier is usually the first noticeable conflict among Hispanic patients and health care providers. An interpreter can assist with communication; however, health care providers must be aware of distortions in communication that may result from the interpreter's translation skills or lack of medical knowledge. When addressing the Hispanic patient, health care providers should respectfully use the patient's last name instead of first name. Health care providers should learn to correctly pronounce patients' names to demonstrate interest and consideration. Whenever possible, visual aids should be used to demonstrate health procedures.

Pregnancy in the Hispanic Population

In addition to the sociodemographic characteristics previously discussed, there are cultural and sociodemographic factors that contribute to the delivery of health care to Hispanic pregnant women. Hispanics tend to marry and start a family earlier than most Americans. Hispanic women have higher birth and fertility rates than non-Hispanics. In June 1990, the overall U.S. population showed a birthrate of 67.0 per 1,000 American women aged 15-44; the rate for Hispanic women was 93.2. They often have relatives or friends living at home; often another family (e.g., a couple with or without children or a part of another family) lives with the family on a temporary or even a somewhat permanent basis.

Hispanics are the ethnic group most likely to have late or no prenatal care (12.1% of Hispanics compared with 4.1% of non-Hispanic whites; "Hispanic

Health," 1990). In 1989, 56.7% of Mexican American mothers, 60.8% of Central and South American mothers, and 62.7% of Puerto Rican mothers received prenatal care in the first trimester compared with 82.7% of white mothers. Whereas 1.1% of white mothers received no prenatal care, 4.9% of Mexican American, 4.8% of Puerto Rican, and 4.2% of Central and South American mothers received no prenatal care (National Center for Health Statistics, 1991).

Hispanic women, especially those of Cuban and Mexican origin, have the lowest proportion of premature deliveries. The incidence of low birth weight for Hispanics falls between that for non-Hispanic blacks and whites and varies by Hispanic subgroup. Cuban Americans (5%), Mexican Americans (5.6%), and Central and South Americans have lower birth weight rates than Puerto Ricans (9.6%). Puerto Ricans are also more likely to have the highest incidence of infant mortality (9.6%) among Hispanic subgroups. On the other hand, Hispanics have a higher proportion of overweight newborns than the national average. Abortion, adoption, and artificial insemination are less acceptable to Hispanic Americans than to non-Hispanic Americans.

Research suggests that factors associated with a Mexican cultural orientation may protect against the risk of low birth weight. An analysis of the Hispanic Health and Nutrition Examination Survey (HHANES) found that U.S.-born Mexican Americans were at increased risk for low birth weight (Scribner & Dwyer, 1989). Dowling and Fisher (1987) found that the infant mortality rate among Mexican Americans, in spite of lower socioeconomic status, was less than half that of whites. These two studies indicated that for Mexican Americans, there was some sociocultural protection from the effects of urban poverty in the United States.

Cultural Factors in Providing Health
Care to Hispanic Pregnant Women

Hispanics vary in the level of acculturation into the U.S. Anglo American culture. Some Hispanics in the United States are fifth generation and are completely acculturated; some are newly arrived immigrants bringing their culture and customs. The cultural beliefs about pregnancy and woman abuse in Hispanics vary by their level of education and their level of acculturation. The guidelines for the delivery of health care to middle-class, acculturated, battered Hispanic pregnant women would be the same as for middle-class, battered Anglo pregnant women. Thus, the following discussion generally relates to the low-income, less educated, and unacculturated Hispanics in the United States.

The Hispanic Family

Today, the Hispanic family is evolving and its roles are changing. Even low-income Hispanic families are changing their traditional values and beliefs.

In general, Hispanics have a strong family network and are very family oriented. Family unity is very important, as is respect and loyalty to the family. Cooperation rather than competition among family members is stressed. The family is perceived as the chief link with the community, providing a source of social support. The extended family includes not only relatives but often non-blood relatives such as the best man (*padrino*) and maid of honor (*madrina*), and godparents (*compadre* and *comadre*). The extended family is a vital support system, and help is generally not sought until advice is obtained from the family, extended family, and friends.

Traditional Hispanic families are hierarchical in form, with special authority given to elderly family members, the parents, and males. Sex roles are clearly delineated, and the father assumes the role of the primary authority figure. The traditional role of the mother and wife is subordinate to that of her husband. Her primary interests include bearing children and caring for her family, her home, and her close kin. In these families, women are in a dependent position and seldom have any input into their health care decisions. In such cases compliance with treatment requires involvement of the male figure at home. This is his responsibility because illness is considered a family problem.

When someone is ill, several family members, usually including the mother, intervene to assist the ill person to return to health. When a patient is hospitalized, he or she usually has several family members attending to his or her needs whether it be bathing, dressing, or feeding. Health care providers need to recognize that patients need to have their family near for physical, emotional, and spiritual support. When making major health care decisions, health care providers must not only talk with the patient but must also discuss the care plan with the family. Health care providers need to allow the family to assist with as much of the patient care as they safely can.

A strong reliance on the family has also proven to have adverse effects on the use of health care services during illness. Family members are encouraged to seek help (curative measures) within the family first, except when illness is very serious (Anderson et al., 1986). On the other hand, favorable results of recent studies concerning infant mortality, low birth weight infants, and prematurity among different ethnic groups suggest that this increased familial support during a stressful period may produce a "protective sociocultural effect" that attenuates some of the negative factors associated with the Hispanic culture (Dowling & Fisher, 1987).

Religion

Religion plays a very important role in the day-to-day lives of many Hispanic people. Their religious background is usually Catholic and they are actively involved with the church. Their religious beliefs are related to views that (a) sacrifice in this world is helpful to salvation, (b) being charitable to others is a virtue, and (c) a person should endure wrongs done against him or her. The consequences of these beliefs are that many Hispanic women have difficulty in behaving assertively. They feel that problems and events are meant to be and cannot change.

Many Hispanic people develop close relationships with their pastor. Some Hispanic families have symbols of crosses, pictures of Jesus and their favorite saints, and even small shrines in their homes. Many Hispanics feel that they have limited control over nature and that God gives health and sends illnesses for a reason. Thus, they believe that their health is fatalistic; that is, if they are good Christians, they will be happy and not become ill. They feel that if they do get ill, it is because they did or thought something that was considered evil in the eyes of their God. Thus, having faith in God is imperative to recovery from illness.

When in the hospital, some Hispanic families use promise-making; shrines; and offerings of medals, candles, and prayers to assist their loved ones through recovery or peaceful death. Health care providers should allow religious rituals to be performed as long as they do not endanger the patient. Awareness of their importance and support for them are important, because this allows for more open communication. Recognizing and accepting indigenous beliefs and practices when planning care, and incorporating them into the plan, will facilitate compliance and cooperation. For example, any medical product, such as an IUD or an oral contraceptive, that alters bodily functions must fit reasonably well within a woman's conceptions about the workings of her body and what affects her sense of well-being. Otherwise, its use will be discontinued.

Health Care Beliefs

Health care providers should also be aware of the inherent health subculture of some Hispanics. This consists of a very different set of beliefs and practices (such as the use of herbs, teas, and massage therapies) to treat symptoms of illness as well as acute and chronic health conditions. Many Hispanics, according to Leininger (1978), believe that the body must function as a whole with a balance of hot and cold substances in the body. Surgery, for example, imposes a great threat to their "wholeness." Health care providers need to be considerate and understanding of these beliefs. The "hot and cold" theory is a prominent concept of this health subculture. Many Hispanics are concerned with keeping a proper balance of temperature and moistness in the body. Health is balanced by the four humors of the body (blood, phlegm, black bile, and yellow bile). Blood is hot and wet; yellow bile is hot and dry; phlegm is cold and wet; black bile is cold and dry. Foods, diseases, and medications are classified as either "hot" or "cold." Cold materials are used to treat hot diseases and vice-versa.

For example, hot diseases such as rashes, kidney diseases, ulcers, and fever can be treated with mannitol, bicarbonate, milk of magnesia, chicken, fruits, and honey. Hispanics are careful to follow culturally prescribed practices with regard to food and exposure to air of different temperatures. Extremes of heat, cold, dryness, and moistness may give rise to anxiety, which affects the sense of well-being. Because pregnancy is considered a hot condition, these women will avoid iron and vitamin supplements (also considered hot) because it is believed that they will upset the body's natural balance. Health care providers play an essential role in the care of the maternity patient. Therefore, they must ask the patient what they can eat and what combination of foods that they feel will be helpful to treat their condition. Advising the patient to take the supplements with fruit juice (classified as "cool"), helping to maintain the proper balance of hot and cold in the body, may encourage compliance.

Fallen fontanelle (*caida de mollera*) can affect newborns. Many Hispanic women practice *cuarentena,* a postpartum lying-in period following birth that lasts 40 days. This is a time of isolation for the mother. During this period, the woman is to rest, stay very warm, and avoid bathing and exercising. Special foods designed to restore warmth to the body are taken. Disregarding these practices is believed to lead to aches and pains in later life. Hispanic women are less likely to believe in drugs for treatment of ailments, and they often lack confidence in physicians, psychiatrists, and other counselors for treatment of medical and emotional problems.

Research has shown that less than 5% of Hispanic women use lay persons (faith healers), including *curanderos* (Mexican), *espiritistas* (Puerto Rican), and *santeros/santeras* (Cuban), for health advice and folk treatments. Faith healers may give women instructions on how to negotiate a better situation for themselves and their children. The woman may be given herbs to make an infusion to drink herself or to serve to her mate that will be calming. She may also be instructed to do some ritualistic maneuvers for a specific saint (e.g., light a certain number of candles at church, pray to a specific saint at the home altar, fast, make novenas, and so forth). Religious ceremonies and rituals, red ribbons, red cloths, and other charms may be used to prevent the evil eye (*mal de ojo*), spells (*brujeria*), bad air (*mal aire*), or fright (*susto*) from affecting mother and child. If the lay practitioners are unsuccessful, the family will use the hospital as the last resort. Some Hispanic women who do not believe in lay practitioners will sometimes seek the services of a faith healer if illness does not respond to medical treatment. Health care providers should not be concerned with allowing patients to practice traditional health measures along with orthodox treatments, unless they prove to be contraindicated.

Scope of Woman Abuse in Hispanic Women

There are conflicting data about the prevalence of woman abuse in the Hispanic population. The reporting mechanisms that allow us to know the extent of child abuse do not exist for woman abuse. Therefore, the true extent of woman abuse, in general, and the extent of woman abuse during pregnancy in Hispanics, in particular, is not known. Indications are that violence during pregnancy may be the most common form of family violence during the perinatal period (Richwald & McCluskey, 1985).

In a national study, Straus and Smith (1990) found a higher prevalence of wife abuse in the Hispanic population than in African American or white American ethnic groups. One out of four Hispanic women was abused. Specifically, the rate of severe assaults on wives, which could be considered a measure of wife beating, was more than double that of non-Hispanic white families. Abused Hispanic women tended to have married at a younger age, had larger families, and stayed in relationships longer. Similarly, they were poorer, less educated, and had been abused for a longer period of time than their non-Hispanic counterparts.

Other research studies that have included pregnant Hispanic women do not support these findings, at least during pregnancy. McFarlane, Parker, Soeken, and Bullock (1992) investigated a cohort of 691 white, black, and Hispanic pregnant women and detected a 17% prevalence of physical and sexual abuse. Fourteen percent of the Hispanic women reported physical abuse during pregnancy compared with 20% of African American and white American women. The authors also reported that severity of abuse during pregnancy was significantly worse for white women. In two studies examining violence and substance abuse during pregnancy, there was no indication that the prevalence of woman abuse was higher in the Hispanic population (Amaro, Fried, Cabral, & Zuckerman, 1990; Berenson, Stiglich, Wilkinson, & Anderson, 1991). However, these two studies (Amaro et al., 1990; Berenson et al., 1991) showed that Hispanic women reported the longest duration of abuse.

Kantor, Jasinski, and Aldarondo (1994) reported that being born in the United States increased the risk of wife assaults by Mexican and Puerto Rican husbands. Other studies reported no significant differences in the severity and frequency of abuse between Hispanic and white American women (Gondolf, Fisher, & McFerron, 1988; Sorenson & Telles, 1991; Torres, 1991). Browne and Bassuk (1997) found that Puerto Rican sheltered women were less likely to report a lifetime history of partner violence or its medical sequelae than were non-Hispanic white sheltered women, even after adjustment for age, educational level, and housing status. The authors, who studied 436 sheltered women, including Anglo Americans, Puerto Ricans, blacks, and other ethnic groups, also found no ethnic differences in the prevalence of abuse by current partners.

Studies of woman abuse have identified several causal factors that are associated with minority ethnic status and with poverty, such as unemployment, stress, and powerlessness, which support the importance of considering sociocultural factors in the delivery of health care (Kaufman Kantor & Straus, 1987; Straus, Gelles, & Steinmetz, 1980). When sociocultural influences are considered, a greater incidence of woman abuse in Hispanic families, compared to other groups, is anticipated. Stressors relative to immigration status (e.g., lack of English proficiency, prejudice), stressors stemming from environmental sources (e.g., work, school, finances), and other family and cultural variables also contributed to woman abuse (Perilla, Bakeman, & Norris, 1994). The stress of acculturation has also been described as having a great impact on the mental health of Hispanics (Padilla, 1975; Vega, Kolody, & Valle, 1986). In particular, differing levels of acculturation and acculturative stress have produced various types of marital conflict, which led to battering (Carillo & Marrujo, 1984). The types of marital conflict have included sex role expectations, family obligations and relationships, and the permissible amount of contact with persons and institutions associated with the host culture (i.e., the United States).

Research has shown that the greater the number of children in the home, the higher the incidence of battering (Poma, 1987). Poma (1987) attributed this to the stress related to parenting. Education has been described as a significant preventive measure against psychological distress (Kessler, 1979).

Migration to large urban areas in the United States, participation in the labor force, and women's changing family sex roles have contributed to Hispanic women's changing role within the family. Changing family roles have increased Hispanic women's responsibilities, which has led to increased stress and cultural conflicts. Young age with larger households, less education, and lower-paying jobs shape the realities of Hispanic women's lives and put them at risk for battering and psychological distress.

Health Care of Battered Hispanic Pregnant Women

The choices that a Hispanic woman has in response to her battering situation are the same as any other woman has—leave or try to work out the relationship. However, the Hispanic woman faces many barriers if she decides to leave. She must endure the many stresses resulting not only from the abusive relationship but also the socioeconomic and political factors that surround the Hispanic community.

Unfamiliarity with Anglo American customs and culture, a marginal economic situation with little or no insurance coverage, language barriers, low levels of education, and a tradition of family-centered living patterns combine to isolate Hispanic women from information about health practices and health facilities of mainstream Anglo American society (Poma, 1987) and information about resources for battered women.

Delay in prenatal care is associated with adverse outcomes, as evidenced by the high incidence of low birth weight newborns born to women with absent or delayed prenatal care (Bullock & McFarlane, 1989). The signs of physical abuse, such as a black eye or bruises, may keep pregnant women from leaving their homes. If the abuser uses a control tactic such as isolation, the woman is further deprived of the opportunity to seek care. A battered woman's delay in obtaining needed prenatal care may be due to threats, isolation, lack of transportation, or fear of exposing the obvious physical signs of abuse; usually, it is a combination of reasons. In a study of African American, Anglo, and Hispanic women, battered participants across ethnic groups sought prenatal care 6.5 weeks later on average than nonabused women (Taggart & Mattson, 1996).

Barriers that Hispanic battered women face in seeking assistance for their battering include their social and economic condition in the United States. Due to the cultural gap, Hispanic women most often refuse to confide in a doctor or health care provider about their home situation. Even when the woman is on the verge of losing her life, she will find it extremely hard to go outside her cultural group to seek help. The health care providers must proceed cautiously when assessing the nature and extent of the violence to avoid imposing the health care provider's own values on the woman's interpretation and handling of the situation. Thus, health care providers need to be sensitive and adept at assessing and planning interventions with Hispanic battered women.

Culturally Relevant Interventions

The challenge to health care providers as they seek to meet the needs of Hispanic battered women is to find methods of intervention and empowerment that address both the environment and the internal factors that affect Hispanic women's well-being. Empowerment must be initiated and experienced by those who see themselves as powerless for empowerment to be meaningful and long lasting. In reality, one cannot empower someone else. Others can strengthen and support individuals who view themselves as powerless. Empowerment occurs by enhancing strengths, promoting the development of the skills necessary to mobilize resources, and providing the necessary resources. In working with Hispanic women, empowering them to cope with and improve their economic and social reality is of utmost importance. Hispanic women should be educated regarding the cycle of violence, resources and strategies to deal with the abusive relationship, information about women's rights, and the social realities of woman abuse. Referrals to self-help and mutual help groups are critical elements in helping Hispanic women cope with their abuse.

A battered Hispanic pregnant woman with low income faces several barriers. These include limited access to adequate prenatal care and limited services to empower her to cope with her abusive relationship. Health care agencies and health care providers need to be culturally sensitive so that they can intervene appropriately. It is particularly important that agencies have mechanisms in place to deal with language barriers.

Health care providers themselves, working with Hispanic pregnant women, can create barriers in the health care system by not understanding or accepting the many ways in which the Hispanic culture perceives and treats pregnancy. The prenatal visit provides the social opportunity to foster a good patient-health care provider relationship, which will facilitate a positive outcome of the labor and delivery experience by decreasing anxiety and fear of the unknown. According to Poma (1987), women are more open to change during this period because it is for the benefit of their families. This provides a good teaching opportunity. Once a relationship of trust is established, Hispanics are more accepting of advice and suggestions concerning new health care ideas. Questions about battering should be included in every routine history taken during pregnancy. McFarlane and Parker (1994a) offer a short, yet effective tool (the five-question Abuse Assessment Screen) to identify battered women (see Chapter 16 in this volume). This tool has been translated into Spanish and has proven effective in identifying Hispanic women who have been battered.

Health care providers need to learn to intervene from within the social organization of the Hispanic culture. Prenatal services for battered Hispanic pregnant women need to be provided in a systematic and acceptable manner using the family and kinship structure. This will facilitate screening, education, and guidance without upsetting the frequently precarious security of this period. Not only is it important for health care providers to provide culturally relevant care to the Hispanic woman, health care providers need to also be ready to intervene on her behalf when appropriate. Leininger (1978) proposes that the most important professional skill that Hispanics look for in a health care provider is interpersonal skill, and genuine interest in them as a cultural group. It is important for the health care provider to understand the worldview of the Hispanic woman to establish rapport and to be genuinely interested in her welfare.

22

Clinical Interventions With Battered Migrant Farm Worker Women

Rachel Rodriguez

Most of the fruits and vegetables we eat were planted, harvested, and packed by migrant farm workers, yet many of us do not know anything about this population. We are unaware of their deplorable living conditions and the fact that they often work for less than minimum wage, under difficult and dangerous circumstances. We are unaware of the assaults on their dignity due to racism and injustice. We are unaware that the people who harvest our food often go hungry.

To live under these oppressive conditions causes stressors that most of us cannot easily imagine. Before you can understand the dynamics of domestic violence for this population, you must have a sense of what it means to be a migrant farm worker. In this chapter, I will attempt to describe the general conditions of migrant life from which you can then begin to understand the scope of the problem of domestic violence for migrant farm worker women and their families. I will share the strategies we have currently developed and our hopes for the future.

The Migrant Lifestyle

Little has changed for migrant farm workers during the past 30 years. Their living and working conditions remain among the most hazardous in this country. Exposure to pesticides, extremes of weather, and overcrowding are just a few of the harsh realities of migrant life (Wilk, 1986). Low wages and harsh living conditions contribute to the potential for poor health that is virtually inevitable for the migrant farm worker (Slesinger, 1992). A migrant farm worker is described by the federal government as "an individual whose principal employment within the last 24 months is in agriculture on a seasonal basis and [who] establishes a temporary abode for employment purposes" (Migrant Health Program, 1992). Contrary to popular belief, migrant farm workers do not just work in the fields harvesting vegetables. They also work in plant nurseries, packing houses, and many even work cutting and preparing Christmas trees. They usually leave their homes in the southern part of the United States, for example, Texas and Florida, in mid- to late April and return to their permanent homes as early as August or as late as November.

Migrant farm workers generally travel through established migration circuits or have particular transmigration patterns. The patterns migrant farm workers travel have also been described as "migrant streams" and were delineated by specific regions of the country. For example, migrants from Florida were said to travel through the "eastern stream," which includes all the states on the eastern U.S. coast. Migration circuits have become a more descriptive term as a migrant family may either have several established locations for work or, given the tenuous nature of the job, must travel to wherever they can find work (personal communication, K. Mountain, Migrant Clinicians Network, December 3, 1996). Migrant farm workers continue to be primarily Latinos (60%), many U.S. born from southwestern states such as Texas, Arizona, and California (Office of Migrant Health, 1992; Zuroweste, 1991). Migrants from Mexico and Central America are also commonly seen working in U.S. agriculture. Mexican migrants may come from the border states, but today they also come from deep in Mexico, such as the states of Chiapas, Oaxaca, and Guanajuato. Migrant farm workers from Central America generally come from Guatemala, Nicaragua, or El Salvador. Indigenous populations from Latin America, such as the Mixtecs, are also seen working in farm work as are Southeast Asians (Hmong, Laotian), African Americans, and Haitians.

Traveling thousands of miles each year, migrant laborers and their families often live in deplorable housing conditions. Some live in migrant camps, but today many growers around the country have chosen to close their labor camps instead of upgrading to meet housing codes. As a result, migrant families must look for housing that is often expensive and in poor condition. Overcrowding becomes a problem as several families must live together to make the housing costs affordable. (I have seen as many as 20 people in one small apartment.) As a result, many farm workers become homeless while they are working. Testimony by farm workers to the National Advisory Council on Migrant Health revealed that migrants were living in garages, cars, caves, boxes, tents, and chicken coops. In many cases, housing is tied to the work and becomes a vicious cycle. If a farm worker does not have housing, he or she will not be able to find work and if there is no work, then there is no housing. Farm workers described their problems with housing in the following manner:

Since we arrived we went to live with one farmer and he rented a cabin to us. We're not going to speak bad of that man that allowed us to have the cabin, but we don't have water to drink, there is not bathrooms to take baths, and we have four children. . . . Now there are a lot of people who are making a living in the same way but are unable to find adequate housing, consequently having to live under trees. What's even worse, the foremen even charged them for sleeping under the trees. (National Advisory Council on Migrant Health, 1993, p. 17)

Effects of Migrant Life on Health

Documentation regarding the health status of migrant farm workers is lacking. Although there is regional and anecdotal information suggesting that farm workers are at risk for poor health, there is a paucity of reliable research data. The studies that exist include epidemiological studies of infectious or chronic disease and medical use patterns (Arbab & Weidner, 1986; Chi, 1985; Dever, 1991). Dever (1991) reviewed 6,969 charts from patients attending migrant health centers across the country and describes the most common health problems found among migrant farm workers. These problems included infectious disease, diabetes, hypertension, and contact dermatitis. He also found that 40% of migrant farm workers who visited these health clinics suffered from multiple health problems. Domestic violence was not reported as a health problem because it did not appear in the charts (personal communication, A. Dever, March 1994).

Arbab and Weidner's (1986) study also found that infectious disease was a primary health problem for migrant farm workers. An audit of 936 charts found that farm workers who were living in conditions that denied them clean water and sanitation facilities had a clinic use rate for diarrhea that was 20 times higher than that of the urban poor in a control group. Fevers of unknown origin were 120 times more common than in the control group.

The Health of Migrant Farm Worker Women

Migrant life is particularly difficult for women. It is estimated that 70% of women work in the fields (Smith & Gonzalez, 1992). After these women work 10 to 12 hours in the fields, their workday continues with housework and child care. Women often mention being tired and having no time to rest. These long workdays preclude much interaction with other women in the camps. Describing life in the camps, one woman stated, "You rarely see women talking to each other. There is no time to worry about the other person" (Rodriguez, unpublished data, 1992). Because agricultural work requires a substantial amount of physical strength and stamina, it is not surprising that migrant farm workers are generally a young population. Consequently, most women are of childbearing age and at risk for complications of pregnancy due to their harsh living and working conditions. Even though this risk is obvious, data regarding pregnancy outcomes and infant mortality rates are scarce. The following provides some indication of the problems of migrant farm worker women. Watkins, Larson, Harlan, and Young (1990) found that migrant farm worker women were less likely to access prenatal care in the first trimester and received less prenatal care than the general population. A study in California (Slesinger, Christensen, & Cautley, 1986) found an infant mortality rate of 30 per 1,000 live births among migrant farm workers, compared with 14 per 1,000 live births in the general population of the United States. This same study reported a mortality rate of 46 per 1,000 migrant children younger than 5 years.

DeLa Torre and Rush (1989) found that 24% of women in their sample (*N* = 148) experienced one or more miscarriages or stillbirths. This was comparable to the findings of similar studies cited by the authors in San Diego and Tulare Counties that reported miscarriages and stillbirths for migrant women of 28% and 31%, respectively. A study of migrant farm worker women in Colorado (Littlefield & Stout, 1987) documented 32.5% of their sample *(N = 120)* experiencing at least one miscarriage or abortion. Infant mortality was reported for this sample at 12.5%.

None of the studies cited discussed the problem of domestic violence or identified domestic violence as a contributor to poor health outcomes. As stated previously, Dever's review of 6,969 charts did not identify domestic violence as a health problem. Although clinicians and migrant farm worker women have had much anecdotal information regarding the severity of domestic violence in this population, research data on this problem did not exist until very recently.

Domestic Violence Among Migrant Farm Workers

Data regarding the presence of domestic violence in relationships among migrant farm workers have only recently become available. The development of the Practice-Based Research Network (PBRN) on Family Violence, created by the Migrant Clinicians Network in 1994, has been primarily responsible for the data that have been generated to date. The origin of the PBRN came as a result of both formal and informal discussions by migrant health clinicians about the problem of domestic violence in their practice. These clinicians were concerned about the number of battered women they were seeing in their practice and their relative insecurity about how to address this problem. As a result, the PBRN was developed to begin documenting the problem of domestic violence for this population.

Since the development of the PBRN, surveys using an adapted version of the four-question Domestic Violence Assessment Form (McFarlane, Christoffel, Bateman, Miller, & Bullock, 1991) have been conducted in 12 migrant health centers around the country who are members of the network. A pilot study was conducted in 1994 to test the adaptation of the form. Results of this survey revealed 35% of migrant women reporting physical abuse and 21% reporting forced sexual activity ($N = 112$) (Migrant Clinicians Network, 1995). The current survey in progress since 1995 continues to identify a high number (25%) of migrant farm worker women ($N = 304$ to date) reporting physical abuse within the past year (see Figure 22.1). In the current survey, 16% of migrant women have reported forced sexual activity within the past year (see Figure 22.2). In all but a rare case, the perpetrators of the abuse have been husbands or boyfriends.

The survey continues to be used and new sites are being included in the network. Plans are in place to expand the network beyond the current survey and provide members with an opportunity to develop new directions for the research network. Participants have been able to use their involvement in the PBRN to increase awareness of the problem among their colleagues and promote strategies within their health centers that can address the needs of battered migrant farm worker women and their families.

Migrant Farm Worker Women Speak
About Domestic Violence

Focus groups with migrant farm worker women in migrant camps in the Midwest have provided much needed information regarding the context of the violence in these women's lives. During the summer of 1994, focus groups were conducted with migrant farm worker women using the following question to open the discussion: "Have you ever known anyone who was physically abused by their partner? Tell me about that." This question was especially helpful given that migrant farm workers are not generally open to discussing personal problems directly. The "third person" (Rodriguez, 1993) has proven quite successful in facilitating discussion of personal issues with farm workers.

Women discussed many of the reasons why they do not talk about the violence in their lives and how they deal with it. The reasons these women gave for staying in their relationships were related to the social pressure migrant women often face in their own communities and the need to keep the family together for the sake of their children. The participants in these focus groups said that this (domestic violence) was not a problem that women would readily talk about. Some of the comments from the women included the following: "We'll die first before we say anything because no one will say, 'I am being abused' . . . none of us talk about such things . . . no one . . . no one." "If I have problems in my house, I wont' even tell my own mother. Because that's my problem, she has her own. We try to resolve our own problems by ourself."

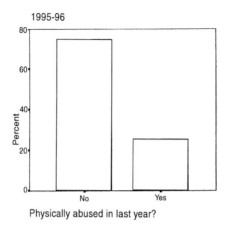

Figure 22.1. Physical Abuse Within the Past Year

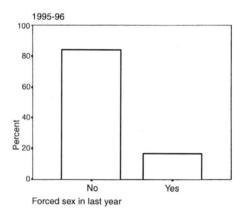

Figure 22.2. Forced Sex Within the Past Year

Staying in the relationship for the sake of the children was reflected in the following statements: "It's just that many women think that they will take away our children and then one says, 'No, my children go before me, I'll take it [the abuse] until my children grow up.' " "There was a woman who told us that she didn't have her papers when she was with her husband and he used to threaten her that he would take away the children . . . every time he would think she would leave him, he would say the same thing, that he was going to tell Immigration."

The social stigma attached to leaving a relationship is one reason many women chose to stay in the relationship. Women were often classified as "good" or "bad" depending on their marital status. Women alone were characterized as women of "the bad life." One woman stated, "You don't divorce your husband, you don't leave your husband. Remember you said for better or for worse. If that's what you got, that's what you got." Leaving was a frightening prospect because women felt they did not have the skills to be on their own. For example, they thought that if they knew how to drive, speak English, or become citizens, then they might be able to leave. Also, many of these women had not been socialized to be alone. Their dilemma is best described in the words of this woman: "It's a very big step. It's like trying to jump a mountain this wide, what if you land in the middle?"

Migrant Farm Worker Women Take Action:
Lideres Campesinas *en Accion*

In 1995, the Centers for Disease Control in conjunction with Lideres Campesinas and the Migrant Clinicians Network developed the Lideres Campesinas Domestic Violence Outreach and Education project. The project was designed to provide a mechanism for migrant farm worker women to share information and resources about domestic violence. Over the prior 18 months, over 50 women have been trained to become liaisons between their communities and service providers around the issue of domestic violence. Each of the women has participated in a 2-day training to learn basic information about domestic violence, legal rights of battered women (particularly undocumented immigrant women), and the services that are available to help survivors of domestic violence.

During the first year of the project, 36 migrant farm worker women, representing 12 different areas of the state of California, received the training. These women then conducted workshops in their local areas and provided information to over 400 other migrant women. The women took advantage of every opportunity to provide information about domestic violence to others in their communities. They talked to women on buses, in beauty shops, at parties, and in the fields. As a result, the Lideres Campesinas were able to provide over 17,000 people with information about domestic violence.

The second year of the project focused on the women becoming leaders in their communities advocating for the rights of battered migrant farm worker women. Another 25 women recently completed a 2-day training to further their skills. During this year, they conducted training sessions for health care providers, social service providers, and law enforcement. They continue to provide information through workshops for women in their communities and individual support as needed. They are becoming partners with health care and other service providers to create an understanding of the needs of migrant farm worker women and promote changes in the service sector to better serve this population.

Unidos Against Domestic Violence

To create a coordinated system of service provision for migrant farm worker women and their families living in violent relationships, Unidos Against Domestic Violence was recently formed in Wisconsin. The group was formed to address the needs of Latino migrant and settled-out migrant communities. The purpose of the group is to develop a comprehensive approach to enhancing existing services that currently do not provide culturally appropriate services. The idea was to create partnerships between existing migrant service providers and other health, social service, and legal services providers. This partnership will build on the cultural expertise of existing migrant providers as well as the trust that has already been established within the migrant community by these providers.

A number of activities are planned as a result of the action plan developed at their first meeting. A few of these activities include cross-training of all providers using a comprehensive curriculum developed by Unidos Against Domestic Violence, creating linkage agreements between migrant service providers and domestic violence service providers, memberships on boards of migrant service agencies and domestic violence agencies by representatives of both groups, and cross-training of existing court translators around the issue of domestic violence for migrant farm workers as well as training service providers to become translators in the court system. These are just a few of the actions planned by and for Unidos Against Domestic Violence in Wisconsin.

Future Directions

The progress to date has been the result of the dedication of service providers, policymakers, researchers, and migrant farm worker women who have been willing to take risks. Working in partnership, they have opened up the discussion of this very intimate problem in a population that had not yet wanted to recognize or talk about the violence that they were living. Although we have opened the door, we have yet to walk through it and develop strategies that can support migrant farm worker families' desire to live in peace. As we continue to work toward this goal, I will share with you our hopes and plans for the future.

Building on the creation of the PBRN, the Lideres Campesinas project in California, and Unidos Against Domestic Violence in Wisconsin, a new project has been proposed that will create a truly comprehensive approach to practice, research, and community outreach for domestic violence among migrant farm worker populations. Interstate networks of service providers (health, domestic violence, social service, and legal) will evolve from the intrastate networks to provide a continuity of services for battered migrant women and their families. Clinicians working in migrant health centers can join the PBRN in their state and collect data that will assist them in program planning and fund-raising for their own domestic violence programs. Replication of the Lideres Campesinas project can occur in migrant communities around the country that can collaborate with professionals as members of the interstate networks.

Much of this work is currently being done as part of the Wisconsin/Texas Domestic Violence project. With the creation of Unidos Against Domestic Violence and the first steps toward replication of the Lideres Campesinas project completed in the summer and fall of 1996, the vision is becoming reality. The migrant health center in Wisconsin is currently a member of the PBRN and has been actively involved in the work of both Unidos Against Domestic Violence and the replication of the Lideres Campesinas project. Additionally, a multidisciplinary course for graduate students at the University of Wisconsin–Madison was offered for the first time in summer 1996. Plans are in place to offer a similar course at the University of Texas Health Science Center, School of Nursing, in San Antonio. The goal of this course offering is to generate a commitment from future practitioners to work in solidarity with marginalized populations in the area of domestic violence.

It is our vision to create a safety net for battered migrant farm worker women that will extend beyond traditional health care and other institutional settings and into migrant communities and households. In this way, a woman will be assured of finding knowledgeable, caring individuals who can guide her to resources regardless of her circumstances.

23

Issues in Providing Care for Rural Battered Women

Nancy Fishwick

Awareness of the nature and extent of violence against women has steadily grown in the United States over the past two decades. However, social policy and program development achievements have not addressed the particular needs of battered women in rural areas. This lack of attention is largely attributable to paradoxical myths about rural life: that rural life is tranquil, pure, and nonviolent or that violence against women is an acceptable aspect of daily rural life.

Are the experiences and needs of rural battered women any different than those of women in urban areas? Women in rural areas of the United States experience abuse from intimate adult partners in ways similar to that experienced by women in urban or suburban areas. The abuse may take the form of physical, psychological, or sexual assault. Although the fundamental nature of abusive relationships crosses all geographic, social, and cultural boundaries, rural women are faced with particularly enormous challenges when they attempt to end the abuse in their lives.

Is it possible to compare the experiences and needs of battered women from the forests of northern New England, the coal fields of Appalachia, the vast farms and ranches of the Midwest and Great Plains, the deserts of the Southwest, and the rural coastal communities of the Northwest? Although diversity of cultural values, norms, and traditions abounds in rural America as much as in urban areas, there are common threads that bind the lives of rural women who are abused by their partners.

To understand and address the needs of rural battered women, a closer look at rural life in the United States is needed. This chapter presents an overview of rural life, rural women, and domestic violence in rural areas. Excerpts from interviews with rural battered women are used to illustrate certain points. The chapter concludes with specific strategies for health and social service providers to improve their care of rural battered women.

Rural Life

The term *rural* is defined in a variety of ways. For example, the U.S. Census Bureau defines an area as rural if the population is less than 2,500 people or the area is open countryside. In contrast, the Office of Management and Budget uses the terms *metropolitan statistical area* (MSA) and *nonmetropolitan statistical area* to separate areas. With this designation, some small towns and sparsely populated areas may fall within an MSA, whereas large towns that are distanced from an MSA may be designated as nonmetropolitan. The inconsistent definitions may affect the economic resources of rural areas because the definitions are used for the allocation and distribution of federal and state funds for health and social programs, housing, and other financial aid. For instance, federal or state funds for programs and shelters for battered women and their children usually are designated to serve a certain population size rather than a geographic area. Consequently, shelters in rural, sparsely populated areas must serve women in a vast geographic area, which means that some women will be many miles from the nearest shelter.

Quality of Rural Life

The term rural conjures up a variety of mental images. The characteristics that make rural areas appealing also can be the characteristics that make them difficult places in which to live. For example, the remoteness from urban areas may be a welcome relief, or it may create a sense of isolation from society. The sense of kinship, neighborliness, and being known to all in the community may foster a sense of connectedness and support, but it also may be viewed as a lack of privacy that results in reluctance to disclose personal concerns that may not be held in confidence. And living simply and independently with few modern amenities may be satisfying, but it also involves hardship, toil, and deprivation.

Demographics. Rural Americans tend to have less formal education than do urban dwellers. College education is rarely available in rural areas, although some colleges now operate rural satellite campuses and also have courses available through telecommunication. Rural residents who finish high school and go to college often relocate to urban areas for satisfactory employment. The lack of opportunities for higher education limits the rural woman's qualifications for satisfactory employment and thwarts her ability to be the sole support of a family if she leaves an abusive partner.

Although affluence and middle-range incomes are present, the average income of rural Americans is consistently lower than that of urban dwellers. Rural poverty rates are as high as, or higher than, urban poverty for every racial and ethnic group analyzed by the U.S. Census Bureau. In addition, rural unemployment rates exceed urban unemployment rates; in 1986, unemployment was 26% higher in rural areas than in urban areas. Poverty is particularly profound in the Appalachian area, the Mississippi Delta, on Native American reservations, and in rural communities of high Mexican American concentration.

Substandard housing abounds in rural areas. Lack of indoor plumbing and electricity persists among those who cannot afford them. Although people are more likely to own, rather than rent, their home, there is heavy reliance on trailer homes that lose value. Furthermore, an owner may own the home but not the land it sits on; mineral rights may belong to private corporations that may eventually want to extract minerals from the land. The rural battered woman who wishes to remain in a particular geographic area may find that safe, affordable, adequate housing is scarce or nonexistent.

Transportation and Communication. Transportation can be difficult in rural areas because of great distances, fewer routes, poor road conditions, and reliance on private vehicles for travel. People without private vehicles are particularly disadvantaged because of the lack of public transportation. The rural battered woman trying to escape an assault may not have a driver's license or may not have access to a vehicle in working order. Abusive partners often deny use of the family's vehicle by keeping the keys hidden from the battered woman, or by deliberately disabling a vehicle to prevent her from leaving.

Communication in rural areas is hampered by the great distances between people, and, for many, lack of telephone service. Television and radio communication remains poor in some areas, although the availability of home satellite dishes has improved reception for many rural residents. Domestic violence programs and shelters for rural battered women and their children have difficultly disseminating information about their services because of the restricted means of communication.

Many rural homes are without telephones because of their remoteness or because of the expense. Although neighbors may be willing to permit use of a telephone, the distance might be too great to be of practical use during an assault; after the assault, a woman may hesitate to make calls where they would be overheard by others. Even if a telephone is available, a woman may be reluctant to make a crisis call if it involves a long-distance toll because the telephone number would be listed on the telephone bill for her abusive partner to see.

Rural Values. Rural populations continue to be generally conservative in personal behavior and political philosophy. Surveys indicate that when compared with urban residents, rural residents favor greater difficulty in obtaining a divorce, oppose teenagers having access to contraceptives, strongly oppose premarital sex, profess to adherence to religious beliefs and customs, and are less tolerant of minority rights. Self-reliance, independence, and solving one's problems without assistance from others, particularly not from officials or "outsiders," is highly valued in rural communities. This value of self-reliance often places the burden of resolving the abuse on the rural battered woman.

Rural Health. Another distorted image of rural America is that of abundant health from living in a clean environment, engaging in physically demanding work, and being away from the stress and dangers of urban life. On the contrary, rural Americans experience higher infant mortality and a higher prevalence of chronic health conditions such as emphysema, hypertension, and coronary heart disease than do urban Americans. Accidents comprise the major cause of death and disability in rural areas. The accidents often are related to occupation, resulting from operating heavy machinery used in farming, mining, and forestry industries. Heavy tools, guns for hunting, and other potential weapons are commonplace in rural homes, which places battered women in danger of lethal injury.

Mental health problems and substance use are prevalent in rural areas, but there are few accessible treatment programs. Alcohol and other drug abuse is widely implicated in assaults against female partners, with women reporting more serious assaults against them when the batterer is intoxicated. However, investigators have not found a consistent cause-and-effect relationship between the two events; some abusive men are not alcohol or drug users, whereas some men who are alcohol or drug abusers are nonviolent. The rural battered woman may also be an abuser of alcohol or drugs. Chemically dependent women have a high prevalence of abuse in childhood or in adult relationships. The use of alcohol or drugs may be a means of self-medicating pain and fear. A woman who lived in an island fishing community premedicated herself every afternoon in anticipation of her husband's return from the boat:

> I would get all my housework done and then I would wait for him to come home. And I would have a couple of drinks, just in case . . . just in case. If he'd had a good catch that day and was in a good mood, then everything was OK. But if he had a bad day, then I got it. I got it really bad.

In addition, the drugs a woman abuses may be medications prescribed by health care professionals for relief of the anxiety, depression, insomnia, or chronic pain that results from abusive and violent living conditions. One woman with a neurological disability related:

> I usually had a supply of different tranquilizers that the doctors prescribed for painful muscle spasms. I used those tranquilizers for a lot more than muscle spasms, believe me. The doctors had no idea what was going on at home.

Rural residents clearly are at a disadvantage in the lack of accessible health services. Small rural hospitals have been closing at an alarming rate in the past decade, leaving people without timely emergency and hospital care. Rural areas lack primary health care services, although access has improved in some regions with the recruitment of nurse practitioners, nurse-midwives, and physician assistants. Availability of prenatal and obstetric care, never in abundance, has been further compromised by the recent trend of family practice physicians, who are the usual medical providers in rural areas, giving up maternity care because of rising malpractice insurance premiums.

Rural Women

Women in rural areas share many of the problems and inequities that concern women everywhere. Resolving problems or coping with them is more difficult in rural areas because of isolation from the larger society, lack of resources, and living within a cultural tradition of restricted roles for women. Women's roles in rural communities reflect traditional gender roles: Women are full-time home-makers and providers of child care. Rural women marry younger, remain married longer, and have their first pregnancy earlier than do urban women.

For rural women, home management responsibilities may involve arduous labor without modern appliances, raising and preserving food for winter use, and "making do" with few resources. The ability to achieve results despite tremendous obstacles is a source of pride for rural women; perseverance and self-sufficiency are viewed as positive attributes. Women also are skilled providers of lay health care in rural areas; traditional remedies and self-care strategies are crucial to the maintenance of physical health needed for rural work.

Despite the long tradition of women staying in the home, rural women increasingly are joining the labor force to supplement an inadequate single income or because they have become a single head of the household. Unfortunately, rural women have a narrow range of occupational choices because of limited education, limited variety of jobs, and travel restrictions. They usually must take low-skill, low-wage jobs that have little job security and poor benefits. Women who want to work outside the home are further limited by the scarcity of child care facilities in rural communities. Rural women also are confronted with persistent, often derogatory, sex role stereotyping in the workplace. For example, the first women coal miners had to overcome the traditional belief that a woman's presence in a deep mine would cause a cave-in.

Domestic Violence in Rural Areas

Domestic violence is as prevalent in rural areas as it is in urban areas. However, the characteristics of rural life, the rural health care system, and the cultural traditions of rural residents have contributed to a lack of attention to rural battered women. Domestic violence is less visible because of the geographic isolation of rural families, reluctance of rural women to come forward, lack of advocacy programs and shelters for battered women and their children in rural areas, and lack of research and media attention to domestic violence in rural America.

A process of systematic isolation from social networks and sources of potential help is a key characteristic of abusive relationships in general. In rural areas, the social isolation of the battered woman is compounded by geographic isolation; a mountain range, prairie, or forest may lie between the battered woman and sources of help.

In general, women who are abused by their partners initially attempt to resolve the abuse by themselves. If the abuse continues, women may turn to informal sources of support and help, such as family members and friends. If needed, women eventually may turn to more formal sources of help, such as law enforcement officials, clergy, social workers, health care professionals, and women's support groups and programs. This pattern seems to hold true for rural women, although cultural traditions and lack of resources severely restrict the rural woman's help-seeking activities. Appalachian women who had been physically abused by their husbands described the strong sense of marital obligation and desire to hold their families together that compelled them to resolve the abuse alone. Although the women did not believe they deserved the abuse, they saw few options to their current situation and felt ill prepared to support themselves and their children without their partners.

Informal and Formal Sources of Help

When rural battered women turn to family members, friends, and neighbors for assistance, they are taking a risk that their disclosure of abuse will be ignored or ridiculed or that they will be held responsible for the problem. Potential helpers may be reluctant to become involved in another family's problems because involvement is perceived as interfering or causing embarrassment for that family. It is thought best to "look the other way" and leave them alone to resolve their own problems. In many cases, when a woman marries a man in a rural area, they establish their home in the vicinity of the husband's family. In times of crisis, the rural battered woman is limited to seeking assistance from the abuser's family, who may be unresponsive to her needs.

Law Enforcement. The lack of anonymity in rural areas discourages women from seeking help from law enforcement agencies unless their safety, or that of their children, is in serious jeopardy. The responding police officer may be a neighbor, a member of the woman's family or social circle, a member of her abuser's family, or one of his friends. The police response to a battered woman's call for help depends on many factors, such as the relationship between the officer and the abuser, the officer's belief of the woman's story, the officer's attitude toward domestic violence and toward women in general, and the laws and customs of that region and state regarding removal of the abuser from the premises. Police may, in fact, be concerned and willing to help the woman regain safety, but they are unable to offer reliable protection from harm. They cannot guard her from future assault, nor can they transport her to distant safety if regulations forbid it. In addition to an uncertain police response, the rural battered woman realizes that police activities and any criminal charges may appear in the local newspaper, which will lead to unwanted attention.

In the best of circumstances, a woman who pursues her legal right to press charges and obtain a protection order from an abusive husband or partner encounters a confusing, expensive, and time-consuming maze of legal personnel, procedures, and regulations. Battered women who seek legal assistance in rural areas face even greater obstacles in the legal system. Because there are fewer legal personnel in rural areas, the success of a woman's legal action depends on the knowledge and attitudes of the local attorneys, prosecutor, and judge toward domestic violence, and on the personal ties between court personnel and her abuser. In addition, remote areas may have a judge available to hold court only a few times a year; thus, the safety of the battered woman who has pressed charges against her abuser is jeopardized until the case is heard in court.

Clergy. Rural inhabitants tend to rank themselves as being more religious than urban dwellers. It is natural, then, for rural women in abusive relationships to seek counsel from their clergy. Traditionally, the religious community has responded to family violence with silence. When women have turned to their clergy for assistance, they have been told to forgive endlessly, to renew their dedication as wife and mother, and to resolve the problem by themselves. This sense of spiritual responsibility deeply affects rural women's responses to abuse by their partners. However, the religious community has become more aware of the need to educate clergy about the dynamics of family violence and to take an active role in assisting those involved. A Catholic woman who was seen in a rural hospital's emergency department for severe injuries sustained from her husband related:

The nurses were pretty direct in asking me if my husband had done this to me. But I was real concerned because my husband had made me swear to God that I wouldn't tell [who did this]. The priest knew me quite well . . . he may have known what was going on even though I never told him. So I had the nurses call the priest and he came right down to the hospital. He explained to me that I had been under duress from my husband and that God would not hold me to that vow . . . so I talked it over with the nurses and we got the police involved. They all seemed to know, step by step, what to do.

Health Care Professionals. When the battered woman turns to health care providers for assistance, the response is unpredictable. Health care providers may overlook signs of battering, ignore a woman's disclosure of abuse, acknowledge the battering but not view it as being germane to health care, or hold the battered woman responsible for her abuse. Seeking help from health care providers involves risks for rural battered women. In small hospitals or other rural clinical settings, ancillary and professional staff are likely to know the battered woman and her batterer.

The lack of anonymity means that her disclosure of abuse may become known to the batterer; she is well aware that he may retaliate with further abuse when she is discharged from the clinical setting. Fear that her children will be removed from the home because of being an "unfit" mother also keeps many women from disclosing abuse in health care settings. A woman who lives in a remote wooded area discussed visits to the regional rural health center for care of her diabetes:

Now I'm not about to tell what's going on at home to anyone at that clinic. Two of his cousins work there. If they find out that I mentioned this, they will just report it back to him [her husband]. And that would make life even worse for me.

Providing Care for Rural Battered Women

Providing health or social service care of battered women in rural areas differs from providing care for women in urban and suburban areas, not in specific interventions, but in the broad scope of care that is needed. Health and social service practitioners in rural areas must function as generalists rather than specialists. The rural practitioner must be able to apply broad-based professional knowledge and provide care in diverse family- and community-based settings to meet the needs of rural residents. Rural practitioners also are familiar with the people they serve through social roles in the community as well as through professional-client roles.

Community education, assessment of all women clients for abuse, interventions that empower women, and forming links with local shelters and programs for battered women are common themes in providing care for battered women. Although rural areas may lack specialized services for battered women, practitioners can take advantage of opportunities that arise in daily rural life to assist battered women. The rural context creates special problems for the practitioner who wishes to have a positive impact on the problem of domestic violence in the community. For example, the health or social service practitioner who is a newcomer to the community, or considered an "outsider," may encounter community resistance when the provocative topic of domestic violence is broached. Gaining acceptance and trust from the community takes time and diplomatic negotiation. Battered women's shelters in rural areas can attest to the skepticism and resistance of rural communities when the programs were first developed. According to the staff of one rural shelter, diplomatic conduct helped to dispel the community's view of staff as homewreckers and "man-hating lesbians."

Community Education

Effective education regarding domestic violence in rural areas can be conducted informally in daily conversations with community residents. Approaches that are more systematic and formal may target local police, attorneys, court personnel, clergy and their congregations, political leaders, health care providers, and social service professionals. Local dentists need to be included in educational efforts because they repair the damage to teeth and jaws inflicted on a woman by an assaultive partner. Mental health care providers in the area also need to be included in educational efforts because they often help women who experience depression, anxiety, substance abuse, and suicidal or homicidal thoughts that may result from living in fear of assault from an abusive partner. Supportive networks in rural areas are more likely to thrive through direct, personal contact with the people involved rather than through mailings or telephone calls. Once people are aware that a local practitioner is concerned about domestic violence, that individual often becomes a resource and referral for battered women needing assistance.

Assessment for Abuse

Clinical Settings. Health care and social service providers in all clinical settings encounter women who are in abusive relationships, although the abuse often goes unrecognized. Direct, simple questions that provide an opportunity to disclose abuse need to be included in routine intake procedures; for example, health histories for women clients seen in emergency departments, well-woman care settings, prenatal care settings, or in hospital or home care should include questions that permit disclosure of abuse. Questions such as "Have you been, or are you being, physically or emotionally hurt by your partner?" or "Do arguments with your partner become physical?" permit a woman to discuss behaviors that have been directed toward her that she has not yet labeled as abusive. Rural practice often allows for continuity of care. Each visit is an opportunity to build trust and convey concern, so women may eventually feel more comfortable in disclosing private information.

The practitioner must be alert to the woman who misses appointments or seems reluctant to let the practitioner come to the house. Although missed appointments or refused home visits may be unrelated to abuse, women who have visible injuries may want to let them heal before being seen by anyone, or they may not want a visitor to come to the house when their abuser is present.

Community Settings. In rural areas, assessment for abuse should occur not only with all women clients in professional care settings but also in daily activities and places where women congregate: in the grocery store, the laundromat, the beauty salon, and in women's religious and civic groups. In addition to visible evidence of injury, the health or social service practitioner should be alert to subtle clues that a woman is being abused, such as a woman using heavy make-up or wearing high-necked, long-sleeved garments to cover bruises; expressions of fear of her partner; inability to participate in community activities because of absolute dependence on her partner for his permission to participate or for transportation or money; disappearance from her usual activities for days or weeks at a time; or reluctance of the partner to let the woman away from his watchful eyes and ears.

Response to Disclosure of Abuse

When abuse is disclosed, rural women have needs similar to those of urban women: The woman needs privacy and time in which to tell her story of abuse, and she needs to know that the practitioner is listening, believes her, and is concerned for her safety and well-being. Alternatives to living with the abuse need to be explored, information about available resources needs to be shared, and the woman's decisions must be supported. Use of the telephone should be offered to the woman; the clinical visit may be a rare opportunity for her to make calls in private to family or friends who might offer help, police, attorneys, or shelters. The scheduling of further visits should also be offered because an appointment may provide one of the few "legitimate" reasons for her to leave her abuser's watchful eye; she can use the visit to gather further information.

Battered women are at high risk for becoming homicide victims or they may ultimately kill their batterer. Consequently, danger assessment is an important component of professional care. The Danger Assessment tool developed by Campbell is an important resource for health care and social service practitioners (see Chapter 18 in this volume). Indicators of escalating danger to the woman include the presence of weapons in the home and threats to use them, increasingly severe physical assaults, increasingly aggressive behavior outside the home, and battering during pregnancy.

Whether the level of danger is believed to be low or high, safety planning is an essential component of the response to disclosure of abuse. Safety plans do not ensure safety; however, the discussion serves an important function for engaging the woman in advanced planning to improve future safety. Strategies for various contingencies can be developed, including learning exit routes from each room in the house and from the house itself, making arrangements for a safe place to stay in advance of a crisis, keeping a set of keys to the house and automobile hidden, keeping some money (including coins for a public telephone) and important identification papers in a secure location, and memorizing the telephone number of the regional domestic violence program and police department.

Resource Development

The rural practitioner who is well accepted in the community is in a unique position to influence local policy and develop resources for battered women. Resource development need not be done from scratch; forming links with existing resources in the region and networking with successful battered women's programs in other rural areas provides an important starting point. The National Coalition Against Domestic Violence (NCADV) has published two resources that are vital for rural practitioners. One publication is a national directory of battered women's shelters and programs (NCADV, 1991a). The rural practitioner can contact the closest program and request assistance in helping local battered women. Staff in existing programs and shelters often are available to provide community education about domestic violence, describe their services, and work with the practitioner to develop services for women in remote areas. The second important publication is the *Rural Task Force Resource Packet* (NCADV, 1991b) in which model programs in rural areas are described for replication.

In summary, the challenge of providing care to rural battered women can be met with innovative strategies that respect the advantages and the limitations inherent in rural life. The rural practitioner who is dedicated to being part of the solution of violence against women will be confronted with community resistance, victim-blaming attitudes, and seemingly insurmountable obstacles at times. Building links with the wider community working with battered women will ensure needed support for the rural practitioner. The concerned rural practitioner can serve as a catalyst for change; ultimately, however, peaceful rural communities will be created through the collaborative efforts of all who reside there.

Resources

Nursing

Nursing Network on Violence Against Women International
1801 H Street, Suite B65-165
Modesto, CA 95354
304-347-1254

Association of Women's Health, Obstetric and Neonatal Nursing
700 14th Street, N.W., Suite 600
Washington, DC 20005-2019
202-662-1600

American Academy of Nursing, Expert Panel on
    Violence Policy Nursing Leadership
600 Marilyn Avenue, S.W., Suite 100 West
Washington, DC 20024-2571
202-651-7066

American College of Nurse Midwives
818 Connecticut Ave, N.W., Suite 900
Washington, DC 20006
202-728-9864

International Association of Forensic Nurses
6900 Grove Road
Thorofare, NJ 08086

Nursing Summit on Domestic Violence
DHHS Nursing Leadership
Frances Page—Office of Women's Health
200 Independence Avenue, S.W., Rm. 728-F
Washington, DC 20201
202-690-6373

Emergency Nursing Association
216 Higgins Road
Park Ridge, IL 60068-5736
708-698-9400

American Nurses Association
600 Maryland Avenue, S.W.
Suite 100 West
Washington, DC 20024-2571
202-651-7066

National Policy and Advocacy

Family Violence Prevention Fund & National Health Resource Center
383 Rhode Island Street, Suite 304
San Francisco, CA 94103-5133
415-252-8900
1-800-313-1310

National Domestic Violence Hotline
1-800-799-SAFE

National Coalition Against Domestic Violence
119 Constitution Avenue, N.E.
Washington, DC 20002
202-544-7358

National March of Dimes
17171 West Nine Mile Road, Suite 1240
Southfield, MI 48075
Mary Ellen Gleason
810-423-3200

NOW Legal Defense and Education Fund
National Policy and Advocacy
1000 16th Street, #700
Washington, DC 20036
202-331-0066

Black Women's Health Network
Principal Ama R. Saran Association
156 Sunset Avenue, N.W.
Atlanta, GA 30314
404-659-1560

National Resource Center
3320 N. Street, N.W., #171
Washington, DC 20007

National Governmental Organizations

Centers for Disease Control, Division of Violence Prevention
Family & Intimate Violence Prevention Team
4770 Buford Hwy, Mailstop k-20
Atlanta, GA 30341-3724
770-488-4349

U.S. Department of Justice
Office of Violence Against Women
Bonnie Campbell
950 Pennsylvania Avenue, N.W., Rm. 5302
Washington, DC 20530
202-616-8894

Health-Related Programs

AYUDA
Immigrant Battered Women—Legal Services and Advocacy
1736 Columbia Road, N.W.
Washington, DC 20009
202-387-0434

American Medical Association
Department of Mental Health
515 North State Street
Chicago, IL 60610

International Organizations

World Health Organization
Office of Women's Development
CH 1211
Geneva 27-Switzerland

PAHO (Pan American Health Organization)
Women's Health and Development
525 23rd Street, N.W.
Washington, DC 20037
202-974-3000

Health and Development Policy Project
6930 Carroll Avenue, Suite 430
Takoma Park, MD 20912
Lori Heise
301-270-1182

For hospital- and health care setting-based programs, see Chapter 2.

References

Abbott, J., John, R., Loziol-McLain, J., & Lowenstein, S. (1995). Domestic violence against women: Incidence and prevalence in an emergency department population. *Journal of the American Medical Association, 273*(22), 1763-1767.

Achenbach, T. M., & Edelbrock, C. S. (1983). *Manual for the Child Behavior Checklist and Revised Child Behavior Profile.* Burlingame: University of Vermont Press.

Aguirre, B. E. (1985). Why do they return? Abused wives in shelters. *Social Work, 30,* 350-354.

Aguirre-Molina, M., & Molina, C. (1994). Latino populations: Who are they? In C. W. Molina & M. Aguirre-Molina (Eds.), *Latino health in the U.S.: A growing challenge* (pp. 3-22). Washington, DC: American Public Health Association.

Albers, P., & Medicine, B. (1983). *The hidden half: Studies of plains Indian women.* Lanham, MD: University Press of America.

Amaro, H., Fried, L. E., Cabral, H., & Zuckerman, B. (1990). Violence during pregnancy and substance use. *American Journal of Public Health, 80*(5), 575-579.

American Board of Forensic Odontology. (1986). Guidelines for bite mark analysis. *Journal of the American Dental Association, 112*(3), 383-386.

American College of Obstetricians and Gynecologists. (1989). *The battered woman* (ACOG Technical Bulletin). Washington, DC: Author.

American Medical Association. (1992a). *Diagnostic and treatment guidelines on child physical abuse and neglect.* Chicago: Author.

American Medical Association. (1992b). *Diagnostic and treatment guidelines on domestic violence.* Chicago: Author.

American Medical Association, Council on Ethical and Judicial Affairs. (1992). Violence against women: Relevance for medical practitioners. *Journal of the American Medical Association, 267,* 3184-3189.

American Psychiatric Association. (1994). *Diagnostic and statistical manual of mental disorders* (4th ed.). Washington, DC: Author.

Anderson, R. M., Giachello, A. L., & Aday, L. (1986). Access of Hispanics to health care and cuts in services: A state-of-the-art overview. *Public Health Reports, 101,* 238-265.

Arbab, D., & Weidner, L. (1986). Infectious disease and field water supply and sanitation among migrant farm workers. *American Journal of Public Health, 76*(6), 694-695.

Asante, M. K. (1990). *Kemet, Afrocentricity and knowledge.* Trenton, NJ: African World.

Asbury, J. (1987). African American women in violent relationships: An exploration of cultural differences. In R. L. Hampton (Ed.), *Violence in the black family: Correlates and consequences* (pp. 89-105). Lexington, MA: Lexington Books.

Ashby, M. R., Gilchrist, L. D., & Miramontez, A. (1987). Group treatment for sexually abused American Indian adolescents. *Social Work With Groups, 10*(4), 21-32.

Astin, M. C., Lawrence, K. J., & Foy, D. W. (1993). Post-traumatic stress among battered women: Risk and resiliency factors. *Violence and Victims, 8*(1), 17-28.

Bachman, G., Moeller, T., & Benett, J. (1988). Childhood sexual abuse and the consequences in adult women. *Obstetrics and Gynecology, 71,* 631-642.

Bachman, R., & Coker, A. (1995). Police involvement in domestic violence: The interactive effects of victim injury, offender(s) history of violence and race. *Violence and Victims, 10*(2), 91-106.

Bachman, R., & Saltzman, L. E. (1995). *Violence against women: Estimates from the redesigned survey.* Washington, DC: U.S. Department of Justice.

Bailey, J. E., Kellermann, A. L., Somes, G. W., Banton, J. G., Rivera, F. P., & Rushford, N. P. (1997). Risk factors for violent death of women in the home. *Archives of Internal Medicine, 157,* 777-782.

Baldwin, J. A. (1986). African (black) psychology: Issues and synthesis. *Journal of Black Studies, 16,* 235-249.

Bass, D. (1992). *Helping vulnerable youths: Runaways and homeless adolescents in the United States.* Washington, DC: National Association of Social Workers Press.

Bass, E., & Davis, L. (1990). *The courage to heal: A guide for women survivors of child sexual abuse.* New York: Harper and Row.

Beauchamp, T. L., & Childress, J. F. (1994). *Principles of biomedical ethics* (4th ed.). New York: Oxford University Press.

Beckstead, J. W., Rawson, R. D., & Giles, W. S. (1979). Review of bite mark evidence. *Journal of the American Dental Association, 99*(1), 69-74.

Bendtro, M., & Bowker, L. (1989). Battered women: How can nurses help? *Issues in Mental Health Nursing, 10,* 169-180.

Benson, B. W., Cottone, J. A., Bomberg, T. J., & Sperber, N. D. (1988). Bite mark impressions: A review of techniques and materials. *Journal of Forensic Sciences, 33*(5), 1238-1243.

Benton, D. A. (1986). Battered women: Why do they stay? *Health Care for Women International, 7,* 403-411.

Berendes, H. W. (1977). Methods of family planning and the risk of low birth weight. In D. M. Reed & F. J. Stanley (Eds.), *The epidemiology of prematurity.* Baltimore: Urban and Schwartzenberg.

Berenson, A. B., Stiglich, N. J., Wilkinson, G. S., & Anderson, D. G. (1991). Drug abuse and other risk factors for physical abuse in pregnancy among white non-Hispanic, black, and Hispanic women. *American Journal of Obstetrics and Gynecology, 164,* 1491-1499.

Bergman, B., & Brismar, B. (1990). Battered wives: Measures by the social and medical services. *Postgraduate Medical Journal, 66*(771), 28-33.

Bergman, B., & Brismar, B. (1991). A 5-year follow-up study of 117 battered women. *American Journal of Public Health, 81*(11), 1486-1489.

Bergman, B., Brismar, B., & Nordin, C. (1992). Utilization of medical care by abused women. *British Medical Journal, 305,* 27-28.

Bergman, B., Larsson, G., Brismar, B., & Klang, M. (1989). Battered wives and female alcoholics: A comparative social and psychiatric study. *Journal of Advanced Nursing, 14,* 727-734.

Berland, D., Homlish, J., & Blotcky, M. (1989). Adolescent gangs in the hospital. *Bulletin of the Menninger Clinic, 53,* 31-43.

Bernard, G. W., Vera, H., Vera, M., & Newman, G. (1982). Til death do us part: A study of spouse murder. *Bulletin of the American Academy of Psychiatry and the Law, 10,* 271-280.

Berrios, D. C., & Grady, D. (1991). Domestic violence: Risk factors and outcomes. *Western Journal of Medicine, 155*(2), 133-135.

Bilinkoff, J. (1995). Empowering battered women as mothers. In E. Peled, P. G. Jaffe, & J. L. Edleson (Eds.), *Ending the cycle of violence: Community responses to children of battered women.* Thousand Oaks, CA: Sage.

Bland, R., & Orn, H. (1986). Family violence and psychiatric disorder. *Canadian Journal of Psychiatry, 31,* 129-137.

Block, R. (1985). *Specific of patterns over time in Chicago Homicide.* Chicago: Criminal Justice Authority.

Blum, R. W., Harmon, B., Harris, L., Bergeison, L., & Resnick, M. D. (1992). American Indian-Alaska Native youth health. *Journal of the American Medical Association, 267*(12), 1637-1644.

Bohn, D. K. (1990). Domestic violence and pregnancy: Implications for practice. *Journal of Nurse-Midwifery, 35,* 86-98.

Bohn, D. K. (1993). *The health effects of domestic violence before and during pregnancy among urban American Indian women in Minnesota.* Doctoral dissertation, Rush University. University Microfilms No. 9406044.

Bohn, D. K., Jones, E., & Jene, T. (1995). [The prevalence and health effects of violence against women in an urban nurse-midwifery practice]. Unpublished raw data.

Bohn, D. K., & Parker, B. (1993). Domestic abuse and pregnancy: Health effects and implications for nursing practice. In J. C. Campbell & J. C. Humphreys (Eds.), *Nursing care of survivors of family violence.* St. Louis, MO: C. V. Mosby.

Bolton, F. G., & Bolton, S. R. (1987). *Working with violent families.* Newbury Park, CA: Sage.

Breslau, N., Davis, G. C., Andreski, P., & Peterson, E. (1991). Traumatic events and posttraumatic stress disorder in an urban population of young adults. *Archives of General Psychiatry, 48,* 216-222.

Breslin, F. C., Riggs, D. S., O'Leary, K. D., & Arias, I. (1990). Family precursors: Expected and actual consequences of dating aggression. *Journal of Interpersonal Violence, 5,* 247-258.

Brooks, R. (1994). Children at risk: Fostering resilience and hope. *American Journal of Orthopsychiatry, 64*(4), 545-553.

Brooks-Gunn, J., & Furstenberg, F. (1989). Adolescent sexual behavior. *American Psychologist, 4*(2), 249-258.

Brown, J., & Rayne, J. T. (1989). Some ethical considerations in defensive psychiatry: A case study. *American Journal of Orthopsychiatry, 59,* 534-541.

Brown, M. A. (1986). Social support during pregnancy: A unidimensional or multidimensional construct? *Nursing Research, 35,* 4-9.

Browne, A. (1987). *Battered women who kill.* New York: Free Press.

Browne, A. (1988). Family homicide: When victimized women kill. In V. B. Van Hasselt, R. L. Morrison, A. S. Bellack, & M. Hersen (Eds.), *Handbook of family violence* (pp. 271-289). New York: Plenum.

Browne, A., & Bassuk, S. S. (1997). Intimate violence in the lives of homeless and poor housed women: Prevalence and patterns in an ethnically diverse sample. *American Journal of Orthopsychiatry, 67*(2), 261-278.

Buel, S. (1994). Domestic violence: Safety for women. *AMA Newsletter, 1*(3).

Buffalohead, P. (1985). Farmers, warriors, traders: A fresh look at Ojibway women. *Minnesota History, 21*(3), 236-244.

Bullock, L. (1987). *Battering and pregnancy: Effect on infant birthweight.* Unpublished master's thesis, Texas Woman's University, Houston.

Bullock, L., & McFarlane, J. (1989). The birth weight/battering connection. *American Journal of Nursing, 89*(9), 1153-1155.

Butts, J., Snyder, H., Finnegan, T., Aughenbaugh, A., & Poole, R. (1994). [Juvenile court statistics]. Pittsburgh, PA: National Center for Juvenile Justice.

Campbell, D. W., Campbell, J. C., King, C., Parker, B., & Ryan, J. (1994). The reliability and factor structure of the Index of Spouse Abuse with African-American battered women. *Violence and Victims, 9,* 259-274.

Campbell, J., Pliska, M. J., Taylor, W., & Sheridan, D. (1994). Battered women's experiences in emergency departments: Need for appropriate policy and procedures. *Journal of Emergency Nursing, 20,* 280-288.

Campbell, J. C. (1981). Misogyny and homicide of women. *Advances in Nursing Science, 3*(2), 67-85.

Campbell, J. C. (1986). Nursing assessment for risk of homicide with battered women. *Advances in Nursing Science, 8*(4), 36-51.

Campbell, J. C. (1989a). A test of two explanatory models of women's responses to battering. *Nursing Research, 38,* 18-24.

Campbell, J. C. (1989b). Women's responses to sexual abuse in intimate relationships. *Women's Health Care International, 8,* 335-347.

Campbell, J. C. (1992). "If I can't have you, no one can": Power and control in homicide of female partners. In J. Radford & D. Russell (Eds.), *Femicide: The politics of woman killing.* Boston: Twayne.

Campbell, J. C. (1993). Posttraumatic stress in battered women: Does the diagnosis fit? *Issues in Mental Health Nursing, 14,* 173-186.

Campbell, J. C. (1995). Prediction of homicide of and by battered women. In J. Campbell (Ed.), *Assessing dangerousness: Violence by sexual offenders, batterers, and child abusers* (pp. 96-113). Thousand Oaks, CA: Sage.

Campbell, J. C., & Alford, P. (1989). The dark consequences of marital rape. *American Journal of Nursing, 89,* 946-949.

Campbell, J. C., Anderson, E., Fulmer, T. L., Girourd, S., McElmurray, B., & Raff, B. (1993). Violence as a nursing priority: Policy Implications. *Nursing Outlook, 41*(1), 89-92.

Campbell, J. C., & Campbell, D. W. (1996). Cultural competence in the care of abused women. *Journal of Nurse-Midwifery, 41*(6), 457-462.

Campbell, J. C., Harris, M. J., & Lee, R. K. (1995). Violence research: An overview. *Scholarly Inquiry for Nursing Practice: An International Journal, 9*(2), 104-125.

Campbell, J. C., & Humphreys, J. C. (Eds.). (1993). *Nursing care of survivors of family violence.* St. Louis, MO: C. V. Mosby.

Campbell, J. C., Kub, J., Belknap, R. A., & Templin, T. (1997). Predictors of depression in battered women. *Violence Against Women, 3*(3), 276-293.

Campbell, J. C., Kub, J., & Rose, L. (1996). Depression in battered women. *Journal of the American Medical Women's Association, 51*(3), 106-110.

Campbell, J. C., McKenna, L. S., Torres, S., Sheridan, D., & Landenburger, K. (1993). Nursing care of abused women. In J. C. Campbell & J. C. Humphreys (Eds.), *Nursing care of survivors of family violence* (pp. 248-299). St. Louis, MO: C. V. Mosby.

Campbell, J. C., Miller, P., Cardwell, M. M., & Belknap, R. A. (1994). Relationship status of battered women over time. *Journal of Family Violence, 9,* 99-111.

Campbell, J. C., & Parker, B. (in press). Clinical nursing research on battered women and their children: A review. In A. S. Hinshaw, S. Feetham, & J. Shaver (Eds.), *Clinical nursing research review.* Thousand Oaks, CA: Sage.

Campbell, J. C., Poland, M. L., Waller, J. B., & Ager, J. (1992). Correlates of battering during pregnancy. *Research in Nursing and Health, 15,* 219-226.

Campbell, J. C., Pugh, L. C., Campbell, D., & Visscher, M. (1995). The influence of abuse on pregnancy intention. *Women's Health Issues, 5*(4), 214-223.

Campbell, J. C., Rose, L., & Kub, J. (in press). Voices of strength and resistance: Women's responses to battering over time. *Journal of Interpersonal Violence.*

Campbell, J. C., & Sheridan, D. J. (1989). Emergency nursing interventions with battered women. *Journal of Emergency Nursing, 15,* 12-17.

Campbell, J. C., & Stuart, E. (1989). Assessment of patterns of dangerousness with battered women. *Issues in Mental Health Nursing, 10,* 245-260.

Campbell, R., Sullivan, C. M., & Davidson, W. S. (1995). Depression in women who use domestic violence shelters: A longitudinal analysis. *Psychology of Women's Quarterly, 19,* 237-255.

Carbonell, J. L., Chez, R. A., & Hassler, R. S. (1995). Florida physician and nurse education and practice related to domestic violence. *Women's Health Issues, 5*(4), 203-207.

Carillo, R. A., & Marrujo, R. (1984). *Acculturation and domestic violence in the Hispanic population.* Unpublished manuscript.

Carlson, B. (1977). Battered women and their assailants. *Social Work, 22,* 455-471.

Carlson, B. E. (1990). Adolescent observers of marital violence. *Journal of Family Violence, 5,* 285-299.

Carmen, E. H., Rieker, P. P., & Mills, T. (1984). Victims of violence and psychiatric illness. *American Journal of Psychiatry, 141,* 378-383.

Cascardi, M., Langhinrichsen, J., & Vivian, D. (1992). Marital aggression, impact, injury, and health correlates for husbands and wives. *Archives of Internal Medicine, 152,* 357-363.

Cascardi, M., & O'Leary, K. D. (1992). Depressive symptomatology, self-esteem, and self-blame in battered women. *Journal of Family Violence, 7*(4),249-259.

Cazenave, N. (1981). Black men in America: The quest for manhood. In H. P. McAdoo (Ed.), *Black families* (pp. 176-185). Beverly Hills, CA: Sage.

Cazenave, N., & Straus, M. (1979). Race, class and network embeddedness and family violence. *Journal of Comparative Family Studies, 10,*281-300.

Centerwall, B. S. (1984). Race, socioeconomic status, and domestic homicide: Atlanta, 1971-1972. *American Journal of Public Health, 74,* 813-815.

Chalk, R., & King, R. (1998). *Evaluation of family violence interventions.* Washington, DC: National Research Council, National Academy Press.

Chalmers, B. (1983). Psychosocial factors and obstetric complications. *Psychological Medicine, 13,* 333-339.

Chapman, J. D. (1989). A longitudinal study of sexuality and gynecologic health in abused women. *Journal AOA, 89,* 946-949.

Chester, B., Robin, R. W., Koss, M. P., Lopez, J., & Goldman, D. (1994). Grandmother dishonored: Violence against women by male partners in American Indian communities. *Violence and Victims, 9*(3), 249-258.

Chi, P. (1985). Medical utilization patterns of migrant farm workers in Wayne County, New York. *Public Health Reports, 100*(5), 480-490.

Chiodo, G. T., Tilden, V. P., Limandri, B. J., & Schmidt, T. A. (1994, January). Addressing family violence among dental patients: Assessment and intervention. *Journal of the American Dental Association, 125,* 69-75.

Christopoulos, C., Cohn, D. A., Shaw, D. S., Joyce, S., Sullivan-Hanson, J., Kraft, S. P., & Emery, R. (1987). Children of abused women: I. Adjustment at time of shelter residence. *Journal of Marriage and the Family, 49,* 611-619.

Coffey, V. (1998). *One woman's story.* Presented at the Society of General Medicine National Conference, Chicago.

Collins, B. G. (1993). Reconstruing codependency using self-in-relation theory: A feminist perspective. *Social Work, 38*(4), 470-476.

Columbus, I., Day-Garcia, B., Wallace, B., & Walt, M. A. (1980). *Battering and the Indian woman.* Unpublished manuscript.

Committee on Health Care for Homeless People. (1988). *Homelessness, health, and human needs.* Washington, DC: Institute of Medicine, National Academy Press.

Counts, D., Brown, J., & Campbell, J. (1992). *Sanctions and sanctuary: Cultural analysis of the beating of wives.* Boulder, CO: Westview.

Creasy, R. K., & Heron, M. A. (1981). Prevention of preterm birth. *Seminars in Perinatology, 5*(3), 295-302.

Crowell, N., & Burgess, A. (Eds.). (1996). *Understanding violence against women.* Washington, DC: National Academy Press.

Cummings, J. S., Pellegrini, D. S., Notarius, C. I., & Cummings, E. M. (1989). Children's responses to angry adult behavior as a function of marital distress and history of interparent hostility. *Child Development, 60,* 1035-1043.

Cummings, N., & Mooney, A. (1988). Child protective workers and battered women's advocates: A strategy for family violence intervention. *Response, 11,* 4-9.

Curry, M. A., Campbell, R. A., & Christian, M. (1994). Validity and reliability testing of the prenatal psychosocial profile. *Research in Nursing and Health, 17,* 127-135.

Daly, M., Singh, L., & Wilson, M. (1993). Children fathered by previous partners: A risk factor for violence against women. *Canadian Journal of Public Health, 84,* 209-210.

Daly, M., & Wilson, M. (1990). Is parent-offspring conflict sex-linked? Freudian and Darwinian models. *Journal of Personality, 58*(1), 163-189.

Dannenberg, A. L., Carter, D. M., Lawson, H. W., Ashton, D. M., Dorfman, S. F., & Graham, E. H. (1995). Homicide and other injuries as causes of maternal death in New York City, 1987 through 1991. *American Journal of Obstetrical Gynecology, 172,* 1557-1564.

Danziger, E. (1978). *The Chippewas of Lake Superior.* Norman: University of Oklahoma Press.

Davidson, T. (1978). *Conjugal crime: Understanding and changing the wife-beating pattern.* New York: Ballantine.

Davis, K. (1995, November). Keynote address. The African American Conference on Mental Health, Atlanta, GA.

Davis, L. V., & Carlson, B. E. (1987). Observation of spouse abuse: What happens to the children? *Journal of Interpersonal Violence, 2,* 278-291.

Dearwater, S. R., Coben, J. H., Nah, G., Campbell, J. C., McLoughlin, E., Glass, N. E., & Bekemeier, B. (in press). Prevalence of domestic violence in women treated at community hospital emergency departments. *Journal of the American Medical Association.*

DeBruyn, L. M., Hymbaugh, M. A., & Valdez, N. (1988). Helping communities address suicide and violence: The special initiatives team of the Indian Health Center. *American Indian and Alaska Native Mental Health Research, 1*(3), 56-65.

DeLahunta, E. A. (1995). Hidden trauma: The mostly missed diagnosis of domestic violence. *American Journal of Emergency Medicine, 13*(1), 74-76.

DeLa Torre, A., & Rush, L. (1989, January-February). The effects of health care access on maternal and migrant seasonal farm worker women, infant health of California. In *Migrant Health Newsline clinical supplement.* Austin, TX: National Migrant Resource Program.

Dennis, R. E., Key, L. J., Kirk, A. L., & Smith, A. (1995). Addressing domestic violence in the African American community. *Journal of Health Care for the Poor and Underserved, 6*(2), 284-293.

Dever, A. (1991). Profile of a population with complex health problems. In *Migrant Clinicians Network monograph series* (pp. 1-16). Austin, TX: Migrant Clinicians Network.

DiMaio, D. J., & DiMaio, V. J. M. (1989). *Forensic pathology.* New York: Elsevier.

Dobash, R. E., & Dobash, R. (1979). *Violence against wives: A case against the patriarchy.* New York: Free Press.

Dobash, R. E., & Dobash, R. (1988). Research as social action: The struggle for battered women. In K. Yllö & M. Bograd (Eds.), *Feminist perspectives on wife abuse* (pp. 51-74). Newbury Park, CA: Sage.

Dobbie, B., & Tucker, B. (1990). The perceived health needs of abused women. *Canadian Journal of Public Health, 81,* 470-471.

Domestic Abuse Intervention Project. (1990). *Power and control: Tactics of men who batter* (An educational curriculum). Duluth: Minnesota Program Development.

Dowling, P. T., & Fisher, M. (1987). Maternal factors and low birthweight infants: A comparison of blacks with Mexican-Americans. *Journal of Family Practice, 25*(2), 153-158.

Drake, Y. K. (1972). Battered women: A health care problem. *Image, 14,* 40-47.

Drossman, D. A., Leserman, J., Nachman, G., Li, Z., Gluck, H., Toomey, T. C., & Mitchell, M. (1990). Sexual and physical abuse in women and functional or organic gastrointestinal disorders. *Annals of Internal Medicine, 113,* 828-833.

Dutton, D., & Painter, S. L. (1981). Traumatic bonding: The development of emotional attachments in battered women and other relationships of intermittent abuse. *Victimology: An International Journal, 29,* 139-155.

Dutton, M. A. (1992). *Empowering and healing the battered woman.* New York: Springer.

Dutton, M. A. (1993). *Understanding women's responses to domestic violence: A redefinition of battered woman syndrome. Hofstra Law Review, 21,* 1191-1194.

Earl, D., & Smith, H. K. (1991). Adolescent involvement in Kansas City gangs. *Missouri Medicine, 88*(10), 699-701.

Eby, K., Campbell, J. C., Sullivan, C., & Davidson, W. (1995). Health effects of experiences of sexual violence for women with abusive partners. *Women's Health Care International, 16,* 563-576.

Egley, L. C., & Ben-Ari, A. (1993). Making *Tarasoff* practical for various treatment populations. *Journal of Psychiatry & Law, 21,* 473-501.

Elbow, M. (1982). Children of violent marriages: The forgotten victims. *Social Casework, 63,* 465-471.

Elliott, B. A., & Johnson, M. M. (1995). Domestic violence in a primary care setting: Patterns and prevalence. *Archives of Family Medicine, 4*(2), 113-119.

Emery, R. (1989). Family violence. *American Psychologist, 44*(2), 321-328.

Emery, R. E. (1982). Interparental conflict and the children of discord and divorce. *Psychological Bulletin, 92,* 310-330.

Ericksen, J., & Henderson, A. D. (1992). Witnessing family violence: The children's experiences. *Journal of Advanced Nursing, 17,* 1200-1209.

Eth, S., & Pinoos, R. (1985). *Post-traumatic stress disorder in children.* Washington, DC: American Psychiatric Press.

Fagan, J., & Browne, A. (1994). Violence between spouses and intimates: Physical aggression between women and men in intimate relationships. In *Understanding and preventing violence: Vol. 3. Social influences.* Washington, DC: National Academy Press.

Fagan, J., Stewart, D., & Hansen, K. (1983). Violent men or violent husbands? Background factors and situational correlates. In R. Gelles, G. Hotaling, M. Straus, & D. Finkelhor (Eds.), *The dark side of families* (pp. 49-68). Beverly Hills, CA: Sage.

Farley, R. (1986). Homicide trends in the United States. In D. F. Hawkins (Ed.), *Homicide among black Americans* (pp. 13-27). New York: University Press of America.

Feld, S. L., & Straus, M. A. (1989). Escalation and desistance of wife assault in marriage. *Criminology, 27*(1), 141-161.

Feldmann, T. B. (1988). Violence as a disintegration product of the self in posttraumatic stress disorder. *American Journal of Psychotherapy, 42,* 281-289.

Ferraro, K. J., & Johnson, J. M. (1983). How women experience battering: The process of victimization. *Social Problems, 30,* 325-337.

Fildes, R., Reed, L., Jones, N., Martin, M., & Barrett, J. (1992). Trauma: The leading cause of maternal death. *Journal of Trauma, 32,* 643-645.

Finkelhor, D., Hotaling, G., & Sedlak, A. (1991). *Missing, abducted, runaway and throwaway children in America.* Washington, DC: U.S. Department of Justice, Office of Justice Program.

Fischler, R. S. (1985). Child abuse and neglect in American Indian communities. *Child Abuse & Neglect, 9,* 95-106.

Flitcraft, A. H., Hadley, S. M., Hendricks-Matthews, M. K., McLeer, S. V., & Warshaw, C. (1992). *Diagnostic and treatment guidelines on domestic violence.* Chicago: American Medical Association.

Frisch, M. B., & MacKenzie, C. J. (1991). A comparison of formerly and chronically battered women of cognitive and situational dimensions. *Psychotherapy, 28*(2), 339-344.

Fromson, T., & Durborow, N. (1997). *Insurance discrimination against victims of domestic violence.* Philadelphia: Women's Law Project and the Pennsylvania Coalition Against Domestic Violence.

Furniss, J. (1981). A general review of bite mark evidence. *American Journal of Forensic Medicine and Pathology, 2*(1), 49-52.

Gage, R. (1990). Consequences of children's exposure to spouse abuse. *Pediatric Nursing, 16*(3), 258-260.

Garmezy, N. (1981). Children under stress: Perspectives on antecedents and correlates of vulnerability and resistance to psychopathology. In A. I. Rabin, J. Arnoff, A. M. Barclay, & R. A. Zucker (Eds.), *Further explorations in personality* (pp. 70-81). New York: Wiley Interscience.

Garmezy, N. (1983). Stressors of childhood. In N. Garmezy (Ed.), *Stress, coping and development in children* (pp. 43-84). New York: McGraw-Hill.

Gary, F. (1991). Sociocultural diversity and psychiatric mental health nursing. In F. Gary & C. Kavanagh (Eds.), *Psychiatric mental health nursing* (pp. 136-162). Philadelphia: J. B. Lippincott.

Gary, F., Campbell, D., & Serlin, C. (1996). African American women: Disparities in health care. *Journal of the Florida Medical Association, 83*(7), 489-493.

Gary, F., & Lopez, L. (1995). [Focus groups with law enforcement officers in a semirural community]. Unpublished data.

Gary, F., Moorhead, J., & Warren, J. (1996). Characteristics of troubled youths in a shelter. *Archives of Psychiatric Nursing, 10*(1), 41-48.

Gary-Hopps, J., Penderhughes, E., & Shunkar, R. (1995). *The power to cure: Clinical effectiveness with overwhelmed clients.* New York: Free Press.

Gazmararian, J. A., Lazorick, S., Spitz, A., Ballard, T. Saltzman, L., & Marks, J. (1996). Prevalence of violence against pregnant women. *Journal of the American Medical Association, 275*(24), 1915-1920.

Gelles, R. (1980). Violence in the family: A review of research in the seventies. *Journal of Marriage and the Family, 42,* 873-885.

Gelles, R. J. (1974). *The violent home: A study of physical aggression between husbands and wives.* Beverly Hills, CA: Sage.

Gelles, R. J. (1975). Violence and pregnancy: A note on the extent of the problem and needed services. *Family Coordinator, 24,* 81-86.

Gelles, R. J. (1988). Violence and pregnancy: Are pregnant women at greater risk of abuse? *Journal of Marriage and the Family, 50,* 841-847.

Gelles, R. J., & Straus, M. A. (1988). *Intimate violence: The causes and consequences of abuse in the American family.* New York: Simon & Schuster.

Gelles, R. J., & Straus, M. A. (1990). The medical and psychological costs of family violence. In M. A. Straus & R. J. Gelles (Eds.), *Physical violence in American families: Risk factors and adaptations to violence in 8,145 families.* New Brunswick, NJ: Transaction Publishing.

Gielen, A. C., O'Campo, P. J., Faden, R. R., Kass, N. E., & Xue, X. (1994). Interpersonal conflict and physical violence during the childbearing year. *Social Science and Medicine, 39,* 781-787.

Gin, N. E., Rucker, L., Frayne, S., Cygan, R., & Hubbell, A.F. (1991). Prevalence of domestic violence among patients in three ambulatory care internal medicine clinics. *Journal of Internal Medicine, 6,* 317-322.

Giorgi, A. (1987). *Phenomenology and psychological research.* Pittsburgh, PA: Duquesne University Press.

Gleason, W. J. (1993). Mental disorders in battered women: An empirical study. *Violence and Victims, 8,* 53-68.

Goetting, A. (1988). Patterns of homicide among women. *Journal of Interpersonal Violence, 3,* 3-20.

Goetting, A. (1989). Men who kill their mates: A profile. *Journal of Family Violence, 4,* 285-296.

Gold, M. H., Roenigk, H. H., Jr., Smith, E. S., & Pierce, L. J. (1989). Evaluation and treatment of patients with human bite marks. *American Journal of Forensic Medicine and Pathology, 13*(2), 140-143.

Goldberg, W. G., & Tomlanovich, M. C. (1984). Domestic violence, victims, and emergency departments: New findings. *Journal of the American Medical Association, 251,* 3259-3264.

Gondolf, E. (1985). *Men who batter: An integrated approach for stopping wife abuse.* Holmes Beach, FL: Learning Publications.

Gondolf, E. W., Fisher, E., & McFerron, J. R. (1988). Racial differences among shelter residents: A comparison of Anglo, black and Hispanic battered women. *Journal of Family Violence, 3*(1), 30-51.

Gonik, B., & Creasy, R. K. (1986). Preterm labor: Its diagnosis and management. *American Journal of Obstetrics and Gynecology, 154*(1), 3-8.

Gordon, I., Shapiro, H. A., & Berson, S. D. (1988). *Forensic medicine* (3rd ed.). Edinburgh: Churchill Livingstone.

Greydanus, D., Ferrell, E., Sladkin, K., et al. (1990). The gang phenomenon and the American teenager. *Adolescent Medicine: State of the Art Review, 1,* 55-69.

Gridley, M. (1974). *American Indian women.* New York: Hawthorn.

Grisso, J. A., Wishner, A. R., Schwarz, D. F., Weene, B. A., Homes, J. H., & Sutton, R. L. (1991). A population based study of injuries in inner-city women. *American Journal of Epidemiology, 134*(1), 59-68.

Gross, T. P., & Rosenberg, M. L. (1987). Shelters for battered women and their children: An under-recognized source of communicable disease transmission. *American Journal of Public Health, 77,* 1198-1201.

Grossman, D. C., Milligan, B. C., & Deyo, R. A. (1991). Risk factors for suicide attempts among Navajo adolescents. *American Journal of Public Health, 81*(7), 870-874.

Gunn Allen, P. (1985). Violence and the American Indian woman. *Working Together to Prevent Sexual and Domestic Violence, 5*(4), 1-3.

Haber, J. (1985). Abused women and chronic pain. *American Journal of Nursing, 85,* 1010-1012.

Hadley, S., Short, L., Lesin, N., Zook, E. (1995). Women Kind: An innovative model of health care response to domestic abuse. *Women's Health Issues, 5*(4), 189-198.

Hadley, S. M. (1992). Working with battered women in the emergency department: A model program. *Journal of the Emergency Nurses Association, 18*(1), 18-23.

Hamberger, L. K., Saunders, D. G., & Hovey, M. (1992). Prevalence of domestic violence in community practice and rate of physician inquiry. *Family Medicine, 24,* 283-287.

Hare, N. (1979). The relative psycho-socio-economic suppression of the black male. In W. D. Smith, K. H. Burlew, M. H. Moseley, & W. M. Whitney (Eds.), *Reflections on black psychology* (pp. 359-381). Washington, DC: University Press.

Hart, B. (1988). Beyond the "duty to warn": A therapist's "duty to protect" battered women and children. In K. Yllö & M. Bograd (Eds.), *Feminist perspectives on wife abuse* (pp. 234-248). Newbury Park, CA: Sage.

Hartup, W. (1989). Societal relationships and their developmental significance. *American Psychologist, 44*(2), 120-126.

Hatcher, R. A., Guest, F., Stewart, F., Stewart, G. K., Trussell, J., Cerel, S., & Cates, W. (1986). *Contraceptive technology 1986-1987.* New York: Irvington.

Hawkins, D. F. (1987). Devalued lives and racial stereotypes: Ideological barriers to the prevention of family violence among blacks. In R. L. Hampton (Ed.), *Violence in the black family: Correlates and consequences* (pp. 190-205). Lexington, MA: Lexington Books.

Hawkins, D. F. (1993). Inequality, culture, and interpersonal violence. *Health Affairs 80,* 80-95.

Heise, L., Pitanguy, J., & Germain, A. (1994). *Violence against women: The hidden health burden* (World Bank Discussion Paper No. 255). Washington, DC: World Bank.

Helton, A. S. (1986). Battering during pregnancy. *American Journal of Nursing, 86,* 910-913.

Helton, A. S., McFarlane, J., & Anderson, E. T. (1987). Battered and pregnant: A prevalence study. *American Journal of Public Health, 77,* 1337-1339.

Henderson, A. D. (1989). Use of social support in a transition house for abused women. *Health Care for Women International, 10,* 61-73.

Henderson, A. D. (1990). Children of abused wives: Their influence on their mothers' decisions. *Canada's Mental Health, 38*(2/3), 10-13.

Henderson, A. D. (1993). Abused women's perceptions of their children's needs. *Canada's Mental Health, 41*(1), 7-11.

Henderson, A. D., & Ericksen, J. R. (1994). Enhancing nurses' effectiveness with abused women: Awareness, reframing, support, education. *Journal of Psychosocial Nursing and Mental Health Services, 32*(6), 11-15.

Henderson, D., Sampselle, C., Mayes, J., & Oakley, D. (1992). Toward culturally sensitive research in a multicultural society. *Health Care for Women International, 13,* 339-350.

Hendricks-Matthews, M. (1991). Conversion disorder in an adult incest survivor. *Journal of Family Practice, 33,* 298-300.

Herman, J. (1992). *Trauma and recovery.* New York: Basic Books.

Herman, J. L. (1986). Histories of violence in an outpatient population. *American Journal of Orthopsychiatry, 56,* 137-141.

Herrell, I. C. (1993). *Health care issues affecting Hispanic women, infants, and children* (Prepared for roundtable discussion on critical health care issues affecting Latino children and Latinas in the United States). Washington, DC: U.S. Department of Health and Human Services, Health Resources and Services Administration.

Hershorn, M., & Rosenbaum, A. (1985). Children of marital violence. *American Journal of Orthopsychiatry, 55*(2), 260-266.

Herzog, E., & Sudia, C. E. (1973). Children in fatherless families. In B. M. Caldwell & H. N. Riciuti (Eds.), *Review of child development research* (Vol. 3). Chicago: University of Chicago Press.

Hickerson, H. (1971). The Chippewa of the upper Great Lakes: A study in sociopolitical changes. In E. Leacock & N. Lurie (Eds.), *North American Indians in historical perspective.* New York: Random House.

Hilberman, E., & Munson, K. (1978). Sixty battered women. *Victimology: An International Journal, 2,* 460-470.

Hillard, P. J. (1985). Physical abuse in pregnancy. *Obstetrics and Gynecology, 66,* 185-190.

Hislop, T. G., Threfall, W. J., Gallagher, R. P., & Band, P. R. (1987). Accidental and intentional violent deaths among British Columbia Indians. *Canadian Journal of Public Health, 78*(4), 271-274.

Hisnanick, J. J. (1994). Comparative analysis of violent deaths in American Indians and Alaska Natives. *Social Biology, 41*(1-2), 96-109.

Hispanic Health and Nutrition Examination Survey, 1982-1984: Findings on health status and health care needs. (1990). *American Journal of Public Health, 80*(Suppl.), 1-70.

Hoff, L. A. (1990). *Battered women as survivors.* London: Routledge.

Holden, G., & Ritchie, K. (1991). Linking extreme marital discord, child rearing, and child behavior problems: Evidence from battered women. *Child Development, 62,* 311-327.

Holtz, H., & Furniss, K. (1993). The health care provider's role in domestic violence. *Trends in Health Care, Law, and Ethics, 8,* 47-53.

Horowitz, D., & O'Brien, M. (1989). In the interest of the nation. *American Psychologist, 44*(2), 441-445.

Horowitz, M. J. (1986). A review of posttraumatic and adjustment disorders. *Hospital and Community Psychiatry,* pp. 241-249.

Hotaling, G. T., & Sugarman, D. B. (1990). A risk marker analysis of assaulted wives. *Journal of Family Violence, 5,* 1-3.

Hudson, W., & McIntosh, S. (1981). The Index of Spouse Abuse: Two quantifiable dimensions. *Journal of Marriage and the Family, 43,* 873-888.

Hughes, H. M. (1982). Brief interventions with children in a battered women's shelter: A model preventive program. *Family Relations, 31,* 495-502.

Hughes, H. M. (1988). Psychological and behavioral correlates of family violence in child witnesses and victims. *American Journal of Orthopsychiatry, 58,* 77-90.

Hughes, H. M., & Marshall, M. (1995). Advocacy for children of battered women. In E. Peled, P. G. Jaffe, & J. L. Edleson (Eds.), *Ending the cycle of violence: Community responses to children of battered women* (pp. 121-144). Thousand Oaks, CA: Sage.

Humphrey, J. A., Hudson, R. P., & Cosgrove, S. (1981). Women who are murdered: An analysis of 912 consecutive victims. *OMEGA, 12,* 281-288.

Humphreys, J. (1989). *Dependent-care directed toward the prevention of hazards to life, health, and well-being in mothers and children who experience family violence.* Unpublished doctoral dissertation, Wayne State University, Detroit, MI.

Humphreys, J. (1990). Dependent-care directed toward the prevention of hazards to life, health, and well-being in mothers and children who experience family violence. *MAINlines, 11,* 6-7.

Humphreys, J. (1991). Children of battered women: Worries about their mothers. *Pediatric Nursing, 17,* 342-345.

Humphreys, J. (1993). Children of battered women. In J. C. Campbell & J. C. Humphreys (Eds.), *Nursing care of survivors of family violence* (pp. 107-131). St. Louis, MO: C. V. Mosby.

Hyman, & Chez, R. A. (1995). *Mandatory reporting of domestic violence by health care providers: A misguided approach.* San Francisco: Family Violence Prevention Fund.

Indian Health Service. (1993). *Regional differences in Indian health.* Washington, DC: Department of Health and Human Services, Public Health Service, Indian Health Service.

Indian Health Service. (1995). *Trends in Indian health.* Washington, DC: Department of Health and Human Services, Public Health Service, Indian Health Service.

Institute of Medicine. (1994). *Reducing risks for mental disorders.* Washington, DC: National Academy Press.

Institute of Medicine. (1995). *Recommendations for research on the health of military women.* Washington, DC: National Academy Press.

Jack, D. (1991). *Silencing the self.* Cambridge, MA: Harvard University Press.

Jacobson, S. F. (1994). Native American health. *Annual Review of Nursing Research, 12,* 193-213.

Jaffe, P., Wolfe, D. A., Wilson, S., & Zak, L. (1986a). Emotional and physical health problems of battered women. *Canadian Journal of Psychiatry, 31,* 625-629.

Jaffe, P., Wolfe, D., Wilson, S. K., & Zak, L. (1986b). Family violence and child adjustment: A comparative analysis of girl's and boy's behavioral symptoms. *American Journal of Psychiatry, 143*(1), 74-77.

Jaffe, P., Wolfe, D., Wilson, S., & Zak, L. (1986c). Similarities in behavioral and social maladjustment among child victims and witnesses to family violence. *American Journal of Orthopsychiatry, 56*(1), 142-146.

Jaffe, P. G., Wolfe, D. A., & Wilson, S. K. (1990). *Children of battered women.* Newbury Park, CA: Sage.

Johnson, B. S. (1993). *Psychiatric mental health nursing.* Philadelphia: J. B. Lippincott.

Joint Commission on the Accreditation of Healthcare Organizations. (1990). *Accreditation manual for hospitals* (Vol. 1). Chicago: Author.

Joint Commission on the Accreditation of Healthcare Organizations. (1992). *Accreditation manual for hospitals.* Chicago: Author.

Joint Commission on the Accreditation of Healthcare Organizations. (1996). *Accreditation manual for hospitals.* Chicago: Author.

Jonsen, A. R., Siegler, M., & Winslade, W. J. (1986). *Clinical ethics* (2nd ed.). New York: Macmillan.

Joseph, J. (1997). Woman battering: A comparative analysis of black and white women. In G. K. Kantor & J. L. Jasinski (Eds.), *Out of darkness: Contemporary perspectives on family violence.* Thousand Oaks, CA: Sage.

Jouriles, E. N., Murphy, C. M., & O'Leary, K. D. (1989). Interspousal aggression, marital discord, and child problems. *Journal of Consulting and Clinical Psychology, 57,* 453-455.

Jouriles, E. N., Pfiffner, L. J., & O'Leary, S. O. (1988). Marital conflict, parenting, and toddler conduct problems. *Journal of Abnormal Child Psychology, 16*(2), 197-206.

Jurik, N. C., & Winn, R. (1990). Gender and homicide: A comparison of men and women who kill. *Violence and Victims, 5,* 227-242.

Justice Research and Statistics Association. (1996). *Criminal Justice Issues in the States 1996 Directory, Vol. 13.* Washington, DC.

Kalmuss, D. G., & Straus, M. A. (1984). Wife's marital dependency and wife abuse. *Journal of Marriage and Family, 44,* 277-286.

Kantor, G. K., Jasinski, J. L., & Aldarondo, E. (1994). Sociocultural status and incidence of marital violence in Hispanic families. *Violence and Victims, 9*(3), 207-222.

Kassierer, J. P. (1991). Firearms and killing threshold. *New England Journal of Medicine, 325*(23), 1647-1650.

Kaufman Kantor, G., & Straus, M. A. (1987). The "drunken bum" theory of wife beating. *Social Problems, 34,* 213-230.

Kehoe, A. (1983). The shackles of tradition. In P. Albers & B. Medicine (Eds.), *The hidden half: Studies of Plains Indian women.* Lanham, MD: University Press of America.

Kellam, S., Ensminger, M., & Turner, R. (1977). Family structure and the mental health of children: Concurrent and longitudinal community-wide studies. *Archives of General Psychiatry, 34,* 1012-1022.

Kellermann, A. L., & Mercy, J. A. (1992). Men, women, and murder: Gender-specific differences in rates of fatal violence and victimization. *Journal of Trauma, 33,* 1-5.

Kemp, A., Green, B., Hovanitz, C., & Rawlings, E. (1995). Incidence and correlates of posttraumatic stress disorder in battered women: Shelter and community samples. *Journal of Interpersonal Violence, 10*(1), 43-55.

Kempe, C., Silverman, F. N., Steele, B. F., et al. (1962). The battered child syndrome. *Journal of the American Medical Association, 181,* 17-24.

Kennedy, M. (1991). Homeless and runaway youth mental health issues: No access to the system. *Journal of Adolescent Health, 12,* 576-579.

Kerouac, S., Taggart, M. E., Lescop, J., & Fortin, M. F. (1986). Dimensions of health in violent families. *Health Care for Women International, 7,* 413-426.

Kessler, R., McGonagle, K., Nelson, C., Hughes, M., Swartz, M., & Blazer, D. (1994). Sex and depression in the National Comorbidity Survey: II. Cohort effects. *Journal of Affective Disorders, 30,* 15-26.

Kessler, R. C. (1979). A strategy for studying differential vulnerability to the psychological consequences of stress. *Journal of Health and Social Behavior, 20*(2), 100-108.

Ketterlinus, R., Henderson, S., & Lamb, M. (1990). Maternal age, sociodemographics, prenatal health and behavior: Influences on neonatal risk status. *Journal of Adolescent Health Care, 11,* 423-431.

King, M. C. (1988). Helping battered women: A study of the relationship between nurses' education and experience and their preferred models of helping. *Dissertation Abstracts International, 49,* 3105.

King, M. C., & Ryan, J. (1989). Abused women: Dispelling myths and encouraging intervention. *Nurse Practitioner, 14,* 47-58.

King, M. C., & Ryan, J. (1991). Advocacy protocol for abused women. In *Proceedings of the National Perinatal Association Annual Conference.* Boston.

King, M. C., Perri, M., & Ryan, J. (1987). *Reaching out to battered women.* Northampton, MA: Stone Circle.

King, M. C., Torres, S., Campbell, D., Ryan, J., Sheridan, D., Ulrich, Y., & McKenna, L. S. (1993). Violence and abuse of women: A perinatal health care issue. *AWHONN's Clinical Issues in Perinatal and Women's Health Nursing, 4,* 163-172.

Klingbeil, K. (1986). Interpersonal violence: A comprehensive model in a hospital setting—From policy to program. In *Surgeon General's workshop on violence and public health.* Washington, DC: U.S. Department of Health and Human Services, Public Health Service.

Kohl, J. (1985). *Kitchi-Gami: Life among the Lake Superior Ojibway.* St. Paul: Minnesota Historical Society Press.

Koranda, A. (1993, January). *Child witnesses of domestic violence: How it hurts and how to help.* Paper presented at the 5th National Conference on Violence Against Women, Orlando, FL.

Koss, M. P., Gidycz, C. A., & Wisniewski, N. (1987). The scope of rape: Incidence and prevalence of sexual aggression and victimization in a national sample of higher education students. *Journal of Consulting and Clinical Psychology, 55,* 162-170.

Kovanis, G. (1990, October 19). Young peacemakers: Students are schooled in settling conflicts without help of adults. *Detroit Free Press,* pp. 1A, 15A.

Krestan J., & Bepko C. (1990). Codependency: The social reconstruction of female experience. *Social Work, 60,* 216-232.

Kurz, D. (1987). Emergency department responses to battered women: Resistance to medicalization. *Social Problems, 34,* 501-513.

Landenburger, K. (1989). A process of entrapment in and recovery from an abusive relationship. *Issues in Mental Health Nursing, 10,* 209-227.

Landenburger, K. M. (1988). Conflicting realities of women in abusive relationships (Doctoral dissertation, University of Washington, 1987). *Dissertation Abstracts International, 49*(2), 362B.

Landenburger, K. M. (1991, May). *Difficulties encountered in women's decisions to leave abusive relationships.* Paper presented at the 24th annual Communicating Nursing Research Conference, Albuquerque, NM.

Langlois, N. E. I., & Gresham, G. A. (1991). The ageing of bruises: A review and study of the colour changes with time. *Forensic Science International, 50,* 227-238.

Layzer, J. I., Goodson, B. D., & deLange, C. (1985). Children in shelters. *Response, 9,* 2-5.

Lazere, E. B., & Leonard, P. A. (1989). *The crisis in housing for the poor: A special report on Hispanics and blacks.* Washington, DC: Center on Budget and Policy Priorities.

Leacock, E. (1981). *Myths of male dominance: Collected articles on women cross-culturally.* New York: Monthly Review Press.

League of Women Voters. (1971). *Indians of Minnesota* (2nd ed.). St. Paul, MN: Author.

Ledray, L. E. (1992a). The sexual assault examination: Overview and lessons learned in one program. *Journal of Emergency Nursing, 18*(3), 223-230.

Ledray, L. E. (1992b). The sexual assault nurse clinician: A fifteen year experience in Minneapolis. *Journal of Emergency Nursing, 18*(3), 217-222.

Ledray, L. E. (1993). Sexual assault nurse clinician: An emerging area of nursing expertise. *AWHONN's Clinical Issues in Perinatal and Women's Health Nursing, 4*(2),180-190.

Leininger, M. (1978). *Transcultural nursing concepts: Theories and practices.* New York: Wiley.

Lempert, L. B. (1996). Women's strategies for survival: Developing agency in abusive relationships. *Journal of Family Violence, 11,* 269-290.

Leong, G. B., Eth, S., & Silva, J. A. (1992). The psychotherapist as witness for the prosecution: The criminalization of Tarasoff. *American Journal of Psychiatry, 149,* 1011-1015.

Lerner, J. M., & Simmons, C. H. (1966). Observer's reaction to the "innocent victim." *Journal of Personal and Social Psychology, 4,* 203-210.

Lewis, D. (1975). The black family: Socialization and sex roles. *Phylon, 36,* 221-237.

Lewis, D., Shanok, S., Cohen, R., Kligfeld, M., & Frisone, G. (1980). Race bias in the diagnosis and disposition of violent adolescents. *American Journal of Psychiatry, 137,* 1211-1216.

Lewis, J. A. (Ed.). (1993). Domestic violence [Special issue]. *AWHONN's Clinical Issues in Perinatal and Women's Health Nursing, 4*(3).

Limandri, B. J. (1987). The therapeutic relationship with abused women. *Journal of Psychosocial Nursing, 25,* 9-16.

Limandri, B. J. (1989). Disclosure of stigmatizing conditions: The discloser's perspective. *Archives of Psychiatric Nursing, 3,* 69-78.

Limandri, B. J., & Tilden, V. P. (1996). Nurses' reasoning in the assessment of family violence. *IMAGE: Journal of Nursing Scholarship, 28,* 247-252.

Littlefield, C., & Stout, C. (1987). *Access to health care: A survey of Colorado's migrant farm workers.* Denver: Colorado Migrant Health Program.

Lockart, L. L. (1985). Methodological issues in comparative racial analysis: The case of wife abuse. *Research and Abstracts, 13,* 35-41.

Lopez, L., & Gary, F. (1996). Logical responses to youth who run away from home: Implications for psychiatric nursing and mental health practice. *Journal of Psychosocial Nursing and Mental Health Services, 33*(3), 9-15.

Lujan, C., DeBruyn, L. M., May, P. A., & Bird, M. E. (1989). Profile of abused and neglected American Indian children in the Southwest. *Child Abuse & Neglect, 13*(4), 449-461.

Lussier, L. (1982, August). Indian community tackles domestic violence. *The Circle,* pp. 7, 8, 11.

Lynch, V. A. (1991). Forensic nursing in the emergency department: A new role for the 1990's. *Critical Care Nursing Quarterly, 14*(3), 69-86.

MacLeod, L. (1980). *Wife battering in Canada: The vicious circle.* Ottawa: Minister of Supply and Service.

MacLeod, L. (1987). *Wife battering and the web of hope: Progress, dilemmas, and visions of prevention.* Ottawa: Health & Welfare Canada.

Makepeace, J. (1981). Courtship violence among college students. *Family Relations, 30,* 97-102.

Mann, C. (1987). Black women who kill. In R. L. Hampton (Ed.), *Violence in the black family: Correlates and consequences* (pp. 157-186). Lexington, MA: Lexington Books.

Mann, C. R. (1990). Black female homicide in the United States. *Journal of Interpersonal Violence, 5,* 176-201.

March of Dimes Birth Defects Foundation. (1986a). *Crimes against the future* [Film]. White Plains, NY: March of Dimes.

March of Dimes Birth Defects Foundation. (1986b). *Protocol of care for the battered woman.* White Plains, NY: March of Dimes.

Martin, D. (1976). *Battered wives.* San Francisco: Glide.

Martin, J., & Pence, E. (Producers). (1988). *Bah-ma-di-zi-win: The journey* [Film]. Duluth: Minnesota Program Development.

Martin, M., Hunt, T., & Hulley, S. (1988). The cost of hospitalization for firearm injuries. *Journal of the American Medical Association, 260*(20), 3048-3050.

Martin, S. L., English, K. T., Andersen, K., Cilenti, D., & Kupper, L. (1996). Violence and substance use among North Carolina pregnant women. *American Journal of Public Health, 86,* 991-998.

Maxson, C., Little, M., & Klein, M. (1988). Police response to runaway and missing children: A conceptual framework for research and policy. *Crime & Delinquency, 34*(1), 84-102.

Maxwell, J. A. (1978). *America's fascinating Indian heritage.* Pleasantville, NY: Reader's Digest Association.

McCauley, J., Kern, D. E., Kolodner, K., Dill, L., Schroeder, A. F., DeChant, H. K., Ryden, J., Bass, E. B., & Derogatis, L. R. (1995). The "battering syndrome": Prevalence and clinical characteristics of domestic violence in primary care internal medicine practices. *Annals of Internal Medicine, 123*(10), 744-781.

McFarlane, J. (1989). Battering during pregnancy: Tip of an iceberg revealed. *Women & Health, 15,* 69-83.

McFarlane, J. (1991). Battering in pregnancy. In C. M. Sampselle (Ed.), *Violence against women: Nursing research, education, and practice issues.* New York: Hemisphere.

McFarlane, J., Christoffel, K., Bateman, L., Miller, V., & Bullock, L. (1991). Assessing for abuse: Self-report versus nurse interview. *Public Health Nursing, 8,* 245-250.

McFarlane, J., & Parker, B. (1994a). *Abuse during pregnancy: A protocol for prevention and intervention.* White Plains, NY: March of Dimes.

McFarlane, J., & Parker, B. (1994b). Abuse during pregnancy: An assessment and intervention protocol. *American Journal of Maternal and Child Nursing, 19,* 321-324.

McFarlane, J., Parker, B., & Soeken, K. (1996a). Abuse during pregnancy: Associations with maternal health and infant birth weight. *Nursing Research, 45*(1), 37-42.

McFarlane, J., Parker, B., & Soeken, K. (1996b). Physical abuse and substance use during pregnancy: Prevalence, interrelationships and effects on birthweight. *Journal of Obstetric, Gynecologic and Neonatal Nursing, 25*(4), 313-320.

McFarlane, J., Parker, B., Soeken, K., & Bullock, L. (1992). Assessing for abuse during pregnancy: Severity and frequency of injuries and associated entry into prenatal care. *Journal of the American Medical Association, 267*(23), 3176-3178.

McFarlane, J., Parker, B., Soeken, K., Silva, C., & Reel, S. (1998). Safety behaviors of abused women after an intervention during pregnancy. *Journal of Obstetric, Gynecologic and Neonatal Nursing, 27*(1), 64-69.

McIntire, M. (1988, June). *Societal barriers faced by American Indian battered women.* Paper presented at the National Women's Studies Association Conference, Minneapolis, MN.

McKenna, L. S. (1986). Social support systems of battered women: Influence on psychological adaptation. *Dissertation Abstracts International, 47,* 1895A.

McLeer, S. V., & Anwar, R. (1989a). The role of the emergency physician in the prevention of domestic violence. *Annals of Emergency Medicine, 16,* 1155-1161.

McLeer, S. V., & Anwar, R. (1989b). A study of battered women presenting in an emergency department. *American Journal of Public Health, 79,* 65-66.

McLeer, S. V., Anwar, R. A. H., Herman, S., & Maquiling, K. (1989). Education is not enough: A system's failure in protecting battered women. *Annals of Emergency Medicine, 18*(6), 651-653.

McLoughlin, E., Lee, D., Letellier, P., & Salber, P. (1993). Emergency department response to domestic violence—California, 1992. *Morbidity and Mortality Weekly Report, 42,* 617-619.

McNair, L. D. (1992). African American women in therapy: An Afrocentric and feminist synthesis. *Women and Therapy, 12,* 5-19.

Mejo, S. L. (1990, August). Post-traumatic stress disorder: An overview of three etiologic variables, and psychopharmacologic treatment. *Nurse Practitioner,* pp. 41-45.

Mercy, J. A., & Saltzman, L. (1989). Fatal violence among spouses in the United States, 1976-85. *American Journal of Public Health, 79,* 595-599.

Merritt-Gray, M., & Wuest, J. (1995). Counteracting abuse and breaking free: The process of leaving revealed through women's voices. *Health Care for Women International, 16,* 399-412.

Migrant Clinicians Network. (1995). *Suffering in silence.* Austin, TX: Author.

Migrant Health Program. (1992). [Program information sheet]. Washington, DC: Public Health Service.

Miller, J. (1976). *Toward a new psychology of women.* Boston: Beacon.

Miller, J. B. (1991). The development of women's sense of self. In J. V. Jordan, A. G. Kaplan, J. B. Miller, I. P. Stiver, & J. L. Surrey (Eds.), *Women's growth in connection* (pp. 11-28). New York: Guilford.

Mills, M. J., Sullivan, G., & Eth, S. (1987). Protecting third parties: A decade after *Tarasoff. American Journal of Psychiatry, 144,* 68-74.

Mills, T. (1985). The assault on the self: Stages in coping with battering husbands. *Qualitative Sociology, 8*(2), 103-123.

Mills, T., Rieker, P. P., & Carmen, E. H. (1984). Hospitalization experiences of victims of abuse. *Victimology, 9,* 436-449.

Milner, J. S., & Gold, R. G. (1986). Screening spouse abusers for child abuse potential. *Journal of Clinical Psychology, 42,* 169-172.

Milner, J. S., Robertson, K. R., & Rogers, D. L. (1990). Childhood history of abuse and adult child abuse potential. *Journal of Family Violence, 5,* 15-34.

Monahan, J. (1993). Limiting therapist exposure to *Tarasoff* liability: Guidelines for risk containment. *American Psychologist, 48,* 242-250.

Monahan, J., & Steadman, H. J. (1996). Violent storms and violent people: How meteorology can inform risk communication in mental health law. *American Psychologist, 51,* 931-938.

Monsma, J. (1984). *The children of battered women: Perceptions and interpretations of wife abuse.* Unpublished field study, Wayne State University, Detroit, MI.

Moone, J. (1994). *Juvenile victimization: 1987–1992* (Fact Sheet Publication #17). Washington, DC: U.S. Department of Justice.

Moore, T., Peeler, D., Weinberg, B., Hammond, L., Wheedle, J., & Weider, L. (1990). Research on children from violent families. *Canada's Mental Health, 38*(2/3), 19-23.

Murphy, S. P., Castillo, R. O., Martorell, R., & Mendoza, F. (1990). An evaluation of food group intakes by Mexican-American children. *Journal of the American Dietetic Association, 90*(3), 388-393.

Myers, L. (1987). Stress resolution among middle-aged black Americans. In R. L. Hampton (Ed.), *Violence in the black family: Correlates and consequences* (pp. 237-245). Lexington, MA: Lexington Books.

National Advisory Council on Migrant Health. (1993). *Under the weather: Farm worker health* (A compendium of farm worker testimony before the National Advisory Council on Migrant Health). Rockville, MD: Bureau of Primary Health Care.

National Center for Health Statistics. (1991). Advance report on final natality statistics, 1989. *Monthly Vital Statistics Report, 40*(Suppl.).

National Coalition Against Domestic Violence. (1991a). *1991 National directory of battered women's shelters and programs.* Washington, DC: Author.

National Coalition Against Domestic Violence. (1991b). *Rural task force resource packet.* Washington, DC: Author.

Nechas, E., & Foley, D. (1994). *Unequal treatment: What you don't know about how women are mistreated by the medical community.* New York: Simon & Schuster.

Neuman, B., & Young, R. (1972). A model for teaching total person approach to patient problem. *Nursing Research, 21*(3), 264-269.

Newberger, E., Barkan, S., Lieberman, E., McCormick, M., Yllö, K., Gary, L., & Schechter, S. (1992). Abuse of pregnant women and adverse birth outcomes: Current knowledge and implications for practice. *Journal of the American Medical Association, 267*(17), 121-123.

Newcomb, M., & Bentler, B. (1989). Substance use and abuse among children and teenagers. *American Psychologist, 44*(2), 242-248.

Nibert, D., Cooper, S., Ford, J., Fitch, L. K., & Robinson, J. (1989). The ability of young children to learn abuse prevention. *Response, 12,* 14-20.

NiCarthy, G. (1982). *Getting free: A handbook for women in abusive relationships* (2nd ed.). Seattle, WA: Seal.

Niethammer, C. (1977). *Daughters of the earth: The lives and legends of American Indian women.* New York: Macmillan.

Norbeck, J., & Anderson, N. (1989). Psychosocial predictors of pregnancy outcomes in low-income black, Hispanic, and white women. *Nursing Research, 38,* 204-209.

Norbeck, J., & Tilden, V. (1983). Life stress, social support and emotional disequilibrium in complications of pregnancy: A prospective multivariate study. *Journal of Health and Social Behavior, 24,* 30-46.

Norton, I. M., & Manson, S. M. (1995). A silent minority: Battered American Indian women. *Journal of Family Violence, 10*(3), 307-318.

Novella, A. (1992). From the Surgeon General, U.S. Public Health Service. *Journal of the American Medical Association, 267*(23), 31-32.

Nurius, P. S., Furrey, J., & Berliner, L. (1992). Coping capacity among women with abusive partners. *Violence and Victims, 7*(3), 229-243.

O'Campo, P., Gielen, A. C., Faden, R. R., & Kass, N. (1994). Verbal abuse and physical violence among a cohort of low-income pregnant women. *Women's Health Issues, 4*(1), 29-37.

Office of Juvenile Justice and Delinquency Prevention. (1994). *Fact sheet No. 12.* Washington, DC: U.S. Department of Justice.

Office of Migrant Health. (1992). *A strategy for reaching migrant and seasonal farm workers.* Washington, DC: Migrant Health Program.

Okun, L. E. (1986). *Woman abuse: Facts replacing myths.* Albany: State University of New York Press at Albany.

Old Dog Cross, P., & Hunter, W. B. (1990). Violence. In Indian Health Service, *Indian health conditions.* Washington, DC: U.S. Department of Health and Human Services, Public Health Service, Indian Health Service.

Ontario Native Women's Association. (1989). *Breaking free: A proposal for change to aboriginal family violence.* Thunder Bay, Ontario: Author.

Osofsky, J., Wewens, S., Hann, D., & Fick, A. (1993). Chronic community violence: What is happening to our children? *Psychiatry, 56,* 36-45.

Padilla, A. M. (1975). *Acculturation: Theory, models, and some new findings.* Washington, DC: American Association for the Advancement of Science.

Pagel, M., Smilkstein, G., Regen, H., & Montano, D. (1990). Psychosocial influences on newborn outcomes: A controlled prospective study. *Social Science and Medicine, 30,* 597-604.

Pagelow, M. D. (1992). Adult victims of domestic violence: Battered women. *Journal of Interpersonal Violence, 7*(1), 87-120.

Parker, B. (1993). Abuse of adolescents: What can we learn from pregnant teen-agers? In J. C. Campbell (Ed.), *Domestic violence* (pp. 363-370). Philadelphia: J. B. Lippincott.

Parker, B., & McFarlane, J. (1991). Nursing assessment of the battered pregnant woman. *Maternity Child Nursing Journal, 16,* 161-164.

Parker, B., McFarlane, J., & Soeken, K. (1994). Abuse during pregnancy: Effects on maternal complications and birthweight in adult and teenage women. *Obstetrics and Gynecology, 84,* 323-328.

Parker, B., McFarlane, J., Soeken, K., Torres, S., & Campbell, D. (1993). Physical and emotional abuse in pregnancy: A comparison of adult and teenage women. *Nursing Research, 42,* 173-178.

Parker, B., & Schumacher, D. (1977). The battered wife syndrome and violence in the nuclear family of origin: A controlled pilot study. *American Journal of Public Health, 67,*(8), 760-761.

Parker, B., & Ulrich, Y. (1990). A protocol of safety: Research on abuse of women. *Nursing Research, 39*(4), 248-250.

Patterson, G., DeBaryshe, B., & Ramsey, E. (1989). A developmental perspective on antisocial behavior. *American Psychologist, 44*(2), 329-335.

Pellegrino, E. D. (1987). Altruism, self-interest, and medical ethics. *Journal of the American Medical Association, 285,* 1939-1940.

Perilla, J. L., Bakeman, R., & Norris, F. H. (1994). Culture and domestic violence: The ecology of abused Latinas. *Violence and Victims, 9*(4), 325-339.

Petersen, R., Gazmararian, J. A., Spitz, A. M., Rowley, D. L., Goodwin, M. M., Saltzman, L. W., & Marks, J. S. (1997). Violence and adverse pregnancy outcomes: A review of the literature and directions for future research. *American Journal of Preventive Medicine, 13,* 366-373.

Pfouts, J. H. (1978). Violent families: Coping responses of abused wives. *Child Welfare,* pp. 101-110.

Piasecki, J. M., Manson, S. M., Biernoff, M. P., Hiat, A. B., Taylor, S. S., & Bechtold D. W. (1989). Abuse and neglect of American Indian children: Findings from a survey of federal providers. *American Indian and Alaska Native Mental Health Research, 3*(2), 43-62.

Plichta, S. (1992). The effects of woman abuse on health care utilization and health status: A literature review. *Women's Health Issues, 2*(3), 154-163.

Plichta, S. B. (1997). Violence, health and the use of health services. In M. Falik & K. Collins (Eds.), *Women's Health: The Commonwealth Fund survey* (pp. 237-272). Baltimore: Johns Hopkins University Press.

Poma, P. A. (1987). Pregnancy in Hispanic women. *Journal of the National Medical Association, 79*(9), 929-935.

Porter, C., & Villarruel, A. (1993). Nursing research with African American and Hispanic people: Guidelines for action. *Nursing Outlook, 41*(2), 59-67.

Porter, K. (1993). Poverty in rural America: A national overview. In S. Jones (Ed.), *Sociocultural and service issues in working with rural clients* (pp. 51-68). Albany, NY: Rockefeller College.

Prato, L., & Braham J. (1991). Coordinating a community response to dating violence. In B. Levy (Ed.), *Dating violence: Young women in danger* (pp. 153-163). Seattle, WA: Seal.

Radford, J., & Russell, D. (Eds.). (1992). *Femicide: The politics of woman killing.* Boston: Twayne.

Ramirez, R. (1991, March 10). Violence at home grips alien women. *San Francisco Examiner.*

Randall, T. (1993). Clinicians' forensic interpretations of fatal gunshot wounds often miss the mark. *Journal of the American Medical Association, 269*(16), 2058-2061.

Rapkin, A. J., Kames, L. D., Darke, L. L., Stampler, F. M., & Naliboff, B. D. (1990). History of physical and sexual abuse in women with chronic pelvic pain. *Obstetrics and Gynecology, 76*(1), 92-96.

Rasche, C. E. (in press). Stated and attributed motives for lethal violence in intimate relationships. *Proceedings of the Homicide Work Group Meetings.*

Rath, G. D., Jarratt, L. G., & Leonardson, G. (1989). Rates of domestic violence against adult women by men partners. *Journal of the American Board of Family Practitioners, 2,* 227-233.

Ratner, P. A. (1993). The incidence of wife abuse and mental health status in abused wives in Edmonton, Alberta. *Canadian Journal of Public Health, 84*(4), 246-249.

Rawson, R. D., Ommen, R. K., Kinard, G., Johnson, J., & Yontis, A. (1984). Statistical evidence for the individuality of the human dentition. *Journal of Forensic Sciences, 29*(1), 245-253.

Resnick, H., Kilpatrick, D., Dansky, B., Saunders, B., & Best, C. (1993). Prevalence of civilian trauma and posttraumatic stress disorder in a representative national sample of women. *Journal of Consulting & Clinical Psychology, 6*(6), 984-991.

Rice, D. P., & MacKenzie, E. J. (1989). *Cost of injury in the United States: A report to Congress.* San Francisco: Institute for Health & Aging, University of California and Injury Prevention Center, Johns Hopkins University.

Richwald, G. A., & McCluskey, T. (1985). Family violence during pregnancy. In D. B. Jeliffe & E. F. T. Jeliffe (Eds.), *Advances in international maternal and child health* (Vol. 5). Oxford, UK: Oxford University Press.

Rodriguez, R. (1989). Perception of health needs by battered women. *Response, 12*(4), 22-23.

Rodriguez, R. (1993). Violence in transience: Nursing care of migrant battered women. *AWHONN's Clinical Issues in Perinatal and Women's Health Nursing, 4,* 437-440.

Rodriguez, R. (1996, October 3). President's Hispanic Education Commission releases report. *Black Issues in Higher Education, 13*(16), 6-7.

Rogers, C. (1951). *Client-centered therapy.* Boston: Houghton-Mifflin.

Rosenbaum, A., & O'Leary, K. D. (1981). Children: The unintended victims of marital violence. *American Journal of Orthopsychiatry, 51*(4), 692-699.

Rosenberg, M. (1965). *Society and the adolescent self image.* Princeton, NJ: Princeton University Press.

Rosenberg, M., Stark, E., & Zahn, M. (1986). Interpersonal violence: Homicide and spouse abuse. In J. Last (Ed.), *Public health and preventive medicine* (12th ed., pp. 1399-1426). Norwalk, CT: Appleton-Century-Crofts.

Rosenfeld, R. (1997). Changing relationships between men and women: A note on the decline of intimate partner homicide. *Homicide Studies, 1*(1), 72-83.

Rotheram-Borus, M., Koopman, C., & Ehrhardt, A. (1991). Homeless youth and HIV infection [Special issue]. *American Psychologist, 46,* 1188-1197.

Rotheram-Borus, M. J. (1991). Serving runaway and homeless youth. *Family Community Health, 14,* 23-32.

Rotheram-Borus, M. J. (1993). Suicidal behavior and risk factors among runaway youth. *American Journal of Psychiatry, 150*(1), 103-107.

Roy, M. (1982). Four thousand partners in violence: A trend analysis. In M. Roy (Ed.), *The abusive partner* (pp. 17-35). New York: Van Nostrand.

Ryan, J., & King, M. C. (1989). A study of the health care needs of women experiencing violence in their lives. In *Proceedings of the Third Nursing Network Conference on Violence Against Women.* Concord, CA: Nursing Network on Violence Against Women.

Sampselle, C. M., Petersen, B. A., Murtland, T. L., & Oakley, D. J. (1992). Prevalence of abuse among pregnant women choosing certified nurse-midwife or physician providers. *Journal of Nurse-Midwifery, 37,* 269-273.

Sassetti, M. R. (1993). Domestic violence. *Primary Care, 20*(2), 289-304.

Saunders, D. G. (1992). Posttraumatic stress symptom profiles of battered women: A comparison of survivors in two settings. *Violence and Victims, 9*(1), 31-44.

Saunders, D. G., & Browne, A. (1991). Domestic homicide. In R. T. Ammerman & M. Hersen (Eds.), *Case studies in family violence* (pp. 379-402). New York: Plenum.

Saunders, D. G., Hamberger, L. K., & Hovey, M. (1993). Indicators of women abuse based on a chart review at a family practice center. *Archives of Family Medicine, 2,* 537-543.

Saylor-Buggs, G. (1996). *Minority health issues.* Washington, DC: Office of Minority Health.

Schechter, S. (1987). *Guidelines for mental health practitioners in domestic violence cases.* Washington, DC: National Coalition Against Domestic Violence.

Schei, B., & Bakketeig, L. S. (1989). Gynecological impact of sexual and physical abuse by spouse: A study of a random sample of Norwegian women. *British Journal of Obstetrics and Gynecology, 96,* 1379-1383.

Schei, B., Samuelsen, S. O., & Bakketeig, L. S. (1991). Does spousal physical abuse affect the outcome of pregnancy? *Scandinavian Journal of Social Medicine, 19,* 26-31.

Scribner, R., & Dwyer, J. H. (1989). Acculturation and low birthweight among Latinos in the Hispanic HANES. *American Journal of Public Health, 79*(9), 1263-1267.

Sebbio, S. R. (1996). *Battered women's relationships with their mates and predictors of continued battering over time.* Unpublished thesis.

Shaffer, D., & Canton, D. (1984). *Runaway and homeless youth in New York City: A report to the Ittleson Foundation.* New York: Ittleson Foundation.

Sheridan, D. J. (1993). The role of the battered women specialist. *Journal of Psychosocial Nursing, 31*(11), 31-37.

Sheridan, D. J. (1996). Forensic documentation of the battered pregnant women. *Journal of Nurse-Midwifery, 41*(6), 467-472.

Sheridan, D. J., & Taylor, W. K. (1993). Developing hospital-based domestic violence programs, protocols, policies, and procedures. *AWHONN's Clinical Issues in Perinatal and Women's Health Nursing, 4*(3), 417-482.

Short, L., Hennessy, M., & Campbell, J. C. (1996). Tracking the work. In R. Berk & P. Rosse (Eds.), *Building a coordinated response* (pp. 59-72). Chicago: American Medical Association Press.

Silvern, L., & Kaersvang, L. (1989). The traumatized children of violent marriages. *Child Welfare, 68,* 421-436.

Simeonsson, R. J. (Ed.). (1994). *Risk, resilience, and prevention: Promoting the well-being of all children.* Baltimore: Brookes.

Slesinger, D. (1992, Summer). Health status and needs of migrant farm workers in the United States: A literature review. *Texas Journal of Rural Health,* pp. 227-233.

Slesinger, D., Christensen, B., & Cautley, E. (1986). Health and mortality of migrant farm worker children. *Texas Journal of Rural Health,* pp. 46-54.

Smith, G., & Gonzalez, A. (1992). Hazardous conditions in the lives of migrant farm workers. *Texas Journal of Rural Health,* pp. 46-54.

Snyder, D. K., & Scheer, N. S. (1981). Predicting disposition following brief residence at a shelter for battered women. *American Journal of Community Psychology, 9,* 559-566.

Snyder, H., Sickmund, M., & Poe-Yamagata, E. (1996, February). *Juvenile offenders and victims: 1996 update on violence.* Washington, DC: Office of Juvenile Justice and Delinquency Prevention, U.S. Department of Justice.

Sogannaes, R. F., Rawson, R. D., Gratt, B. M., & Nouyer, B. N. (1982). Computer comparison of bitemark patterns in identical twins. *Journal of the American Dental Association, 105,* 449-452.

Sorenson, S. B. (1996). Violence against women: Examining ethnic differences and commonalities. *Evaluation Review, 20*(2), 123-145.

Sorenson, S. B., & Telles, C. A. (1991). Self-reports of spousal violence in a Mexican-American and non-Hispanic white population. *Violence and Victims, 6*(1), 3-15.

Sorofman, B. (1986). Research in cultural diversity. *Western Journal of Nursing Research, 8*(1), 121-123.

Stanton, B., Xiaoming, L., Black, M., Ricardo, I., Galbraith, J., Kaljee, L., & Feigelman, S. (1994). Sexual practices and intentions among preadolescent and early adolescent low-income urban African-Americans. *Pediatrics, 93*(6), 966-973.

Stark, E. (1990). Rethinking homicide: Violence, race, and the politics of gender. *International Journal of Health Services, 20,* 3-26.

Stark, E. (1994, Winter). Where do we go from here? In *NCADV Voice, special edition: Domestic violence as a health issue* (pp. 15-17). Washington, DC: National Coalition Against Domestic Violence.

Stark, E., & Flitcraft, A. (1985). Spouse abuse. In *Surgeon General's workshop on violence and public health.* Washington, DC: U.S. Department of Health and Human Services, Public Health Service.

Stark, E., & Flitcraft, A. (1988). Women and children at risk: A feminist perspective on child abuse. *International Journal of Health Services, 18,* 97-118.

Stark, E., & Flitcraft, A. (1992). Spouse abuse. In J. Last & R. Wallace (Eds.), *Public health and preventive medicine* (13th ed., pp. 1040-1062). Norwalk, CT: Appleton and Lange.

Stark, E., & Flitcraft, A. (1995). Killing the beast within: Woman battering and female suicidality. *International Journal of Health Services, 25*(1), 43-64.

Stark, E., Flitcraft, A., & Frazier, W. (1979). Medicine and patriarchal violence: The social construction of a private event. *International Journal of Health Services, 9,* 461-493.

Stark, E., Flitcraft, A. Z., Zuckerman, D., Grey, A., Robinson, J., & Frazier, W. (1981). Wife abuse in the medical setting. *Domestic Violence Monograph Series, 7*(7), 7-41.

Stauffer, D. M. (1986). The trauma patient who is pregnant. *Journal of Emergency Nursing, 12*(2), 89-93.

Stavrou-Peterson, K., & Gamache, D. (1988). *My family and me: Violence free: A domestic violence prevention curriculum.* St. Paul: Minnesota Coalition for Battered Women.

Stewart, D. E., & Cecutti, A. (1993). Physical abuse in pregnancy. *Canadian Medical Association Journal, 149,* 1257-1263.

Stout, K. D. (1991). Intimate femicide: A national demographic overview. *Journal of Interpersonal Violence, 6,* 476-485.

Straus, M. A. (1979). Measuring intrafamily conflict and violence: The Conflict Tactics (CT) Scale. *Journal of Marriage and the Family, 41,* 75-88.

Straus, M. A., & Gelles, R. J. (1986). Societal change and change in family violence from 1975 to 1985 as revealed by two national surveys. *Journal of Marriage and the Family, 48,* 464-479.

Straus, M. A., & Gelles, R. J. (1988). How violent are American families? In G. Hotaling, D. Finkelhor, J. Kirkpatrick, & M. Straus (Eds.), *Family abuse and its consequences: New directions for research.* Newbury Park, CA: Sage.

Straus, M. A., & Gelles, R. J. (Eds.). (1990). *Physical violence in American families: Risk factors and adaptations to violence in 8,145 families.* New Brunswick, NJ: Transaction Publishing.

Straus, M. A., Gelles, R. J., & Steinmetz, S. K. (1980). *Behind closed doors: Violence in the American family.* Garden City, NY: Anchor.

Straus, M. A., & Smith, C. (1990). Violence in Hispanic families in the United States: Incidence rates and structural interpretations. In M. A. Straus & R. J. Gelles (Eds.), *Physical violence in American families: Risk factors and adaptations to violence in 8,145 families* (pp. 341-367). New Brunswick, NJ: Transaction Publishing.

Strube, M. J., & Barbour, L. S. (1984). Factors related to the decision to leave an abusive relationship. *Journal of Marriage and the Family, 46,* 837-844.

Suggs, N. K., & Inui, T. (1992). Primary care physicians' response to domestic violence. *Journal of the American Medical Association, 267,* 3157-3160.

Taggart, L., & Mattson, S. (1996). Delay in prenatal care as a result of battering in pregnancy: Cross-cultural implications. *Health Care for Women International, 17,* 25-34.

Takeuchi, D., & Uehara, E. (1996). Ethnic minority mental health services: Current research and future conceptual directions. In B. Levin & J. Petrila (Eds.), *Mental health services.* New York: Oxford University Press.

Tarasoff v. Regents of the University of California (1974).

Tarasoff v. Regents of the University of California, 551 p. 2d 334 (1976).

Thomas, P., & Lowitt, N. R. (1995). A traumatic experience. *New England Journal of Medicine, 333,* 307-310.

Tilden, V. P. (1989). Response of the health care delivery system to battered women. *Issues in Mental Health Nursing, 10,* 309-320.

Tilden, V. P., Schmidt, T. A., Limandri, B. J., Chiodo, G. T., Garland, M. J., & Loveless, P. A. (1994). Factors that influence clinicians' assessment and management of family violence. *American Journal of Public Health, 84,* 628-633.

Tilden, V. P., & Shepherd, P. (1987a). Battered women: The shadow side of families. *Holistic Nursing Practice, 1,* 25-32.

Tilden, V. P., & Shepherd, P. (1987b). Increasing the rate of identification of battered women in an emergency department: Use of a nursing protocol. *Research in Nursing and Health, 10,* 209-215.

Tolman, R., & Bhosley, G. (1991). *Abused and battered: Social and legal responses of family violence: Social institutions and social change* (pp. 113-122). New York: Aldine de Gruyter.

Tomes, H. (1995). Research and policy directions in violence: A developmental perspective. *Journal of Health Care for the Poor and Underserved, 6*(2), 146-151.

Torres, S. (1987). Hispanic-American battered women: Why consider cultural differences? *Response, 10,* 20-21.

Torres, S. (1991). A comparison of wife abuse between two cultures: Perceptions, attitudes, nature and extent. *Issues in Mental Health Nursing, 12,* 113-131.

Tuma, J. (1989). Mental health services for children: The state of the art. *American Psychologist, 44*(2),188-199.

Turner, S. F., & Shapiro, C. H. (1986, September-October). Battered women: Mourning the death of a relationship. *Social Work,* pp. 372-376.

Ulrich, Y. C. (1989a). Formerly abused women: Relation of self concept to reason for leaving. *Dissertation Abstracts International, 50,* 2344B.

Ulrich, Y. C. (1989b). [Transcripts from 3-hour audiotaped interviews]. Unpublished raw data.

Ulrich, Y. C. (1991). Women's reasons for leaving abusive spouses. *Health Care for Women International, 12,* 465-473.

Ulrich, Y. C. (1994). What helped most in leaving spouse abuse: Implications for interventions. In J. Campbell (Ed.), *AWHONN'S Clinical issues in perinatal and women's health nursing* (pp. 385-390). Philadelphia: J. B. Lippincott.

Ulrich, Y. C. (1998). *Women in recovery from spouse abuse: Releases to leave.* Unpublished manuscript.

U.S. Bureau of the Census. (1991, March). *The Hispanic population in the United States* (Current Population Report, Series P-20, No. 455). Washington, DC: Government Printing Office.

U.S. Department of Health and Human Services. (1990). *Healthy People 2000: National health promotion and disease prevention objectives* (DHSS Publication No. 95-50212). Washington, DC: Government Printing Office.

U.S. Department of Health and Human Services. (1991a). *Healthy People 2000.* Washington, DC: Author.

U.S. Department of Health and Human Services. (1991b). *Setting the national agenda for injury control in the 1990s.* Washington, DC: Author.

U.S. Department of Health and Human Services. (1993). *Depression in primary care* (AHCPR Publication Nos. 30550 and 30551). Rockville, MD: Author.

U.S. Department of Health and Human Services, Public Health Service. (1995). *Healthy People 2000: Midcourse review and 1995 revisions.* Washington, DC: Author.

U.S. General Accounting Office. (1989). *Homelessness: Homeless and runaway youth receiving services at federally funded shelters.* Washington, DC: Author.

U.S. Surgeon General. (1985). *Surgeon General's workshop on violence and public health.* Washington, DC: U.S. Department of Health and Human Services, Public Health Service.

Urbancic, J., Campbell, J. C., & Humphreys, J. (1993). Student clinical experiences in shelters for battered women. *Journal of Nursing Education, 32,* 341-346.

Uzzell, O., & Peebles-Wilkins, W. (1989). Black spouse abuse: A focus on relational factors. *Western Journal of Black Studies, 13,* 10-16.

Vale, G. L., & Noguchi, T. T. (1983). Anatomical distribution of human bite marks in a series of 67 cases. *Journal of Forensic Sciences, 28*(1), 61-69.

Varvaro, F. F., & Lasko, D. L. (1993). Physical abuse as cause of injury in women: Information for orthopaedic nurses. *Orthopaedic Nursing, 12*(1), 37-41.

Veatch, R. M., & Fry, S. T. (1987). *Case studies in nursing ethics.* Philadelphia: J. B. Lippincott.

Vega, W. A., Kolody, B., & Valle, R. (1986). The relationship of marital status, confident support, and depression among Mexican immigrant women. *Journal of Marriage and the Family, 48,* 597-605.

Walker, L. (1979). *The battered woman.* New York: Harper and Row.

Walker, L. E. (1984). *The battered woman syndrome.* New York: Springer.

Walker, L. E., & Edwall, G. E. (1987). Domestic violence and determination of visitation and custody in divorce. In D. J. Sonkin (Ed.), *Domestic violence on trial: Psychological and legal dimensions of family violence* (pp. 127-152). New York: Springer.

Walker, L. E. A. (1985). Feminist therapy with victim/survivors of interpersonal violence (pp. 203-214). In L. B. Rosewater & L. E. A. Walker (Eds.), *Handbook of feminist therapy.* New York: Springer.

Wallace, A. (1986). *Homicide: The social reality.* Sydney: New South Wales Bureau of Crime Statistics and Research.

Warren, B. (1982). *Issues relating to American Indian women.* Unpublished manuscript.

Warren, J., Gary, F., & Moorhead, J. (1995). Self-reported experiences of physical and sexual abuse among runaway youths. *Perspectives in Psychiatric Care, 30,* 23-28.

Warshaw, C., & Ganley, A. L. (1996). *Improving the health care response to domestic violence: A resource manual for health care providers* (D. Lee, N. Durborow, & P. R. Salber, Eds.). San Francisco: Family Violence Prevention Fund.

Watkins, Larson, Harlan, & Young. (1990). A model program for providing health services for migrant farm worker mothers and children. *Public Health Reports, 6,* 567-576.

Weatherford, J. (1991). *Native roots: How the Indians enriched America.* New York: Fawcett Columbine.

Weingourt, R. (1985). Wife rape: Barriers to identification and treatment. *Journal of Psychotherapy, 39*(2), 187-192.

Weingourt, R. (1990). Wife rape in a sample of psychiatric patients. *Image: Journal of Nursing Scholarship, 22,* 144-147.

Weinstock, R., & Weinstock, D. (1988). Child abuse reporting trends: An unprecedented threat to confidentiality. *Journal of Forensic Sciences, 33,* 418-431.

Weissman, M., & Klerman, G. (1992). Depression: Current understanding and changing trends. *Annual Review of Public Health, 13,* 319-339.

Westra, B., & Martin, H. P. (1981). Children of battered women. *Maternal-Child Nursing Journal, 10,* 41-54.

White v. Illinois, 90-6113, Opinions of the U.S. Supreme Court, 50, 15 (1992).

White, E. (1985). *Chain, chain, change.* Seattle: Leaf. (From the College of Nursing, University of Florida, Gainesville)

Whitley, N. (1985). *A manual of clinical obstetrics.* Philadelphia: J. B. Lippincott.

Wilbanks, W. (1986). Criminal homicide offenders in the U.S.: Black vs. white. In *Homicide among black Americans* (pp. 43-55). Lanham, MD: University Press of America.

Wilk, V. (1986). Farm worker occupational health and field sanitation. In *Migrant Health Newsline— Compendium of clinical supplements 1985-87.* Austin, TX: National Migrant Resource Program.

Wilk, V. A. (1993). Health hazards to children in agriculture. *American Journal of Industrial Medicine, 24*(3), 283-290.

Williams, G. (1983). Responsible sexuality and the primary prevention of child abuse. In G. Albee, S. Gordon, & H. Lihenburg (Eds.), *Promoting sexual responsibility and preventing sexual problems* (pp. 251-272). Hanover, NH: University Press of New England.

Williams, O. (1989). Sexual conquest and patterns of black-on-black violence: A structural-cultural perspective. *Violence and Victims, 4,* 257-274.

Wilson, E. F. (1977). Estimation of the age of cutaneous contusions in child abuse. *Pediatrics, 60*(5), 750-752.

Wilson, M. (1989). Child development in the context of the Black extended family. *American Psychologist, 44*(2), 380-385.

Wilson, M., & Daly, M. (1993). Spousal homicide risk and estrangement. *Violence and Victims, 8*(1), 3-16.

Wilson, M., Johnson, H., & Daly, M. (1995). Lethal and nonlethal violence against wives. *Canadian Journal of Criminology, 37,* 331-362.

Wolfe, D. A., Jaffe, P., Wilson, S. K., & Zak, L. (1985). Children of battered women: The relation of child behavior to family violence and maternal stress. *Journal of Consulting and Clinical Psychology, 53,* 657-664.

Wolfe, D. A., Zak, L., Wilson, S., & Jaffe, P. (1986). Child witnesses to violence between parents: Critical issues in behavioral and social adjustment. *Journal of Abnormal Child Psychology, 14,* 95-104.

Wolk, L. E. (1982). *Minnesota's American Indian battered women: The cycle of oppression.* St Paul: St. Paul American Indian Center, Battered Women's Project.

Woods, S. J., & Campbell, J. C. (1993). Post traumatic stress in battered women: Does the diagnosis fit? *Issues in Mental Health Nursing, 14,* 173-186.

World Bank. (1993). *World development report: Investing in health.* Oxford, UK: Oxford University Press.

World Health Organization. (1997). *Violence against women: A priority health issue.* Geneva: Author.

Yates, A. (1987). Current status and future direction of research on the American Indian child. *American Journal of Psychiatry, 144,* 1135-1142.

Yates, G., MacKenzie, R., Pennbridge, J., & Cohen, E. (1988). A risk profile comparison of runaway and non-runaway youth. *American Journal of Public Health, 78,* 820-821.

Yllö, K., & Bograd, M. (1988). *Feminist perspectives on wife abuse.* Newbury Park, CA: Sage.

Young, W. W., Bracken, A. C., Goddard, M. A., Matheson, S., & the New Hampshire Sexual Assault Medical Examination Protocol Project Committee. (1992). Sexual assault: Review of a national model protocol for forensic and medical evaluation. *Obstetrics and Gynecology, 80*(5), 878-883.

Zachariades, N., Koumoura, F., & Konsolaki-Agouridaki, E. (1990). Facial trauma in women resulting from violence by men. *Journal of Oral Maxillary Surgery, 48,* 1250-1253.

Zeanah, C. (1994). The assessment and treatment of infants and toddlers exposed to violence. *Zero to Three, 14,* 29-37.

Zierler, S., Feingold, L., Laufer, D., Velentgas, P., Kantrowitz-Gordon, I., & Mayer, K. (1991). Adult survivors of childhood sexual abuse and subsequent risk of HIV infection. *American Journal of Public Health, 81,* 572-575.

Zuroweste, E. (1991). Migrant Clinicians Network testimony before Hispanic caucus. In *Migrant clinical supplement.* Austin, TX: Migrant Clinicians Network.

Index

About the Editor

Jacquelyn C. Campbell, PhD, RN, FAAN, received her BSN from Duke University, her MSN from Wright State University, and her PhD from the University of Rochester. Her honors include membership in the American Academy of Nursing and a Kellogg National Leadership Fellowship. She is currently the Anna D. Wolf Endowed Professor and Director of the doctoral programs at Johns Hopkins University School of Nursing with a joint appointment in the School of Hygiene and Public Health. She is the principal investigator of five National Institutes of Health, DOD, or Centers for Disease Control major funded research studies on battering and author or coauthor of more than 50 publications on the subject, including *Nursing Care of Survivors of Family Violence, Sanctions and Sanctuary,* and *Assessing Dangerousness,* and two forthcoming texts from Sage, *Drawing the Line* and *Beyond Diagnosis: Advocacy Health Care for Battered Women and Their Children.* She has worked with wife abuse shelters and policy-related committees on domestic violence for more than 15 years. She is currently on the board of directors of the House of Ruth, a shelter in Baltimore, the Family Violence Prevention Fund in San Francisco, and the Institute of Medicine's Board on International Health.

About the Contributors

Debra Gay Anderson, RN, PhD, is a National Research Service Award postdoctoral fellow in family nursing at the Oregon Health Sciences University, Portland, Oregon. Her current research is with homeless women, families, and domestic violence. She is principal investigator on the study titled "Factors Influencing Homelessness in Women," National Institute of Nursing Research/NIH.

Diane K. Bohn, DNSc, CNM, RN, is Assistant Professor at the University of Minnesota, School of Nursing. She is also a certified nurse-midwife and president of the Nursing Network on Violence Against Women International. Recent publications include "Nursing Care of Native American Battered Women" (*AWHONN'S Clinical Issues in Perinatal and Women's Health Nursing,* 1993) and "Domestic Violence and Pregnancy: Implications for Practice" (*Journal of Nurse-Midwifery,* 1990).

Diane M. Brockmeyer, M.D. is a resident in internal medicine at the Brigham and Women's Hospital in Boston, Massachusetts. She began doing domestic violence clinical work and education while a medical student at the University of California, Davis. She has also worked as a visiting medical fellow on this topic at the National Institute of Justice.

Linda F. C. Bullock, PhD, RN, is Assistant Professor at the Sinclair School of Nursing, University of Missouri-Columbia. She obtained her BS and MS degrees in nursing from Texas Woman's University and her PhD in public health from the University of Otago in New Zealand. Her research interests have been in the area of maternal child health and public health with focuses in the area of domestic violence and social support.

Doris Williams Campbell, PhD, FAAN, is Director of Diversity Initiatives for the University of South Florida Health Sciences Center, Tampa, and Professor in the Colleges of Nursing and Public Health. She is a member of the Governor's Task Force on Domestic Violence, State of Florida and the State of Florida Clemency Panel for Domestic Violence Review. Her research interest is in violence against women with a special focus of research and practice issues related to violence and abuse in the lives of African American women and abuse during pregnancy.

Mary Ann Curry, RN, DNSc, FAAN, is Professor in the School of Nursing, Oregon Health Sciences University. Research interests are prenatal psychosocial risk factors, including domestic violence; methods to improve women's identification and disclosure of abuse; and prenatal interventions effective in reducing psychosocial risk and improving pregnancy outcome. Recent publications include (with R. A. Campbell and M. Christian) "Validity and Reliability Testing of the Prenatal Psychosocial Profile" (*RINAH,* 1994).

Susan Dersch, RN, founded and is coordinator of AWARE, a hospital-based support and advocacy program in St. Louis, Missouri serving battered women. She has over 14 years of experience working as a battered women's advocate with community woman abuse services and 12 years as a nurse practicing in women's health. She currently serves as Vice President of the Nursing Network on Violence Against Women International and is also cofounder of WEB: Women, Elderly and Battered, a community partnership between battered women's agencies and elder services addressing the issue of older battered women.

Janet R. Ericksen, RN, MA, is Assistant Professor in the School of Nursing at the University of British Columbia in Vancouver, British Columbia. In addition, she is a nurse-counselor with the Sexual Assault Service at British Columbia Women's Hospital in Vancouver. Her research interests are in two areas: violence against women, in particular its effects on child witnesses; and ethical decision making. Her publications include articles and book chapters reflecting these interests.

Nancy Fishwick, PhD, RN, CS, is Assistant Professor, University of Maine, School of Nursing. She is a family nurse practitioner with research and clinical interest in the primary health care needs of rural populations, domestic violence in rural areas, and women's disclosure of abuse to health care providers. Her current research addresses health care experiences and disclosure of rural women who are in abusive relationships.

Kathleen K. Furniss is a nurse practitioner in women's health employed at the Women's Health Initiative at the University of Medicine and Dentistry of New Jersey and in private practice with six physicians and a midwife at Associates in Women's Health Care in Wayne, New Jersey. She is a volunteer at Jersey Battered Women's Services in Morristown, New Jersey, and is involved with research on the health status of battered women in shelters and outpatient settings. She recently contributed to a monograph titled *Current Practice Issues in Adolescent Gynecology.*

Faye Annette Gary, EdD, FAAN, in her active practice, has provided services to troubled youth and their families for more than two decades. Her research interests highlight designs to improve the human condition through the promotion of health, management, and rehabilitation. She has worked as a teacher, trainer, practitioner, and consultant in more than 15 countries. She was the recipient of the Book of the Year award from the American Journal of Nursing Company; Volunteer of the Year, Marion County, Florida; the Governor's Medallion for Outstanding Services to youth and families; and the Honorary Human Rights Award, American Nurses Association.

S. Marie Harvey is Director of Research at the Center for the Study of Women in Society and Associate Professor of Public Health in the Department of Anthropology at the University of Oregon. She is also a cofounder and Associate of the Pacific Institute for Women's Health. One major branch of her work is in population psychology. For the past 15 years, she has conducted research examining sociodemographic and psychosocial aspects of contraceptive sexual behavior and abortion. She is currently principal investigator on a 2-year study funded by the Centers for Disease Control on reproductive decision making and HIV prevention among Mexican immigrant men and their female partners.

Angela D. Henderson is Associate Professor of Nursing at the University of British Columbia. She has authored a dozen publications on various aspects of women's transition from violent relationships to living independently with their children. She is a founding member of the Feminist, Research, Education, Development, and Action Center on Violence Against Women in Vancouver, one of five federally funded centers for research into violence. Current research interests include supportive parenting classes for women whose children have witnessed violence and the role of nursing in addressing the needs of abused women.

Janice Humphreys, PhD, RN, CS, PNP, is Assistant Professor in the Department of Family Health Care Nursing, University of California, San Francisco. She has provided nursing care to battered women and their children since 1980. She has used her nursing practice as a basis for a program of research that addresses the human responses of battered women and their children. Recent publications include "The Work of Worrying" (*Scholarly Inquiry for Nursing Practice,* 1995) and "Dependent-Care by Battered Women: Protecting Their Children" (*Health Care for Women International,* 1995).

M. Christine King, EdE, RN, is Associate Professor in the School of Nursing, University of Massachusetts at Amherst. She has a doctorate in counseling and consulting psychology and is a clinical nurse specialist in child and adolescent health. Her research and clinical interests are in the area of women's and children's health, violence and abuse, and school health and school nursing. She is Codirector of the Primary Health Care Project for Abused Women and is currently establishing a federally funded comprehensive school health program and school-based health center in an urban high school.

Kären M. Landenburger is Associate Professor of Nursing at the University of Washington, Tacoma. She received her PhD in nursing from the University of Washington, Seattle, where she completed her postdoctoral work in women's health. Her area of expertise is community health with an emphasis on women as a population at risk. Her current research and practice focus is on violence against women. She is actively involved at community and state levels in educating health professionals about domestic violence as a social issue and about the needs of women who seek care.

Barbara J. Limandri is Associate Professor in Mental Health Nursing at the Oregon Health Sciences University School of Nursing. She is also a psychiatric-mental health nurse practitioner, with her primary clinical and research focus on family and domestic violence. Her current research is an outcome study regarding improving abused women's self-efficacy with a psycho-educational group format.

Mary Carter Lominack, MEd, is Executive Director of the Shelter for Help in Emergency in Charlottesville, Virginia, and is a subcommittee member of the Virginia Commission on Family Violence Prevention. Related work includes serving as a board member on Virginians Against Domestic Violence and as Vice-Chair of the Charlottesville-Albermarle Council on Sexual and Domestic Violence, of which she is a founding member.

Judith McFarlane, RN, Dr.PH, conducts research, funded by the Centers for Disease Control, on abuse during pregnancy; the effects of abuse on maternal, infant, and child health; and the effectiveness of clinical interventions to prevent abuse to women. Since 1984, she has authored seminal studies on abuse during pregnancy and its connection with low birth weight. Her research findings have been presented to congressional committees, included in the national health objective (Healthy People 2000), and used by clinicians in the United States and abroad to set standards of care for pregnant women.

Catharine E. Oliver, RN, BSN, MSN, is Clinical Nurse Specialist, Maternal Child Unit, for Hutzel Hospital Detroit Medical Center. She is an adjunct faculty member for the University of Detroit Mercy. She teaches clinical information on the childbearing family. She received her BSN in 1972 and her MSN in 1978, both from Wayne State University, College of Nursing. Her research is focused on battery and its significance in the prenatal period. She has led various workshops and discussion groups on violence for community groups and the Neonatal Nurse Practitioner Program at Wayne State, and the physician's assistance program at the University of Detroit Mercy.

Deborah Page-Adams, PhD, is Assistant Professor at the University of Kansas School of Social Welfare with research interests in violence against women, asset-based antipoverty strategies, and community revitalization. She teaches graduate social policy and social administration courses, in addition to a course titled "Ending Violence Against Women: Individual, Community, and Policy Practice." Her current research projects include a quantitative analysis of the impact of home ownership on safety from marital violence.

Barbara Parker, PhD, RN, FAAN, is Professor of Nursing and Director of the Center for Nursing Research at the University of Virginia School of Nursing. She has conducted several studies on violence against women with J. McFarlane of Texas Women's University. The first study documented the frequency and severity of violence against pregnant women. She and McFarlane recently completed a second 3-year study to test an intervention for abuse during pregnancy. She has published extensively on violence against women.

Rachel Rodriguez, PhD, RN, is Assistant Professor at the University of Texas Health Science Center at San Antonio School of Nursing, San Antonio, Texas. She has conducted several studies on health care issues and domestic violence affecting migrant farm workers. Recent publications include "Promoting Health Partnerships With Migrant Farm Workers" (in J. McFarlane and E. Anderson, eds., *Community as Partners,* 1996) and "Family Violence and Migrant Women; Implications for Practice" (*Migrant Clinicians Network Clinical Supplement,* 1993).

Josephine Ryan, DNSc, RN, is Associate Professor at the University of Massachusetts at Amherst School of Nursing. Her research interests are in the area of women's health especially as that is affected by violence and abuse. She is Codirector of the Primary Care Project for Abused Women and is a member of the Massachusetts Nurses Association Task Force on Domestic Violence, the Nursing Research Consortium on Violence and Abuse, and the Nursing Network on Violence Against Women International. Her current faculty practice area is in a comprehensive school health center in an urban vocational technical high school, where her research will focus on teen dating violence.

Daniel J. Sheridan, RN, recently completed his PhD at Portland's Oregon Health Sciences University (OHSU) School of Nursing. He has been working with survivors of domestic and family violence since 1978. As a family violence clinical nurse specialist, he created the Family Violence Program at Chicago's Rush-Presbyterian-St. Luke's Medical Center. In 1990, he created the Domestic Violence Intervention Team at OHSU's University Hospital. Through his clinical experiences as an emergency department nurse and working with thousands of domestic and family violence survivors, he was one of the pioneers in forensic nursing, and he lectures extensively around the country.

Karen L. Soeken, PhD, is Associate Professor at the University of Maryland School of Nursing. She has been involved in extensive research in the psychological effects of stress on health behaviors and other various health care issues. Recent publications include (with J. McFarlane and B. Parker) "Physical Abuse, Smoking and Substance Use During Pregnancy: Prevalence, Interrelationships and Effects on Birth Weight" (*Journal of Obstetric, Gynecologic and Neonatal Nursing,* 1996) and (with J. McFarlane and B. Parker) "Abuse During Pregnancy: Effects on Maternal Health and Infant Birth Weight" (*Nursing Research,* 1996).

Virginia P. Tilden is Professor and Associate Dean for Research at the Oregon Health Sciences University, School of Nursing, Portland, and Associate Director for the Center for Ethics in Health Care, Oregon Health Sciences University, Portland. She is also principal investigator on the study titled "Family Decision Making: Withdrawing Life Support From Incapacitated Patients," National Institute of Nursing Research/NIH.

Sara Torres, PhD, RN, FAAN, is Associate Professor and Chair of the Department of Psychiatric and Community Health at the University of Maryland School of Nursing in Baltimore. Academic and research interests focus on the Hispanic community: family violence, cross-cultural health care, mental health of Hispanic women, and substance abuse. Her awards include the U.S. Surgeon General's Exemplary Service Award and the Ildura Murillo Rhode Award for Educational Excellence by the National Association of Hispanic Nurses. She has been funded by the National Institutes of Health to conduct research on Hispanic battered women and published the first article in a refereed journal on this topic.

Yvonne Campbell Ulrich, PhD, RN, is a postdoctoral scholar at the University of Washington, Center of Women's Health Research in the School of Nursing. There, in an interdisciplinary research project, she is studying abused women and their children's help-seeking patterns in an HMO. Since 1985, her research and practice has been directed to abused women and their strengths. Her research has focused on women's reasons for leaving and what helps them most in leaving and is based on in-depth interviews with over 60 women. Her practice included conducting community support groups for women deciding to end the abuse and most recently, cofacilitating a support group for homeless women aimed at preventing violence.